# AS Law

*AS Law* covers the content of AS Law for AQA and OCR students in a stimulating and reader-friendly style. Subjects are broken down into manageable parts, with clear headings, sub-headings, photographs, diagrams, boxes and illustrations. A glossary of commonly encountered legal terms also helps those new to the subject understand some of the more technical words and phrases.

Each chapter contains a number of common features designed to aid learning, including:

- This topic enables you – an introduction to each chapter outlining learning objectives that also explain why the subject is important to the study of law
- Developing the subject – explains a particularly important or difficult point in more detail
- Useful websites – a list of websites that enable students to access primary law materials, which will support chapter-by-chapter reading
- It's a fact! – highlights interesting and contemporary applications of the legal principle under discussion
- Let's look at the cases – examines a particular case in more detail in the context of the chapter discussion
- Hints and Tips – suggests revision topics and strategies bearing in mind the questions that could well come up in an exam

With revision quizzes, quick tests and sample questions and answers included within the textbook alongside additional online material, this text covers AS Law in a stimulating and exciting manner. Designed for sixth form and college students, it brings law to life by profiling famous legal figures and examining law in films, fiction, non-fiction and on the internet while fulfilling all syllabus requirements.

Praise for the first edition:
"This is a good book which I would willingly recommend to students." Carol Edwards, *The Law Teacher* (2004) Volume 38, No. 1

**Minel Dadhania** was a co-author on the first edition. A former student of Kingsbury High School, Minel holds a first class honours degree in Law from the London School of Economics and Political Science and acts as a private tutor for A-level Law students.

**Andrew Mitchell**, LLB, PGCE, started his career as a Lecturer in Law and Business at De Montfort University (Lincoln) and now teaches AS and A2 Law at Kingsbury High School.

This book is supported by a companion website designed to keep *AS Law* up to date and to provide interactive resources for students.

Key features include:

- Glossary of legal terms
- Useful web-links to information resources and important websites
- Revision quizzes for students
- Celebrity cases relating to key areas of the law
- Self-test essay questions with answer plans for students
- Tri-annual updates

**Visit the companion website at:**

**www.routledgecavendish.com/textbooks/9781845680329**

# AS Law

## Second Edition

Andrew Mitchell

LONDON AND NEW YORK

First edition published 2003 by Cavendish Publishing Ltd
Second edition first published 2007 by Routledge-Cavendish
2 Park Square, Milton Park, Abingdon, OX14 4RN

Simultaneously published in the USA and Canada
by Routledge-Cavendish
270 Madison Ave, New York, NY 10016

*Routledge-Cavendish is an imprint of the Taylor & Francis Group, an informa business*



Typeset by RefineCatch Limited, Bungay, Suffolk
Printed and bound in Great Britain by TJ International, Padstow, Cornwall



*British Library Cataloguing in Publication Data*
A catalogue record for this book is available from the British Library

*Library of Congress Cataloging in Publication Data*
A catalog record for this book has been requested

ISBN 10: 1–84568–032–4 (pbk)
ISBN 13: 978–1–84568–032–9 (pbk)

# Contents

# Acknowledgements

Welcome to the second edition of the book that began life as *AS Level Law* and now sits before you as *AS Law*. Not only has it a different title, but it is also quite a different animal. For a start, Minel Dadhania has not been able to contribute to this edition, though I am indebted to her for her excellent work on the first edition and for permitting me to use what remained of that book. Then the Government decided to bombard Parliament with lengthy and complex legislation to inconvenience law teachers and students everywhere: this edition, written just three years from the first, has had to take into account the Courts Act 2003, the Criminal Justice Act 2003, the Serious Organised Crime and Police Act 2005 and the *pièce de résistance*, the Constitutional Reform Act 2005. I can't think of many other A-levels that are affected by such a deluge of new material as examinations loom. Can you? And then on top of that, I have tried very hard to address some of the comments received about the first edition. Thanks to all of the law teachers who have contributed to this process, and also to the students who have given me feedback. My experiences on the editorial board of the A-level Law Review (Philip Allan) have also been instructive and I offer thanks to my colleagues accordingly. This second edition therefore contains much more to *do*, think about and *discuss*, whilst also, I hope, continuing to fulfil its original brief as a sound, thorough examination text that will enable students of all abilities to reach their potential.

Both the new cover image and the exceptional photographs of legal London that punctuate this text were created by Steve Foster and I am very grateful to him for his skill, generosity and hard work in preparing these; my thanks also to Vinicius Pereira for donning the hoodie! Steve and Vinnie work with me at Kingsbury High School and in some respects this feels like an in-house production: my thanks to Atul Patel and colleagues in the Business Education department; to Paul Irving for his helpful comments on the first edition and for making the teaching of law a team effort; to James Appleby for his willingness to offer technical help at a moment's notice; to Jill, Jo and the Library/OLC team; and to Clem Chung, Head Teacher, Michael Senior, Director of Sixth Form Studies and other members of the school's senior management team for their continued support.

I am also proud to give credit, in this second edition, to members of the law department at the University of Huddersfield, who succeeded, between 1991–94, in triggering an interest in the law that has so far shaped my professional career and given me opportunities like this one; and also to my former colleagues at De Montfort University for supporting and developing my enthusiasm. I believe, with hindsight, that the supervision of Dr Rob Widdicombe and Professor Neil Hawke at the latter institution was an especially valuable experience and taught me a great deal about the writing process in this field.

Lastly, I am privileged to have such supportive friends and family, in London and Lincoln, and so say cheers to the Mitchells (Mo, Jan), Vicki and Graham Davis, the Dadhanias and the Rothwells.

Every effort has been made to attribute source material clearly and accurately, with appropriate credit given to the respective authors. In the event that a copyright issue has been left unresolved, the publisher will be pleased to remedy the situation at the first opportunity. Routledge-Cavendish has afforded me every assistance in the writing of this second edition and I thank Sonny Leong and Zoe Botterill for initially pushing the project forward and to Madeleine Langford, Benjamin Roberts, Paula Devine, Constance Sutherland, Kara Milne and the production team (including Bob Banbury and colleagues at RefineCatch Ltd) for working so hard in seeing it through to completion. Any errors in this book are my responsibility and mine alone.

*Andrew Mitchell*
*London, August 2006*

## Postscript

This book aims for a statement of the law as at **August 2006.** I have tried to take account also of statutory provisions not yet in force, but scheduled for commencement. The references I have made to the Prime Minister, unless otherwise stated, are therefore to Mr Tony Blair, and those to the Government, unless otherwise stated, are to the Labour Government which was elected for a third term in 2005. Many changes may of course occur during the life of this edition. I will therefore endeavour to keep readers aware of any major changes to the English legal system via the **companion website** (www.routledgecavendish.com/textbooks/9781845680329) for this book.

# Dedication

This book is dedicated to my law students, past and present, whose interest, enthusiasm and successes make teaching and writing about the law such a pleasure.

# Table of cases

# Table of legislation

## Secondary legislation

## European law

# INTRODUCTION

This book sets out to provide a clear introductory text on English law and thorough coverage of the AS Law specifications, presenting the subject in a sufficiently interesting and stimulating way so that it appeals both to students and law teachers. It is intended as a guide and reference work for AS Law and as an aid to revision. The main purposes of this Introduction are:

- To consider, briefly, the question **'What is law?'**
- To explain the **structure** and **format** that have been used for the book.
- To offer some flavour of its **contents** and ways of **learning the law**.

## WHAT IS LAW?

Law represents a set of rules that can be **enforced** in society. The enforcement of legal rules is formal, generally taking place in courts or tribunals, and leads either to **sanctions**, in the form of punishments, or **remedies**, in the form of financial compensation or the protection of certain rights. Legal rules therefore differ from other rules of behaviour in society, such as habits, traditions and moral rules, in that they have formal consequences. This book concerns **English law**, which is the law in England and Wales. Scotland and Northern Ireland, by and large, have their own legal arrangements.

The law has significance throughout our lives – for example, ages of consent and eligibility, and laws relating to education, further and higher education, work and pensions – and even **pre-birth** (through the laws on fertilisation, embryology and abortion) and **post-grave** (through the operation of wills). Some of the dilemmas facing the courts are incredibly difficult,

### Developing the subject: What sort of issues does the law deal with?

Law is a fascinating area of study because it is so wide-ranging. It covers:

- *Everyday situations:* such as parking and road traffic law; the buying and selling of goods and land; births and marriages; medical procedures; the formation and operation of businesses.
- *Particular problems:* such as acts of violence or property damage; accidents at work; rail or air disasters; businesses creating environmental damage; and social issues such as smoking in public places and anti-social behaviour.
- *Constitutional issues:* such as challenges to the decisions of Government Ministers and local councils; and claims that the police have exceeded their powers and infringed the human rights of suspects.
- *International disputes:* such as matters of extradition about terrorist suspects held in the UK and wanted for trial by other countries, and those captured abroad and sought by the UK authorities.

raising social, political and ethical considerations, as the following case focus illustrates.

## Let's look at cases: Some recent dilemmas faced by the courts

Consider the following questions that have had to be resolved by the courts in recent times:

- Could a male-to-female transsexual, regarded in law as 'male', carry out all the roles required of her as a police officer, including searches of female suspects? (*A v Chief Constable of West Yorkshire Police*, 2004: the House of Lords found that she could.)
- Could a Muslim pupil challenge the uniform requirements of her school and insist on wearing the jilbab, a long cloak covering all but face and hands? (*R (Shabina Begum) v Governors of Denbigh High School*, 2006: the House of Lords found that she could not, reversing a decision of the Court of Appeal.)
- Could Christian religious schools seek an exemption on the law banning corporal punishment (eg, physical punishments in school) as part of their 'duty to discipline children'? (*R (Williamson and others) v Secretary of State for Education and Employment*, 2005: the House of Lords found that they could not.)
- Could a couple be permitted to use a controversial form of stem-cell 'tissue typing' to produce a child that could act as a tissue donor for their seriously ill son? (*R (Quintavelle) v Human Fertilisation and Embryology Authority*, 2005: the House of Lords found that the 'tissue typing' process could be authorised.)
- Could a boy under 16 who had admitted to the criminal offence of sexual intercourse with a girl under 16 argue that his human rights had been infringed because the law treated him as the 'accused' and the girl as the 'victim'? (*E v Director of Public Prosecutions*, 2005: the Divisional Court of the Queen's Bench Division found that he could not.)
- Could a parent secure a declaration that would give her the right to know about, and determine, medical treatment relating to contraception, sexually transmitted diseases and abortion for her child, aged under 16? (*R (Sue Axon) v Secretary of State for Health*, 2006: the Divisional Court of the Queen's Bench Division found that the parent could not be granted such a declaration.)

These are the sorts of issues you might encounter, and discuss, as your legal studies progress.

The American writer, **Scott Turow**, once quoted one of his lecturers at Harvard Law School as saying, 'the law . . . is so broad a reflection of the society, the culture, that it is ripe for the questions posed by any field of inquiry: linguistics, philosophy, history, literary studies, sociology, economics, mathematics'. The list could easily be added to. Many students now usefully combine their legal studies with business, geography, psychology, medicine, politics or the sciences.

## CIVIL LAW AND CRIMINAL LAW

The main distinction that all students of law have to learn is between the body of rules known as civil law and those rules known as criminal law.

Civil law expresses those areas of law that deal with **legal disputes between individuals and/or businesses.** For example, disputes that relate to commercial agreements between businesses; or between an employer and employees; or following a medical operation that has gone wrong and caused injury to the patient; or situations where a consumer has bought a product, or paid for a service, which proves to be less than satisfactory. In these sorts of situations, the law will be **enforced** by those persons who feel that they have lost out, or suffered harm or an injury. They will take out a **lawsuit** – which may be funded by the individual, or with help from funds set aside by the Government – against the body or person whom they believe to be legally responsible for the loss or injury. This is the process of **litigation**. The person who takes out the lawsuit (a 'litigant') is called the **claimant**, and he or she will **sue** the party he or she believes to be responsible, known as the **defendant**. The claimant will be seeking a **remedy** for the dispute or problem.

The most common civil remedy is in the form of financial compensation and is referred to as **damages**. However, sometimes other civil remedies might be sought: for example, an **injunction** might be applied for in order to stop the defendant from carrying out a certain activity or practice if it is causing a nuisance. Civil lawsuits will generally begin in either the **county court** or the **High Court**, depending on the nature and size of the claim. The word 'claimant' replaced the term 'plaintiff' during reforms to the civil justice system in the 1990s (see Chapter 6 for details of the reforms). Therefore, to avoid confusion, references to civil cases in this book will use the new terminology of 'claimant', irrespective of whether cases pre-date or post-date the reforms.

The other main branch of law is called the **criminal law**. This is concerned with **punishing** an individual or business for acting contrary to the laws of the State. While the civil law is left to the individual to enforce, victims of criminal offences will take action themselves only on very rare occasions, since the crime is an offence against the State and the State will therefore seek to bring the offender to justice on behalf of the victim. The State is represented by a number of enforcing agencies, most prominently the police and the **Crown Prosecution Service (CPS)**, who develop the case against the suspect, known as the **defendant**, so that it can be brought to court. This action is referred to as a **prosecution**. A successful prosecution leads to criminal **sanctions** being imposed on the defendant in the sentencing process, such as imprisonment, fines, or sentences that require services to the community. Criminal trials are heard either by the **magistrates' courts** or by the **Crown Court**, depending on the seriousness of the crime.

## THE STRUCTURE OF THE BOOK

### Part one

The first five chapters of this book cover what are generally referred to as the **sources of law** (OCR/WJEC) or **law-making** (AQA) topics. Most law in England and Wales has its origins, or sources, in two places: **Parliament** and the **courts**. Chapter 1 examines the way in which Parliament makes law, taking account of its place within the British constitution and the varied influences on its law-making (including the **law reform** bodies). It also notes the increasing significance of the **European Convention on Human Rights**,

**IT'S A FACT!**

Civil law actually makes a larger contribution to English law than criminal law, yet television and other media tend to reinforce the idea that law is mainly about crime. A university degree in law, for example, focuses largely on civil law topics, such as contract, tort and property.

following the incorporation of the Convention into English law by the Human Rights Act 1998. Chapter 2, on **delegated legislation**, focuses on types of law created by bodies *other than* Parliament, but which Parliament has authorised. Chapters 3 and 4 describe law-making in the courts through the processes of **statutory interpretation** and **judicial precedent** respectively. Chapter 5 introduces **European Community law**, a very important source of law that is, in certain areas of policy, superior to English law.

## Part two

Chapters 6 to 11 concern the procedures, processes and people of the English legal system: for OCR, the **English Legal System** topics, for WJEC the **machinery of justice** and **legal personnel** topics; and for AQA, the **dispute-solving** topics. Chapter 6 looks at **civil** and **criminal procedure** (including **police powers**) and the **courts**, whilst Chapter 7 focuses on **tribunals** and other forms of **dispute resolution** to be encountered in your legal studies. These are complemented by thorough coverage of the **judges** to be found in the courts (Chapter 8) and also of the members of the public who are involved in the hearing of cases, either as **lay magistrates** or **jurors** (Chapter 9). Chapters 10 and 11 provide a practical introduction to the **legal profession** – solicitors, barristers and legal executives – and the ways in which legal information, advice and representation can be delivered to the public. The issue of whether the English legal system allows ordinary people real **access to justice** is discussed here.

## Part three

It is in Chapters 12–15 that the first two parts of this book are brought together and you can begin to apply the law and gain broader perspectives on the subject. This part is of greater interest to those taking the AQA specifications, although some OCR and WJEC AS coverage is included here (on **sentencing**, for example). Chapter 12 provides an introduction to **criminal law** and focuses on **non-fatal offences against the person**. Chapter 13 looks at the main elements of establishing a **civil legal claim** in the **tort of negligence**. Chapter 14 outlines the consequences of committing a criminal offence by explaining the sanctions, or punishments, which may be imposed as **sentences** on offenders; and considers the **civil damages (compensation)** which will be awarded to a victim of the tort of negligence. Chapter 15 is called '**Experiencing the law**' and aims to extend your studies through exploration of the law in media (such as film, television and literature).

## THE FORMAT OF THE BOOK

Every chapter in this book begins with '**This topic enables you to . . .**', a short section that highlights the importance of the topic in relation to others, and reveals patterns and themes that offer a broader understanding and awareness of law. Too often, topics are revised in isolation rather than as part of a larger whole. It is hoped that this book will give you the confidence to adopt a wider perspective.

You will find that the text of each chapter is broken up with summary tables and illustrations, and that some chapters, including this Introduction, contain additional features. Thus, the main text contains the key principles and areas for learning and revision, whilst the tables, illustrations, etc. are designed to reinforce your knowledge and understanding, and test your recall and application. The additional features include: **Developing the subject** boxes (providing additional detail to supplement earlier comments); **Let's look at cases** (focusing on key cases in the topic); **It's a fact!** (raising short points of interest), a variety of boxed **Exercises**; occasional **Talking points** (raising issues to prompt discussion and further reading); **Profiles** (focusing on famous legal figures); and **Talking from experience** (providing snapshots of a variety of legal environments).

Every chapter ends with **Hints and Tips** on the topics being studied. These are designed to aid your understanding of the foregoing coverage and help with your revision. This book is supported by an **online companion** (**www.routledgecavendish.com/textbooks/9781845680329**) which has two features to support the coverage of topics:

- **Revision activities** (with answers)
- **Suggested approaches** to answering **sample questions**

A general comment that applies to all of the hints and tips is that candidates should take care with grammar, punctuation and use of language in responding to questions, placing particular emphasis on the correct use of 'legal terminology'. A **glossary** has been included in the book to assist this process. You will find that key words and phrases are featured in bold in the text; if you are unsure of what such a word means, you will find a short explanation of the key terms in the glossary.

The chapters in this book contain **useful website addresses** for you to further your reading and understanding, though Chapter 15 contains sites that are *generally* useful to your studies. You are encouraged to bear these sites in mind and to check this chapter out. It also contains a range of recommendations relating to law films and books, plus advice about furthering your studies.

Coverage of the European Union and its related body of law, **European Community** (**EC**) **law**, can be found in Chapter 5 of this book. It is difficult to know where exactly to put this topic, given its importance as a **source of English law**. The processes and institutions of the European Union may seem very unfamiliar to you at the start of your course, though EC law is a fascinating topic, bringing historical, cultural and political aspects to legal studies. Your teacher will advise you on the best approach, and perhaps you will choose to refer to the EC law chapter when you feel confident about the general workings of the English legal system.

## GENERAL POINTS ON LEARNING THE LAW

One of the main features you will encounter in studying AS Level Law is the need to remember examples of **statute law** (Acts of Parliament) and **common law** (law developed by cases).

The titles of **statutes** tend to describe the aim, scope or subject of the legislation and the year in which the Act was formally created: for example, the Racial and Religions Hatred Act 2006. Acts are often made up of many parts, with sections and subsections within them. Sometimes you will be required to refer to one of the sections of an Act because of its legal significance: for example, in writing about the UK's obligations under EC law, it would make sense to refer to section 2 of the European Communities Act 1972. Adopting the usual abbreviation, this book will refer to such a section as **s 2**. Statutory sections are not easy to learn, though once you have a fair understanding of the legal framework being presented by an Act, some of the individual sections become more memorable and make greater sense.

Case law, on the other hand, represents the reported facts and decisions of cases that have come before the civil and criminal law courts over the years. The more important cases form **precedents** (or principles) that may be applied in future situations. Although there is much to learn, do not let yourself be overwhelmed by cases. There may be several cases that are similar to each other, not in factual terms but in principle, so learn the principle first and then just a few main cases to illustrate this principle.

If you find it difficult to remember cases, there are many ways of trying to overcome this. A basic aim in learning case law is to know, for each case, **what happened** and **what the court decided**. So what methods can be used? A popular method of learning cases is to give them nicknames. Take the tort case of *Grant v Australian Knitting Mills* (1936). This can be remembered as 'the case of the dangerous underpants', as the facts related to underwear that, owing to the manufacturer's negligence, caused harm to the unfortunate customer. Other methods include the use of pictures to illustrate a case. Sometimes this can be a simple representation of the case – for example, a snail in a ginger beer bottle for the landmark case of *Donoghue v Stevenson* (1932) (see Chapter 13) – but on other occasions, an illustration will not only aid the memory but also provide a fuller understanding of the facts. Such methods are subjective and you will have your own favoured approach, but it does seem to be generally good advice to **learn by association**. Lastly, you do *not* have to learn dates of cases for examinations. Therefore, while the decision has been taken to give dates for each case so that you can appreciate how the law has developed over time, do not lose sleep trying to remember all of them.

Researching for short **homework** essays throughout the year is important because you add to your knowledge about the subject and you will, through this process, remember some of the information. Exchanging these pieces of work with your friends is often a good idea (once these have been marked!) as you learn a lot from collaborative work, and it reveals ways of improving your own work and different styles of writing which you may wish to adopt. After all, your friends may approach the subject from differing perspectives, and use other cases and examples that might spark your interest and ideas. **Debates** and **class discussion** are also very useful for appreciating differing views on the subject.

I hope you enjoy this book and find it a useful companion for your studies in AS Law.

# The British constitution, law reform and the parliamentary legislative process

This topic enables you:

- To appreciate the role of Parliament as the dominant law-making power in the British constitution.
- To identify the influences on Parliament from law reform bodies, pressure groups and campaigners.
- To understand the law-making processes within Parliament.
- To identify the powers in the British constitution.
- To recognise that there are limits to the supremacy of Parliament in law-making.
- To take account of the importance of European Community (EC) law and its impact on the English legal system (to be read in conjunction with Chapter 5).
- To appreciate the far-reaching significance of some parliamentary law, such as the Human Rights Act 1998.

Most of this chapter will concern itself with the way in which law is made by **Parliament.** Parliament creates written law referred to as **legislation** or **statute law.** Legislation or statutes passed by Parliament take the form of **Acts of Parliament.** You can see from the illustration below, and from Chapters 1–5, that there are four main **sources of law** in the English legal system, of which Acts of Parliament are seen as the dominant source:

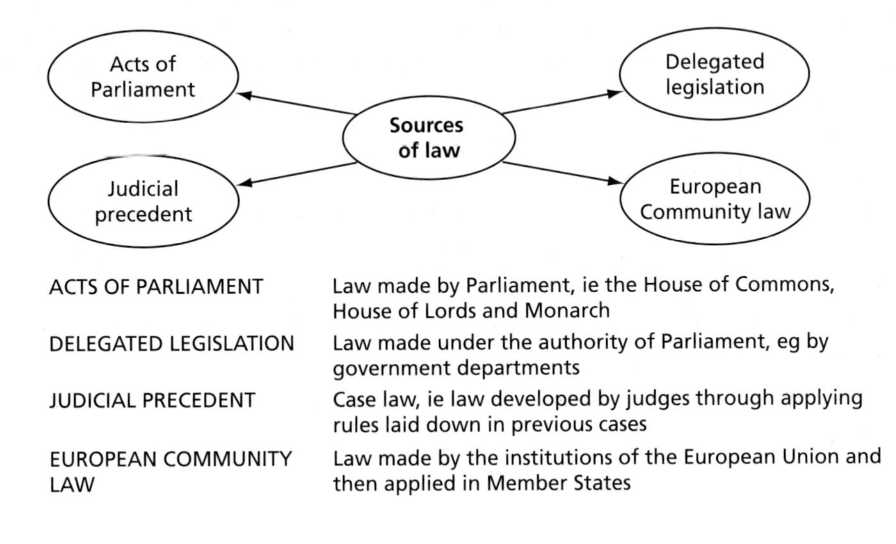

In order to understand Parliament's law-making role, it is first necessary to consider the **place of Parliament within the British constitution** and to describe its **relationship with the other constitutional powers.**

## THE BRITISH CONSTITUTION AND CONSTITUTIONAL THEORY

What are people referring to when they talk about **'the constitution'**? It is easier to imagine this if the constitution is declared in some form: for example, the United States has a written constitution, which sets out the limits of presidential government. However, the position is complicated in Britain, because the constitution is a product of historical development and has never been reduced to one written code or document. Therefore, on a simple level, the British constitution is an example of an **unwritten constitution.**

Nevertheless, whether written or unwritten, a constitution will, in practice, define limits for Government and administration in a nation State. **In short, the constitution sets out the way in which a country will be run.** Three aspects are generally defined in any constitution:

- The way in which power is balanced between the institutions (or governing bodies) of the nation State.
- The limits to the powers exercised by such institutions, imposed to safeguard the rights and freedoms of individuals.
- The extent to which individual rights and freedoms within the nation State are protected.

The three institutional powers in the British constitution are, according to the **'separation of powers'** theory, the **executive** (Government: the administration that runs the country); the **legislature** (Parliament: the institution of law-making); and the **judiciary** (judges: the adjudicators in disputes).

Of the three institutional powers, constitutional theorists have identified **Parliament** as being the **supreme law-making body**. Parliament can make, or unmake, any laws that it wants. This is the theory of **parliamentary sovereignty**.

An additional theory is the **rule of law** as developed by the 19th-century theorist **Dicey**. This places an importance on **law as a check on the arbitrary exercise of power** by Government; and stresses that **no one individual is 'above the law'**, thus ensuring equality of treatment for all before the courts.

Table 1.1 summarises what is meant by the **'constitution'** and the **main constitutional theories.**

**IT'S A FACT!**

**A written constitution for the UK?**

Stephen Hockman, QC, as Chairman of the Bar Council, wrote to *The Times* on 8 February 2006 to suggest an important target to be achieved by 2015, the 800th anniversary of the first major constitutional landmark, *Magna Carta*: the 'enactment of a codifying measure which would contain in a **single piece of legislation** all the key constitutional principles and procedures which underpin the governance of the country'. It remains to be seen whether this will lead to a campaign to reform Britain's famously 'unwritten' constitution, though the approaching anniversary focuses minds on Britain's unique constitutional heritage, whilst stimulating debate about future constitutional arrangements. David Cameron, as Leader of the Conservative Party, has proposed a British 'Bill of Rights' in the same spirit, but he has done so more as a response to dissatisfaction with the Human Rights Act 1998 than in an attempt to achieve a written constitution for the UK (for a summary of this proposal, and the responses to it, see *The Week* magazine, 1 July 2006).

Table 1.1 The constitution and constitutional theories

*What is a constitution?*

- Either written (eg, US constitution) or unwritten and based on historical development (eg, British constitution).
- Sets out how a country should be run.
- Lays down the powers of the governing bodies in the country.
- Takes into account the relationship between the governors and the governed.
- Sets out powers and duties of the governors and the rights and freedoms of the governed (citizens).

*What are the main constitutional theories?*

| *Separation of powers* | *Parliamentary sovereignty* | *Rule of law* |
|---|---|---|
| That there are three main powers in the constitution and that these should remain separate. The three powers are:<br>• Executive (Government)<br>• Legislature (Parliament)<br>• Judiciary (Judges)<br>Through separation, each acts as a check on the other. Therefore, power is not concentrated in one area. | That of the three main powers in the constitution, Parliament is the supreme law-making body. (See later comments in this section.) | That the three main powers of the constitution must observe the rule of law. This means:<br>• There is a check on the power of the Government in its decision-making.<br>• That no one is above the law – all are equal before the courts. |

## Developing the subject 1.1: Focus on the separation of powers and the rule of law

The separation of powers theory is that the constitutional powers are to some degree separate, thereby ensuring that there are checks and balances in the system, thus limiting the power of Government and enabling the judiciary to have independence in reaching legal judgments on disputes. The value of this separation of powers theory, if applied in practice, is that it avoids totalitarian government: in Nazi Germany, for example, the evils of the system occurred because there were no checks and balances, and Hitler's regime exercised dominance over all of the powers of the State. The judiciary lacked necessary independence and the executive controlled the legislature. The practical consequences were horrendous.

The rule of law clearly places limits on the exercise of powers by the Government and protects the rights of citizens. The rule of law theory, like the separation of powers, emphasises the need for keeping the institutions and their processes within reasonable limits so as to avoid totalitarianism.

## The development of the British constitution

Oliver Cromwell, architect of the English Civil War and Parliamentarian, commemorated at Westminster

The constitution has evolved over time, with two main strands of historical development: first, the **changing relationship** between the **monarchy, executive and Parliament**; and, second, the **landmark reforms** that have extended rights and liberties and delimited constitutional powers. These are summarised by Table 1.2 below and explained in 'Developing the subject 1.2' opposite.

## The role of the Crown in the British constitution

The title **'the Crown'** is given to the monarch or sovereign of the country, that is, the **Royal Head of State**. The British monarch is also the Head of the Church of England and Head of State for assenting countries within the Commonwealth (an association of former colonial nations). In its practical operation, the Crown represents the **monarch** and, more significantly, the Government of the day – the **executive** – that has responsibility for governing the country, and can call upon **'royal prerogative'** powers that have been established during the historical development of the common law.

The **Crown** has legal significance in two main respects:

- Through exercise of the **royal prerogative.**
- Through **Crown immunity.**

Table 1.2 The development of the British constitution

| *Changing relationship between the monarchy, executive and Parliament* | *Landmark reforms extending rights and freedoms and setting the boundaries of constitutional powers* |
|---|---|
| • Kings and Queens have **absolute power** up to 17th century.<br>• **English Civil War** takes place, in which Parliament stands up to the monarchy.<br>• **Glorious revolution** of **1688**, following the civil war, gave Parliament dominance over the monarchy.<br>• Since 1688, **Parliament has gained power** at the monarchy's expense.<br>• Parliament develops procedures to keep executive governance in check. | • **Magna Carta 1215**: first real attempt to set out constitutional powers and give rights and freedoms to citizens.<br>• **Act of Settlement 1701**: provided for judicial independence from the other constitutional powers.<br>• **Extension of voting rights (19th/20th centuries)**: led to **parliamentary democracy**.<br>• UK joins the **European Community** in 1973 and therefore becomes subject to **European Community law**. |

## The Crown and the 'royal prerogative'

In his landmark work on the *Law of the Constitution* (1885), **Dicey** defined the **royal prerogative** in the following terms:

> The prerogative is the name for the *remaining portion of the Crown's original authority*, and is therefore . . . the name for the *residue of discretionary power* left at any moment in the hands of the Crown, whether such power be in fact exercised by the King [or Queen] him[her]self or by his [her] Ministers. (emphasis added)

In simple terms, therefore, the prerogative represents that part of the Crown's power that has survived historical reforms and can still be exercised.

## Developing the subject 1.2: Notable events in the historical development of the British constitution

Kings and Queens tended to wield **'absolute' power** in affairs of State prior to the seventeenth century. The turning point came with the **English Civil War (1642–1648)** and the battle between the Royalists (represented by the 'Cavaliers'), who supported the monarch, King Charles I, and the Parliamentarians (represented by the 'Roundheads'), led by Oliver Cromwell, who sought to challenge the monarch's powers. In bringing the relationship between the powers of the monarch and Parliament to the fore, it was not long before a settlement was reached which sought to define the appropriate balance of these powers. This settlement resulted from the **'Glorious Revolution' of 1688**, in which King William III (William of Orange) agreed to a **'bill of rights'** for the protection of individual rights and liberties, and parliamentary dominance over the monarchy was declared. After 1688, Parliament continued to gain power at the monarch's expense, to the extent that the monarch is today a largely ceremonial figure with very limited powers (see further discussion of the Crown in this chapter).

As for constitutional landmarks, the **Magna Carta of 1215**, signed by King John and the major feudal landowners, is still seen as a reference point for the protection of civil liberties. It required that every man accused of a crime should be given a fair trial and be judged by his peers, and that the legal system be free of bribery and corruption. These principles are of continuing relevance today. The right to a fair trial, for example, is now explicitly protected in law under the **Human Rights Act 1998**, a very recent landmark in the development of the British constitution. This Act brings many of the rights and freedoms laid down in the **European Convention on Human Rights** into English law.

Other notable developments in history include the **Act of Settlement 1701**, which provided judges with freedom from interference by the other constitutional powers; and the widening of public participation in the political process, with the extension of certain **voting rights** to men in the nineteenth century and to women in the first half of the twentieth century, thus creating, over time, a parliamentary democracy. However, perhaps the most significant constitutional development of all has been the UK's participation as a Member State of the **European Community (EC)** (now European Union, or EU) since 1973. This has meant that the British constitution is subject to the exercise of powers and processes by a further set of institutions. EC law which describes the law developed by the institutions of the European Union, is superior to English law, and there is little doubt that when the UK joined the EC it gave away aspects of its own parliamentary sovereignty (see Chapter 5). A constitutional question that remains contentious is whether the UK can, in any circumstances, withdraw from the European Union.

**Tasks for developing learning:**

(1) Create a time-line to illustrate the development of the British constitution.
(2) Carry out research into the constitutional reforms implemented by the Labour governments since 1997. Add the results to your time-line.

In practice, common law prerogative powers are rarely exercised by the monarch; and if they are, they are exercised in appearance rather than in substance. Maitland, the great legal historian, once wrote 'the Crown does nothing but lie in the Tower of London to be gazed at by sightseers' – a comment that emphasises the ceremonial rather than the legal role of the Crown as reflected by the monarch in the British constitution. This is the **Crown acting as the 'Queen (or King) in Parliament'**. The following examples of the royal prerogative illustrate the point.

## The prerogative powers of the 'Queen in Parliament'

- The monarch has the prerogative power to **open new parliamentary sessions** and to **dissolve Parliament for the purposes of a general election.** The former power is illustrated by the **Queen's (or King's) Speech** during the State Opening of Parliament, a ceremonial occasion in which the monarch reads a speech prepared by the **Government** outlining its proposals for new laws.
- The monarch has the prerogative to give the '**royal assent**' to legislation, thus formally making Bills (draft legislation) into operative Acts of Parliament. However, this is a formality rather than a power (the last time power was exercised by the monarch in such circumstances was as long ago as 1707). It used to be the case, historically, that the monarch signed all Bills, but today assent can be given by the signing of general documents to announce the giving of assent to the two Houses of Parliament. It is unrealistic to assume that the monarch reads the Bills that have been given assent, though detailed briefings will have been provided.
- The monarch has prerogative powers to **appoint and dismiss the Prime Minister of the country**, though, rather like the earlier examples, this is a matter of **political convention** rather than informed choice. Here, the monarch merely follows the choice of the political party with a majority in the House of Commons and appoints the leader of that party as Prime Minister after a general election victory. Moreover, the monarch will accept the resignation of a Prime Minister who loses a **'vote of no confidence'** in Parliament, or who leads a party to **defeat at the general election.**

We can see, therefore, that Crown powers as exercised by the monarch are limited in practice.

## The executive and its exercise of prerogative powers

A further dimension of the prerogative can be found in situations where the exercise of **Crown powers** is undertaken by the **executive** in times of war or emergency, or for the protection of overriding public interests. There have been occasions, for example, where the Government has attempted to justify its activities as a legitimate extension of the royal prerogative to **safeguard national security**. The exercise of the prerogative has far more significance, and deeper political implications, in the hands of the executive as a representation of the Crown, than with the monarch.

## Crown immunity from legal action

Part of the character of the Crown is that it is an entity with powers and rights as distinct from the citizens of the State. For this reason, the Crown enjoys **legal immunity** in certain respects because of its status. The origins of Crown immunity lie in the maxim that **'the King can do no wrong'**. It is still the case that the monarch cannot be sued in a personal capacity, though servants of the Crown – such as Government departments and other executive bodies and institutions – can be subject to **civil legal action** in the areas of contract and tort (Crown Proceedings Act 1947).

With regard to criminal law, the constitutional position is very controversial since the royal prerogative suggests that the Crown is immune from criminal prosecution. There is a fear that such a power allows the security services, in the name of the Crown, to obtain intelligence and maintain security through criminal activities, such as burglary and unlawful surveillance. However, this area is subject to the developing legal framework of human rights law, following the passing of the **Human Rights Act 1998** (see pp 27–34 below), even though some of the rights are limited to take into account the need for 'national security'.

The box to the right summarises the role of the Crown in the British constitution.

**SUMMARY BOX: WHAT IS THE CROWN?**

***Refers either to:***

- Queen or King (**monarch**); or
- Government (**executive**).

Both may exercise certain **royal prerogative powers**.

***What Crown powers does the monarch exercise?***

***Powers of the Queen (or King) in Parliament***

- Open **new Parliamentary sessions**.
- **Dissolve Parliament** for a general election.
- Give **royal assent** to legislation.
- Appoint and dismiss the **Prime Minister**.

*These are seen as 'conventions' rather than powers.*

***Crown immunity***

- Maxim: **'The King can do no wrong'**.
- King or Queen cannot be subject to legal action.
- Crown servants can be subject to legal action.

## PARLIAMENT AND ITS LAW-MAKING ROLE: PRESSURES FOR LAW REFORM

We now turn to the dominant law-making power in the British constitution, according to theory: the **legislature**, represented by **Parliament**. This section looks at the way in which Parliament makes statute law, taking into account the influences on it and the procedures to be followed.

Statutes are examples of **primary legislation**. This type of legislation must be distinguished from secondary legislation, which assumes the form of statutory instruments (regulations, orders in council) and byelaws, and is otherwise known as **delegated legislation**. Delegated legislation is covered in Chapter 2 of this book.

Primary legislation is the written law made by **Parliament** in the form of Acts of Parliament (statutes). The word 'Parliament' needs some explanation. It refers generally to a democratically elected chamber with law-making powers. In English law, the Parliament has two parliamentary chambers. The two chambers are the directly elected **House of Commons**; and the **House of Lords**, a non-elected chamber that includes appointed life peers and a limited

The Clock Tower, enclosing the bell that gives it the name 'BIG BEN', a prominent feature of the Houses of Parliament, Westminster

**Talking points: critically examining the British constitution**

*To what extent are the constitutional theories reflected in the practical workings of the British constitution?*
*Are the three main powers really separated?*
On the face of it, there are **three institutional powers** and there are **checks and balances** between them:

- Parliament acts as a **check** on the Government, through debates and by amending, delaying and sometimes even defeating Government proposals.
- Judges act as a **check** on the Government by hearing challenges to Government decisions in **judicial review** cases, on the basis that the decisions have been made unreasonably or exceed the legal powers available. Judges can also consider whether the Government, or Parliament, has acted in a manner **compatible with the European Convention on Human Rights**.

However, did you know that:

- The Government can be found within Parliament, so the **executive** and the **legislative** branches of the British constitution are to some extent 'fused'. The Government represents the party with the largest number of MPs in Parliament and all of the senior members of the Government, including the Prime Minister, are MPs. Therefore, if the Government has a large majority of MPs in Parliament it can wield an enormous amount of power, which Opposition MPs will find difficult to check effectively.
- The **House of Lords**, being the unelected chamber of Parliament, is not so easily under the control of a powerful Government, but it can only amend Government legislation and seek to hold it up. If the House of Lords chooses to delay Government legislation, the Government can force it to back down by using the **Parliament Acts 1911** and **1949**.
- Until the **Constitutional Reform Act 2005**, the senior members of the judiciary breached the separation of powers: the Lord Chancellor's roles involved the executive (as a member of the Cabinet at the heart of Government), the legislative (as Speaker in the House of Lords) and judicial (as head of the judiciary and serving 'law lord' on the Judicial Committee of the House of Lords); the senior judges also had seats in the House of Lords. However, the **2005 Act** includes reforms which pass the Lord Chancellor's role as head of the judiciary to the Lord Chief Justice; remove senior judges from entitlement to seats in the Parliamentary chamber of the House of Lords; and will replace in due course, the Judicial Committee of the House of Lords with a Supreme Court.

Moreover, do not accept the other constitutional theories at face value. You should ask:

- *Is Parliament really sovereign?*
- *Does the rule of law have practical relevance?*

By Chapters 1–5 of this book, you should start to think more critically about these questions. For example, is Parliament truly sovereign when there are other significant law-makers in the British constitution, when some legislative power is devolved to regional assemblies (such as the Scottish Parliament) and when EC law can override UK law? How can the Government square its desire to protect national security through identity cards, the lengthy detention of terrorism suspects and increased stop and search powers with individual civil liberties and fundamental human rights? To what extent do the Government's anti-terrorism measures breach the rule of law? To what extent should a Government lower its own legal standards – for example, by accepting evidence gained via the torture of a prisoner held in a foreign jail – to pursue suspected terrorists? At what constitutional price should national security be achieved?

number of hereditary peers (that is, members by birth). As we have seen, the House of Lords also has a **judicial committee**, and in this capacity is the **highest appeal court** in the English legal system (see Chapter 6); its role will be replaced by a **Supreme Court** when the **Constitutional Reform Act 2005** comes fully into effect.

**IT'S A FACT!**

**1.1: Primary legislation and secondary (delegated) legislation**

In 2004, Parliament passed 44 Acts of Parliament (primary legislation), comprising 38 Public Acts and 6 Private Acts (see coverage below).

Over the same period, however, some 3,452 pieces of delegated (secondary) legislation were passed by Government Ministers and other bodies under Parliament's authority (see Chapter 2 for elaboration). These figures were taken from the House of Commons Library update: see www.parliament.uk/commons/lib/research/notes/snsg-02911.pdf

So even though Acts of Parliament are the dominant sources of law in the British constitution, they are outnumbered by small, technical pieces of delegated legislation, which are being passed at a remarkable rate.

## Law reform and the influences upon parliamentary law-making

So where does the law-making process begin? The origins of law-making may be quite diverse.

The most obvious source is a new Government that has come to power. The Government will be elected on the basis of a document known as a **manifesto**. Each political party has a manifesto during the election and, in effect, is saying to voters, 'vote for us if you like what we have to say about how the country should be run'. Therefore, informed voters will choose the party with the manifesto that most appeals to them. A party that is elected for

Government will claim that the majority of votes affords them a **'political mandate'** for making changes, and often these involve either new laws or changes to existing ones. The Government will often get its way in making the law because it has a **majority of representatives** in the **House of Commons** (known as **Members of Parliament – MPs**). The **House of Lords**, in which the Government may or may not have a majority, is **restricted to delaying laws** for **up to one year** (under the **Parliament Act 1949**) rather than defeating them altogether.

## Let's look at cases: Challenging the Hunting Act 2004

The case of *R (Jackson and Others) v Attorney General* (2005), involving a challenge to the constitutional validity of the Hunting Act 2004, started in the Queen's Bench Divisional Court and ended up, via the Court of Appeal, in the House of Lords. The case had been brought by pro-hunting supporters who wanted to see the 2004 Act declared invalid, but not one of the courts found for the claimants.

*So what was the background to this case?*
The case centred on the way in which the Hunting Act had been passed through Parliament. The House of Commons, the elected (and therefore 'legitimate') chamber of Parliament had clearly voted in favour of the Bill to ban fox-hunting, but the House of Lords had persistently refused to accept the Bill. With a compromise out of reach, the Government resorted to the Parliament Acts 1911 and 1949 to force the Bill through Parliament and give effect to the will of the elected chamber. The Parliament Acts can be used when, in line with the 1949 Act's amendments to the 1911 Act, the House of Lords has rejected a Bill in two successive parliamentary sessions. This triggers the Act's automatic presentation for Royal Assent, subject to the further proviso that a year must have passed – between the original second reading of the Bill and its second successive passage through the House of Commons – for the provisions to take effect. Since the Bill to ban fox-hunting met these criteria, the Parliament Acts were invoked and the Royal Assent was given, thus creating the Hunting Act 2004.

*So what constitutional objections were raised against this Act?*
The claimants argued, amongst other things, that (1) Acts of Parliament were not constitutionally valid unless approved by *both* Houses of Parliament; (2) the Parliament Act 1949 had accordingly been passed without the consent of the House of Lords and so was itself invalid; (3) the Parliament Act 1949 was, in fact, delegated legislation and not primary legislation, and so could not validly increase the power of the House of Commons at the expense of the House of Lords.

The general rule is that no court can declare an Act of Parliament invalid, since that would undermine the concept of **parliamentary sovereignty** (*Pickin v British Railways Board*, 1974), but the House of Lords heard this case on the basis that a matter of constitutional law had to be resolved, which Parliament, itself, could not answer. To find otherwise would amount to a breach of the **rule of law**, since this would leave an important question of law unresolved.

*Why did the claimants lose their case?*
Senior judges in all three of the courts dismissed these arguments. Acts of Parliament could be valid without the consent of the House of Lords; whilst this might be perceived to erode checks and balances, leaving the House of Commons at the control of a strong Government, this was not a new position. The Parliament Acts have been used before, in 1991 pushing through the War Crimes Bill (to allow for the prosecution of 'war criminals' from World War II), in 1998 to give effect to a Bill allowing proportional representation for European Parliamentary Elections and in 2000 to enact the Sexual Offences (Amendment) Bill, which

reduced the age of consent for homosexual activity to 16. The Parliament Act 1949 was clearly to be regarded as an Act of Parliament, rather than delegated legislation, from the wording of the 1911 Act; and it did not seek to increase the powers of the House of Commons, but rather to place limits on the powers of the unelected House of Lords. As Lord Bingham concluded in the House of Lords, the Parliament Act 1949 and the Hunting Act 2004 were Acts of Parliament of full legal effect.

**Tasks**

(1) The Parliament Act 1911 was passed because Conservative hereditary peers in the House of Lords had begun to overstep the mark in rejecting the constitutional and social legislative programme of a popular Liberal Government, which dominated the House of Commons. Compare this situation with the controversy over the Hunting Act 2004. To what extent might it be said that Governments are too willing in modern times to invoke the Parliament Acts 'not for the major constitutional purposes for which the 1911 Act was invoked, but to achieve objects of more minor or no constitutional import' (Lord Bingham)?

(2) Summarise the Parliament Act procedures and make a brief set of notes on this important constitutional case.

(3) Why is it important to have 'checks and balances' within a constitution? Consider whether the decision of the House of Lords in this case 'erodes' those checks and balances in the British constitution?

(4) What does this case tell you about the relationship between the respective powers of the Crown, Commons, Lords and Government? Use your answer to draw up a list of evaluative points about the legislative process.

The Government will often **consult widely** before proceeding with substantial changes to the law. After a proposal has been made, the next stage of law-making is often the production of consultation documents: a **Green Paper** is a document outlining the Government's proposals for the purposes of further discussion; more significantly, a **White Paper**, taking into account one round of discussion, is a document containing a detailed explanation of the proposed legal changes. Although the consultation process can be long and at times frustrating for those seeking law reform, it ensures that the laws are carefully considered and subject to wide-ranging scrutiny and informed comment. The Government will be criticised if it announces changes without having carried out adequate consultation, as illustrated by the Government's handling of reforms affecting the Lord Chancellor and constitutional position of the senior judiciary (see Chapter 8 for elaboration).

However, the impetus for new law does not always arise from Government proposals. The following sources are also very relevant.

## Public opinion

At times, the public can demand new laws, usually encouraged by media campaigns. Public concern about dangerous dogs, for example, led to swiftly made – and now often criticised – legislation (the **Dangerous Dogs Act 1991**).

### Campaigns by pressure groups

**Pressure groups** are those organisations that seek to influence the direction of law and policy on the basis of particular **interests** or **causes**. The pressure groups that most readily spring to mind are those that support certain causes:

these will often be seen in newspapers or on television campaigning about issues such as health, human rights, consumer protection and the environment. Anyone can join a cause group, and popular examples include the **Royal Society for the Protection of Birds (RSPB), Greenpeace, Amnesty International** and **Compassion in World Farming.** If a pressure group begins to reflect mass public opinion, and the membership of the group rises, it can exert a great deal of pressure on law-makers. It is certainly true, for example, that by the late 1980s, environmental pressure groups had influenced legislation on the need for industries to protect the environmental media of air, water and land. More recently, a battle of cause groups – the **League Against Cruel Sports** in one corner, and the **Countryside Alliance** in the other – raged over the Government's proposal to ban hunting with hounds, with the resulting legislation, the **Hunting Act 2004**, favouring the former, leaving the latter to carry out a series of unsuccessful legal challenges in the courts (see *R (Jackson and Others) v Attorney-General* on pp 15–16, a challenge rejected by the House of Lords in October 2005).

The **interest pressure groups** may be less familiar to you, but are perhaps even *more* influential in the law-making process. This is often because they are consulted at an early stage by the Government and are therefore heavily involved in the law-making process. Interest groups differ from cause groups in that they represent the **interests of a specified membership**. The most obvious examples of interest groups are the **Trades Union Congress** (TUC), representing workers, and the **Confederation of British Industry** (CBI), representing business and management. The debates between these bodies have influenced a great deal of **employment legislation.**

### Private Members' Bills

Here, a **Member of Parliament**, without the official support of the Government or his/her party, puts forward an idea for legal change. This is an opportunity for ideas to be presented to Parliament which would otherwise be ignored because they are divisive within the political parties. A Private Member's Bill was the source, for example, of the Act that abolished the death penalty in this country: the **Murder (Abolition of the Death Penalty) Act 1965**. Another famous example is the **Abortion Act 1967**, which had been introduced as a Bill by the Liberal MP, David Steel.

MPs may also use such Bills to push an issue of **particular concern to their constituents:** for example, Stephen Pound, a Labour MP, brought a Private Member's Bill to the House of Commons on the issue of neighbour disputes arising from trees and high hedges on property boundaries. Whilst this Bill did not succeed in its passage through Parliament it nevertheless influenced Part 8 of the Government's subsequent Anti-Social Behaviour Act 2003.

### The need for a legal response to changing circumstances

Sometimes law-making is required quickly because of changing circumstances. Here, **secondary, delegated legislation** is used at times because it is more flexible than primary legislation. However, primary framework legislation is often required to deal with extreme circumstances. The terrorist attack on the US World Trade Center in 2001 prompted the UK Government to create primary legislation to combat terrorism (**Anti-Terrorism, Crime**

**and Security Act (ATCSA) 2001**). The only problem with this situation is that legislation can be rushed into force without its consequences being properly thought through, and this may mean that the law is less effective, in practice, than it should be. Indeed, the House of Lords, in 2004, declared the regime created by the ATCSA to subject foreign terrorist suspects to indefinite detention without trial to be **incompatible** with the European Convention on Human Rights (*A and Others v Secretary of State for the Home Department*, 2004) and forced the Government to re-think its response to terrorism.

### Legal changes prompted by the requirements of European Community law

The importance of European Community law, which is covered in depth in Chapter 5, is such that the UK has an **obligation to give effect to European Community legislation**. An example is provided by the **Equal Treatment Framework Directive**, which obliged the UK to pass laws, in 2003, to outlaw discrimination in the workplace on the grounds of sexual orientation and religious belief.

### Legal changes prompted by the requirements of the European Convention on Human Rights

We will see on pp 27–34 the wider impact that this Convention is having on English law following the **Human Rights Act 1998**. However, an example of a decision of the **European Court of Human Rights (ECtHR)** which led to parliamentary law reform (**Gender Recognition Act 2004**) is the case of *Goodwin v UK* (2002), which highlighted the inequalities in the current law relating to transsexual rights.

### Legal changes prompted by the law reform bodies/agencies

Attempts have been made over the years to make the system of **law reform** more logical. As the list of categories above shows, new laws can arise from so many different sources, and yet it has long been understood that law reform requires careful consideration and informed discussion.

The most significant law reform body is the **Law Commission**, which is an independent, full-time agency set up systematically to reform the law. The Law Commission was itself the product of primary legislation – the **Law Commissions Act 1965** – reflecting Parliament's anxiety to reform the law in a consistent manner. The Act states that the Law Commission's role is to **keep the law under review**. The Law Commission responds to proposals from judges, academics, the legal profession and others on the sorts of reform projects that need to be undertaken. The Law Commission has been very successful in encouraging law reform. Between 1966 and 2004, 114 reports have made reform recommendations that have been implemented (by contrast with 20 reports in which reforms were rejected). Examples commonly given of the Law Commission's role in reforming the law include:

- the **Unfair Contract Terms Act 1977** (which considers contract terms that seek to exclude or limit liability to the potential detriment of the other party or parties to the contract);

- the **Supply of Goods and Services Act 1982** (which creates terms to be implied into all contracts for the supply of services); and
- the **Contract (Rights of Third Parties) Act 1999** (which gives third parties, that is, those persons not directly involved in a contract but nevertheless affected by it, the ability to enforce certain contractual rights).

More recently, the Law Commission's reports on hearsay evidence in criminal proceedings (1997), double jeopardy and prosecution appeals (2001), bail and human rights (2001) and evidence of bad character in criminal proceedings (2001) have all been implemented in the **Criminal Justice Act 2003**. It also suggested reforms implemented in the **Domestic Violence, Crimes and Victims Act 2004** and recently published a well-received proposal to simplify the framework for **unfair terms in contracts** (2005). However, the Commission's attempts to **codify** the criminal law – perhaps its biggest project – have not been so successful and have been only partially implemented.

## Developing the subject 1.3: The Law Commission

The Law Commission structure includes **five full-time commissioners** (including a High Court Judge as Chairman on a three-year secondment) heading respective departments – **common law and commercial law; criminal law; public law; property, family and trust law; statute law** – within which can be found solicitors, barristers, academics, parliamentary draftsmen and a number of graduate research assistants. Each department usually has a number of projects on the go. The Law Commission is both proactive, in planning projects for the attention of the Lord Chancellor, and reactive, in that it responds to Government requests to investigate law reform possibilities in specific areas. Its first stated aim is to '***ensure the law is as fair, modern, simple and cost-effective as possible***' and as such it is engaged not only in the process of developing **new proposals**, but also in **consolidating** the existing statute law in an area, suggesting **revisions** to statutes (with a particular interest in updating, or removing, old and obsolete laws and eliminating loopholes), and, at its most ambitious, **codifying** whole frameworks of law (thus reducing years of common law and statutory development to single 'codes' or pieces of legislation).

A review of the Law Commission's work, the **Halliday Report (2003)**, was favourable and said that the Commission's contribution to law-making was 'held in high esteem', thus echoing the Lord Chancellor's view prior to the report that the 'Law Commission is a highly respected and expert body, with a fine record of producing well-argued recommendations for law reform'.

At the time of writing, the Law Commission is developing proposals for a reform of the **law of murder**, building on an earlier report into the **partial defences to murder**. It hopes to 'bring the law of murder into the twenty-first century' and has put forward for consultation a structure of three tiers of homicide:

- **First degree (top tier) murder:** murder with intention to kill, for which the mandatory life sentence would be reserved.
- **Second degree (second tier) murder:** where killing results through reckless indifference to causing death or there was an intention to cause serious harm, but not death. Here, there would be some flexibility in the sentence.
- **Manslaughter (third tier):** killing by gross negligence or intention to cause harm, but not serious harm.

**Research task:**
Visit www.lawcom.gov.uk/murder.htm and have a look at the proposals for murder (for general interest). The final recommendations should be available by the time you read this book. Monitor the progress of these reform proposals. Will they ever be implemented? Should they be implemented? See also Ian Yule's article on reforming murder in the A-level Law Review, Vol I Issue 2 (January 2006), at p 2, and coverage of relevant update cases – such as *R v Holley* – in Chapter 4 of this book. You might encounter this area of reform in your A2 studies, so make sure you keep a clippings file just in case.

Another type of law reform agency with great significance is the **ad hoc committee**, with **Royal Commissions** being the most important examples of these. **Royal Commissions** have prompted a great deal of law reform in the criminal justice system (with the **Runciman** and **Philips Commissions** being especially important in relation to criminal law procedures and police powers), though they have had less success in terms of civil law. The **Pearson Commission of 1978** was perceived as a notable failure, in that the Government did not take up a number of proposals relating to the law on personal injury. Royal Commissions have **advantages** in that they attract resources to carry out their work and are staffed by a broad range of experts, both legal and non-legal. However, the opportunities for following up important themes and issues are limited since Royal Commissions generally disband after they have delivered their reports. This increases the likelihood that law will develop in a **piecemeal fashion** rather than on the basis of logical progression. Ad hoc committees more generally are established to look at particular problems or situations that have occurred, and their influence on law reform will vary. Inquiries, such as those held into rail disasters or high-profile murders, are a form of ad hoc committee. Two recent ad hoc committees with great influence on law reform are the **Woolf Commission on Civil Justice** and the **Auld Review of the Criminal Justice System**. The implications of these law reform reports are considered later in this book (see Chapters 6 and 9, respectively).

For technical law reform – those reforms referred to as 'lawyers' law' because they relate, say, to the specific wording of statutes rather than to issues of general policy – two bodies operate on an advisory basis. The **Law Reform Committee** deals with narrow matters of civil law; and the **Criminal Law Revision Committee** operates likewise in criminal law. A result of the **Woolf Commission on Civil Justice**, mentioned above, is that other bodies (namely the **Civil Justice Council** and the **Legal Services Commission**) now keep the civil law under review, thus overshadowing the Law Reform Committee. Moreover, the Criminal Law Revision Committee has not sat since the mid-1980s. Both agencies are **part-time** and staffed by legal practitioners (for example, judges, barristers and solicitors) and academic lawyers (for example, professors of law at universities). It remains to be seen how long these two technical bodies will continue to have an influence on law reform in the English legal system.

Another related source of influence on law reform are the **academic law journals** published by university presses, and also highly respected textbooks. These often contain a critical examination of the current law and may influence the direction of reforms. Lord Bingham, in leading the House of Lords to overrule the *Caldwell* (1981) recklessness test in the landmark criminal law case of *R v G and R* (2003) (see also Chapters 4 and 12), remarked that: '*A decision was not, of course, to be overruled or departed from simply because it met with disfavour in learned journals. But a decision which attracted reasoned and outspoken criticism by the leading scholars of the day, respected as authorities in the field, must command attention*'.

### Judicial decisions

Judicial decisions can make new law through contributing to the **development of common law**, that is, the set of legal rules created through decisions in the courts over time (see Chapters 3 and 4 for elaboration). Clear examples of law-making, from judges in the courts, include the House of Lords' decision in *Ghaidan v Godin-Mendoza* (2004) that homosexuals in long-term loving relationships should enjoy the same tenancy rights as heterosexual couples; and the House of Lords' decision in *R v R* (1992) to recognise the offence of 'marital rape', after years of confusion. However, because these issues relate to 'public policy', primary legislation is often seen as preferable to judicial law-making. Developments in the common law may lead to **statutory law reform**, and may serve as an inspiration for law reformers to tackle certain issues.

So, as we have seen, there are many influences that may suggest a change in the law and the need for primary legislation. When the proposed change has taken shape, the next stage is for the outline to be drafted into the form of a **Bill**. It is this document, in effect a draft law, which will then proceed, if supported, through Parliament and become, after several distinct stages, an **Act of Parliament**.

Figure 1.1 summarises the **influences on parliamentary law-making** that stimulate **law reform**.

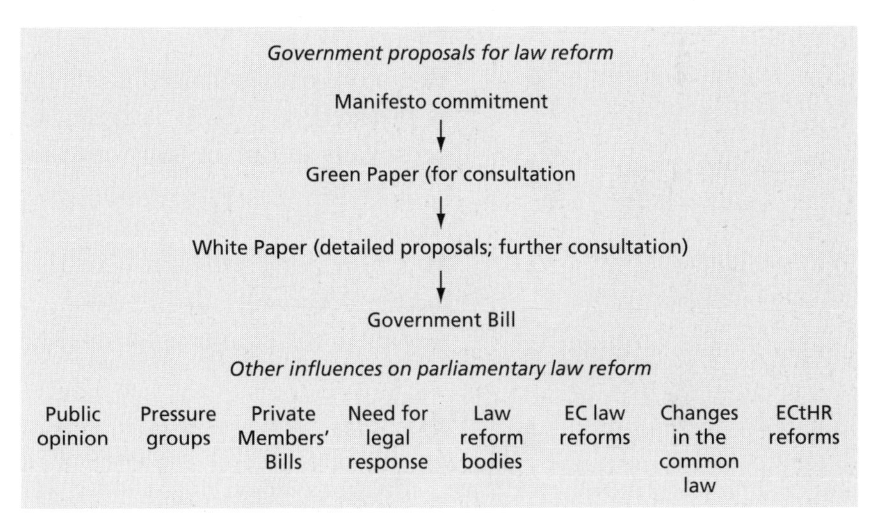


Figure 1.1 Influences on parliamentary law-making

## Bills

Bills may be divided into two main forms: **Public Bills** and **Private Bills**.

### Public Bills

These affect the law **in general** and have relevance for a wide range of persons, organisations and areas. **Public Bills** include:

- **Government Bills.** Government Bills are brought forward by Ministers: for example, the **Secretary of State for Trade and Industry** will be responsible for Bills relating to business regulation, consumer protection and fair trading. Government Bills are likely to succeed in becoming Acts of Parliament because the Government has a **majority of seats** in the House of Commons;

and the House of Lords, even if opposed to the Bill, can *only* **delay** the process of implementation. The Government can try to ensure that it gets all its members voting in favour of a Bill it has put forward by using the **Whip system,** which requires MPs to vote with their party. MPs rarely defy the Whips (that is, those politicians given the job of enforcing the system) for fear of damaging their chances of promotion within the Government. On occasions, the Government has suspended MPs who refused to follow the Whip in a crucial vote. In fact, the **House of Lords** provides a good check on Government Bills by suggesting sensible amendments and influencing the policy direction of the new law. The vast majority of Acts considered in this book – such as the **Criminal Justice Act 2003** and the **Courts Act 2003** – originated as Government Bills.

- **Private Members' Bills (PMBs)**. Despite their name, PMBs are types of Public Bill since they affect the general law. A recent example is the **Christmas Day (Trading) Act 2004,** which was introduced as a Bill by Labour MP Kevan Jones to prohibit the opening of large stores on Christmas Day in order to protect workers and offer time for families to come together. However, these Private Members' Bills rarely have the support of Government, and therefore it is a struggle for the individual MPs to get these Bills successfully through Parliament. Members of the House of Lords can also initiate these types of Bills, but these are known as **Private Peers' Bills.** A recent example is the **Assisted Dying for the Terminally Ill Bill,** initially introduced in 2004 by Lord Joffe, scrutinised by a House of Lords Committee and then re-introduced, with amendments, in 2005. Peers share similar difficulties to those experienced by MPs in making progress with these types of Bills. The Assisted Dying for the Terminally Ill Bill 2005, for example, was defeated on second reading in the House of Lords (May 2006).

### Private Bills

Private Bills affect only a **limited area or range of persons**. In certain, very rare, situations they might only relate to one or two people and are then referred to as Personal Bills. They are far less common than Public Bills and arise through petitioning from outside bodies or campaigners. A recent example is the **Mersey Tunnels Act 2004,** which enables local transport authorities in Merseyside to use surplus money from the operation of road toll schemes for the improvement of local public transport services. Private Bills have their own special procedures in Parliament, allowing for objections from members of the public to be submitted formally and taken into account.

Table 1.3 summarises the main types of Bills that may be encountered.

If a Bill affects only a limited area or range of persons, and yet has wider significance for the nation, it might be classed as a **hybrid Bill.** For example, the **Crossrail Bill** is before Parliament at the time of writing which would give effect, if passed, to an east-west rail link across Central London. A hybrid bill is treated as a **Private Bill** for the purposes of parliamentary procedure.

Table 1.3 Public and Private Bills

| *Public Bills* | *Private Bills* |
|---|---|
| Bills that propose **general changes** in the law:<br>• **Government Bills** (brought forward by Ministers heading Government departments).<br>• **Private Members' Bills** (brought forward by individual MPs). | Bills that propose changes in the law that **affect only specific areas or persons**.<br>These are brought to Parliament by outside bodies.<br>These Bills are relatively rare. |

## THE PARLIAMENTARY LAW-MAKING PROCESS: HOW A PUBLIC BILL BECOMES AN ACT

The **formal process of statute creation** (that is, the passing of a Bill to an Act) can be described as a six-part process, though note that the first five parts are repeated in the next House of Parliament (for example, most Bills start off in the House of Commons and then go to the House of Lords, so *both* Houses follow parts one to five). The **House of Lords** can **delay a Bill** or **seek amendments**, but they *cannot* **prevent** the elected House of Commons from passing a Bill for more than a year: if they seek to do so, the **House of Commons** can use powers in the **Parliament Acts 1911 and 1949** to force the legislation through Parliament (as occurred with the **Hunting Act 2004**, see pp 15–16).

The term '**readings**', which you will see below, is maintained for historical purposes and refers to the times when, prior to the introduction of printing, Bills were read out in the parliamentary chamber. Clearly, today MPs can obtain a printed copy of the Bill for reference. It is also necessary to point out that some Bills are '**fast-tracked**' through Parliament. This is largely reserved for Bills that are *not* contentious (that is, unlikely to cause great debate or argument).

### First reading

This is seen as something of a **formality** and consists merely of introducing the Bill to Parliament so that MPs can prepare for further discussion.

### Second reading

This is a very important stage of the Bill's passage through Parliament, since the Minister in charge of the Bill explains the main aims and objectives of the proposed law and answers any questions MPs may have. It is at this stage, often, that lively **debate** ensues. A vote will be taken at the end of the second reading, and if sufficient approval is given, the Bill will proceed to the Committee stage. 'Sufficient approval' may mean that enough MPs shout 'Aye' rather than 'No'; or where this is not clear, the MPs take a **formal vote**. The formal votes are also based on 'Ayes' and 'Noes', though these opinions are expressed by MPs choosing to walk through one of the designated **division lobbies** adjoining the parliamentary chamber. The MPs who choose to walk through the 'Aye' lobby will be counted as against those who walk through the 'No' lobby.

## Committee stage

This stage of the Bill's passage through Parliament is significant because it allows for detailed examination of the Bill by a small group of MPs (forming a **Standing Committee**) with an interest in its contents; and it is also the first occasion when amendments can be added. Votes will be taken on any amendments, within the confines of the Committee. Some very important or controversial Bills may be heard by a Committee of the whole House, but these occasions will be rare.

## Report stage

The results of the Committee stage are reported back to the whole House. Clearly, if there was a Committee of the whole House this stage will not be necessary. MPs can, at this point, suggest **further amendments** to the Bill. Votes will take place on proposed amendments.

## Third reading

This is the final overview stage of the Bill's passage, whereby it is considered in its amended form as a whole. MPs engage **in further debate**. The Bill then goes to the **next House** for these steps to be repeated and further amendments made and agreed. If a Bill is particularly controversial then disagreements between the two Houses may lead to a 'ping-pong' process, in which issues are batted back and forth between them until a compromise is reached. In 2006, the **Terrorism Bill 2005** and the **Identity Cards Bill 2005** were 'ping ponged' between the Houses, though the Government managed, in both cases, to steer these through Parliament and onto the statute book.

## Royal assent

Once the Bill has completed the parliamentary process in both Houses of Parliament then it is ready to become an Act. To give effect to this, the Queen has to give her assent. In modern times, the Queen merely signs her **general consent** to the Bills passed in each parliamentary session, and such assent is usually communicated to the relevant House by its Speaker. As we have seen, this is one of the few residual powers of the Crown in the British constitution, but as you will note, it is a formality rather than a power to be exercised freely by the Queen.

Table 1.4 summarises the stages through which a Bill has to pass on the way to becoming an Act of Parliament.

# THE CONCEPT OF PARLIAMENTARY SOVEREIGNTY

Reference has already been made at pp 8–9 to the constitutional theory of **parliamentary sovereignty**, and this underlines the importance of primary legislation. Parliamentary sovereignty means that:

(a) **Parliament** is the **supreme law-making body** in the British constitution. Parliamentary law should therefore **prevail** over all other sources of law. This means that Acts of Parliament are superior to, and can therefore override, the common law rules made by judges. If it appears that primary legislation is out of date – and this is noted by judges in relevant cases that come before them – the enacted legislation will nevertheless remain in force until **expressly or impliedly repealed** (cancelled out).

(b) **Parliament** can **make any laws that it wants.** This follows from an acceptance of Parliament as the supreme law-making body and is both subject to, and supported by, the **doctrine of implied repeal.** This amounts to a practical rule that a differing later statute dealing with a subject in an earlier statute, in the absence of any express statement, **impliedly repeals the earlier statute.** The doctrine requires that **no Parliament bind its**

Table 1.4 The passing of a Government Bill

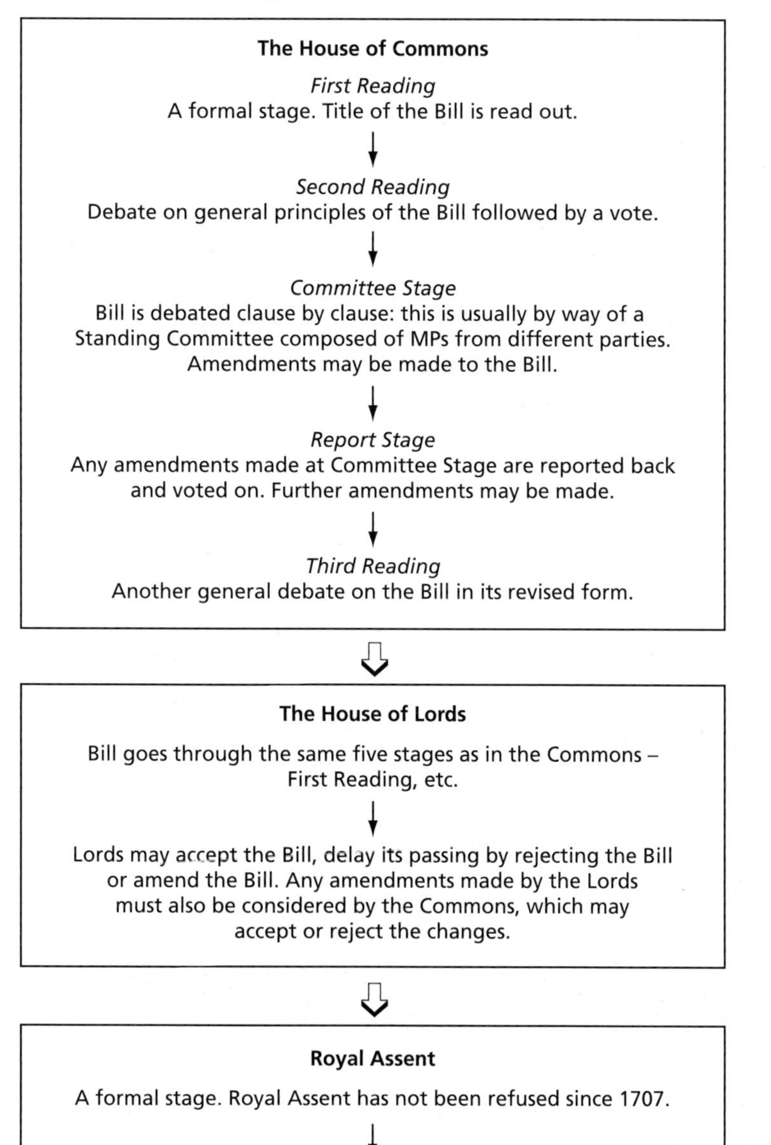

**successors** (that is, for no Parliament to make laws that will restrict law-making in future Parliaments), and thereby allows for freedom in law-making. Moreover, since Parliament is of a superior status to the courts, the traditional view is that judges cannot question or challenge Acts of Parliament.

## Limitations to parliamentary sovereignty

The above points represent the **theory of parliamentary sovereignty**, but is **Parliament really the supreme law-making body in practice?** It is not difficult to find limitations to the supremacy concept. As Chapter 2 indicates, statistically speaking, Acts of Parliament are not the dominant form of written law produced each year. A far greater body of law-making is carried out by **Government Ministers**, amongst others, in the form of **secondary – or 'delegated' – legislation.** While this legislation is dependent on primary legislation for its development, there is far more of it produced than Acts of Parliament, and the parliamentary controls over it are relatively limited.

Moreover, it is now accepted that judges *do* make law, and the **common law** has contributed large bodies of law independent of statutory intervention (see Chapter 4, for example). This is seen particularly in the areas of contract and tort law, where common law development far outweighs statutory provisions and has given rise to new forms of liability, such as that in tort relating to nervous shock.

Parliament is also sensitive to **public opinion**, and the Government's plans for law-making will reflect this. Therefore, the idea that Parliament can do what it wants is constrained by practical reality.

One of the most significant limitations on the concept of parliamentary sovereignty is that of **entrenched** laws, that is, those that for historical, social or political reasons have become embedded within the constitution. It is highly unlikely, for example, that Parliament would dismantle the recent policy of **devolution**, which has granted some legislative power to a Scottish Parliament: it would be difficult for any future Parliament to repeal such powers. The problem of entrenched laws raises question marks about the rule that Parliament shall not bind its successors.

It is difficult to find a better illustration of the latter point than the UK's membership of the European Union. The UK joined the then European Community in 1973, as effected by the **European Communities Act 1972.** This statute is entrenched as a matter of 'political reality': because of the UK's status as a Member State, English law is subject to the laws of the institutions of the European Union and the UK is a participant in, and a recipient of, social, economic and political policies. The constitutional writer, Wade, has argued that this marks a 'constitutional revolution' in that Parliament did, in impact, bind its successors back in 1972. Those who argued against membership of the European Community in 1972 tried to insert a clause into the European Communities Bill safeguarding UK sovereignty. They failed. There is little doubt that since 1 January 1973, **parliamentary sovereignty** has been *limited* by membership of the European Union and the impact of European Community law, a point underlined by the furious debates that have taken place in the UK – and other Member States – about the significance of the **Draft European Union Constitution** (see also Chapter 5).

A more recent reform that has had a further diluting effect on the sovereignty principle is that of the **Human Rights Act 1998**, which implements, to a large extent, the **European Convention on Human Rights**. While there is some debate about the status of the Convention, it has far-reaching implications for English law. One of the most significant points is that Parliament now has to pass Bills which are 'compatible' with the Convention, unless **specific derogations** from the Convention are made (in other words, it is made clear that Convention rights will be waived, say, for reasons of national security). This means that **Parliament can no longer do precisely what it wants**. The Act also permits judges to **declare Acts of Parliament 'incompatible'** with the Convention, thus undermining the sovereignty principle that Parliament is the supreme law-making body in the Constitution and that Acts of Parliament cannot be challenged in the courts. It can be argued, of course, that in practice Parliament's role is secured, because it can refuse to respond to a judicial 'declaration of incompatibility' under the Human Rights Act (a luxury it is not afforded, incidentally, under the separate regime of EC law, where EC law *must* be followed). However, the fact that judges are now able to challenge the validity of Acts is highly significant, and reflects a discernible shift in the separation of powers.

Table 1.5 overleaf summarises the issue of **parliamentary sovereignty**.

## THE HUMAN RIGHTS ACT 1998: SOME QUESTIONS ANSWERED

The 2 October 2000 marked the beginning of radical legal change in this country when English law substantially incorporated the **European Convention on Human Rights ('the Convention')**. While claimants seeking to establish that their rights have been breached have been able to take their cases to the **European Court of Human Rights (ECtHR)** in **Strasbourg**, the implementation of the **Human Rights Act 1998** provides for the enforcement of such rights in the English courts. The following summary answers some key questions about this important legal change.

### What is the European Convention on Human Rights?

As a response to the horrors of World War II, the Convention provided a framework for the protection of fundamental rights and freedoms. It was created in 1950 and gained the status of an international treaty in 1953. It has since been ratified by over 40 States. For many of these States, the formal acceptance of the Convention as an international treaty *automatically incorporated* Convention rights into their domestic legal systems. This did *not* occur in the UK for a number of reasons (the lack of a written constitution being a significant factor).

Therefore, although the UK was an original signatory of the Convention, it chose not to incorporate its terms into English law. The UK did, in 1966,

Table 1.5 Nature and limits of parliamentary sovereignty

*What is parliamentary sovereignty?*

In theory:

- Parliament is the supreme law-making body.
- Parliamentary law is superior to all other types of law.
- Parliament can make any laws that it wants.
- Parliament can unmake any laws (through express or implied repeal).
- Parliaments are not bound by their predecessors, so have freedom to make new law.

*But is parliamentary sovereignty limited in practice?*

| *Limitation to sovereignty theory* | *Brief description* |
|---|---|
| Delegated legislation | See Chapter 2. More delegated legislation than primary legislation – so is this the dominant form of law, in practice? |
| Common law | See particularly Chapters 4 and 13. Law made by judges has contributed whole areas to English law, without the need for statutes – so Parliament has not been involved. |
| Public opinion | Parliament cannot create laws that the public will not tolerate. Therefore, practical limits to law-making power. |
| Entrenched laws | Some parliamentary laws clearly bind successor Parliaments – what sort of Parliament would seek to repeal the Independence Acts? |
| European Community law (brought into English law by the European Communities Act 1972) | See Chapter 5. Parliament is now subject to the laws made by the European Union institutions – it is no longer the dominant law-maker in some areas of policy. For the UK to withdraw from the European Union would create huge practical, constitutional and legal difficulties. |
| European Convention on Human Rights (incorporated by the Human Rights Act 1998) | See below. Laws must now be compatible with the Convention. Judges can declare Acts to be incompatible with the Convention. |

recognise the authority of the European Court of Human Rights (ECtHR) to hear, and adjudicate on, complaints from UK citizens, but again it chose not to incorporate the Convention.

Despite calls for incorporation in the 1980s and early 1990s, the Conservative Government always resisted the move on both policy and practical grounds. A new Labour Government in 1997, however, promised to bring about incorporation of the Convention into English law and swiftly introduced a Human Rights Bill to Parliament. The resulting statute was the **Human Rights Act 1998**. The Act received its royal assent in November 1998, but did not come into force in England and Wales until 2 October 2000. One reason for the gap between royal assent and the Act coming into force was the need to train judges and magistrates and recruit more of them.

The **rights** protected by the **Articles (Arts) of the Convention**, and contained within **Schedule 1** to the **Human Rights Act 1998**, include:

- a right to life (Art 2);
- rights prohibiting torture (Art 3);
- rights prohibiting slavery and forced labour (Art 4);
- rights to liberty and security (Art 5);
- a right to a fair trial (Art 6);
- a right to privacy and family life (Art 8);
- a right to marry (Art 12); and
- rights against discrimination (Art 14).

There are also established rights relating to freedom of thought, expression, religion and assembly.

## Is the European Convention on Human Rights a source of EC law?

No. The European Convention on Human Rights is *quite separate* from the European Community. The European Convention on Human Rights was made in 1950 by a body called the Council of Europe. Cases on human rights matters brought under the Convention go to the ECtHR in Strasbourg (and now also to English courts). The European Community (EC), on the other hand, was not created until 1957 and brings Member States together to achieve common economic and social aims. The EC, now referred to as the European Union (EU), consists of (currently) 25 Member States and is governed by a set of institutions that include the European Court of Justice in Luxembourg. Do *not* confuse the **EU's European Court of Justice** with the **Council of Europe's European Court of Human Rights.**

## How does the Human Rights Act 1998 incorporate the Convention into English law?

The Human Rights Act 1998 requires that, as far as possible, primary legislation and delegated legislation are made **compatible** with the Convention. If such legislation comes before the courts and is found not to be compatible, the courts have the power to make a **declaration of incompatibility** under **s 4** of the **1998 Act.** This acts as an encouragement to Government and Parliament to make the necessary amendments – via primary or delegated legislation – to ensure compatibility.

The UK courts can hear any cases in which claimants allege that their rights have been breached by **public authorities** (that is, the State or bodies with functions of a 'public nature', for example, the NHS, Police, etc) under ss 6 and 7 of the Human Rights Act 1998. In determining these cases, previous decisions of the ECtHR should be taken into account, thus affecting the system of judicial precedent, discussed in Chapter 4. Moreover, s 3 requires courts to read and give effect to legislation **'so far as it is possible to do so'** in order to achieve **compatibility with Convention rights,** thus necessitating a **purposive approach to interpretation,** as discussed later in Chapter 3. The Act gives a degree of discretionary power to the court, under s 8, in awarding remedies or relief to claimants who have suffered a breach of their rights (for example, damages, injunctions and remedies available under the judicial review procedure). It does *not* incorporate Art 13 of the ECHR – 'Everyone whose (Convention) rights and freedoms . . . are violated shall have an effective remedy before a national authority' – though claimants reserve the right to take their cases to the Strasbourg court (ECtHR) if all domestic appeals have been exhausted.

Table 1.6 summarises some of the main features of the Human Rights Act 1998.

Table 1.6 Main features of the Human Rights Act 1998

- Concerns situations where claimants have suffered a **violation of rights** by **public authorities**.
- Rights are contained in the **Articles** of the **European Convention on Human Rights,** which can be found in **Schedule 1** to the **1998 Act.**
- Rights can be **enforced in the English courts.**
- Judges have the job of **interpreting these rights** and **developing the common law** accordingly.
- Judges **must** take into account the **previous decisions** of the **European Court of Human Rights.**
- Judges must give effect to Convention rights **'so far as it is possible to do so'.**
- Judges can make a **declaration of incompatibility** if an Act before the courts is seen to be incompatible with the Convention.
- Judges can award **remedies** or **relief** for any breach of rights.
- If a claimant is not successful in the English courts, there is a **right of appeal** to the **European Court of Human Rights** in Strasbourg.

## Overview of some of the impacts of the Human Rights Act 1998 so far . . .

At the time of writing, the **Human Rights Act 1998** has been in force for over five years and perhaps a measure of its success is the amount of controversy it has generated over that period. One of the aims of the Act was to create a **'rights culture'** and the extent to which this has begun to challenge traditional power relationships has generated lots of debate about the scope and exercise of State powers and the sort of rights that individuals can legitimately expect to be protected. However, if some politicians get their way, the Act might become a victim of its own success, with sections of the media clearly alarmed by its implications (see, for example, coverage in *The Sunday Telegraph*, 14/5/06), Tony Blair suggesting it be amended and David Cameron, leader of the Conservative Party, arguing for its repeal.

Particular issues raised have included:

- A shift in the power relationship between **judges** and the other constitutional powers. The judges' ability, in particular, to make **declarations of incompatibility** in respect of primary legislation (of which there had been ten examples by 2004, excluding those reversed on appeal) has, according to Professor David Feldman (2005), marked 'a major move *away* from the

. . . principle of **parliamentary sovereignty**'. In addition, the **separation of powers** has been strengthened, with the judiciary keeping Parliament and the Government in check, and thus protecting the **rule of law**.

- **Political controversy** arising from the uses to which the Human Rights Act has been put featuring in 557 court cases in 2002–2003 and currently running at 400 cases per year (*The Times*, 26/12/05). For example, the Conservative Party's commitment, prior to the 2005 General Election, to review the Act on the grounds of the 'compensation culture' it had created. Conservatives were particularly concerned by decisions that provided rights to gypsies and travellers, and to prisoners. The Government has also, at times, lost its patience with the judges – David Blunkett, when Home Secretary in 2003, was quoted as saying that he was 'fed up' debating issues in Parliament only for judges to overturn the decisions made and, more recently, Tony Blair described a decision giving refugee-status to nine Afghan nationals who had hijacked a plane as 'an abuse of common sense' – though it has introduced amended legislation to Parliament to address **declarations of incompatibility** so far.
- The capacity of the Act to affect relationships between private individuals as well as between citizens and public authorities. Under s 6 of the Act, the courts as a 'public authority' are under a duty to apply and develop the law in a way that is compatible with Convention rights. Therefore, if areas of common law can develop compatibly with Convention rights then the Act will be of relevance to **private disputes**. This has proved especially relevant in a number of high profile disputes between celebrities and newspapers or magazines, in which celebrities have sought to rely on a **right to privacy** (**Art 8**) and the media has claimed **freedom of expression** (**Art 10**).

## Let's look at cases 1.2: The right to privacy cases

The following cases in the English courts have considered the relationship between: the common law protections relating to privacy, including the tort of breach of confidence, and the right to privacy in Art 8 of the ECHR; the potential for Art 8 to be raised in essentially private disputes; and the relationship between the Art 8 right to privacy and the Art 10 right to freedom of expression.

*Douglas and Zeta-Jones v Hello! Ltd (2000)*
The Hollywood couple, Michael Douglas and Catherine Zeta-Jones, together with *OK!* magazine, successfully claimed damages, but not an injunction, in a claim against *Hello!* magazine, which had published unauthorised photographs of the couple's wedding. *OK!* magazine had been given an exclusive contract for the wedding, which *Hello!*, its rival, had sought to undermine. At the Court of Appeal stage, Lord Justice Sedley expressed the view that English law would now, following the Human Rights Act 1998, uphold a *general right to privacy* under Art 8. However, the case was resolved, instead, by common law relating to commercial secrets (breach of confidence) and data protection law.

*Wainwright v Home Office (2003)*
Two prison visitors, suspected of carrying drugs, had been strip-searched in a manner that breached established Codes of Practice and caused them distress

and psychiatric injury. The trial judge found that Mrs Wainwright could establish a claim in tort based on the Art 8 breach of privacy. However, the Court of Appeal and the House of Lords, in subsequent appeals, did not accept that view. Lord Hoffmann made it clear that he was unconvinced by arguments that equated a right to *respect for* privacy with a general right to privacy in English law.

*Campbell v MGN (2004)*
Here the supermodel, Naomi Campbell, sued the *Daily Mirror* (owned by MGN) when it published photographs and a story about her attending a drugs clinic. Her tort claims included the common law breach of confidence, which the House of Lords accepted could be informed by the values of Art 8, and that specific instances, such as the breach of confidential information, could allow Art 8 to outweigh the newspaper's Art 10 (freedom of expression) defence. Lord Hope, in particular, seemed to recognise a *specific right to privacy* action for misuse of private information based on Art 8 that can be contrasted with the unwillingness, in *Wainwright*, to recognise a *general right to privacy*. Campbell won the case, leaving the *Daily Mirror* with a large bill for costs. (See also Chapter 11.)

The point of these cases seems to be that whilst incorporation of the European Convention on Human Rights in the Human Rights Act 1998 is not immediately changing English common law, it is, over time, influencing the rights available.

## Some landmark decisions of the English courts relating to the Human Rights Act 2000

*R (on the application of Anderson) v Secretary of State for the Home Department* (2002) – the House of Lords found that English law in respect of mandatory life sentences, and the Home Secretary's role in determining the period to be served, was incompatible with the Art 6 right to a fair trial, since this should be a matter for the judiciary (an interesting case, particularly in its defence of the **separation of powers** within the British constitution). The Government subsequently introduced provisions to address these concerns to Parliament and they were subsequently passed as part of the **Criminal Justice Act 2003**.

*Bellinger v Bellinger* (2003) – the House of Lords found that English law was in breach of the Art 8 right to privacy and the Art 12 right to marry when a transsexual was unable to enter a valid marriage because the law would not recognise her changed gender. The Government – also under pressure on the problems faced by transsexuals after the European Court of Human Rights found the UK to be in breach of rights in *Goodwin v UK* (2002) – subsequently acted on the **declaration of incompatibility** by introducing a **Gender Recognition Bill** to Parliament (now an Act).

*Ghaidan v Godin-Mendoza* (2004) – the House of Lords, by interpreting English law compatibly with the Art 14 Convention right prohibiting discrimination, found that surviving members of same-sex relationships were to be treated in the same way as husband or wife and granted secure rights of tenancy. Thus, the *Mendoza* decision prevented discrimination on the grounds of sexual orientation in tenancy law.

*A v Secretary of State for the Home Department* (2004) – the House of Lords found that the Anti-Terrorism, Crime and Security Act 2001, which allowed for the indefinite detention of foreign terrorism suspects without trial, breached the Art 5 right to liberty and the Art 14 right prohibiting discrimination (since this procedure was provided only for foreign suspects). Some of the Law Lords saw this as an opportunity to defend the **rule of law** against an over-powerful executive, with Lord Hoffmann's comment that 'the real threat to the nation . . . comes not from terrorism but from laws such as these' receiving a great deal of media comment. The Government responded by introducing another controversial **Prevention of Terrorism Bill** to Parliament (now an Act) to address concerns about liberty (replacing indefinite detention with house arrest in the form of 'control orders') and discrimination (the new provisions apply to all terrorism suspects). Even this response, however, has not found favour in the courts (see Chapter 8, at p 164).

## The impact of the European Court of Human Rights (ECtHR)

The ECtHR in Strasbourg has heard lots of UK cases since 1966 and even today, with the European Convention on Human Rights incorporated in English law, applicants unable to gain a remedy in the national courts continue to take their cases there. Indeed, those at school should thank the ECtHR for the fact that caning, birching and spanking are no longer permitted for bad behaviour: a ban on corporal punishment in the UK being influenced by a number of ECtHR cases relating to the Art 3 right not to suffer degrading treatment and the Art 8 right to respect for private life (such as *X v UK* (1981) and *Costello-Roberts v UK* (1995)). The impact on society of such rulings is undeniable. Chapter 1 ends, then, with a very brief round-up of recent ECtHR cases and some discussion points.

## Some recent ECtHR cases

- *Steel and Morris v UK* (2005): in the 'McLibel' case, where two animal rights protesters (Steel and Morris) were sued for libel by McDonald's, the ECtHR held that the proceedings had been conducted unfairly because the defendants had been denied legal aid. (Breach of Art 6 ECHR: damages and costs awarded.)
- *Bubbins v UK* (2005): the failure to incorporate Art 13 of the ECHR in the Human Rights Act 1998 had left the applicant (Bubbins) without a remedy in the national courts. She had sought, and been denied, legal aid, to challenge the investigation of the Police Complaints Authority, and an inquest, into the shooting of her brother by police during a 'siege'. A police marksman had fired the fatal shot when the brother, apparently drunk, had brandished a replica pistol. (Breach of Art 13 ECHR: damages and costs awarded.)
- *B and L v UK* (2005): the UK was in breach of Art 12, the right to marry, when the statutory framework for marriages prevented a valid marriage being achieved between a father-in-law and daughter-in-law. (Costs awarded.)

**Talking points 1.2: Human rights and the British constitution**

*Reviewing coverage of the Human Rights Act 1998 in Chapter 1, it is worth thinking about and discussing some of the issues raised by this important constitutional reform. Consider the following:*

- To what extent has the Human Rights Act 1998 supported the principles of the British constitution?
- Has the Act given the judges too much power?
- Are there any cases in this chapter, or that you have seen in the media, that have particularly impressed you? Are there, likewise, any cases that you think should not have been brought?
- Is there too much talk today about rights, at the expense of responsibilities?
- Has the rights culture had a positive impact on the UK?

- *Hirst v UK* (2005): the UK was in breach of the right to free elections, as laid down in a protocol to the ECHR, when it automatically denied the right to vote to Mr Hirst, one of 48,000 convicted prisoners, under the Representation of the People Act 1983. The ECtHR left it to the UK Parliament to remedy this situation. (Costs awarded.)

**Exercise for Chapter 1: Recap quiz**

(1) Which **constitutional theory or feature** represents:

(a) checks and balances between executive, legislature and judiciary?
(b) a check on arbitrary power and an insistence that no individual is above the law?
(c) the Queen's remaining powers and those assumed by the executive in certain circumstances?
(d) the dominance of parliamentary law over other types of law?
(e) the sharing of some sovereign executive or legislative power with the regions?
(f) the UK's entrenched status, since 1973, of being a Member State?
(g) the enforcement of the ECHR in the national courts?
(h) the lack of a single written code of fundamental principles?

**Options**: parliamentary sovereignty; Human Rights Act 1998; unwritten constitution; rule of law; prerogative powers; separation of powers; EC law obligations under the European Communities Act 1972; devolution.

(2) Which **influence on Parliament or specific law reform body** is suggested in the following examples:

(a) a campaign by the National Farmer's Union to influence a Bill on agriculture?
(b) a full-time body, created by statute, which keeps the law under constant review?
(c) a Bill put forward on a single issue by an MP or peer?
(d) any form of law reform body that is set up to tackle a specific issue and then disbands once its report has been published?
(e) a change initiated by judicial decisions in the courts?

**Options**: *ad hoc* committees; pressure groups; private members' Bill; common law; Law Commission.

(3) Which **stages of the process of statute creation (parliamentary law-making)** are represented by the following summaries:

(a) Minister explains Bill, followed by major debate and vote?
(b) Queen formally approves a Bill that has passed through both Houses?
(c) Bill formally introduced to Parliament?
(d) Feedback to Parliament on scrutiny of a Bill by Standing Committee?
(e) Final reading stage?
(f) Scrutiny of a Bill by Standing Committee?

**Options:** first reading; second reading; committee stage; report stage; third reading; royal assent.

For Answers, please turn to p 333.

## Useful website addresses

| | |
|---|---|
| BBC News Politics (A–Z of Parliament) | www.news.bbc.co.uk/i/hi/uk_politics |
| Department for Constitutional Affairs | www.dca.gov.uk |
| European Court of Human Rights | www.echr.coe.int |
| Law Commission | www.lawcom.gov.uk |
| Liberty | www.liberty-human-rights.org.uk |
| Parliament (Bills/Acts) | www.parliament.uk |
| *Materials directly for AS studies:* | |
| John Deft (St Brendan's Sixth Form College) | www.stbrn.ac.uk/other/depts/law |
| Asif Tufal | www.a-level-law.com |

**HINTS AND TIPS**

This section of the exam specifications is a challenging one for students *and* teachers, because (a) it is so broad in scope; and (b) it informs most other topics in the sources of law area. Before developing the comment in (b), let's first address (a): how can this broad topic be broken down? What should, with confidence, be revised?

- Role of the **Queen in Parliament** (eg, conventions, royal assent).
- Influences on **Parliament** and **law reform** (eg, role of bodies such as the Law Commission).
- From a Bill to an Act of Parliament – referred to as the process of **statute creation** (eg, first reading, second reading, etc – and with some appreciation of the roles of Government, Parliament and Queen).
- The doctrine of **parliamentary sovereignty** and the **limits** placed on it (eg, EC law, devolution, the European Convention on Human Rights etc).

Around these central topics, the remainder of Chapter 1 has been about context-setting: ensuring that you understand the relationships between the powers in the British Constitution; and providing some additional knowledge on how certain sources of law have affected sovereignty (such as the European Convention on Human Rights, as incorporated by the Human Rights Act 1998).

For the topics bullet-pointed above, make sure you revise enough so that you can *describe* and *explain* the areas and provide *examples*; also make sure you note down any critical comments about these roles, concepts and processes, and also their perceived strengths, in order that you can offer some *evaluation* for each one.

Turning attention to my earlier comment (b), the broad nature of this topic means that you have to plan ahead for the possibility of **mixed topic questions**. However, don't worry about this, since some of the links between topics are easy to spot. Here are some likely combinations of topics in this chapter with topics covered later in this book:

- Parliament's law-making role as illustrated by statute creation, might be *contrasted* with other forms of law-making (see, for example, delegated law-making in Chapter 2, and judicial law-making in Chapter 4).
- The concept of parliamentary sovereignty might be *contrasted* with its limitations: such as delegated legislation (Chapter 2) or EC law (Chapter 5). Brief coverage of the Human Rights Act 1998, from this chapter, would be relevant here.

This chapter informs your general understanding of the sources of law and will allow you, in time, to evaluate the other topics in Chapters 2–5.

# Delegated legislation

2

This topic enables you:

- To appreciate that primary legislation is often supplemented by different types of secondary, technical legislation.
- To show the extent of legislation that may be passed.
- To indicate that legislation can be made by a range of bodies and organisations under authority from primary legislation.
- To appreciate the scale of law-making that occurs in the English legal system.
- To understand the relationship between the creation of secondary legislation and constitutional legal theory.

By volume, secondary, or delegated, legislation is the largest source of legislation in the English legal system. In 1998, there were 3,319 pieces of UK delegated legislation compared with only 49 pieces of primary legislation. In 2001, there were some 4,147 pieces of UK delegated legislation! So what is this mass of legislation concerned with? Who reads it all? Is it all 'good law'?

## WHAT IS DELEGATED LEGISLATION?

The word '**delegate**' means to pass power to another person. Delegated legislation is therefore formed when **Parliament** has delegated power to other persons or bodies. The authority to make these laws is laid down in **primary legislation** (Acts of Parliament). Consider the example set out in Developing the subject 2.1.

### Developing the subject 2.1: How delegated legislation is made

The specific power to make delegated legislation is contained in an enabling provision or enabling section of the Parent/Enabling Act. The relevant section in the Environment Act 1995, s 97, states that the 'appropriate Ministers' (then Secretary of State for the Environment and Minister of Agriculture) may 'by regulations make provision for, or in connection with, the protection of important hedgerows in England and Wales'. This provision has the effect of identifying the person/body responsible for creating new law (Secretary of State/Minister); determining the type of secondary legislation to be made (regulations); and prescribing the focus required by that law (the protection of important hedgerows in England and Wales). The outcome of the process, then, is the creation of a new piece of delegated legislation: the **Hedgerows Regulations 1997**.

On a simple level, therefore, it can be said that the **Hedgerows Regulations** are the offspring of the main primary legislation, the Environment Act 1995. For this reason, the 1995 Act might be referred to as the **'Parent Act'**.

Alternatively, such primary legislation can be called an **Enabling Act**, because it has enabled further law to be made (see Developing the subject 2.1 on p 37).

Table 2.1 Comparing the volume of Acts of Parliament and UK delegated legislation (Statutory Instruments) between 1997 and 2004

| *Year* | *Acts of Parliament Figures relate to Public General Acts (ie, those Acts originating as Public Bills)* | *Delegated legislation in the form of Statutory Instruments* |
|---|---|---|
| 1997 | 69 | 3,114 |
| 1998 | 49 | 3,319 |
| 1999 | 35 | 3,488 |
| 2000 | 45 | 3,424 |
| 2001 | 25 | 4,147 |
| 2002 | 44 | 3,271 |
| 2003 | 45 | 3,354 |
| 2004 | 38 | 3,452 |

*Source:* Cracknell, R (2004) *Acts and Statutory Instruments: Volume of Legislation 1950–2004* (House of Commons Library) – www.parliament.uk/commons/lib/research/notes/snsg-02911.pdf

Table 2.2 Making delegated legislation

| *Example of Act of Parliament passing power to another person/body* | *Example of person/body to whom such power to make law is passed* | *Example of the type of delegated legislation which results from this process* |
|---|---|---|
| **Environment Act 1995 (a general Act to protect and enhance the environment)** | **Secretary of State for the Environment; and Minister of Agriculture** | **Hedgerows Regulations 1997 (technical laws to provide protection for important environmental habitat features, that is, important hedgerows)** |

## WHY IS THERE A NEED FOR DELEGATED LEGISLATION?

While Acts of Parliament can provide the broad framework for areas of law, more detailed technical rules are often required to address specific issues. For example, the Race Relations Act 1976 (Parent Act) sets out the broad principles of protection against racial discrimination in the workplace, but through its enabling provisions the power is given to the appropriate Minister to address specific issues. As a consequence, delegated legislation (such as the **Race Relations Act 1976 (Amendment) Regulations 2003**, which, amongst other things, add a separate definition of racial harassment) has since been passed under the Act.

Delegated legislation is also used to implement a great deal of **technical EC law**, under s 2(2) of the European Communities Act 1972. Examples of such legislation in the consumer protection context include the **Unfair Terms in Consumer Contracts Regulations 1999** and the **Sale and Supply of Goods to Consumers Regulations 2002.**

**IT'S A FACT! 2.1**

That the offence of using a hand-held mobile telephone whilst driving is laid down in a piece of delegated legislation: the **Road Vehicles (Construction and Use) (Amendment) (No. 4) Regulations 2003**, amending an earlier piece of delegated legislation created in 1986.

**IT'S A FACT! 2.2**

EC law-inspired delegated legislation often creates rights for individuals: see the **Employment Equality (Sexual Orientation) Regulations 2003** and the **Employment Equality (Religion or Belief) Regulations 2003**, which extend UK employment law to protect workers from harassment and discrimination on the grounds of sexual orientation and religious belief.

The Human Rights Act 1998 includes an unusual, and controversial, use for delegated legislation – for making swift amendments to primary legislation that is seen as incompatible with the European Convention on Human Rights. Such powers, arising from a so-called '**Henry VIII clause**' in the Act, enable Ministers to make primary legislation 'compatible' with the Convention. These powers are rarely found in legislation and secondary legislation cannot generally be used to amend primary legislation without express parliamentary authorisation. However, these powers will also be available to the Government if they are necessary to meet EC law obligations, as the Court of Appeal found in *Oakley Inc v Animal Ltd*, 2005, reversing a decision of the Chancery Division that had placed a limit on Government powers in this regard.

The **need for delegated legislation** is highlighted by the following advantages:

- Law is made by specialists in the field (such as a relevant Government department or a local authority with local knowledge), and often follows consultation with a wider body of expert opinion.
- Delegated legislation is easier and quicker to make than Acts of Parliament. This is useful given the pressures on Parliamentary time and the need to legislate for emergencies and to address social and technological changes.
- Delegated legislation supplements the broad aims and principles of primary legislation with detailed rules, and can be used to amend and update Acts of Parliament, thus contributing to legal frameworks that are both comprehensive and relevant.

## WHAT ARE THE MAIN TYPES OF DELEGATED LEGISLATION?

### Orders in Council

**Orders in Council** enable the Government to make law in the name of the Queen, through a group of ministers sitting as the **Privy Council**. For practical purposes, the Government will seek to make law in this way because it avoids going through the full Parliamentary process of law-making. Orders in Council are mainly used to meet any **national emergencies** that might arise in the future, such as threats to the supply and distribution of food, water, fuel or other 'essentials of life'.

## Let's look at cases: A recent successful challenge in the courts to an Order in Council

In *R (Bancoult) v Secretary of State for Foreign and Commonwealth Affairs* (2006), the Divisional Court of the Queen's Bench Division found, on an application for judicial review (see later coverage in this chapter), that the Order in Council titled the **British Indian Ocean Territory (Constitution) Order 2004** should be quashed on the grounds that it was both unlawful and irrational.

The case has a very interesting history, stretching back to the 1960s when the UK allowed the US military to locate a strategic military base in Diego Garcia, in the Chagos Islands, and therefore evicted all the inhabitants of the islands. This judicial review action was taken by Olivier Bancoult, who had been a child at the time of eviction, and who is leading a campaign to allow those evicted to return to the islands. The Order in Council had explicitly prevented this option of return for exiled islanders. Lord Justice Hooper, in giving his judgment, pointed out that an Order in Council could not be defended merely by reference to the Queen's prerogative powers (see also Chapter 1) since: 'The decision was in reality that of the Secretary of State, not of her Majesty, and was subject to a challenge by way of judicial review in the ordinary way.' Counsel for the Chagos islanders, Sir Sydney Kentridge, QC, was reported in *The Times* (12/4/06) as commenting that the whole matter was 'a very sad and by no means creditable episode in British history.'

A more common use of delegated orders is to bring an Act of Parliament, or parts of it, into effect. Such **Commencement Orders** are necessary because Acts are often brought into effect part by part. Not all sections of an Act will automatically come into effect upon the point of royal assent. Orders are generally published in the form of **Statutory Instruments** (see also 'Regulations', below).

## Regulations

Regulations are used to supplement the broad aims of primary legislation with detailed, technical rules. The power to make such rules will be delegated to those **Ministers** of the Government who head departments, usually as **Secretaries of State**. Ministers are representatives of the executive, in constitutional terms. Regulations are published in the form of **Statutory Instruments (SIs)**, and sometimes they are referred to in this way. They make up the bulk of the thousands of pieces of delegated legislation created each year.

## Developing the subject 2.2: Regulations

Regulations are especially useful to update primary legislation and adapt the law to changing circumstances. **The Health and Safety at Work etc Act 1974**, for example, is supplemented by a number of detailed regulations that take account of changing conditions in the workplace. Such regulations provide rules on a wide range of workplace activities, from manual handling operations to the use of display screen equipment. An example of one of many such pieces of delegated legislation is the **Management of Health and Safety at Work Regulations 1999**. The impetus for such changes, as so often with technical legal changes relating to standards in the commercial environment, has been a set of **European Community Framework Directives**. It is common for English secondary legislation, in the form of regulations, to be used in implementing new rules from EC legislation.

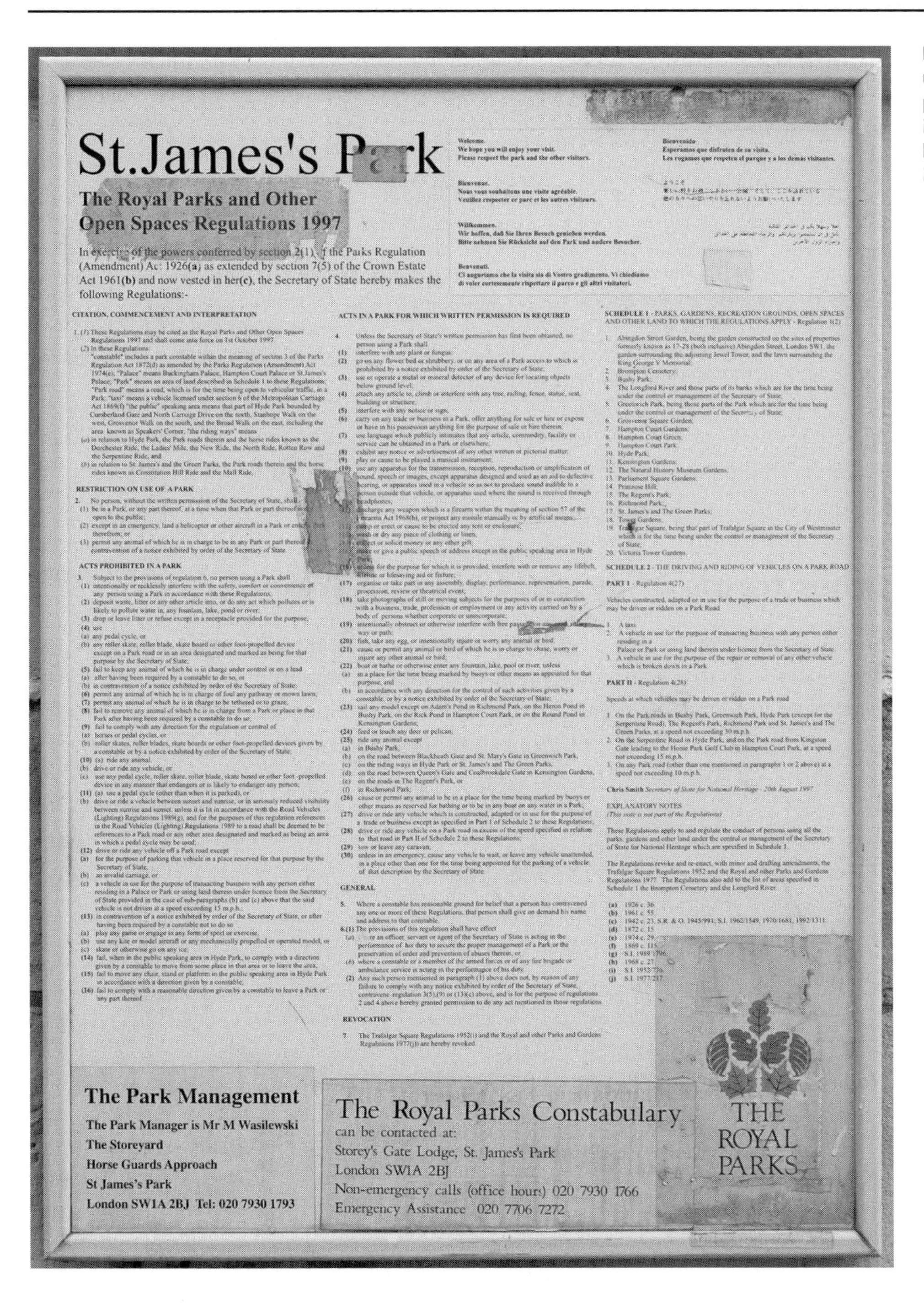


Delegated legislation will often be used for the governance of public parks, as this famous example illustrates. Is there a set of byelaws, or regulations, for your local park?

## Let's look at cases on byelaws: *Boddington v British Transport Police* (1998)

Here, the Enabling Act was the Transport Act 1962, which had authorised the creation of the British Railways Board Byelaws 1965. The byelaw in question prohibited smoking in railway carriages, and Boddington, the defendant, had been caught smoking on a Network South Central service. He was convicted for breaching the provisions of the byelaw.

## Byelaws

Byelaws are exercised by **local authorities** and other designated **public bodies,** for the 'good rule and government' of the area and to prevent local nuisances.

| *Statutory instruments* ↓ | *Orders in Council* ↓ | *Byelaws* ↓ |
|---|---|---|
| Regulations and Orders issued by government departments, eg Motor Cycles (Protective Helmets) Regulations 1980 issued by the Department of Transport. | Issued by the Monarch and Privy Council. Mainly used in times of emergency when Parliament is not sitting. | Issued by local authorities, eg 'no cycling' signs, or by other authorised bodies such as London Transport, eg ban on smoking on trains and the Underground. |

You may find examples of 'byelaws' in local parks, on public transport and in respect of areas of leisure, recreation and sport.

## Other forms of delegated legislation

Law-making powers are also delegated to **professional bodies**, such as the Law Society, to make specific rules governing professional conduct and to the **Church of England's General Synod** which, for example, makes provision for the preservation of church buildings. Table 2.3 summarises the main types of delegated legislation.

Table 2.3 Forms of delegated legislation

| *Type of delegated legislation* | *Made by?* | *Used for?* |
|---|---|---|
| Orders in Council; Orders | Privy Council; Government Ministers | • To declare a 'state of emergency'<br>• To bring parts of Acts of Parliament into effect in the form of Commencement Orders |
| Regulations | Government Ministers | • To add detailed, technical rules to the general legal framework provided by an Act of Parliament<br>• To implement new rules from EC legislation |
| Byelaws | Local authorities and public bodies | • To provide for the 'good rule and government' of local areas and to prevent local nuisances |

## WHY DO WE NEED CONTROLS OVER DELEGATED LEGISLATION?

So far, we know that there is more delegated legislation than Acts of Parliament and that it is made quickly. A mass of legislation is therefore being made by persons *other than* Parliament, without being subject to the full scrutiny of the parliamentary process. This should sound 'warning bells' for the critical reader.

The following *disadvantages* of delegated legislation summarise **why controls are perceived to be needed** over this form of legislation:

- Delegated legislation **undermines parliamentary sovereignty** as persons other than Parliament make a great mass of legislation every year.
- It gives **too much power** to a **politically motivated executive**, thus unbalancing the separation of powers and resulting in a less democratic form of law-making.
- Delegated legislation results in **too much law** and **insufficient controls** over it.
- Parliament's knowledge and understanding of the mass of delegated legislation it authorises is questionable. Lord Walker, in *Greenalls Management Ltd v Commissioners of Customs and Excise* (2005), found some 1992 regulations on VAT '**remarkably obscure**'.
- Delegated legislation does *not* always have to be laid before Parliament; and even if the Enabling Act insists on this, most delegated legislation **automatically becomes law** after 40 days under the '**negative resolution**' procedure, or is pushed through Parliament by the Government under the '**affirmative resolution**' procedure (see pp 44–5 below).
- Delegated legislation is *not* always adequately **publicised.**
- There are also concerns about **sub-delegation of legislation.** Delegated legislation is once removed from primary legislation already, and if that legislation then delegates power even further – to a separate body that is going to enforce the law, for example – legislation becomes remote from its origins.

Delegated legislation is subject to **controls** by Parliament, but these are open to question, as Lord Justice Jacob recently acknowledged in *Oakley Inc v Animal Ltd* (2005). Given the huge mass of legislation being passed, is delegated legislation really subject to sufficient scrutiny? Judicial review controls through the courts are also present, although the procedure is highly specialised and subject to many qualifications.

**IT'S A FACT! 2.3**

That when the **Control of Asbestos at Work Regulations 2002** came into effect in May 2004 – creating a duty on businesses to ensure asbestos risk management for workers, with heavy fines payable for non-compliance – it was estimated that 700,000 UK businesses were in technical breach of the Regulations, with over half of these unaware of their new legal obligations.

## HOW DOES PARLIAMENT 'CONTROL' OR 'ENSURE VALIDITY' OF DELEGATED LEGISLATION?

### Enabling (Parent) Act

The power to delegate lies with Parliament. Therefore, the way in which Parliament drafts the Enabling Act determines the nature and scope of the power given. Parliament can also amend or repeal the enabling powers and revoke or vary pieces of delegated legislation.

**IT'S A FACT!**

For concerns about delegated legislation, and views on why controls are needed over this form of legislation, consider the controversy and debate that ensued when the UK Government sought to get its **Legislative and Regulatory Reform Bill 2005** through Parliament. This Bill – labelled as the 'Abolition of Parliament Bill' and the 'dictatorship Bill' by critics – would enable the Government to make delegated legislation, in the form of Orders, to reform existing legislation or to implement Law Commission proposals. The Government has argued that it needs these powers to make technical changes to the law; and to cut unnecessary regulations, particularly on businesses (who have to cope with too much 'red tape'), in order to improve efficiency and competitiveness.

However, no less than six senior Professors of Law at the University of Cambridge wrote to *The Times* (16/2/06) to complain about the constitutional implications of the Bill, which, they argued, would allow the Government to use delegated legislation to curtail or abolish jury trial and increase Government powers over citizens. The Bill has also been criticised by a cross-party group of MPs, and by Peers in the House of Lords. It has been widely argued that the Bill gives the executive (Government) far too much power at the expense of the legislature (Parliament).

At the time of writing, the Bill is going through the House of Lords, having been subject to numerous changes and safeguards. As originally introduced to Parliament, the Bill contained 63 proposed Government powers and these have been reduced to 27 during the passage of the Bill, together with commitments from Ministers that the Bill, if enacted, would not go beyond the remit of achieving 'better regulation'. It is anticipated that the Bill will be made subject to further safeguards prior to enactment.

## Statutory Instruments Act 1946

Most delegated legislation is published in the form of statutory instruments. Under the **Statutory Instruments Act 1946**, a person will have a defence to a breach of delegated legislation if statutory instruments have not been printed and put on sale as soon as they are made. A problem with this is that statutory instruments, even if issued correctly, are often not adequately publicised.

## Laying delegated legislation before Parliament

It is usually stated in an Enabling Act whether delegated legislation needs to be laid before Parliament. There are two main ways of laying delegated legislation before Parliament:

(a) the negative resolution method; and
(b) the affirmative resolution method.

### Negative resolution method

This is the most common form of laying delegated legislation before Parliament, and reinforces earlier concerns that perhaps such legislation is not subject to appropriate scrutiny. It involves delegated legislation being **laid before Parliament for 40 days**. If, during this period, an MP formally objects to the legislation, and a resolution is carried as a consequence of this objection, the delegated legislation can be annulled. However, this assumes that MPs, and particularly those of the Opposition parties in Parliament, have had time:

(a) to take an interest in a specific piece of delegated legislation, as distinct from all the others being laid at that point in time;
(b) to read the legislation; and
(c) to understand its implications.

More commonly, delegated legislation **lies unchallenged** for the set period and **automatically becomes law** after 40 days. While this position is less than desirable, it is understandable given the large amount of delegated legislation being made. It is difficult to see how this level of 'control' by Parliament can be perceived to be effective.

### Affirmative resolution method

This represents a **more effective** form of control as it involves delegated legislation being **approved by both Houses of Parliament**. Here, because of the importance of the issue on which law is being made, Parliament will have ensured, through the enabling provision, that the affirmative resolution

procedure is used. Such a procedure raises the profile of the delegated legislation and subjects it to greater critical scrutiny. The Hedgerows Regulations, referred to at p 37 above, had to be laid before Parliament in this way to take account of the conflict between farming and environmental interests. In this instance, the parliamentary process was also preceded by a wide-ranging consultation exercise, providing further evidence of its social and political importance.

This method clearly does provide a measure of control over delegated legislation. However, it may be criticised for undermining some of the advantages of delegated legislation (for example, by prolonging the law-making process). Moreover, in circumstances of limited parliamentary time, a large amount of business to get through and a Government majority in the House of Commons, it is difficult to imagine too many occasions where the delegated legislation would not be approved.

## Joint Committee on Statutory Instruments ('Scrutiny Committee')

This committee comprises both MPs from the House of Commons and Peers from the House of Lords. It considers whether statutory instruments are properly made, taking into account the relevant Enabling Act and the Statutory Instruments Act 1946. Whilst the committee focuses on **form and procedure** rather than content, delegated legislation that imposes a new tax, or attempts to have retrospective effect (that is, affects previously settled dealings), will be investigated by the committee and brought to the attention of Parliament. There is no consideration given to the merits of the legislation. The Commons and the Lords also have separate scrutiny committees relating to the delegated law-making process.

## HOW IS DELEGATED LEGISLATION CONTROLLED BY THE COURTS?

Judicial control is provided by the judicial review procedure in the High Court (**Divisional Court of the Queen's Bench**, referred to as the Administrative Court). There are, however, difficulties with pursuing a claim for **judicial review**. The rules are not straightforward, and this makes it difficult for aggrieved citizens to know when, how and whether they can seek to initiate such a claim. Furthermore, judicial review can be both time-consuming and costly for the litigant, who must, at the outset, show a substantial interest in the case to activate the review procedures.

There are two main grounds for judicial control where the delegated power may be declared *ultra vires*, which means exceeding the powers given by the legislation:

(a) the procedural ground; and
(b) the substantive ground.

## Procedural ground for judicial review

This ground enables a citizen to challenge the validity of delegated legislation on the grounds of procedural *ultra vires* where there has been a failure to **follow correct procedures** as laid down in the enabling provisions of an Act of Parliament.

## Substantive ground for judicial review

This ground – substantive *ultra vires* – focuses on alleged abuses of delegated law-making power by administrative bodies. It is therefore concerned with the **content** of delegated legislation.

If delegated legislation is found to be **unreasonable** or **disproportionate**, it may be declared void (of no effect) in whole or in part. Sometimes, a provision might be drafted too wide to achieve its purpose: for example, a byelaw prohibition on the singing of rude songs which would have affected those singing in private as well as in public was an unreasonable prohibition and therefore *ultra vires* (*Strickland v Hayes Borough Council*, 1896).

Another branch of substantive *ultra vires* relates to the actual exercise of delegated powers. It is *ultra vires*, for example, for a local authority with statutory responsibility to provide public washing facilities to establish a commercial laundry instead (*Attorney-General v Fulham Corporation*, 1921).

Table 2.4 opposite summarises the parliamentary and judicial controls over delegated legislation.

### Let's look at cases on procedural *ultra vires*

In the *Aylesbury Mushroom case* (1972), a failure by a Minister to consult an interested party (the Mushroom Growers' Association) when making an Order establishing a Training Board for land-workers meant that the legislation was *ultra vires* in respect of the Mushroom Growers' Association and would apply only to those bodies that had been properly consulted.

By contrast, a recent claim of procedural *ultra vires* by the National Association of Health Stores, relating to Regulations made by a Minister in alleged ignorance of scientific opinion and the benefits of alternative legal approaches, was rejected by the Court of Appeal (*R (National Association of Health Stores) v Secretary of State for Health*, 2005). The Minister had, on the facts, followed the correct consultation procedures for the making of this legislation, which banned the use of the substance kava-kava in foodstuffs.

Table 2.4 Controls over delegated legislation

| *Controls by Parliament* | *Controls by the courts* |
| --- | --- |
| • Nature and scope of the powers to delegate laid down in the Enabling Act. Parliament has the ultimate power to repeal delegated powers.<br>• All statutory instruments issued subject to the legal requirements of the Statutory Instruments Act 1946.<br>• Laying delegated legislation before Parliament by way of the negative resolution method (laid for 40 days, passes unless objections are made).<br>• Laying delegated legislation before Parliament by way of the affirmative resolution method (approval required by both Houses of Parliament).<br>• Delegated legislation is examined by the Joint Committee on Statutory Instruments, also referred to as the Scrutiny Committee. | Delegated legislation may be challenged under the judicial review procedure, on the basis of *ultra vires* (that the delegated power exceeds that provided by the legislation).<br>There are two main grounds of judicial review:<br>• Procedural ground. A person may challenge the validity of delegated legislation on the basis of procedural *ultra vires*. For example, a Minister has failed to follow the correct procedures for making delegated legislation: *Aylesbury Mushroom* case (1972).<br>• Substantive ground. A person may challenge the validity of delegated legislation on the basis of alleged abuses of delegated law-making power, referred to as substantive *ultra vires*. For example, that the use of delegated power exceeds that anticipated by law: *Attorney-General v Fulham Corporation* (1921). |

## Case exercise: *R (BAT UK Ltd) v Secretary of State for Health* (2004)

Tobacco manufacturers used judicial review to challenge the **Tobacco Advertising and Promotion (Point of Sale) Regulations 2004**, which specified restrictions on the advertising of tobacco products in furtherance of the broad, general policy of the Tobacco Advertising and Promotion Act 2002.

The 2004 Regulations limited advertising to areas where tobacco was for sale and laid down additional criteria as to the size and nature of permissible advertising. The tobacco manufacturers argued that these restrictions were disproportionately restrictive and therefore *ultra vires*.

However, the court found in favour of the Secretary of State for Health. Parliament had authorised a ban on the advertising of tobacco products and the 2004 Regulations had not been annulled when laid before Parliament. The Regulations extended no further than was necessary to deliver the objectives that Parliament had laid down in the 2002 Act.

In dismissing the judicial review action, Mr Justice McCombe said 'it was a responsible and proportionate step to have regulated as the Minister did'.

(1) Identify the respective pieces of primary and secondary (delegated) legislation in this case-note. What general term do you think could be used to describe the primary legislation?
(2) Why do you think the case was taken against the Secretary of State for Health?
(3) What court do you think this case was heard in? (Justify your answer.)
(4) List the reasons why the delegated legislation was seen as reasonable and justified in this case.
(5) Explain the comment '*and the 2004 Regulations had not been annulled when laid before Parliament*'.

For Answers, please turn to pp 333–4.

Brian Haw and his protest in Parliament Square against the Iraq war

## Let's look at cases: *R (Haw) v Secretary of State for the Home Department* (2006)

The Government had become concerned by protesters in Parliament Square and sought to use enabling powers in the Serious Organised Crime and Police Act 2005 to effect, by way of a Commencement Order, a ban on future, and continuing, demonstrations. Brian Haw has been the most visible protester in Parliament Square over recent years (see photograph), waging a colourful and eccentric campaign against the UK's military intervention in Iraq and he brought an action for judicial review against the Government, claiming that the Commencement Order was *ultra vires* and should be quashed.

The Divisional Court of the Queen's Bench agreed with Mr Haw. Lady Justice Smith and Justice McCombe, in the majority, took the view that the Commencement Order had the radical impact of transforming the enabling provisions which, on their own, did not create a criminal offence for demonstrations started prior to the Act, into just such an offence. This amounted to an amendment to, and extension of, the primary legislation and parts of the delegated legislation were, accordingly, *ultra vires*. Justice Simon, in the minority, disagreed with this position, arguing that Parliament had passed the Serious Organised Crime and Police Act 2005 for the purpose of banning all demonstrations on Parliament Square, regardless of when these had actually started.

The Court of Appeal upheld the minority view and found in favour of the Secretary of State for the Home Department. The enabling powers should be taken to reflect the purpose of the legislation – to ban all demonstrations, regardless of when they actually started – and so the start of Mr Haw's demonstration should be deemed, in legal terms, as beginning at the point of commencement laid down in the Commencement Order.

You should note that the Court of Appeal preferred the purposive approach to statutory interpretation in this case with Sir Anthony Clarke, Master of the Rolls, pointing out that the 'language used by Parliament was of central importance but that did not mean that it always had to be construed literally' (see Chapter 3 on statutory interpretation).

## Useful website addresses

| | |
|---|---|
| House of Commons Library statistics | www.parliament.uk/commons/lib/research/notes/snsg-02911.pdf |
| Parliament | www.parliament.uk |
| *Materials directly for AS studies*: | |
| John Deft (St Brendan's Sixth Form College) | www.stbrn.ac.uk/other/depts/law |
| Asif Tufal | www.a-level-law.com |

### HINTS AND TIPS

Delegated legislation is a good topic to revise: not too long, reasonably self-contained, and providing a good mixture of factual recall, on the one hand, and subject evaluation, on the other. This chapter has sought to explain delegated legislation in a clear order and using headings that should assist your preparation for examination questions. Table 2.5 provides an at-a-glance revision guide, bearing in mind the sorts of questions that may be asked in this topic.

Table 2.5 Revision guide to delegated legislation

| *Areas of the topic where **description/explanation** is often required* | *Areas of the topic where **analysis/evaluation** is often required* |
|---|---|
| • **What is meant by delegated legislation?**<br>(The process by which law-making power is delegated by an Enabling Act to a person or body other than Parliament.)<br>• **What are the main types of delegated legislation?**<br>(Orders in Council (made by the Privy Council); orders and regulations (made by Government Ministers); byelaws (made by local authorities))<br>• **What are the Parliamentary and judicial controls over delegated legislation?**<br>(Parliamentary controls: control through the Enabling Act; Statutory Instruments Act 1946; laying the legislation before Parliament (affirmative resolution; negative resolution); Joint Committee on Statutory Instruments. Judicial controls: judicial review – procedural *ultra vires* ground; substantive *ultra vires* grounds.)<br>**NB: Wherever possible use examples to illustrate your answers.** | • **What are the advantages of delegated legislation?**<br>(Made by specialists; creation of detailed/technical rules; saves Parliamentary time; consultation; flexible and can adapt to changing circumstances; quick and easy to change, etc.)<br>• **What are the disadvantages of delegated legislation and why do we need controls over delegated legislation?**<br>(Contradicts constitutional theory; less democratic form of law; little publicity given to delegated legislation; too much law being made by the executive, etc.)<br>• **Why is there a need for delegated legislation?**<br>(To supplement broad primary legislation with detailed rules; to bring EC laws into effect; to make 'fast-track amendments' to primary legislation; plus the main advantages – saving Parliamentary time, useful for emergencies, etc.)<br>• **Why is there a need for controls over delegated legislation? How effective are the controls?**<br>(Consider some of the disadvantages of delegated legislation to provide a context for your answer. Issues such as potential abuse of power; law-making power given to the executive at the expense of the legislature; too much law being created, without attendant publicity or debate, etc can be used to inform your judgments about the adequacy of the controls.) |

**Exercise: Revision Quiz**

Identify the words suggested by the following clues. The first letters of each of these words make up a new word that describes the nature of delegated legislation as a source of law.

________ committee: this body, made up of MPs and peers, looks into the making of delegated legislation.

________ Act: the 'parent' of delegated legislation.

________: these are exerted over delegated legislation by Parliament and the courts, though how effective they are provides a common evaluative question.

________: types of delegated legislation used, for example, to bring Acts into effect.

________ resolution: the process where delegated legislation is laid before Parliament for 40 days and passed if unchallenged.

________: the passing of power from one body to another.

________: in evaluation, these include the points that delegated legislation is made by specialists and is quick to make, flexible and useful in emergencies.

________: the type of delegated legislation made by Ministers to supplement Acts with detailed, technical rules.

________: what Parliament has to say if a piece of delegated legislation is to be passed by the affirmative resolution procedure!

For Answers, please turn to p 334.

# 3

# Statutory interpretation

This topic enables you:

- To understand the approaches that judges use to interpret words and phrases in Acts of Parliament.
- To recognise the aids to interpretation to which judges may refer.
- To inform a critical appreciation of constitutional theory, especially parliamentary sovereignty and the separation of powers.
- To contrast constitutional theory with the practical, working relationship between legislature and judiciary.
- To recognise some of the problems with prospective written legislation.
- To appreciate that differences between the judges might lead to differing approaches to interpretation.

Statutory interpretation is the process by which **judges** *apply* and *interpret* the provisions of an Act of Parliament when a case comes before them. **Appeals** turning on the interpretation of words and phrases in Acts of Parliament are an important part of the workload of the higher courts in the English legal system.

## APPROACHES TO STATUTORY INTERPRETATION

The rules or principles of statutory interpretation may be found in two sources: in **statute law** and in **common law**. The common law also provides aids to interpretation in the form of developed **rules of language** and long-established **presumptions**. Further, judges have access to a set of **intrinsic** and **extrinsic aids** to help them in their interpretation of statutes.

This chapter will examine these principles and aids in the following order:

- Statutory rules
- Rules of language
- Common law 'rules' of interpretation
- Extrinsic and intrinsic aids
- Presumptions.

The common law 'rules' are, however, more accurately termed 'approaches', as they are *not* fixed. The judges are free to choose which approach to adopt, depending on the facts of the cases before them. It is only in applying European Community law and European Convention on Human Rights cases that the judges are required to adopt the broader, purposive approach.

**IT'S A FACT!**

**3.1: recent examples of issues before the courts requiring interpretation**

- *Director of Public Prosecutions v Smith* (2006): **Was it an assault occasioning actual bodily harm for a man to cut off his former girlfriend's ponytail?** (The Queen's Bench Divisional Court held yes, dealing with the defence argument that hair was merely dead tissue by pointing out that it was still part of a person's body and that cutting hair without consent, even though it did not cause physical pain, amounted to harm to the health and comfort of the victim.)
- *R v Goodwin* (2006): **Is a Yamaha Waverunner jet ski a 'ship' for the purposes of the Merchant Shipping Act 1995?** (Court of Appeal held not, in allowing the appeal of Mr Goodwin against conviction under the 1985 Act of offences committed by masters of ships. He had been prosecuted because his jet ski had run into another one and caused property damage and personal injury.)
- *Ahmed Amin v Brown* (2005): **Is an Iraqi citizen, resident in Iraq, unable to bring an action in the UK courts because she is an 'enemy alien'?** (Chancery Division held not, finding that the term 'enemy alien', referred to in common law in the seventeenth century, required the individual to be a citizen of a country with which the UK was at war, but the UK was not, in fact, in a state of war with Iraq.)
- *R v H* (2005): **Was the touching of a woman's tracksuit bottoms sufficient for an offence of sexual assault under the Sexual Offences Act 2003?** (Court of Appeal held yes, though distanced itself from the comments of the trial judge that the defendant's earlier comment to the woman, 'Do you fancy a shag?', was a relevant consideration given the strict wording of the Act.)
- *Morris v Commissioners of Revenue and Customs* (2006): **Is a motor home/camper van a 'car' for the purposes of the Income and Corporation Taxes Act 1988?** (The Chancery Division held that it was, so Mr Morris's general use of the motor home as his office was a form of benefit that attracted taxation. Mr Morris's appeal was defeated largely by the broad definition of 'car' in the 1988 Act as 'any mechanically propelled road vehicle'. The judge, Justice Park, in finding against Mr Morris nevertheless conceded that this statutory definition stretched the meaning of 'car' and acknowledged that a motor home was not a car 'in the ordinary sense'.)
- *R (W) v Commissioner of Police of the Metropolis* (2006): **To what extent do police constables and community support officers in uniform have power to remove persons under 16 to their place of residence for the purposes of the Anti-Social Behaviour Act 2003?** (The Court of Appeal heard this appeal, on a hypothetical question given the facts of the case, because the matter was of general public concern and of concern to the police; the court could consider the matter against the actual facts of the case; it would resolve an area of law that the Divisional Court had not addressed; and the 'issues were clear cut'. It was held, on an interpretation of ss 30 and 33 of the Act, that police constables and community support officers can use 'reasonable force', where necessary, to remove a person under 16 from a public place to his or her place of residence, though this power should not be exercised in an arbitrary manner.)
- *And finally . . .* two unresolved questions of statutory interpretation that have appeared as news stories recently and should make you think. First, is Poker, the card game, a 'game of skill' or a 'game of chance'? The answer to this question has significance for any private members club that allows Poker to be played since if it is regarded as the latter (a 'game of chance') then the game can only lawfully be played in a licensed casino. Second, can the winner of a prestigious art prize associated with painting be stripped of his title because the winning piece of work was largely created by charcoal? This matter is, at the time of writing, testing the higher courts in Australia.

## STATUTORY RULES

Parliament attempted to make the job of interpreting statutes easier for judges by passing the **Interpretation Act 1978**. This statute lays down some basic assumptions to ensure, for example, that 'he' also applies to 'she' (unless the contrary is stated) and that uses of the singular form will reflect the plural in application.

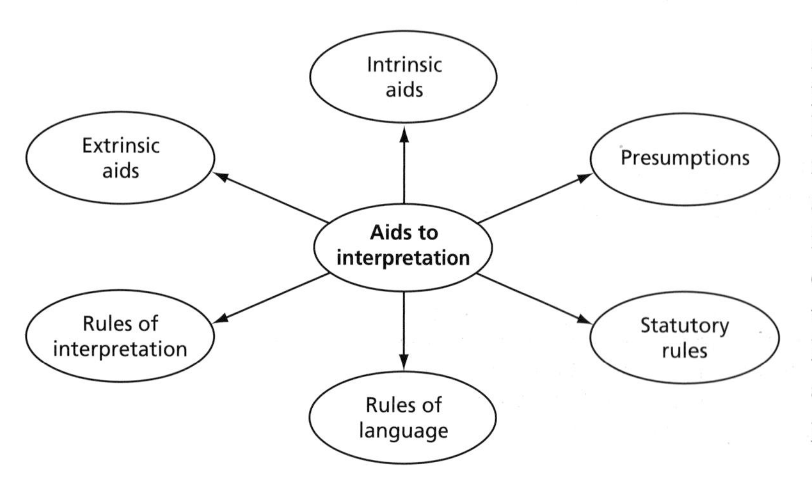


Some statutes contain guidance for judges in the form of **definition or interpretation sections.** In s 68 of the Disability Discrimination Act 1995, for example, a number of important words and phrases are defined, such as 'employment', 'profession' and 'mental impairment'. The extent to which these are helpful to judges will depend on the manner in which they have been drafted. New statutes are accompanied by **'explanatory notes'** to provide further guidance.

## Developing the subject 3.1: Some statutory definitions contrasted

To illustrate the fact that some sections provide more assistance than others, consider s 1(3) of the Companies Act 1985, which reads: 'A private company is any company that is not a public company'. Clearly this, on its own, is not particularly helpful to judges. By contrast, in s 10 of the Theft Act 1968, for the purposes of establishing the offence of aggravated burglary, a 'weapon of offence' is defined as 'any article made or adapted for use for causing injury to or incapacitating a person, or intended by the person having it with him for such use'. This is a more useful definition because it provides elaboration, for interpretation purposes, on the nature of the item that might be used for committing the offence.

## RULES OF LANGUAGE

There are **three** rules of language that might be applied in the process of statutory interpretation. These are:

(a) *ejusdem generis* (the **'same kind'** rule);
(b) *expressio unius est exclusio alterius* (the **'express words exclude others'** rule);
(c) *noscitur a sociis* (the **'read words in context'** rule).

### *Ejusdem generis*

*Ejusdem generis* means the 'same kind' or 'same class'. So, if a statute sets out a list of specific items or objects, any general terms following the list shall be taken to reflect the specific examples given.

### *Expressio unius est exclusio alterius*

This means that the expression of one thing is to the exclusion of another. Here, in contrast to the situation where *ejusdem generis* is employed, there is a list of specific words within the statutory provision but no accompanying general terms. In effect, the **wording of the provision does not give room for further interpretation**. Therefore, if the Act expresses a list of items, any further items or aspects which have not been stated in the provision are by

## Let's look at cases: *Re Stockport Ragged, Industrial and Reformatory Schools (1898)* illustrating the *ejusdem generis* rule

This case involved a statutory provision listing 'cathedral, collegiate, chapter or other schools'. In interpreting the schools that would be covered by 'or other schools' (the general term), the court observed that the specific examples indicated a similar class associated with the Church of England. Therefore, to fall within this general provision, a school would have to be linked to the Church of England.

implication excluded. So, in *R v Inhabitants of Sedgley* (1831), where a tax was imposed, amongst a list of other specific things, on the occupiers of 'coal mines', this provision could not apply to occupiers of other types of mines.

## *Noscitur a sociis*

This means that words in a statute should be **read in their context**. Therefore, to determine the meaning of one word, other accompanying words and sections must be considered.

### Let's look at cases: *Muir v Keay* (1875) illustrating the *noscitur a sociis* rule.

This case concerned a section of the Refreshment Houses Act 1860, which required that 'all houses, rooms, shops or buildings, kept open for public refreshment, resort and entertainment during certain hours of the night' must be licensed. The defendant owned a café that was not licensed. He was convicted at first instance and appealed on the basis of the meaning of 'entertainment', arguing that this would apply only to the playing of music and dancing, which did not take place at the café. However, the first instance verdict was upheld on appeal: applying the *noscitur a sociis rule*, the context of the provision suggested that 'entertainment' related to matters of bodily comfort (bear in mind the accompanying words 'public refreshment, resort . . .') and not to theatrical or musical performances. The café owner therefore had to have a licence under the 1860 Act.

**Table 3.1** summarises the rules of language, using the facts of *Powell v Kempton Racecourse* (1899) to illustrate the application of the rules. In that case, the prohibited conduct was betting, and the *ejusdem generis* approach was used.

Table 3.1 Statutory interpretation: the rules of language

| *Ejusdem generis* | *Expressio unius est exclusio alterius* | *Noscitur a sociis* |
|---|---|---|
| • 'Same kind/class' rule.<br>• If a list of specific items of a similar class or kind is followed by a general term, **the general term will also reflect that class.**<br><br>*Imagine that an Act states that certain conduct will be prohibited in 'houses, offices, rooms or other places'. You are asked to interpret whether that conduct would be illegal on a playing field. Using* ejusdem generis, *what is your answer? Well, the items 'houses, offices, rooms' share the common feature of being indoor places, so the 'other places' must be of the same class. Therefore, since a playing field is outdoors, no offence has been committed: it is not a place of the same class.* | • Expression of one thing is to the exclusion of another.<br>• If there is a list of specific items **but no general term**, the provision will include only those specific items and no more.<br><br>*Imagine that an Act states that certain conduct will be prohibited in 'houses, offices and rooms'. You are asked to interpret whether that conduct would be illegal in a factory. Using the* expressio unius *rule, what is your answer? If you took a strict view here, the word 'factories' has not been expressed, and so this type of indoor place is, by implication, excluded.* | • Words reflect their context.<br>• The meaning of a word is derived from those that surround it.<br><br>*Using the same construction once again, 'houses, offices and rooms', examination will suggest the following context factors:*<br>*(a) All indoor places.*<br>*(b) No distinction drawn between the domestic situation and the business situation.*<br><br>*Regard would also be given to the wider context of the statute in determining whether a certain place fell within the provision.* |

## COMMON LAW APPROACHES TO INTERPRETATION

### The literal rule

For many years the literal rule was the dominant approach to statutory interpretation. It is very simple: if the wording in a statute is **clear**, it can be applied literally. So in the case of *Cutter v Eagle Star Insurance Co Ltd* (1998), in determining whether an insurance company was liable to a person injured in a car-park, the House of Lords found that the relevant Act specified a 'road' and not a 'car-park', so no compensation had to be paid by the company.

Judges may use the extrinsic aid of a **dictionary** to give words their ordinary meaning. Although there has been a *general move away* from the literal approach in recent years, some judges prefer to start with this method and apply the ordinary meaning of the word wherever possible.

#### Let's look at cases: *R v Bentham* (2005) on applying the plain words of the statute

In Bentham, the House of Lords had to interpret the Firearms Act 1968 to determine whether a man who, during a robbery, had used his fingers beneath the fabric of his jacket to suggest he had a gun, should be convicted of possession of an imitation firearm. Looking closely at the precise wording of the statute – 'anything which has the appearance of a firearm . . . whether or not it is capable of discharging any shot, bullet or other missile' – Lord Bingham said that Parliament had clearly intended to legislate about 'imitation firearms', not to create an offence of falsely pretending to have a firearm. Moreover, 'possession' of something requires it to be external to the body and a 'thing' could not possibly refer to a part of the body since a 'thing' was the sort of property that could be confiscated by the State under other criminal legislation. The words of the 1968 Act were plain and therefore no further statutory construction was required. As Lord Bingham concluded, 'Purposive construction cannot be relied on to create an offence which Parliament has not created'. The defendant's conviction for the offence was accordingly quashed.

However, one consequence of an application of the literal approach to interpretation is that it can lead to **harsh** and sometimes **absurd** results. This is because the literal application of words might defeat the broader purposes of the statute, as the case of *London & North-Eastern Railway v Berriman* (1946) illustrates.

## Let's look at cases: *London & North-Eastern Railway v Berriman* (1946)

The case concerned legislation relating to the prevention of accidents on the railways, which stated that it was necessary for a railway company to provide a 'look-out man' while someone was 'repairing or relaying' the railway. On the basis of a breach of this specific legislation, Mrs Berriman wished to make a claim for compensation under the Fatal Accidents Acts 1846–1908 in relation to her husband, who had died while working on the railways. A look-out man had not been present when her husband was killed. The railway company argued that Mr Berriman was merely 'maintaining' the railway rather than 'repairing or relaying' it, so no look-out man had been required. Using a literal interpretation, the House of Lords held in favour of this view. Therefore, the railway company did not have to compensate Mrs Berriman.

The advantages and disadvantages of the literal approach are summarised in Table 3.2.

Table 3.2 The literal approach to interpretation: advantages and disadvantages

| *Advantages* | *Disadvantages* |
|---|---|
| This approach observes the doctrine of parliamentary sovereignty. Consider the comments made by Lord Simonds in *Magor and St Mellons Rural District Council v Newport Corporation* (see further p. 66 below). | Criticism by Professor Michael Zander (of the London School of Economics), among others, that such an approach is lazy, reduces the role of judges to a mechanical task and, with the use of a dictionary, provides the easy option of interpreting difficult problems. |
| This approach satisfies the separation of powers as the judiciary is not given too much power and statutes are interpreted as Parliament enacted them (see Chapter 1). It also encourages certainty in judicial law. | If judges use the literal approach in relation to old statutes they have very limited discretion to adapt to changing times, since social and technological developments may have outpaced the legislation. |

## The golden rule

The golden rule may be used to *qualify* the literal rule. The golden rule applies in two main situations.

- If the statutory wording is **ambiguous**, judges will adopt an interpretation that produces the *least absurd* result, on the basis that it is not the intention of Parliament to promote absurdity.
- If the meaning of a word in an Act is **clear**, but to adopt that meaning would result in absurdity, the literal rule is not adopted as it would be against the public interest to do so.

The advantages and disadvantages of the golden rule are summarised in Table 3.3.

Table 3.3 The golden rule approach to interpretation: advantages and disadvantages

| *Advantages* | *Disadvantages* |
| --- | --- |
| Enables judges to avoid absurdity in the public interest. | What seems absurd to one judge may not be absurd to another. May lead to uncertainty. |
| Provides a check on the strictness of the literal approach and allows for the justification that Parliament's intention would not have been to create an absurd situation. | Shows the beginnings of the drift of power from Parliamentary control to judicial discretion, as courts are not confining themselves to the actual words in the statute. |

## Let's look at cases: Two examples of the golden rule

In *Adler v George* (1964), where an offence in the Official Secrets Act 1920 of obstructing the armed forces in the 'vicinity' of a prohibited place was held to apply when the offence took place within that prohibited place (an RAF station). As Lord Chief Justice Parker pointed out, if would be absurd to say that an offence could be committed close to (in the 'vicinity' of) a prohibited place, but not in the place itself.

In *Re Sigsworth* (1935), a man's estate tried to inherit property under the Administration of Estates Act 1925 after the man had murdered his mother. If the literal rule was adopted then the inheritance could occur, but this would not be in the public interest because it would allow benefits to be gained as a consequence of one person's serious criminal act. Therefore, departure from the literal rule towards the wider interpretation of the golden rule resulted in the court interpreting the statute in a way that prevented the man's estate gaining from his wrongdoing.

# The mischief rule

In its application today, the mischief rule begins by seeking the true intention of Parliament and therefore the purpose for enacting the legislation. Hence, this rule enables judges to consider **extrinsic aids** and look beyond the literal meaning of words in the statute to ascertain the 'mischief', or problem, that the Act was trying to remedy.

**IT'S A FACT! 3.2**

The mischief rule may be traced back to *Heydon's Case* (1584). This was one of the earliest statements on statutory interpretation and required judges to consider, amongst other things, the problems (mischief) that an Act had been required to remedy and the reasons for the Act's approach to achieving that remedy.

## Let's look at cases: *Smith v Hughes* (1960)

A clear, simple example of the application of the mischief rule relates to judicial interpretation of the **Street Offences Act 1959**. It became accepted that the 'mischief', or problem, targeted by this Act was that of members of the public suffering harassment on the streets. Thus, a prostitute – in the case of *Smith v Hughes* – who argued that her conviction under the Act should not be upheld because she was soliciting passers-by from a window, rather than a 'public place or street' as the Act required, did not succeed in her appeal. She was still causing the mischief of harassing members of the public.

In *Corkery v Carpenter* (1951) the question for the Queen's Bench Divisional Court was whether the word 'carriage' in an old statute could be represented, in practice, by a 'bicycle'? The judge considered the intention of Parliament and believed that it could: the mischief that the Act sought to remedy was the problem of drunken people driving street vehicles on the highway, and thus a 'carriage' and a 'bicycle' were seen as equivalent causes of this problem. This case illustrates the usefulness of the mischief rule in allowing judges to **keep up with changing times.**

A further example of this function provided by the mischief rule is the important case of *Royal College of Nursing of the UK v Department of Health and Social Security* (1981).

The advantages and disadvantages of the mischief rule are summarised in Table 3.4.

## Let's look at cases: *Royal College of Nursing of the UK v Department of Health and Social Security* (1981) and the application of the mischief rule.

This case concerned s 1(1) of the Abortion Act 1967: '. . . a person shall not be guilty of an offence under the law relating to abortion when a pregnancy is terminated by a registered medical practitioner.' In seeking to reflect the intention of Parliament, as opposed to a literal view of the actual words used, the House of Lords held that an abortion effected by nursing staff rather than performed directly by a registered medical practitioner would be lawful under the 1967 Act. This was an important decision, not least because a finding of 'unlawful' would have left nurses open to prosecution under the Offences Against the Person Act 1861.

The court looked to the 'mischief' of the Act and found that the statute had insisted on a 'registered medical practitioner' in order to outlaw dangerous 'back-street abortions'. The court also acknowledged that those drafting the 1967 Act could not have foreseen the improvements in medical practice that had allowed nurses a role in abortion procedures. Therefore, the court had identified the mischief that the Act was trying to remedy and given effect to the purpose of the Act (that is, to provide for lawful abortions, carried out in a clean, safe, clinical environment, as distinct from unlawful 'back-street abortions').

Table 3.4 Interpretation under the mischief rule: advantages and disadvantages

| *Advantages* | *Disadvantages* |
| --- | --- |
| Enables judges to look beyond the literal meaning of words in the Act to find the 'mischief' that Parliament was concerned to remedy by passing the legislation. | Judges have discretion to look beyond the plain words of the Act itself, and this may increase judicial power at the expense of legislative power. |
| Allows judges to interpret statutes in the light of changing social, economic and technological circumstances. | Although some of the restrictions on the use of extrinsic aids have relaxed over recent years, there are still sufficient restrictions and controls to make the 'mischief' hard to determine in some cases. |

Although the mischief rule is old in origin and has been of great significance in recent times, there is in fact now a drift towards the **purposive approach.** This is conceptually related to the mischief rule in seeking a broader approach to interpretation.

## The purposive approach

The purposive approach is wider than the mischief rule. According to the **Law Commission,** it looks to the '*positive social purpose*' of legislation rather than focusing on the evil that an Act might have been created to deal with. The purposive approach is therefore a contextual approach. Judges adopting this approach look to the *spirit of the law* rather than at the literal detail. As Lord Diplock pointed out in *Carter v Bradbeer* (1975): 'If one looks back to the actual decisions of this House [of Lords] . . . over the last thirty years one cannot fail to be struck by the evidence of a trend away from the purely literal towards the purposive construction of statutory provisions.'

As we have seen, the purposive approach is suggested by the Human Rights Act 1998, s 3 (see pp 29 and 51 above; see also p 68 below); and as Lord Denning observed in *Bulmer v Bollinger* (1974), it is the required form of interpretation for matters of European Community law. Since the latter case, the trend has become so marked that Lord Millett was able to write recently in the *Statute Law Review*, albeit tongue in cheek, that 'we are all purposive constructionists now'. This confirms the view of Gary Slapper in the *Student Law Review* (2001) that 'the use of a purposive approach by the courts is becoming something of a standard approach since Britain has become more involved in Europe'.

A good case to illustrate the purposive approach is *Coltman v Bibby Tankers* (1987).

### Let's look at cases: *Coltman v Bibby Tankers* (1987).

Here, an employee was killed when a ship sank off the coast of Japan. The employee's representatives argued that his death had been caused in the course of employment because of defects in equipment, referring to the ship provided by the defendants. The question for the court was therefore whether the word 'equipment' in the Employers' Liability (Defective Equipment) Act 1969, which was defined in the Act as including 'any plant and machinery, vehicle, aircraft and clothing', could also include a ship. The House of Lords interpreted the provision purposively, thus giving a broad construction to the effect that 'equipment' did include a ship.

However, use of the purposive approach can sometimes be controversial where the social purpose being recognised is one of **public policy**, an area generally left to Parliament's express intentions. In *Fitzpatrick v Sterling Housing Association Ltd* (1999), for example, the House of Lords interpreted provisions of the Rent Act 1977 purposively in order to allow a close and loving homosexual relationship to fall within the statutory wording of 'family', thus affording security of tenure to the claimant.

However, the House of Lords decision was by majority, with two dissenting judges believing that recognition of homosexual relationships should be left to Parliament and not developed through statutory interpretation in one case. The case of *Ghaidan v Godin-Mendoza* (2004) has nevertheless taken the matter one stage further with the House of Lords finding that to be properly compliant with the Human Rights Act 1998, a homosexual tenant need no longer rely on being part of a 'family' relationship but could instead claim to be the 'surviving spouse' of a homosexual partner. The Court of Appeal has made recent use of the purposive approach in *R(Haw) v Secretary of State for the Home Department* (2006) as discussed in Chapter 2 (p 48).

A further important case that has been credited with furthering the contextual or purposive approach to interpretation is *Pepper (Inspector of Taxes) v Hart* (1993).

### Let's look at cases: *Pepper (Inspector of Taxes) v Hart* (1993)

The case concerned a tax issue. The masters and bursar at an independent school benefited from a concessionary fees scheme that enabled their sons to attend the school for one-fifth of the fee charged to the public. This was, however, a 'taxable benefit' under s 61 of the Finance Act 1976. A dispute arose when the masters and bursar were assessed for income tax on the 'cash equivalent' of that benefit. They argued that since the school was not incurring significant expense in operating the scheme, the 'cash equivalent' was nil.

Both the High Court and the Court of Appeal found for the Inland Revenue (that is, Pepper, the Inspector of Taxes). Hart appealed to the House of Lords. The case could be determined only by interpretation of ss 61 and 63 of the Finance Act 1976, and it became apparent that an examination of parliamentary proceedings prior to the 1976 Act might shed light on the issue. Thus, it was put to the House of Lords that a review of previous authority on the use of *Hansard* (the official record of debates in Parliament) in construing statutory provisions was now in order. The case was eventually decided by a committee of seven judges in the House of Lords. On law, by a majority of 6:1, their Lordships decided that reference to *Hansard* should be allowed as an aid to statutory interpretation, subject to three qualifications:

- The legislation at issue has to be ambiguous or obscure (to such an extent that to use the literal approach would lead to absurdity).
- The material in *Hansard* to be relied upon must consist of statements by a Minister or other promoter of the Bill (the debates at Bill stage being important to interpretation of the Act in practice).
- The statements to be relied on in *Hansard* must be clear and unambiguous.

Hart won the case: the use of *Hansard* favoured his interpretation. This was very significant, as previous authorities had prohibited the use of *Hansard* on the basis of rules that generally excluded extrinsic, or external, aids to interpretation.

The advantages and disadvantages of the purposive approach are summarised in Table 3.5.

## EXTRINSIC AIDS TO INTERPRETATION

We have seen already that judges have some **extrinsic aids** – that is, aids separate to the legislation itself that can be used for interpretation purposes – available to them, ranging from a dictionary to the official records of parliamentary debates, known as *Hansard*. The use of extrinsic aids has become more acceptable recently, particularly after the case of *Pepper v Hart*.

**Talking point: should judges use *Hansard* in interpreting statutes?**

There was much discussion in *Pepper (Inspector of Taxes) v Hart* (1993) about the merits of allowing an extrinsic aid such as *Hansard* to be referred to, and particular concern was expressed about the practical difficulties associated with it, such as the time, effort and expense that legal practitioners might have to incur as a result of searching for useful references in the record of debates. Constitutional concerns about threats to the mutual respect between Parliament and the judiciary were also raised, as was the point that parliamentary debates were perhaps more likely to produce confusion, rather than clarity.

By contrast, the following arguments in favour of admitting *Hansard* (and therefore relaxing the 'exclusionary rule') prevailed:

- It might be the case that the very question of interpretation at issue was considered by Parliament (and would therefore be in *Hansard*) – why should the judges be blind to this?
- Looking at *Hansard* increases the chances of identifying the mischief in an Act, and provides the necessary context and intention for the purposive approach.
- Academic textbooks will often refer to *Hansard* in pursuing a legal argument – so why not allow such references in the courts?
- Strict control over allowing reference to *Hansard* would keep legal costs at a reasonable level.

The impact of *Pepper v Hart* has been considerable, generating a great deal of case law in which *Hansard* has been referred to. It has not, however, always resulted in resolving ambiguities and assisting clarity. Indeed, it has raised questions in many instances rather than answered them. There is a suspicion that some judges use *Hansard* as a method of purposive law-making, contrary, or on a tangent, to the words contained within the Act. Lord Millett has gone so far as to call for the rule established in *Pepper v Hart* to be abolished.

Nevertheless, some cases have revealed the benefits of admitting *Hansard* as an aid to statutory interpretation. The contract case of *Stevenson v Rogers* (1999), which interpreted the words 'in the course of a business' in provisions of the Sale of Goods Act 1979 as applying to a fisherman who sells his boat, and thereby determined the boundaries of a business sale, provides an example of *Hansard* being used to resolve an ambiguity that had plagued the courts for years in cases relating to similar legislation. More recently, *Hansard* was used to show that licensing legislation passed in the 1960s had intended to place the responsibility of alcohol licences on specific individuals rather than on corporate bodies, thus supermarkets could not be prosecuted as 'persons' for breaches of this area of law (*London Borough of Haringey v Marks & Spencer plc* (2004) ).

Table 3.5 The purposive approach to interpretation: advantages and disadvantages

| *Advantages* | *Disadvantages* |
| --- | --- |
| Looks to the spirit of the law, rather than its letter (ie, the actual words used), thus moving away from narrow, technical decisions towards a more flexible, potentially more just approach. | Gives more power to the judiciary, at the expense of the legislature, thus bringing into question parliamentary sovereignty and the separation of powers by allowing judges, in effect, to make new law. (See Chapter 1.) |
| Allows judges to investigate relevant extrinsic aids to resolve ambiguities. | A purposive approach may result in uncertainty in the law and subjective decision-making. |
| Enables judges to keep up with changing times and new developments. | Looks beyond the Act itself to extrinsic aids and the broader context, bringing into question parliamentary intention as evidenced by the plain words of the statute. |

## Official publications developed during law reform

Courts can use these publications as an aid to interpretation. They include **Government White Papers** and reports of law reform agencies such as the **Law Commission.** As Lord Halsbury said in *Eastman Photographic Materials Co Ltd v Comptroller of Patents* (1898), there is often 'no more accurate source of information' as to the **mischief** at which an Act was aimed.

## Academic authorities

Judges can refer to authoritative textbooks, and the views of legal scholars as expressed in books and journal articles, to assist them in interpreting statutory sections. The House of Lords' interpretation of s 1(1) of the Criminal Attempts Act 1981 in *R v Shivpuri* (1987) was heavily influenced by the views of a leading academic, Glanville Williams, in an article for the *Criminal Law Review*. In the more recent case of *R v Bentham* (2005) (see Let's Look at Cases on p 55), Lord Bingham cited an article by Professor Spencer in the *Cambridge Law Journal* in support of his interpretation of the Firearms Act 1968. However, judges do not always agree with the views of authorities and, in *R v S (and others)* (2005), the Court of Appeal (Criminal Division) expressly doubted an opinion contained in the criminal practitioners manual, *Archbold*, on interpreting ss 227 and 228 of the Criminal Justice Act 2003, regarding licence periods for defendants serving extended sentences.

## Explanatory notes

These now accompany all new Acts of Parliament. While Parliament recognises, and welcomes, the inclusion of explanatory notes, Ministers have pointed out that these should not be considered as 'authoritative'. Nevertheless, the courts have been prepared to take these notes into account as an extrinsic aid in respect of delegated legislation.

## Parliamentary debates (*Hansard*)

After a long period of judicial debate as to whether *Hansard* could be referred to when interpreting statutes, we have already seen that the House of Lords in the case of *Pepper v Hart* determined that it could – subject to certain qualifications – on the basis that access to such materials might throw light on parliamentary intention and **purpose**.

## Dictionaries

Judges following the **literal approach** (see pp 55–6 above) tend to use dictionaries to assist their interpretation. The Court of Appeal in *R v Dovermoss* (1995) consulted the Oxford English Dictionary to find the meaning of 'polluting matter'. This was a term used in s 85 of the Water Resources Act 1991. The question was raised when slurry was applied to agricultural land by farmers and polluted an underground spring, but without causing harm to animal and plant life. On a literal reading, 'polluting matter' did not have to be poisonous in its impact to attract a prosecution under this Act.

## Relevance of other statutory authority

This aid to interpretation is illustrated by the case of *Royal Crown Derby Porcelain Co Ltd v Raymond Russell* (1949). Here, words in the **Rent and Mortgage Act 1920**, which had received clear judicial interpretation in a series of cases, enabled a judge considering the **Rent and Mortgage Act 1933,** containing substantially the same words, to apply the interpretation of the previous decisions.

## International Agreements

Parliament has expressly to incorporate **international treaties** and **conventions** for them to be enforced in English law. The primacy of **European Community (EC) law** was, for example, given effect by the **European Communities Act 1972**; and the general incorporation of the **European Convention on Human Rights** through the **Human Rights Act 1998**. The courts will use these sources for interpretation when looking at the incorporating provisions of the English Act. Table 3.6 summarises the extrinsic aids to interpretation.

Table 3.6 Extrinsic aids to interpretation

| *Type of extrinsic aid allowed by the courts* | *Brief description* |
|---|---|
| Documents produced during the law reform process | For example, reports of law reform bodies; White Papers. Good for mischief rule. |
| Academic authorities | For example, authoritative textbooks and journal articles: can provide useful assistance, though views not always accepted by judges. |
| Explanatory notes | Now accompany all Acts. Allowed for interpretation of delegated legislation, though to be confirmed for Acts. |
| Parliamentary debates | Allowed, following *Pepper v Hart*, but subject to three controls (see p 60 above). Good for mischief and purposive approaches. |
| Dictionaries | Very necessary for operation of the literal rule. But is this an 'easy option' for judges? |
| Other statutory authority | Useful if the provision contains a construction common to an earlier Act. |
| International agreements | Useful support for interpreting Acts of incorporation. |

## INTRINSIC AIDS TO INTERPRETATION

The judges may also make some use of intrinsic aids in the interpretation process. Intrinsic aids are so called because they can be found *within* the statute.

## Short title

The short title is a **brief description** of the statute. This will rarely, on its own, be particularly useful for interpretation, though it might provide weight alongside other relevant factors.

## Long title

This is like a **sub-heading supporting the short title** of an Act and can sometimes be used by judges in working towards interpretation. For example, it was used by judges to establish the social purpose and policy of the Abortion Act 1967 in *Royal College of Nursing of the UK v Department of Health and Social Security* (1981). However, the general rule is that the long title should be referred to only if the words in the Act are ambiguous. On the rare occasions that the long title might provide 'the plainest of all guides to the general objectives of a statute', there might not be a need for ambiguity before this is used. This was suggested by Lord Simon in the *Black-Clawson* (1975) case.

## Schedules

These are **supplementary parts of a statute** that offer details required by other parts of the Act and are often referred to directly by statutory provisions. Schedules can be used as an aid to interpretation on this basis.

## Other intrinsic aids

As Lord Reid said in the case of *DPP v Schildkamp* (1971), 'cross-headings, side-notes and punctuation . . . may be taken into account provided that they cannot have equal weight with the words of the Act'. Generally speaking, these will have relevance only if the words of the Act are ambiguous. Table 3.7 summarises the intrinsic aids to interpretation.

Table 3.7 Intrinsic aids to interpretation

| *Types of intrinsic aid allowed by the courts* | *Brief description* |
|---|---|
| Short title | Of little use, on its own. |
| Long title | Useful, particularly if there is ambiguity. Good for the mischief and purposive approaches. |
| Schedules | Support the main provisions of the Act, so may provide useful elaboration. |
| Other intrinsic aids | Include:<br>• Headings<br>• Side-notes<br>• Punctuation.<br>Useful if there is ambiguity in the Act. |

## PRESUMPTIONS

Presumptions assist in the interpretation process by enabling judges to consider certain points to be **'taken as read'**, even though a statute is *silent* on them. The courts will presume that a certain state of affairs, or set of circumstances, exists, unless the contrary is proved directly (a process known as **'rebutting the presumption'**). These are not applied uniformly by judges, so we do not know when courts will rely on the presumptions. Some of the main presumptions are set out below.

## Presumption against an alteration of the common law

The doctrine of parliamentary sovereignty indicates that Parliament can make any law that it wants. Therefore, it can modify the common law, but it must do so in a clear, explicit manner. If the Act is silent, the presumption is that no alteration of the common law was intended.

## Presumptions against a statute having retrospective effect

This means that Acts of Parliament will not apply to past happenings. They will not, for example, make a person whose conduct was legal a criminal, where laws making such conduct illegal came later in time. Therefore Acts are generally **prospective**: they will usually apply only from the date they come into effect, and the courts make this presumption accordingly.

## Presumption that *mens rea* is required for criminal offences

Many criminal offences require two key features: the *actus reus* (guilty act or omission) and the *mens rea* (guilty mind). Therefore, if an Act creates a criminal offence the presumption is that the *mens rea* has to be proved. However, some Acts expressly create **'strict liability'** offences, in which it is necessary for the prosecution to prove only the commission of the Act, not the state of mind. Where strict liability offences are expressly created, the presumption is clearly rebutted. (See also Chapter 12.)

## Presumption that the Crown is not bound by a statute

In *Lord Advocate v Dumbarton District Council* (1990), the Ministry of Defence (MoD), representing the Crown, blocked off part of a road without obtaining consent from the relevant local authorities and was subsequently challenged for doing so. However, in seeking to interpret the relevant statutory powers, the presumption supported the MoD. As Lord Keith commented, 'the Crown is not bound by any statutory provision unless there can somehow be gathered from the terms of the relevant Act an intention to that effect.' Table 3.8 summarises the presumptions.

Table 3.8 Interpretation: presumptions

| *Name of the presumption* | *Application* |
|---|---|
| Presumption against an alteration of the common law | Court presumes the Act will not alter existing common law rules. It will look to the express wording of the Act. |
| Presumption against a statute having retrospective effect | Court presumes the Act will apply only for the future, not to affect past happenings. |
| Presumption that *mens rea* is required for criminal offences | Court presumes the Act will require *mens rea*, but will be mindful of the fact that Acts may expressly create strict liability offences. |
| Presumption that the Crown is not bound by a statute | Court presumes that the Crown will not be bound. It will look to the express wording of the Act. |

## STATUTORY INTERPRETATION IN CONTEXT

### Constitutional theory and statutory interpretation

As we saw from earlier coverage of the constitutional **'separation of powers'**, the three 'powers' in the constitution keep checks and balances on each other. Nevertheless, of the three powers, Parliament is seen as the supreme law-making body in the constitution. This means that judges cannot directly challenge or seek to undermine Acts of Parliament. (However, judges can now declare Acts of Parliament to be incompatible with the European Convention on Human Rights under provisions of the Human Rights Act 1998: see Chapter 1.)

The process of statutory interpretation has traditionally shown great respect for **parliamentary sovereignty** in that judges often choose to give words their literal meanings in interpretation. Indeed, as Lord Simonds famously said in the case of *Magor and St Mellons Rural District Council v Newport Corporation* (1952):

'*The duty of the court is to interpret the words that the legislature has used. Those words may be ambiguous, but even if they are, the power and duty of the court to travel outside them on a voyage of discovery is strictly limited . . . It appears to me to be a naked usurpation of the legislative function under the thin guise of interpretation, and it is guesswork with what material the legislature would, if it had discovered the gap, have filled it in. If a gap is disclosed, the remedy lies in an amending Act.*'

However, in more recent times, and particularly since the United Kingdom's membership of the **European Community** in 1973, the courts have chosen to take a broader approach to interpreting statutes, and have sought to discern parliamentary intention as to the meaning of statutory provisions. This has involved seeking the purpose of the legislation. Clearly, to a judge like Lord Simonds, such a departure from the literal approach undermines the doctrine of parliamentary sovereignty. Still, even where the judges take a wider approach and seek to determine purpose or legislative intent (as Lord Denning MR advocated in *Bulmer Ltd v Bollinger SA* (1974)), they tend to acknowledge the importance of maintaining sovereignty. As (the then Lord Justice) Denning said in his Court of Appeal judgment in the *Magor and St Mellons* case, which provoked Simonds's response, above: '*We do not sit here to pull the language of Parliament . . . to pieces and make nonsense of it. That is an easy thing to do . . . We sit here to find out the intention of Parliament . . . and carry it out, and we do this better by filling in the gaps and making sense of the enactment than by opening it up to destructive analysis*'.

Interestingly, Denning's approach, expressed in the Court of Appeal, has had more influence on interpretation than Simonds's words in the House of Lords' judgment. Certainly, parliamentary sovereignty is now much more open to challenge than in the past.

On occasions, the process of statutory interpretation changes the direction or policy of the law, and there are some judges who object to this on the grounds that it undermines parliamentary sovereignty. The case of *Fitzpatrick v Sterling Housing Association* (1999) provides a clear example of this.

**Exercise: Matching the cases and the rules**

Read the following case summaries and complete the table immediately below, identifying the case name and the rule, approach or presumption it illustrates.

(1) This case asked whether a ship that sank, leading to the death of a man, was an example of 'defective equipment': the House of Lords took the view that it was.
(2) This case concerned whether a defendant found within a prohibited area of an RAF camp was in the 'vicinity' of a prohibited place. In determining this, regard was had to the least absurd result.
(3) In this licensing case, did 'entertainment' refer to bodily comfort or theatrical performance? The court held that the words of the statute supported the former rather than the latter.
(4) What's the difference between a car-park and a road? A crucial distinction for the parties in this sharp-sounding case.
(5) If you're drunk, does it matter whether you are driving a bicycle or a carriage? Apparently not, according to the Queen's Bench Divisional Court in this case.
(6) The Oxford English Dictionary came in handy in this case: it defined 'pollution', though critics might perhaps take the view that it has muddied the waters?
(7) The Crown might just seem ceremonial, but it can block off roads when it wants to!
(8) Don't know the answer to an academic question of taxation? The taxpayer found it, controversially, in parliamentary statements contained in the official record of debates.
(9) It doesn't matter how high up those prostitutes are, we're still feeling harassed – the court's view of a little local difficulty in 1960.
(10) 'Other schools' means Church of England schools, according to interpretation of a nineteenth century education statute.

| *Number* | *Case name* | *Rule, approach or presumption* |
|---|---|---|
| 1 | | |
| 2 | | |
| 3 | | |
| 4 | | |
| 5 | | |
| 6 | | |
| 7 | | |
| 8 | | |
| 9 | | |
| 10 | | |

For Answers, please turn to p 334.

The two European sources of law – **European Community law** and the legal regime associated with the **European Convention on Human Rights** – have had a great influence on sovereignty and, by association, on statutory interpretation. They have both influenced statutory interpretation by requiring use of the purposive approach. This approach ensures that English law reflects European Community law. With regard to the **Human Rights Act** 1998, English judges must now interpret words '*so far as is possible to do so*' to give effect to them as compatible with rights set down in the European Convention on Human Rights (s 3), and take account of the previous case law of the European Court of Human Rights. Since these factors give greater discretion to judges at the expense of Parliament, and show that some aspects of continental law are given greater weight than English law, the doctrine of sovereignty is substantially weakened.

## The judges and statutory interpretation

As we have seen, Lord Simonds and Lord Denning had very different views on statutory interpretation. It is not surprising, therefore, that commentators have observed that there are different types of judge, and that the type of judge will influence the approach that it is used. The jurist **Llewellyn** identified two types of judges. The **grand-style judge**, who would be prepared to act creatively (such as Lord Denning); as contrasted with the **formal-style judge**, who would defer to parliamentary supremacy and follow the strict words of an Act rather than its general intent (such as Lord Simonds). The approach adopted by Lord Simonds may be described as respecting the letter of the law, as opposed to its spirit. **Lord Reid**, in a famous lecture given in 1972 called 'The Judge as Law-Maker', identified three types of judge: the black letter lawyers (who, like the formal-style judges, looked to the letter of the law); the legal reformers (rather like the grand-style judges); and the common sense judges. Lord Denning falls into the latter two categories: he was famous for putting common sense before legal principle, though this often conflicted with the views of formal-style judges.

## The drafting of statutes and the process of statutory interpretation

Traditionally, Acts of Parliament were drafted to allow for every possibility, and so were necessarily long-winded and complex. One of the influences, though, of the UK's membership of the European Community (and now Union) since 1973 has been the recognition that legislation can be drafted in a broader style that provides judges with greater interpretative discretion.

The draftsmen who create statutes cannot foresee all future developments, so in reality they cannot allow for every contingency, however hard they try. As Acts of Parliament have been drafted throughout the centuries, statutory interpretation is important, as the law is based on judges interpreting an Act of Parliament in accordance with changing times. For example, does the old word 'aerodrome' have the same meaning as the more contemporary term 'airport' (*Rolls Royce Ltd v Heavylift Volga* (2000))? Or is the old street vehicle, a 'carriage' under the Licensing Act 1872, the same as the newer form of transport, a bicycle (*Corkery v Carpenter* (1951))? In both cases, the judges interpreted the legislative provisions to give effect to changing times, recognising that for all the practical changes that may have taken place, the aims of the statute would remain the same. This search for **legislative purpose** indicates a trend that is currently prevailing in the area of statutory interpretation.

**IT'S A FACT!**

**New 'plain English' drafting initiative**

In June 2006, Constitutional Affairs Minister, Harriet Harman, prompted a great deal of discussion among lawyers when she announced that a draft Coroner Reform Bill would, for the first time, provide accompanying comments to aid interpretation for each of the clauses in the Bill, including explanation of all references to other legislation. Whereas in the past 'explanatory notes' have been written separately to complement pieces of legislation, the supporting comments in this instance will be *within* the Bill itself. The move has been welcomed by the Campaign for Plain English and this Bill is proposed as the first of many to be drafted in a style that should allow for greater public understanding of legislation. In addition, new initiatives to involve members of the public in discussions on the Coroner Reform Bill and to provide for a period of 'post-legislative' parliamentary review on a Family Court Bill are designed to enhance the scrutiny of legislation.

However, lawyers know only too well the difficulties of drafting and interpretation and have offered a very cautious welcome. Simple wording can still give rise to ambiguity and will be put to the test by unpredictable and fast-changing human activity. As Lord Millett pointed out some years ago, even the most simple constructions – such as the New York traffic sign, 'Fine for Parking' – can cause problems for judges in interpreting their meaning.

**HINTS AND TIPS**

When revising statutory interpretation, divide the topic up into different sections. The **common law approaches** – consisting of the literal, golden, mischief and purposive – should be outlined under separate subheadings, with case examples and evaluative points noted for each. You can do the same with the **three rules of language**, the **extrinsic** and **intrinsic aids**, and so on.

- Make sure you know the purposive approach very well because it is increasingly significant today (confirmed by the creative interpretation being undertaken in human rights cases following the passing of the Human Rights Act 1998 and the great importance of EC law). A contrast between the literal and purposive approaches is always useful for drawing out the differences between judges and for showing the law's ability to keep up with changing times if there is a willingness for it to do so.
- Make sure you know at least one case to illustrate each approach. It is, however, better to know more than one, and ideally some contrasting cases, because the question may ask you to use illustrative examples and to assess the advantages and disadvantages of the approaches.
- Do not forget the background to statutory interpretation when compiling advantages and disadvantages. Constitutional theory, judicial styles and the drafting of statutes all provide the means for evaluating and commenting critically on this topic.
- With regard to the three rules of language, do not worry too much if you find the Latin phrases difficult to revise. Just make sure you can identify these rules, and their respective meanings in English, and learn some examples for each so you can demonstrate your knowledge and understanding of each one.

For further reading on statutory interpretation, and good examination advice, see Chris Turner's articles in *A-level Law Review*, Vol 1, Issue 1, at p 8, and Vol 1, Issue 2, at p 28; and Ian Crawford in *A-level Law Review*, Vol 1, Issue 3, at p 30.

## Useful website addresses

| *Materials directly for AS studies:* | |
| --- | --- |
| John Deft (St Brendan's Sixth Form College) | www.stbrn.ac.uk/other/depts/law |
| Law Weblog (Bournemouth and Pool SF College) | www.sixthforminfo/lawblog/index.php |
| Asif Tufal | www.a-level-law.com |

# The doctrine of judicial precedent

4

This topic enables you:

- To recognise how an important source of law – judicial law-making based on the doctrine of precedent, known as common law – contributes to the English legal system.
- To appreciate that there is a hierarchy of English courts and that this assists the process of precedent through the principle of *stare decisis*.
- To demonstrate the importance of law reporting in recording precedents.
- To develop knowledge relating to the nature of judicial precedent and how it works in practice.
- To understand the role of judges, building on earlier knowledge of the constitution and the separation of powers.
- To consider the doctrine of parliamentary sovereignty and the extent to which this is undermined by judicial law-making.

**Judicial precedent** is a system of **law-making by judges** rather than by Parliament: generally applicable decisions made by judges, referred to as **precedents**, are used as models for future cases, and these are developed on a case-by-case basis to establish areas of law. This process describes the growth of the **common law**. Therefore, judicial precedent is an important source of law and a core topic for any student of the English legal system.

## INTRODUCTION TO JUDICIAL PRECEDENT

The general idea of the precedent system is that the lower courts have to **follow** the decisions of the higher courts because these have precedent-making powers. This is referred to as the doctrine of ***stare decisis*** (which means **'stand by what has been decided'**). Moreover, some of the higher courts, such as the Court of Appeal, are self-binding in principle, whereas the House of Lords has wider discretion to create precedents for all the courts to follow. For the doctrine of precedent to work, future cases have to be decided in the same way as earlier decisions if the facts before the courts are similar, or analogous.

The part of a judicial decision that is binding on future cases is called the ***ratio decidendi***, which represents the legal reasoning for that decision. The precedent may be **binding**, or merely **persuasive**, based on the relative standing of the courts and the way in which the judicial comments in the case have been interpreted.

## Let's look at cases: *Donoghue v Stevenson* and reasoning by analogy

For example, a case that decides that a manufacturer owes a consumer a 'duty of care' because they are 'neighbours' (*Donoghue v Stevenson* (1932): for the facts and further coverage of this case, see Chapter 13) is logically analogous to other 'neighbour' situations, such as the relationship between doctor and patient. Clearly, a doctor owes a duty to take care when treating his or her patients, and any conduct that falls short of this will be actionable in the tort of negligence. By treating **like cases alike**, precedent therefore provides some degree of **certainty**.

The effective practical operation of precedent requires an accurate and reliable recording of **legal judgments in cases (law reports)** and a **clear hierarchy of courts**. English law contains both. Judgments of the superior courts are reported by barristers and published in newspapers (see, for example, *The Times*), journals (for example, the *Criminal Law Review*) and volumes of collected reports (for example, the *All England Law Reports* and the *Weekly Law Reports*). Moreover, a **clear courts hierarchy** has been established by the **Judicature Acts 1873–75**, as amended particularly by the **Courts Act 1971** and the **Supreme Court Act 1981** (see coverage below and elaboration in Chapter 6).

## JUDICIAL PRECEDENT AND THE COURTS HIERARCHY

### The House of Lords

The Judicial Committee of the House of Lords is the **superior court** in English law – to be replaced by a **Supreme Court**, with a similar composition and roles, when the **Constitutional Reform Act 2005** comes fully into effect – although some cases are referred to the **European Court of Justice** (see p 81 below; see also Chapter 5).

The House of Lords hears **appeals on both civil and criminal matters**, particularly those raising **points of law** of **general public importance**. Its decisions are such that they should **bind all lower courts** save for very exceptional circumstances (see later coverage of the Privy Council at p 83). Traditionally, the House of Lords was bound by its own previous decisions. However, this had the effect of stifling legal development, with the law unable to reflect changing times. In 1966, Lord Gardiner, the then Lord Chancellor, issued a Practice Statement to address such concerns. This expressed the view that the House of Lords should be able to **depart from a previous decision** if:

(a) it **was out of date**, thus rendering the precedent less relevant to current times; or
(b) it **was wrong** or **created uncertainty**.

#### Departing from a previous decision seen to be 'out of date'

A good example can be provided by *BRB v Herrington* (1972).

## Let's look at cases: *BRB v Herrington*

In *British Railways Board v Herrington* (1972), the British Railways Board was aware of a defective fence running alongside one of its electrified railway lines. It also knew, as a consequence of this, that people took advantage to take a short-cut across the tracks, and that children had been seen playing on the line. All those who climbed through or over the fence to get on to British Railways Board property were, in legal terms, 'trespassers'. The Board's liability to such trespassers was raised when Herrington, a six-year-old boy, was burnt while playing on a live rail-line and suffered severe injuries. However, an earlier decision of the House of Lords, in *Robert Addie & Sons Collieries v Dumbreck* (1929), in which a four-year-old trespasser was crushed in the wheel of a machine operated by a colliery, had held that there was **no general duty of care to trespassers**. A duty would be imposed only where the occupier had wilfully caused harm to a trespasser. The question for the House of Lords in the *Herrington* case was whether *Addie v Dumbreck* should be followed.

The House of Lords, relying on the **1966 Practice Statement**, held that since social and physical conditions had changed dramatically over the years (including the growth of towns and lack of play areas for children, leading to a temptation to trespass) Addie should no longer be followed. An occupier *should* now owe some **duty of care to trespassers**, which their Lordships referred to as a test of **'common humanity'**. As Lord Wilberforce commented, in support of rejecting the earlier decision: *'It [the decision] takes account, as this House as the final expositor of the common law should always do, of changes in social attitudes, circumstances and general public sentiment'.*

**Questions:**

(1) Identify the precedent the House of Lords had to consider in *BRB v Herrington* (that is, the name of the case and the principle it expressed).

(2) On what grounds did the House of Lords decide to depart from this precedent?

(3) To what extent do you agree with the view that *BRB v Herrington* provides a good justification for the 1966 Practice Statement?

The case of *Miliangos v George Frank (Textiles) Ltd (1976)* provides a further example. Here, the defendant was in breach of contract with a Swiss businessman. A batch of yarn had been supplied, but the defendant had not paid. The claimant sued for the debt, but the issue arose as to the value of currency in which payment could be made: Swiss francs or pounds sterling? The House of Lords was bound by an earlier precedent, *Re United Railways of the Havana and Regla Warehouses Ltd* (1960), which stated that judgments could be enforced by the English courts only in sterling.

However, in view of changes that had occurred in the foreign currency markets and sterling's relative instability at the time of the *Miliangos* case, the House of Lords **overruled its earlier decision** in the *Havana* case. Thus the House of Lords allowed the claimant to enforce judgment in francs rather than sterling. This gave rise to the general proposition that awards of damages no longer had to be in sterling in civil litigation if the contract involved the contract law of another state and involved payment in another currency.

### Departing from a previous decision on the basis that it is wrong or creates uncertainty

A clear example of this situation is provided by the criminal case of *R v Shivpuri* (1987). Shivpuri believed he was carrying a suitcase full of drugs. He was arrested, and it was later discovered that the suitcase did not contain drugs but was actually full of vegetable matter of a similar nature to snuff. The question for the court was whether Shivpuri was guilty of a drug-related offence under the Criminal Attempts Act 1981. In deciding the case, the House of Lords **overruled** its previous decision on the Criminal Attempts Act in *Anderton v Ryan* (1985). In that case, a woman who believed she was in possession of a stolen video recorder was acquitted on the basis that belief did not amount to liability, a decision later criticised by the criminal law scholar, **Glanville Williams** in the *Criminal Law Review*. This critical view influenced the House of Lords in *Shivpuri*. Here, their Lordships held that belief did amount to liability, since it was clear that *Shivpuri* intended to commit a criminal offence and believed that he was in the act of doing so. Lord Bridge made the point in this case that: '*If a serious error embodied in a decision of this House has distorted the law, the sooner it is corrected the better*'.

A more recent example of the House of Lords using the Practice Statement to depart from one of its previous decisions is provided by the case of *R v G and R* (2003), as the following describes.

## Let's look at cases: *R v G and R* (2003), overruling *Caldwell* (1981)

In *R v G and R*, the House of Lords had to determine whether two boys, aged 11 and 12 respectively, could be convicted of criminal damage when they did not, in fact, perceive the risk or danger arising from their conduct.

The boys had been on a late night 'camping expedition', without parental permission. They had entered the backyard of a local supermarket and, finding some newspapers, set light to them to create a fire; they threw some of these burning papers under a plastic wheelie-bin on the site and then left the scene, without extinguishing the fire. Unfortunately, the bin also caught fire and the flames spread as far as the roof of the supermarket. It was estimated that the ensuing blaze caused damage to the value of £1 million.

The boys' defence was that when they left the site they believed the papers would burn harmlessly on the concrete floor. It was accepted, as a matter of fact, that they had not appreciated the extent of the risks their conduct had created. However, under the test for recklessness established by the House of Lords in *Caldwell* (1981) for criminal damage cases, the conduct of the boys would be measured against an objective standard: what would be an obvious risk to an ordinary reasonable bystander? On this basis, the boys were convicted, but their appeal reached the House of Lords as a legal matter of general public importance.

The House of Lords took account of the numerous criticisms of the test in *Caldwell*, from judges (including **Goff, LJ, Ackner, LJ**, and the dissenting judges in the original case); academics (including **Professor Glanville Williams** and **Professor John Smith**); and law reform bodies (the **Law Commission**, in particular). The case of *Elliott v C (a minor)* (1983), which applied *Caldwell*, had caused disquiet when liability for criminal damage – the burning down of a shed – had been imposed on a young girl with learning difficulties, who was largely oblivious to the dangers associated with her conduct (setting light to white spirit).

The House of Lords used its power under the 1966 Practice Statement to depart from *Caldwell*. The *Caldwell* precedent was both **wrong** and **created uncertainty** for the following three reasons:

- The *Caldwell* precedent had been based on a misinterpretation of Parliament's intention with regard to the **Criminal Damage Act 1971**.
- Application of the *Caldwell* precedent led to harsh results in practice (such as *Elliott v C*), with no account taken of ability and capacity in determining recklessness.

- The *Caldwell* precedent brought confusion, rather than clarity, to establishing the mental element required for criminal cases, appearing to create an overlap between recklessness and negligence.

The House of Lords decision in *R v G and R* was welcomed by legal commentators for overruling *Caldwell* and introducing clarity to the law: the test for recklessness should be subjective (taking account of individual characteristics) rather than objective.

**Question:**
To what extent does the case of *R v G and R* illustrate the value of the 1966 Practice Statement?

There is also an example of a case in which the departure from precedent was justified on grounds that the previous decision was **out of date** and **wrongly decided:** *R v R (Rape: marital exemption)* (1992). Here, Mrs R had left her husband. They both intended to get a divorce, but proceedings had not been instituted when the husband forced his way into the wife's parents' house and attempted to have sexual intercourse with her against her will. He was convicted of rape, but appealed on the basis that it was an **old principle of the English common law** that a husband could not be criminally liable for raping his wife. The Court of Appeal upheld his conviction for rape (**Lord Chief Justice Lane** went as far as to say that the old common law rule had become *'anachronistic and offensive and we consider having reached that conclusion to act upon it'*) and the husband appealed to the House of Lords.

The House of Lords was prepared, unanimously, to **depart** from the common law rule, as stated by **Sir Matthew Hale** in **1736**, and uphold the conviction for 'marital rape'. This reflected the fact, as **Lord Keith** pointed out, that the common law is *'capable of evolving in the light of changing social, economic and cultural developments'* and that the *'status of women, and particularly of married women, has changed out of all recognition in various ways'*. However, their Lordships were keen to show respect for the **declaratory theory**, a theory that states the judges should declare the law rather than make it, thus preserving the doctrine of **parliamentary sovereignty**. They pointed out that this was *not* an alteration of the law, but really the removal of a misconception in the existing law, that being the common law 'fiction' of 'mutual matrimonial consent' to sexual intercourse. Nevertheless, objectively speaking, this was an example of **judicial law-making** on an issue of **public policy**, and the judges' insistence that they were merely removing a 'fiction' allowed them to justify taking action rather than leaving Parliament to deal with the matter.

### Significance of the Practice Statement for law-making in the House of Lords

The 1966 Practice Statement emphasised the importance of the doctrine of binding precedent for providing a degree of **certainty in the law**. Such certainty allows for those affected by the law to conduct themselves with a degree of confidence, and provides a sound foundation for the coherent development of legal rules.

**IT'S A FACT!**

**4.1: the importance of certainty**

In 2004, the House of Lords was invited in *Jindal Iron and Steel Co Ltd v Islamic Solidarity Shipping Co* to use the 1966 Practice Statement to depart from an earlier decision (from 1957) interpreting international shipping rules that had proved harsh in application and not always consistent with market practices. However, it refused to do so because a change to shipping rules would lead to uncertainty, bring into question the validity of previous transactions, and affect at least three outstanding disputes. Lord Steyn, in his leading judgment, relied on some eighteenth century wisdom from Lord Mansfield: *'In all mercantile transactions the great object should be certainty . . . Because speculators in trade then know what ground to go upon'* (*Vallejo v Wheeler* (1774)).

However, the 1966 Practice Statement also recognised the **dangers of rigidity** within the system, which could mean that the following of an old precedent might lead to an unjust result in modern times. The effect of the Practice Statement was therefore to encourage House of Lords judges to consider previous decisions as binding in the main, but also **to allow departure** from these **in certain limited circumstances.** The judges were also warned to recognise the dangers that such flexibility could present, and in particular the hazards associated with **retrospective law,** for example where a new decision has a major impact in commercial and financial transactions, particularly where it alters previously settled arrangements.

## Let's look at cases: *Horton v Sadler* (2006)

This case concerned whether a defendant to a tort personal injury claim could raise the technical defence that the claim was time-barred (under the Limitation Act 1980) when this would clearly be inequitable, in the circumstances, to the claimant. The House of Lords had previously decided, in *Walkley v Precision Forgings Ltd* (1979), that the courts should not exercise discretion over the statutory time limits in favour of claimants. However, the *Walkley* decision has long been recognised as giving rise to difficulties and uncertainty in application and the House of Lords, in *Horton v Sadler*, declared that it was wrongly decided. Lord Bingham, leading a five-member unanimous House of Lords, made the point that since the Practice Statement of 1966, the House of Lords had rarely used its power to depart from past decisions, but it had to do so in situations where the rigidity of a past decision was leading to injustice to claimants. He therefore outlined three reasons why the House of Lords in *Horton* could depart from the precedent set in *Walkley*:

- It unfairly deprived claimants of a right that Parliament intended them to have;
- It had forced the Court of Appeal into making a number of fine distinctions which, whilst correct in the circumstances, 'reflect no credit on this area of the law';
- It 'subverted' the 'clear intention of Parliament'.

This decision has the practical impact of allowing judges to exercise their discretion to hear secondary personal injury claims made after the three-year limitation period where it is equitable to do so.

Table 4.1 summarises the position of the House of Lords with regard to precedent.

Table 4.1 Precedent and the Judicial Committee of the House of Lords

House of Lords – key points:

- Most senior appeal court in English law: hears civil and criminal appeals.
- Binds all lower courts, save for exceptional circumstances.

- Traditionally self-binding, up until 1966.
- Practice Statement in 1966 allows House of Lords to depart from previous decisions if out of date or wrong/creating uncertainty in the law.
- Soon to be replaced by a Supreme Court, with similar roles and powers.

*Examples of the House of Lords departing from a previous decision if out of date*

- *British Railways Board v Herrington* (1972) which overruled the previous decision of *Robert Addie & Sons Collieries v Dumbreck* (1929) and extended the civil duty of care to trespassers.
- *Miliangos v George Frank (Textiles) Ltd* (1976) which overruled the previous decision of *Re United Railways of the Havana and Regla Warehouses Ltd* (1960) in allowing awards of damages to be paid in currencies other than sterling.

*Examples of the House of Lords departing from a previous decision if wrong/creating uncertainty*

- *R v Shivpuri* (1987) which overruled the previous decision of *Anderton v Ryan* (1985) on the law relating to criminal attempts.
- *R v G and R* (2003) which overruled the previous decision of *Caldwell* (1981) on recklessness in criminal law.
- *Horton v Sadler* (2006) which overruled the previous decision of *Walkley v Precision Forgings Limited* (1979) on personal injury claims and the rules relating to limitation periods.

*Useful general example*

- *R v R* (1992) which removed uncertainty in the common law that had originated in the eighteenth century and recognised that a husband could be found guilty of raping his wife. This decision also took into account the fact that in denying such an offence, the law had not kept up with changing times.

## The Court of Appeal (Civil Division)

The Court of Appeal is **bound** by the **previous decisions of the House of Lords** (though see coverage of a remarkable exception in *R v James/R v Karimi* (2006) at p 83). It **binds all lower courts**, and is also **self-binding**, *subject to* the **three exceptions** in *Young v Bristol Aeroplane Co Ltd* (1944):

- If a previous decision conflicts with a later House of Lords decision, the **House of Lords decision clearly prevails.**
- If **two previous decisions conflict**, the court must **choose** between them. When Lord Justice Peter Gibson considered this situation in *Starmark Enterprises Ltd v CPL Enterprises Ltd* (2001), he considered there to be freedom of choice: it is '*open to the court to apply the ratio of the earlier decision and to decline to follow the later decision*'.
- The court may **depart** from one of its **previous decisions made *per incuriam*** (that is, made through lack of care). The point is illustrated by *Williams v Fawcett* (1985), where the court realised, in seeking to establish the formalities for a legal notice (a 'non-molestation order'), that its previous decisions were based on a clearly discernible error.

### Concluding comments on precedent in the Court of Appeal (Civil Division)

While for Lord Denning the precedent doctrine unnecessarily *restricted* the proper growth of the law (see p 78), other judges have recognised the benefits

**Talking point 4.1: Precedent in the Court of Appeal (Civil Division) and Lord Denning**

When Lord Denning was Master of the Rolls (1962–82) (see the profile of Lord Denning in Chapter 8), he tried, unsuccessfully, to free the Court of Appeal from the burdens of precedent. According to Smith, Bailey and Gunn (2002): 'Lord Denning, MR, fought, almost single-handed, against the notion that the Court of Appeal should be bound by its own previous decisions at all'.

Lord Denning's line of dissent included a refusal to follow House of Lords' judgments in *Cassell & Co Ltd v Broome* (1972), in which he commented that Lord Devlin's test on awarding 'exemplary damages' in the House of Lords' decision of *Rookes v Barnard* (1964) was 'unworkable' and 'hopelessly illogical and inconsistent'. This led to a chorus of disapproval in the Lords.

According to Judicial Statistics (2004), the Court of Appeal (Civil) hears over 1,000 cases each year (with over 7,000 appeals being entered in the Criminal Division), compared with the 200 or so heard by the House of Lords: therefore the Court of Appeal is, in practice, the final court for many litigants. This justifies Lord Denning's position to some degree. However, if his view were allowed to prevail, the system of precedent would be undermined and the law would become unpredictable. Why break a system that is working? However, as Smith, Bailey and Gunn also point out: 'Since the retirement of Lord Denning, MR, the loyalty of the Court of Appeal to decisions of the House of Lords has not been in question'. (*R v James*/*R v Karimi* (2006) notwithstanding: see later coverage at p 83.)

The case of *Davis v Johnson* (1979) is a famous example where Lord Denning MR, leading a five-member Court of Appeal, sought to overrule a previous Court of Appeal decision on the basis that it was wrongly decided (and therefore did not fall into one of the accepted *Young v Bristol Aeroplane* categories). The case concerned whether the county court had jurisdiction to grant an injunction excluding a spouse from the 'matrimonial home' where that spouse had a proprietary interest in the home. The previous case law decided against such a power for the court, but the Court of Appeal in *Davis* thought that the plain words of the relevant statute, the Domestic Violence and Matrimonial Proceedings Act 1976, did provide for this jurisdiction to be exercised. Lord Denning clearly set out his view: '. . . while the Court (of Appeal) should regard itself as normally bound by a previous decision of the court, nevertheless it should be at liberty to depart from it if it is convinced that the previous decision was wrong'.

The House of Lords did overrule the previous authorities, but strongly stated the view that the Court of Appeal should be bound by its own previous decisions, subject only to the *Young* exceptions. Lord Denning viewed this as a 'crushing rebuff' (a comment that appears in his book, *The Discipline of the Law*, 1979). He had long argued that the Court of Appeal's approach to precedent should be modified along the lines of the House of Lords (that is, the Practice Statement), or through adding to the exceptions in *Young v Bristol Aeroplane*. Lord Salmon, giving judgment in the House of Lords in *Davis v Johnson*, provides a fitting conclusion to this section: 'until such time, if ever, as all his [Denning's] colleagues in the Court of Appeal agree with those views, *stare decisis* must still hold the field'. Post-Denning, it generally prevails without argument.

of the **self-binding principle** being supported by specified exceptions in which discretion can be exercised. This is because precedent in operation accommodates both certainty and flexibility, with the former being maintained to a large extent since flexibility to depart is kept within set limits.

## The Court of Appeal (Criminal Division)

This court is **bound by decisions of the House of Lords** and, in turn, **binds all inferior courts**. The *stare decisis* doctrine **applies less strictly** in the Criminal Division, as here it concerns the **liberty of individuals.**

A good example is provided by *R v Gould* (1969). This case considered whether on a charge of **bigamy**, under the Offences Against the Person Act 1861, a defendant's honest belief (based on reasonable grounds) that at the time of his second marriage his first marriage had been dissolved, amounted to a good defence to the charge. Previous authority, in the form of *R v Wheat* (1921), held that such a defence could not succeed on the basis that bigamy was a **strict liability offence**. Did this have to be followed here?

The Court of Appeal (Criminal Division) **declined** to follow *R v Wheat* and instead recognised the validity of the defence. As **Lord Justice Diplock** stated in the case:

> *In its criminal jurisdiction . . . the Court of Appeal does not apply the doctrine of stare decisis with the same rigidity as in its civil jurisdiction . . .*

> *we should be entitled to depart from the view as to the law expressed in the earlier decision notwithstanding that the case could not be brought within any of the exceptions laid down in Young v Bristol Aeroplane . . .*

However, some later cases have tended to assume that the Court of Appeal (Criminal Division) is **generally bound** by earlier decisions. The best way to look at this court seems to be that it clearly does have **greater flexibility**, in practice, to **depart from previous decisions**, though it will generally exercise such power only to **prevent an injustice** to the defendant.

Table 4.2 summarises the way in which precedent works in the Court of Appeal.

Table 4.2 Precedent and the Court of Appeal

Court of Appeal – key points:

- Hears civil and criminal appeals in separate divisions.
- Hears many more cases than the House of Lords and is therefore the final appeal court for many litigants.
- Bound by the precedents of the House of Lords (but note *R v James*/*R v Karimi* (2006) at p 83 below)
- Binding on all the lower courts.
- Self-binding, subject to three accepted exceptions laid down in *Young v Bristol Aeroplane Co Ltd* (1944).
- Criminal Division has greater flexibility to depart from previous decisions to avoid injustice.

*How precedent works in the Court of Appeal (Civil Division)*

The Civil Division is self-binding, but judges can depart from previous decisions according to the *Young* criteria:

- If a previous decision conflicts with a later House of Lords decision, the House of Lords decision prevails.
- If two previous Court of Appeal decisions conflict, the court must choose between them.
- The Court of Appeal may depart from a previous decision made *per incuriam* (through lack of care) (*Williams v Fawcett* 1985)).

*How precedent works in the Court of Appeal (Criminal Division)*

*Stare decisis* applies less strictly to the Court of Appeal (Criminal Division). Therefore the Criminal Division can depart from previous decisions even if this would *not* fit into one of the *Young* criteria.

An example of the Criminal Division departing from a previous decision is provided by *R v Gould* (1969) which overruled the previous decision in *R v Wheat* (1921) to hold that bigamy was not a strict liability offence.

## Divisional Courts

Divisional Courts of the High Court hear appeals from both civil and criminal first instance courts. In *criminal cases*, the Divisional Court is **bound by** decisions of the **House of Lords** and the **Court of Appeal.** Like the Court of Appeal (Criminal Division), it **may depart from previous decisions to prevent injustice.**

In *civil cases*, the Divisional Courts are **bound by** decisions of the **House of Lords**, the **Civil Court of Appeal** and by their **own previous decisions.** Like the Court of Appeal, the Civil Divisional Courts are **self-binding**, *subject* to the **three exceptions** in *Young v Bristol Aeroplane*.

## The High Court

The High Court is **bound by** the decisions of **House of Lords**, the **Court of Appeal** and **Divisional Courts**, but *not* by its own previous decisions.

Although previous decisions are often followed, this is not always the case. The Court of Appeal might have to resolve the confusion left by several conflicting High Court decisions, as it did in the case of *Froom v Butcher* (1975). Here, the claimant was injured when the car he was driving collided with the defendant's car. The defendant was negligent, but the claimant suffered head and chest injuries which could have been avoided had he worn a seat belt. So did this amount to **contributory negligence** on the claimant's part? After wide judicial disagreement in several cases on the same point in the High Court, this question had to be determined by the Court of Appeal. The Court of Appeal held that failure to wear a seat belt would amount to contributory negligence, with damages being reduced, as a general rule, by 25 per cent.

Sometimes, High Court decisions will have a major impact on the law. A famous example is the development of the **equitable estoppel** doctrine in the case of *Central London Property Trust Ltd v High Trees House Ltd* (1947). In the context of a dispute over a lease agreement, Mr Justice Denning (as he then was) posed a famous 'What if?' question: could one party be stopped from going back on a promise that another party had relied upon, even though there had been no obligation on the first party to make the promise at the outset? This question did not relate specifically to the legal claim before the court, and therefore it could not form part of the *ratio decidendi* (that is, the ground for the decision). However, Denning's comments represent a good example of *obiter dicta* (that is, opinions given by judges that are not directly relevant to the cases before them). Denning argued that *equity* would prevent a party from going back on a promise upon which another party had relied and this became an important **persuasive precedent** to support the extension of equitable principles. It has been of relevance for many later cases.

## Crown Courts, county courts and magistrates' courts

While **bound by all** of the above courts, these courts are generally seen as *not* **self-binding** but merely **persuasive.** This is underlined by the fact that decisions taken at these levels are largely first instance rather than appellate and generally not reported, confirming the earlier point that one of the key features required for the operation of the doctrine of precedent is the system of **law reporting.**

## European courts and their impact on judicial precedent

### The European Court of Justice (ECJ)

Although this court technically stands outside the English courts hierarchy, its decisions – based on references from Member State courts – are very important, since where there is a conflict, **EC law prevails over UK law**. Therefore, the **decisions of the ECJ are binding on the English courts**. The significance of this was underlined in the recent ECJ case of *Commission of the European Communities v Council of the European Union* (2005), which obliges Member States to enforce criminal penalties for breaches of EC environmental laws in national courts, thus extending EC law into areas usually reserved for domestic law.

An important distinction has been drawn, however, between the ECJ's power to make rulings on the law and its role regarding the facts of cases sent from the national courts. In *Arsenal Football Club plc v Reed* (2002) (for facts, see Chapter 5 at p 101), the ECJ had differed from the national courts in its interpretation of the facts of the case, and this was seen as overstepping its powers.

### The European Court of Human Rights (ECtHR)

The English courts are required to **take into account** the past decisions of the ECtHR under **s 2** of the **Human Rights Act 1998**. However, unlike the position relating to EC law, the English courts are under no obligation to follow these decisions (a point confirmed by the House of Lords in *R (Alconbury Developments Ltd) v Secretary of State for the Environment, Transport and the Regions* (2003). In *Leeds City Council v Price and Others* (2005) it was held, by the Court of Appeal, that where an English court was seeking to resolve an issue on which there was a precedent set by the House of Lords and a subsequent conflicting decision of the ECtHR, it was **bound to follow the House of Lords' decision.** In practical terms, this meant that the Court of Appeal allowed a council to exercise its right of possession over land occupied by gypsies by following a House of Lords ruling in a similar case, whereas this action would have been denied had the subsequent ECtHR decision been followed.

# THE NATURE OF PRECEDENT

## Binding and persuasive precedents

### Binding precedents

**Binding precedents** are those that **must be followed by lower courts**, or **by appeal courts that are self-binding**. The binding part of any judgment is the *ratio decidendi*, though sometimes judicial comments made 'by the way' (*obiter dicta*) will attract the status of a binding precedent through years of judicial approval, as illustrated by the *Central London Property Trust Ltd v High Trees House Ltd* case on p 80 above.

The history of a precedent and what judges and legal academics have said about it over the years will be important in determining its **binding** status. The contract case of *Stilk v Myrick* (1809) illustrates this point. Here, to deal with desertion on a ship, the ship's captain offered the remaining crew more money to ensure that the ship got home. When they accepted this offer, and the ship was safely home again, the captain did not go through with his promise to pay the extra amount to the crew. It was held that the sailors had no entitlement to the extra money, since they were merely fulfilling their contractual duties to get their ship home. This decision, made at a level equivalent to the High Court, became very significant as a precedent. This had much to do with the **distinguished nature of the judge** in the case, Lord Ellenborough CJ, and with the favourable comments made about the decision in later cases over a long period of time.

The status of the precedent was such that it was held to be binding in the Court of Appeal (a court higher in the courts hierarchy) in *Williams v Roffey Bros & Nicholls (Contractors) Ltd* (1990). In Williams, the judge acknowledged the importance of *Stilk v Myrick* as a precedent, but **distinguished** the case on its facts. (For the meaning of '**distinguishing**' a judgment, see p 84 below.)

**Exercise 4.1: Identifying cases in the precedent topic and their relationship to the courts hierarchy**

**Task 1**
Identify the cases suggested by the following clues:

(1) This landmark case tells you to avoid short-cuts across railway lines: one unfortunate boy risked it once too often, but the rail company owed him a duty of care for failing to maintain its fences.
(2) This case tells you that certain appeal courts are self-binding, except in three specified situations.
(3) Marrying again? Hold on, haven't you already got a wife? Are you *sure* the first marriage was dissolved? This case lays down the law on bigamy.
(4) A message to all would-be campers: if you are going to start a fire, don't burn newspapers under a wheelie bin in the vicinity of a supermarket. Mind you, the young campers were dealt with sympathetically, in the circumstances.
(5) Denning's inspiring 'what if' moments in this case opened up new ways of thinking about the relationship between equity and contract law.
(6) In this one, Denning – older and in a more senior position – perhaps went a bit far in thinking that precedent didn't really need to be followed: it was the case that earned him a 'crushing rebuff' from the boys upstairs.
(7) A message from Luxembourg: our powers extend to criminal matters, too!
(8) The case for those who would prefer to receive their damages in Swiss francs.

**Case options:** (a) *R v Gould*; (b) *Central London Property Trust Ltd v High Trees House Ltd*; (c) *Miliangos v George Frank (Textiles) Ltd*; (d) *R v G and R*; (e) *BRB v Herrington*; (f) *Davis v Johnson*; (g) *Young v Bristol Aeroplane Co*; (h) *Commission of the European Communities v Council of the European Union*.

**Task 2**
Once you have identified these cases, organise them by reference to the appropriate courts. Which case or cases illustrate the doctrine of judicial precedent in: the House of Lords; Court of Appeal (Civil); Court of Appeal (Criminal); the High Court; European Court of Justice?

For Answers, please turn to p 335.

## Persuasive precedents

**Persuasive precedents** do *not* have to be followed, although judges will exercise their discretion to follow them if the precedent carries sufficient weight (in terms of some of the factors considered above) or suggests a solution to problems in the development of the law.

**Persuasive precedents** arise from the following sources:

- Decisions of courts lower in the court hierarchy. For example, consider cases decided at the High Court level, such as *Central London Property Trust Ltd v High Trees House Ltd* (see p 80, above), which have been followed by the higher appellate courts.
- Decisions of the **Judicial Committee of the Privy Council**. The Privy Council hears appeals from the courts in the following **Commonwealth countries:** Antigua and Barbuda, The Bahamas, Barbados, Belize, British Virgin Islands, Brunei, Cayman Islands, Dominica, Gibraltar, Grenada, Jamaica, Kiribati, Mauritius, Montserrat, New Zealand, St Christopher and Nevis, St Lucia, St Vincent and the Grenadines, Trinidad and Tobago, Turks and Caicos Islands and Tuvalu. The Committee also hears appeals from the **Channel Islands** and the **Isle of Man**, and is the final arbiter in matters arising from exercise of the devolved powers given to **Scotland, Wales** and **Northern Ireland**. The decisions made by the Privy Council are highly respected by the English courts. The case of *R v Thabo Meli* (1954), which you will find as a useful authority in **criminal law** (see Chapter 13), was heard in the Privy Council. Moreover, *Wagon Mound (No 1)* (1961) (see Chapter 12) is another Privy Council case that laid down important rules in the **law of tort.** In exceptional cases, where the Lords of Appeal in Ordinary sitting in their capacity as members of the Judicial Committee of the Privy Council decide in sufficient numbers that a decision will clarify English law, the **Privy Council decision will be binding** over an earlier House of Lords' decision. This situation recently occurred when the Court of Appeal (Criminal) held, in *R v James/R v Karimi* (2006), that the Privy Council's decision on provocation as a partial defence to murder in *R v Holley* (2005) effectively overruled the earlier decision of the House of Lords in *R v Smith* (2001). The Court of Appeal justified following the Privy Council decision in favour of the House of Lords' decision because the Privy Council in *Holley* had been composed of House of Lords judges and a clear majority had decided that *R v Smith* should not remain as the authority on provocation. It should be noted, however, that this decision is limited to the specific circumstances and does *not* alter the general rule that the Court of Appeal should follow decisions of the House of Lords.
- Decisions of courts in **Scotland** and **Northern Ireland** and decisions of **Commonwealth courts**. An Irish case that is often referred to in English decisions, and textbooks, is that of *Schawel v Reade* (1913) relating to the identification of contractual terms between parties. The law of tort, on the other hand, contains many references to Commonwealth cases, such as *The Queen v Saskatchewan Wheat Pool* (1983), a Canadian case of great significance in the area of breach of statutory duty.
- Decisions of **courts in the USA**. For example, the case of *Shuey v US* (1875) is referred to as a precedent when seeking to determine whether an offer made in contract law has been effectively withdrawn via a newspaper advertisement.
- *Obiter dicta* of English judges. *Obiter dicta* are things said in passing by a judge while making his or her speech in the case. They therefore do not form part of the ratio and will be of persuasive rather than binding authority in most cases. Denning's 'What if?' question in *Central London*

*Property Trust Ltd v High Trees House Ltd* (see p 80 above) is a good example of *obiter dicta* being followed by judges in later cases.

## The *ratio decidendi* in practice

It is the *ratio decidendi* part of the judgment that will form the **binding precedent** for future cases to follow. However, there is a problem here, since the *ratio* is not clearly identified within the judgment; therefore, it is for later cases to determine the *ratio* in a previous judgment. The interpretation of a later judge may obviously differ from the intentions of the judge who delivered the original judgment. Moreover, this gives later judges the discretion to find a *ratio*, or to classify a passage within a judgment as a *ratio* or as *obiter dicta*, retrospectively. The tort case of *Hunter v Canary Wharf* (1997) helps to illustrate the difference between the *ratio decidendi* and *obiter dicta*.

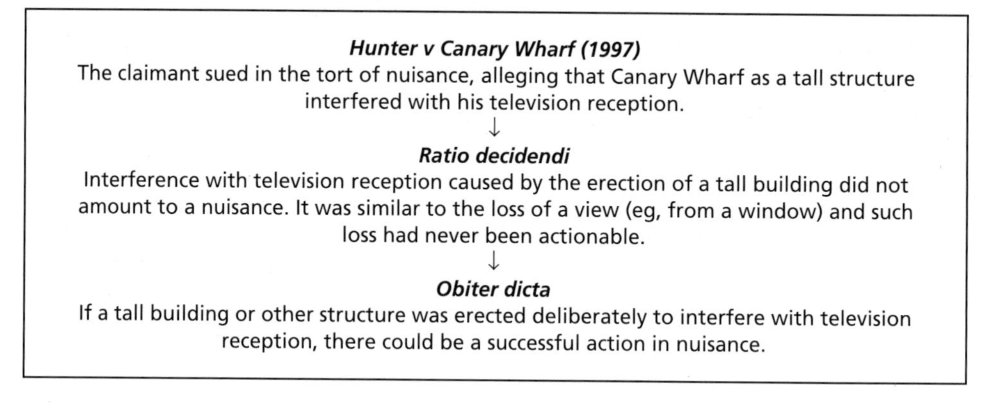
***Hunter v Canary Wharf (1997)***
The claimant sued in the tort of nuisance, alleging that Canary Wharf as a tall structure interfered with his television reception.
↓
***Ratio decidendi***
Interference with television reception caused by the erection of a tall building did not amount to a nuisance. It was similar to the loss of a view (eg, from a window) and such loss had never been actionable.
↓
***Obiter dicta***
If a tall building or other structure was erected deliberately to interfere with television reception, there could be a successful action in nuisance.

## The doctrine of judicial precedent and methods of creating flexibility

The point that *ratios* are determined **retrospectively** means that judges do have **flexibility** in **applying the precedent system**. Other ways in which a judge can exercise flexibility may be summarised as follows.

### Distinguishing

This occurs where a court holds that the *ratio* of a previous case would not find application in the case before the court because it dealt with a different factual situation. For example, this occurred in *Williams v Roffey Bros* (1990), as mentioned at p 82 above, which distinguished the old precedent of *Stilk v Myrick* (1809). Furthermore, the case of *Hartley v Ponsonby* (1857) also distinguished *Stilk*: this was a case with very similar facts to *Stilk* but the sailors were in a much greater state of deprivation and need, and so were forced to go far beyond their mere contractual duties. The sailors were therefore entitled to the extra money that had been promised by their captain in *Hartley*.

### Disapproving

This occurs when a **judge believes that a previous decision was wrongly decided**. This will not result in the case being overruled at this point, though the judicial disapproval may prove persuasive to judges in other cases so that law perceived as flawed is not perpetuated. The decision in the tort case of *Anns v Merton London Borough Council* (1978) (see Chapter 13), both in respect of its contribution to the duty of care principle and its specific relevance to cases relating to the liability of local authorities for property damage caused by defective construction work, was widely disapproved by a number of later cases before being decisively **overruled** by *Murphy v Brentwood District Council* (1991).

### Overruling

This occurs where a court believes that a **previous case is no longer good law** and therefore does not follow it. This does *not* extend to affect the parties in the authorities overruled. As we have seen at pp 73–5 above, this is illustrated by the criminal law cases of *R v Shivpuri* (1986), which overruled the previous House of Lords' decision in *Anderton v Ryan* (1985), and *R v G and R* (2003), which overruled the previous House of Lords decision in *Caldwell* (1981); and by the civil law cases of *British Railways Board v Herrington* (1972), which overruled the decision in *Addie v Dumbreck* (1929), and *Horton v Sadler* (2006), which overruled the decision in *Walkley v Precision Forgings Ltd* (1979) (see pp 72, 73 and 76 above respectively).

### Reversing

This occurs where a **court changes the result of a decision from a lower court** through the **appeal process**. This has the obvious impact of affecting the parties in the case. The libel case of *Grobbelaar v News Group Newspapers Ltd* (2001), discussed in Chapter 9, provides an example here: the House of Lords reversed the decision of the Court of Appeal.

## EVALUATING JUDICIAL PRECEDENT

Below there are listed some **advantages** and **disadvantages** of the system. A central question in evaluating the advantages and disadvantages of precedent will be the extent to which the system accommodates both **certainty** and **flexibility**.

## Advantages

- There is a degree of **certainty** as the precedent system encourages **consistency** (since like cases are treated alike). This means that the system is to some extent predictable, and therefore people can plan ahead with reasonable confidence that they are acting within the law. It is also less costly for litigants.
- There is, correspondingly, a degree of **flexibility**, since judges can **distinguish** cases on their facts.
- This system prevents judges exercising personal prejudices, making the courts' decisions more transparent and creating legal rules that are **objectively acceptable**.

- This system is also flexible because the House of Lords Practice Statement and the other ways of avoiding precedent enable the law to **develop and adapt,** thus keeping up with modern times. It also means that bad decisions can be remedied.
- It has an advantage over legislation as it deals with things that have already occurred (in other words, it can **respond to factual situations**). Therefore the law can be applied in a **practical,** thorough manner.
- The precedent system has enabled **whole areas of law to grow,** with little statutory intervention to accompany them: for example, the laws of **contract** and **tort.**
- This system **allows 'original precedents' to be created** to deal with difficult new legal dilemmas. Famous examples of such cases include *Airedale NHS Trust v Bland* (1993) on the question of whether a life support machine should be switched off when a person was in a persistent vegetative state (it could); and the case of *In Re A* (2000) on the question whether Siamese twins should be separated by an operation when the hospital recommended this, but where the parents had clearly expressed their opposition (separation allowed).
- Legal growth occurs in the light of **practical experience.**

## Disadvantages

- **Judges** are drawn from a **narrow social spectrum.** Their views are therefore less likely to be representative of those of the general public (see also Chapter 8).
- This system is **rigid** as the lower courts have to follow the decisions of higher courts. It can be argued that the Court of Appeal should be allowed to overrule decisions of the House of Lords in certain defined circumstances, as it is often the ultimate court for most litigants. (Note the recent exceptional Court of Appeal decision in *R v James/R v Karimi* (2006)).
- **Judgments** can be **long and unclear,** and so finding the ***ratio*** is not an easy task.
- **In seeking to avoid a precedent,** judges may make distinctions which seem neither logical, nor in line with the general rules that have been developed.
- **Case law** is *not* designed for **coherent legal development:** the law inevitably develops in a piece-meal, incremental fashion, and the directions of such change are not predictable.
- Only the House of Lords is in a position to give an ultimate ruling on an issue before the courts, and it is **extremely expensive** and time-consuming to get a case this far. Even then, the Practice Statement means that the law might not be settled.
- The system of precedent **cannot initiate legal change** since it has to wait for an appropriate case to come before the courts.
- Some judges – notably **Lord Denning** and other 'grand-style' judges (see Chapter 3) – have been **frustrated by the restrictions imposed by the precedent system,** believing them – at times – to **create injustice.**
- Judicial precedent leads to **complex and imprecise bodies of law,** thus encouraging speculative litigation.

**HINTS AND TIPS**

Judicial precedent is one of the larger topics by virtue of the number of case examples that can be used and the potential need to explain both ***stare decisis*** and the **nature of precedents**. That said, however, it is also one of the most interesting topics, and the following suggestions should help you to get to grips with it.

- Using the **illustrations of the courts' hierarchy** in **Chapter 6** to provide your **framework**, create an A3-sized poster of the courts hierarchy with notes for each court relating to the **application of precedent** based on the ***stare decisis*** principle. You could use the following subheadings in relation to each court as prompts for your notes: **bound by**; **binding on**; position relating to **own previous decisions**; and **illustrative cases**. The summary tables for the House of Lords and Court of Appeal at pp 76–7 and 79 above should help you to get started.
- Judicial precedent can be understood only by **reference to cases**, but do not panic when revising: the facts of these cases do not always have to be used in answering examination questions on this topic. The facts have been included for most cases in this chapter so that the authorities are easier for you to understand, but it is the principles represented by these cases that are much more significant in the area of judicial precedent. If you are explaining the courts' hierarchy in an examination, for example, you might deal with the example of ***Shivpuri*** in relation to the House of Lords by writing something along the lines of:
  '*Shivpuri* overruled an earlier interpretation of the Criminal Attempts Act in *Anderton v Ryan* on the basis that it had created uncertainty and led to a great deal of academic criticism. Therefore, *Shivpuri* shows the House of Lords using the 1966 Practice Statement to depart from a previous decision that was widely perceived as having been wrongly decided'.
- **Descriptive questions** on judicial precedent tend to focus on **how the doctrine works or operates**. This allows you to demonstrate knowledge of ***stare decisis***, the **courts hierarchy** and **law reporting**; and also to develop the **nature of precedent**, such as the distinctions between **binding** and **persuasive precedents** and the importance of the ***ratio decidendi***.
- There are **several evaluative issues** that can be raised in this topic, though often the central question will be the extent to which **precedent** successfully *balances* **certainty** with **flexibility**. You should try to understand the ways in which the **operation of the higher courts** provides some **measure of flexibility** (such as the **1966 Practice Statement**; the views of **Lord Denning** on the **Court of Appeal**; and the **importance of the *Young* criteria**), and also how the **judges might seek to avoid following an existing precedent** (through **distinguishing**, for example). The implications of **too much flexibility** might be considered, as might the opposite problem of **too much certainty leading to rigidity**. A popular question for examiners, with these points in mind, is the extent to which the **doctrine of precedent** allows for the law **to develop with changing times**. For a fresh perspective on the topic, see Chris Turner's article on 'Precedent' in *A-level Law Review*, Vol 2, No 1 (Sept 2006) in which he argues, persuasively, that the senior judges pay less heed to the strict doctrine of precedent than is commonly thought.

## Useful website addresses

| | |
|---|---|
| Incorporated Council for Law Reporting | www.lawreports.co.uk |
| Parliament (House of Lords judgments) | www.parliament.uk |
| Privy Council | www.privy-council.org.uk |
| *Materials directly for AS studies:* | |
| John Deft (St Brendan's Sixth Form College) | www.stbrn.ac.uk/other/depts/law |
| Law Weblog (Bournemouth and Poole SF College) | www.sixthform.info/lawblog/index.php |
| Asif Tufal | www.a-level-law.com |

# The European Union and European Community law

This topic enables you:

- To appreciate the historical background of the European Community (EC) and the UK's relationship to it from 1973 to the present day as a Member State of the European Union (EU).
- To understand the nature of EC law and how such law is made by the EU institutions.
- To recognise the extent to which EC law provides rights to citizens in the UK.
- To consider the extent to which EC law has affected principles of the UK constitution, such as parliamentary sovereignty, in practice.

It is no longer possible to study English law without reference to the European legislative process and institutions. This is because the UK's membership of the European Union has meant that English law is now subject to EC law in many areas, and where a conflict arises between the two legal systems, **EC law prevails**.

This chapter refers to **EC law** (that is, the **law of the European Community**). The EC has, in political terms, developed into the **EU** (**European Union**), but since the law and institutions of the Union are grounded in European Community law, the description EC law has been retained. Either EC law or EU law might be encountered on an examination paper, though the coverage here applies to *both* terms in practice.

**IT'S A FACT!**

**5.1: Differences between EC law and the European Convention on Human Rights**

EC law is not the same as the law of the European Convention on Human Rights. As Chapter 1 described, the Convention has been largely incorporated into English law by the Human Rights Act 1998, but this is *not* a source of EC law. It was not made by EC institutions.

The European Convention on Human Rights is, however, increasingly recognised as an *influence* on EC law. For example, the EC institutions and Member States adopted a Charter of Fundamental Rights in the year 2000.

EC law will prevail over English law. By contrast, Convention rights will *not* automatically prevail over English law, since under the Human Rights Act 1998, Parliament can, in theory, ignore a breach of the Convention if it wishes to.

Lastly, try not to confuse the *European Court of Justice* (ECJ, in EC law) with the *European Court of Human Rights* (ECtHR, relating to Convention rights). These are separate courts with differing origins, powers and jurisdictions.

## THE HISTORY AND BACKGROUND OF EC LAW

The development of the EC was a response to the upheaval caused by **World War II (1939–45)** and sought to bring countries together for peace and security in Europe. Six European nations came together – Belgium, France, Luxembourg, The Netherlands, Germany and Italy – to establish this new collaborative framework. The aims of the nations at this stage were to identify common industrial interests and maintain controls over the production of resources that could be put to military use. The first steps of this process were demonstrated in the formation of a **European Coal and Steel Community**

(**ECSC**), the creation of **Euratom** to develop a Europe-wide policy for nuclear energy, and the origins of a **European Economic Community** (EEC), as created by the **Treaty of Rome 1957 (the EC Treaty)**.

The **EEC** introduced a **'common market'** of participating Member States, in which free trade prospered within the market and common tariffs were applied to foreign trade. This became the foundation of the **European Community** (EC), a title that reflected the merger of the 'Communities' in 1967. The **policy aims** of the EC have been based around a set of principles referred to as the **'four freedoms'**:

- Free movement of goods
- Free movement of services
- Free movement of people
- Free movement of capital (money).

In recent years, these economic principles have been supplemented by a great deal of **social policy**, which has also introduced EC law competence over matters such as consumer protection, environmental protection and employment rights.

There were **six Member States** in **1957**; there are now (in 2006) **25**: Austria, Belgium, Cyprus, Czech Republic, Denmark, Estonia, Finland, France, Germany, Greece, Hungary, Ireland, Italy, Latvia, Lithuania, Luxembourg, Malta, The Netherlands, Poland, Portugal, Slovakia, Slovenia, Spain, Sweden and the United Kingdom. The **Treaty of Nice** 2001 has put in place the administrative and political arrangements necessary for enlargement of the EU in future years to 27 Member States.

## THE INSTITUTIONS OF THE EU

The **institutions** are the **governing bodies** of the **European Union** and provide its constitutional and **law-making framework**. Figures 5.1 and 5.2 (see pp 94–5 below) illustrates the relationship between the institutions in the EC law-making process, and you should refer to these as you read about each institution. There are four main institutions:

- The European Commission
- The European Parliament
- The Council of Ministers
- The European Court of Justice.

### The European Commission

The **European Commission** is based in **Brussels (Belgium)**. This is an **executive** institution, providing the **civil service** of the European Union. It is responsible for administering EC law and policies. There are currently **25 Commissioners** in the European Commission, one for each Member State.

The Commission's work is divided into departments known as **Directorates-General**, overseen by the Commissioners, in areas such as Agriculture, Rural

## Developing the subject 5.1: Time-line for the development of EC law and the European Union

Since 1957, the following landmark events have characterised both the development of EC law and the creation of a European Union:

- 1 January 1973 – UK joins the EC (implemented in UK law by the **European Communities Act 1972**; and in EC law by the Treaty of Accession 1972).
- 1986 – the **Single European Act** established a single European economic market via a series of measures designed to remove barriers to trade within the EC and harmonise product standards across Europe.
- 1991 – the **Treaty on European Union** (sometimes referred to as 'the **Maastricht Treaty**' after the city in the Netherlands in which it was agreed) extended the areas of EC competence from economic matters to social and political policies and established three 'pillars' of European law and policy:
  - the **European Communities pillar** relating to the laws and governance (by institutions) of the EC;
  - the **Common Foreign and Security Policy pillar** relating to co-operation across Europe on matters of mutual concern such as peace-keeping and strategic defence;
  - the **Home Affairs and Justice Co-operation pillar** relating to the pooling of legal and police resources to tackle Europe-wide problems such as terrorism, drugs, the protection of children and racism.

  The pillars heralded the creation of a **European Union (EU)** within which the citizenship of Member State nationals would be recognised. Furthermore, this Treaty laid the plans and timetables for **Economic and Monetary Union (EMU)** and the creation of a **single currency** in Europe.
- 1997 – the **Treaty of Amsterdam** extended further into matters of social policy and 'citizenship' (by adopting the Schengen Agreement which removed internal border controls in Europe) and laid plans for wider 'union' membership. It amended the 1957 Treaty, renumbering its Articles.
- 2001 – the **Treaty of Nice** concerned the expansion of the EU to accommodate new Member States.
- 2002 – the **European single currency** became a reality in participating states, with Euro coins and notes in circulation. (The UK has yet to accept the single currency.) The European Coal and Steel Community, one of the foundations of the EC, formally came to an end, with coal and steel issues being absorbed into the Treaty of Rome.
- 2003 – **a draft EU Constitution** was drawn up by a convention headed by the former French President Valéry Giscard d'Estaing.
- 2005 – though scheduled to be ratified by 2006, the Constitution ran into problems when it was rejected by referendums in France and the Netherlands. The UK Government announced in June 2005 that it would suspend a vote on the draft Constitution until some clarification had been provided by EU leaders as to the political future of the document.
- 2006 – it was announced at a Brussels summit in June 2006 that no decision would be made on the EU Constitution until 2008.

Development and Fisheries; Competition; Education and Culture; Economic and Monetary Affairs etc. At the time of writing, **Peter Mandelson** is the UK's Commissioner, with responsibility for **Trade**.

The Commission **proposes secondary EC legislation** for implementation in the Member States. It will **issue 'opinions' to Member States** in danger of breaching EC law. It also **enforces EC law** and **brings Member States** before the **European Court of Justice** for **breaches of EC law**. For this reason, the

Commission is known as the **'guardian of the Treaties'**. It recently brought the UK to the European Court of Justice for breaching an EC Directive on waste control – the UK failed to meet its obligations under EC law when it kept agricultural and mineral waste out of its 'controlled waste' regime (*Commission v UK*, 2005).

## The European Parliament

The **European Parliament** is primarily based in **Strasbourg (France)**, though also in **Brussels (for committees)** and **Luxembourg (for administration)**. This is a **directly elected body** comprising 732 Members of the European Parliament (MEPs), with the most recent elections having been held in June 2004: the UK contributes 78 MEPs. It is *not* a legislative body in the same sense as the UK Parliament, but it does have an *increasingly* **significant role in the EC legislative process** (see further below).

The European Parliament is in a powerful position with regard to the **European Union budget**, and has the **power to remove the Commission** by way of passing a motion of censure (a formal vote of disapproval; please see It's a Fact! box on the left).

**IT'S A FACT!**

**5.2: The European Parliament's strength in financial matters**

In 1998, the European Parliament refused to accept the European Commission's accounts. The Court of Auditors, another institution of the EU, which provides an external audit of EU finances, subsequently discovered fraud and financial mismanagement through investigation of the Commission's accounts. In 1999, the whole Commission resigned, though it seems likely that the Parliament would have invoked its powers had it not done so. Since this episode, the Commission has been committed to financial reforms, and yet the Court of Auditors remains critical of the budget arrangements, and the European Parliament – emboldened by a successful challenge to commissioners in 2004, resulting in the current line-up of the Commission led by José Manuel Barroso – has greater institutional confidence in the exercise of its powers.

The **European Parliament** has **three main types of power** in the **legislative process**:

- **Co-operation procedure.** This law-making procedure applies to laws relating to aspects of the single market, competition, and certain strands of social and environmental policies. The European Parliament is given two readings of legislative proposals from the Commission. This gives the European Parliament time to reach a **'common position'** with the **Council of Ministers** (see below) and allows it to make any amendments. If the European Parliament rejects the proposals the Council of Ministers could still make this legislation, but only by **unanimous vote.**
- **Co-decision procedure.** This is now the **dominant decision-making mechanism** (as introduced by the Maastricht Treaty and extended by the Treaty of Amsterdam 1997). It applies to all areas for which the **Council's 'qualified majority voting' procedure** applies (see below), accounting for most of the single market legal framework, including health and safety as well as environmental and consumer protection laws. It gives the **European Parliament** greater **powers of amendment** and a **veto (or power to block)**, based on an absolute majority of MEPs, over legislation where the European Parliament and Council of Ministers fail to agree. It significantly increases the power of Parliament in the legislative process.
- **Assent procedure.** This procedure, introduced by the Single European Act 1986, exists for certain **major decisions**, such as admitting a new country to the EU. Here, the European Parliament's approval to such decisions is of equal weight to any other institution.

## The Council of Ministers

The main function of the **Council of Ministers** – also known as the **Council of the European Union** – is to **enact legislation proposed by the Commission.** You might wish to remember the old saying: *the Commission proposes, the Parliament discusses, and the Council decides.* However, in doing so please bear in mind that on many legislative matters today, the European Parliament has *co-decision* powers.

The Council of Ministers combines legislative (that is, **law-making**) and executive (that is, **governmental**) functions. The Council is made up of ministers from each Member State. Ministers sit on councils according to the issue for discussion. For example, if it relates to a trade issue then the Minister of Trade from each state will participate.

The **presidency** of the **Council of Ministers** *rotates* on a **six-month basis:** in 2005, for example, Luxembourg held the presidency for the first six months and the UK for the second; and in 2006, Austria, then Finland. A **Committee of Permanent Representatives** (often referred to as COREPER) provides administrative support and continuity for the Council (with officials based in Brussels).

In adopting legislation, **votes are cast by ministers** on the Council. Major decisions require **unanimity** (for example, acceptance of new members in the EU). However, most decisions require **majority voting.** The dominant voting system is that of **qualified majority voting,** which has been extended to cover more areas over the last three Treaties: **Maastricht, Amsterdam,** and **Nice.**

When **Heads of State** get together, this is an extension of the Council of Ministers and known as the **European Council.** It is during such meetings of the European Council – held twice a year – that broader matters of policy are shaped and Treaties are agreed.

### Developing the subject 5.2: Council of Ministers– How qualified majority voting works, in brief

In this system, votes are weighted according to the **size of Member States** (with population size, in particular, taken into account). Therefore, the larger States inevitably qualify for more votes than the smaller States. Enlargement of the EU in 2005 led to arguments about the weighting of votes, particularly between Germany (with 29 votes) and the new entrant, Poland (with 27 votes); the former wanted more, by comparison with what it regarded as a smaller nation. The **UK** is one of four countries with the largest share of weighted votes (29 votes); **Malta,** on the other hand, has the smallest share (3 votes). There are 321 votes in total: a **qualified majority** will be reached if a majority (or in some cases, two-thirds majority) of Member States approve, a minimum of 232 votes is cast in favour of a proposal (over 70 per cent) and that this equates, roughly, to representation of over 62 per cent of the population of the European Union.

## The European Court of Justice

The European Court of Justice (ECJ) is based in **Luxembourg.** It hears two main forms of legal proceedings:

- **Breach of EC law actions** (brought by the Commission as the 'guardian of the Treaties' or, more rarely, by other Member States against those Member States alleged to be in breach of EC law).
- **References from Member State courts** on matters of **EC law** (**Art 234 References**).

The Court is staffed by 25 judges from across the Member States, assisted by eight Advocates-General (legal professionals) who prepare and present the legal arguments for consideration for the benefit of the judges. A **Court of First Instance** was established to ease the workload of the ECJ, though its jurisdiction is much more limited, relating mainly to enforcement of penalties imposed by the ECJ and aspects of competition law.

The ECJ adopts a **purposive (or 'teleological') approach to interpretation.** It is *not* bound by precedent in the traditional sense and so may depart from its own previous decisions. Its decisions will **bind the Member States,** and the ECJ has the **power to fine Member States** that are in breach of their obligations.

Figure 5.1 summarises the role and work of each institution and Figure 5.2 shows the relationship between the institutions in the making of EC law.

**The Council of Ministers**

Composed of government ministers from each Member State – usually the appropriate minister for the business under discussion. For example, if a meeting concerns employment, the UK would send the Secretary of State for Employment.

***Work***

- Main decision-maker and EC law-maker for the EU.

**The Commission**

At least one Commissioner may be appointed by each Member State. Once appointed, Commissioners act in the interests of the EU as a whole.

***Work***

- Policy-makers: the Commission comes up with ideas for new laws and puts forward proposals to the Council.
- Guardians of the Treaties, bringing suspected breaches of the Treaties to the attention of the European Court of Justice.

**The European Parliament**

Composed of MEPs (Members of the European Parliament) directly elected by citizens of Member States.

***Work***

- Advisory body highlighting areas of concern and reporting on them to the Council and Commission, eg global warming.
- Has a role in law making. Under the co-decision process, proposals from the Commission can become law only if the Parliament and Council agree.

**The European Court of Justice (ECJ)**

Composed of one judge per Member State, assisted by Advocates General who give an independent opinion at the end of a case.

***Work***

- Ensures Member States are interpreting EC law correctly (Article 234 references).
- Hears cases involving disputes between Member States.

**Figure 5.1** Institutions of the European Union

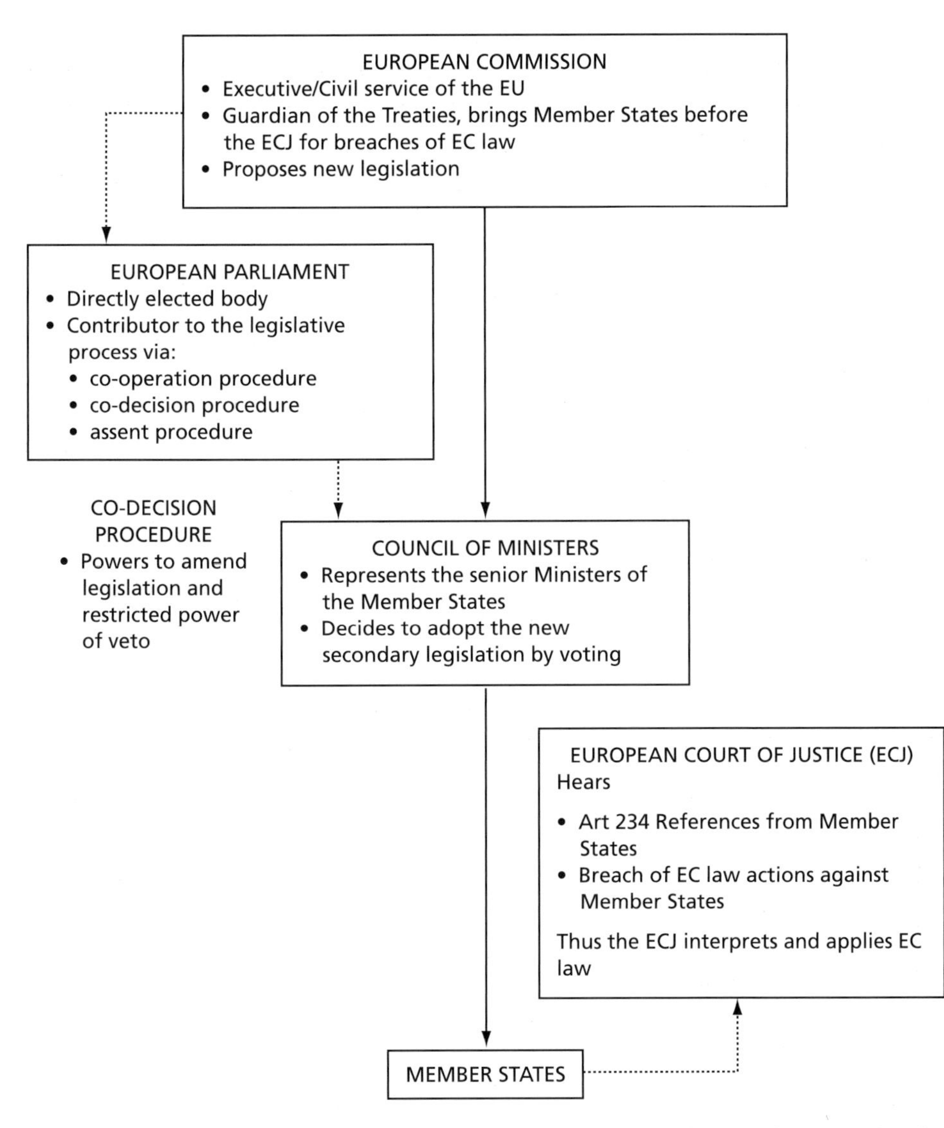


**Figure 5.2** The relationship between the institutions in the creation of EC law (secondary legislation) and the development of EC case law in the European Court of Justice

## THE SOURCES OF EC LAW

There are **three main sources** of EC law:

- Primary sources (the Treaties)
- Secondary sources (Regulations, Directives and Decisions)
- Case law of the ECJ.

## The primary source of EC law

The EC **Treaties** represent the primary source of EC law. They are agreed by the Heads of State at meetings of the European Council (see above at p 93). The **Treaty of Rome 1957** is the founding Treaty (referred to as the **EC Treaty**) and has been amended by the **Single European Act 1986**; the **Maastricht Treaty 1992**; the **Amsterdam Treaty 1997**; and the **Treaty of Nice 2001**.

Provisions of the EC Treaty are called **'Articles'**: they are drafted in a wide, continental style, outlining the general principles of EC law rather than comprising detailed, technical rules. The application and interpretation of Articles is left to the ECJ.

The case of ***Van Gend en Loos*** (1963) (see facts below) states that if Treaty provisions are clear, precise, unconditional or confer rights on an individual, they may be **enforced within Member States** as if they are part of national law. The point that Treaty provisions can be treated as part of national law and have precedence over any national law which conflicts with them is formally known as **direct applicability**. More significantly, however, the practical power for citizens within Member States to enforce their rights provides an example of the **direct effect** principle. This means that **certain Treaty provisions can be enforced by individuals in national courts**. Articles that do not meet the *Van Gend* criteria may require further UK legislation to confer rights and obligations within Member States.

Treaty provisions give rise both to **vertical** and **horizontal direct effect** (see Figure 5.3). **Vertical direct effect** relates to a situation in which rights can be enforced against the State directly, or against 'emanations of the State' such as public bodies or authorities (police, the NHS, Customs & Excise, etc).

By contrast, **horizontal direct effect** relates to a situation in which a citizen wishes to enforce an EC law right against a private enterprise or body (that is, one that is established for personal profit, rather than a publicly-funded body).

Figure 5.3 illustrates the way in which Treaty provisions have both vertical and horizontal direct effect.

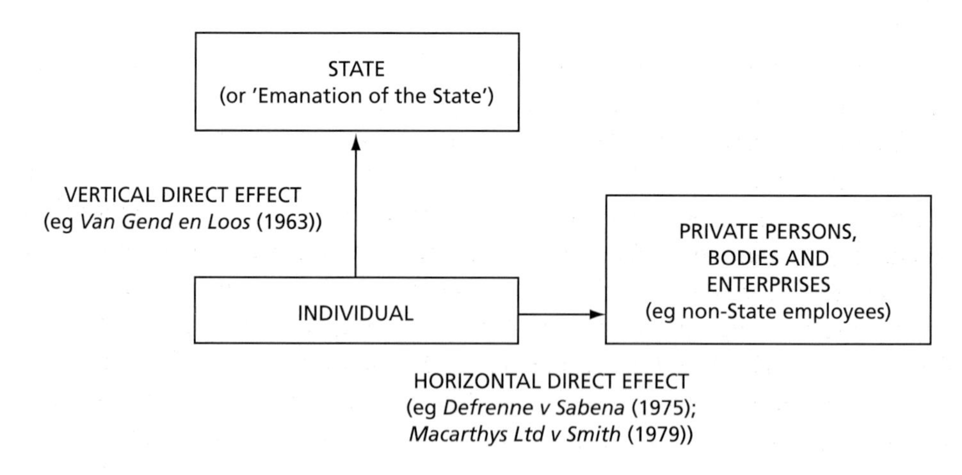


**Figure 5.3** Treaty provisions give rise to both vertical and horizontal direct effects

### Let's look at cases: Treaty Provisions– *Van Gend en Loos*, illustrating vertical direct effect

In *Van Gend en Loos*, there was a breach by the Netherlands of an Article of the EC Treaty relating to the free movement of goods, since the Netherlands charged one of its import companies a duty to import a German glue product into the country. The breach could have been enforced directly against the State by the importers; thus, there was vertical direct effect because the State, in this case the Netherlands, was in breach of EC Treaty provisions and therefore had accountability to its citizens in the national courts.

## SECONDARY SOURCES OF EC LAW

These are provided for in **Art 249** of the **EC Treaty** and are generally the product of the legislative process described at p 95 above (see Figure 5.2).

### Let's look at cases: Treaty Provisions– Examples of horizontal direct effect

The case of *Macarthys Ltd v Smith* (1980) provides a useful example of this. Here, a female employee who believed she was being discriminated against in comparison with male workers successfully exercised her EC legal rights under the EC Treaty (now Art 141) on equal pay for equal work against her employer in the UK courts. The case of *Defrenne v Sabena* (1975) provides a similar example. Here, Defrenne successfully sued her employers, the privately-owned Belgian airline Sabena, for compensation on the grounds that air hostesses and cabin stewards were not paid equally (again relating to what is now Art 141).

### Regulations

These are **directly applicable** in all Member States, that is, they can be **enforced exactly as if they were national law**. They therefore have **vertical direct effect** *and* **horizontal direct effect.** An example of the applicability of Regulations may be seen in the case of *EC Commission v UK: Re Tachographs* (1979). Here, the UK had breached a Regulation when it introduced a voluntary, rather than mandatory, scheme for tachographs (instruments to record driving periods and distance) to be fitted into lorries. More recently, the European Court of Justice, responding to a reference from the UK Court of Appeal in *R (Watts) v Bedford Primary Care Trust* (2006), found that a Regulation supported, rather than denied, a claim by a UK patient for the NHS to authorise medical treatment in another Member State and for the costs of that treatment to be reimbursed.

### Directives

These are **binding**, but the **manner of implementation** is **left to the discretion of the Member States** (within a time limit). Directives have **vertical direct effect only**.

In *Marshall v Southampton Health Authority* (1986), a female employee exercised her EC legal rights (**EC Directive 76/207** on **equal treatment**) to sue her employer, a public body, successfully arguing that the different retirement ages that applied to men and women amounted to sex discrimination. This is an example of vertical direct effect since the health authority, a **public body representing the State**, was held accountable to a citizen exercising her EC rights in the national courts.

## Let's look at cases: Directives– *Van Duyn v Home Office*, illustrating vertical direct effect

The principle of a citizen enforcing an EC Law right applied in *Van Duyn v Home Office* (1974), though here the claim was not successful for other reasons connected to the case. Van Duyn, a Dutch national, was a member of a controversial society known as the Church of Scientology. She wanted to join the UK's branch of the Church but was refused entry by the UK authorities. By denying her entry, the UK was in breach of Directive 64/221, which relates to the free movement of people between the Member States. The UK authorities argued that they were not in breach of the Directive because the UK had not implemented it. However, the ECJ, on an Art 234 Reference, stated that Van Duyn could base her claim on the Directive. Member States cannot rely on their wrongful failure to implement Directives as a defence, since a consequence of doing so would be to deny rights to European citizens.

Although Directives can be enforced against the State, they *cannot*, as a general rule, be **enforced against a private enterprise**. This may result in a person employed by a private enterprise being at a considerable disadvantage. For example, two cases came before the ECJ in 1984 concerning rights of **equal employment** under **Directive 76/207**, but one involved a worker in a **State body** (*Von Colson* (1984)) and the other a **worker in a private company** (*Harz v Deutsche Tradax* (1984)). According to strict application of the **direct effect principle** as it applies to Directives, the former claim could succeed whereas the latter claim would necessarily fail. However, the ECJ found ways of awarding compensation to both claimants, rather than restricting the remedy to the State employee only. This did not ignore the horizontal direct effect principle, but side-stepped it in order to achieve justice.

Figure 5.4 illustrates the way in which **Directives have vertical direct effect.**

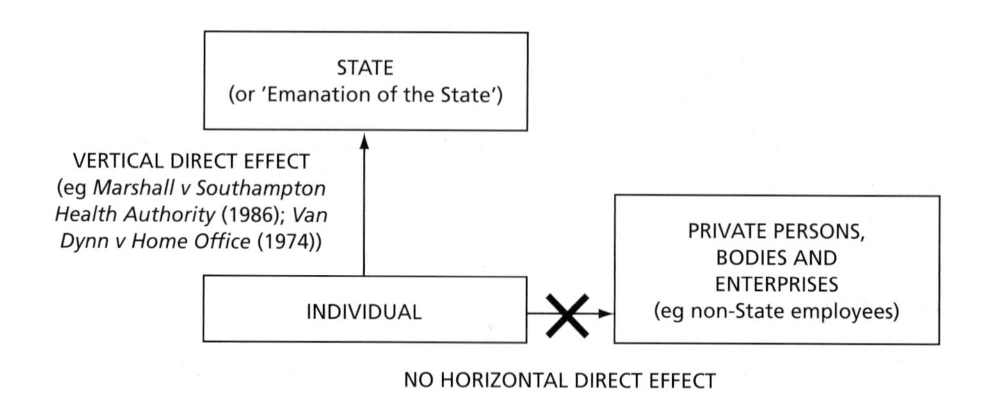


**Figure 5.4** Directives give rise to vertical direct effect only

Thus, certain steps have been taken by the **ECJ** to overcome the problem of 'no horizontal direct effect' of Directives:

- By providing a **wide definition** of the **'State'** or **'emanations of the state'**. For example, in *Foster v British Gas* (1990), the central question was whether British Gas, which was going to be privatised, was an 'emanation of the State'. The ECJ held that it was subject to a **degree of State control** and **providing a public service**. Therefore, Foster could rely on the **Equal Treatment Directive** against British Gas as an 'emanation of the State'. This reasoning was followed in the cases of *NUT v St Mary's Church of England Junior School* (1987), in respect of the **governing body** of a **Church of England school**; and *Griffin v South-West Water Services* (1995) regarding a **privatised utility company**.
- By **interpreting national law in conformity with EC law**. The purposive approach to interpretation gives rise to the **indirect effect principle**, as laid down in the case of *Marleasing* (1990). Here, Spanish company law was in conflict with an EC Directive. National courts were required by the ECJ to interpret law 'in every way possible' to reflect the text and aims of a Directive, thus indirectly giving rights to individuals working in a private enterprise.
- The *Francovich* principle. This principle allowed the **right to compensation from the State for failing to implement EC law**. It derived from the case of *Francovich v Italy* (1990). A Directive required States to set up a scheme to ensure that employees received their outstanding wages if an employer (individual private enterprise) was unable to pay off outstanding debts and had gone into liquidation. The Italian Government did not set up such a scheme, so that when Francovich's employer became insolvent he lost his wages and there was no scheme to compensate him. The ECJ held that Francovich had a **right to compensation** from the Italian Government. Such a right to compensation would be recognised, provided that three criteria were satisfied:
  - that the **purpose of the Directive** was to **grant such rights to individual citizens**;
  - that the **content** of those rights was **clear and precise**; and
  - that there was a **clear link** between the **failure by the State** to **fulfil its obligations** and the **damage suffered by the person affected.**

The *Francovich* case has been followed by *Brasserie du Pêcheur SA v Germany* (1996) and *Factortame (No 3)* (1996) which, on a reference to the ECJ, jointly established the point that the State's liability to an individual will be dependent on the breach being one that is **'sufficiently serious'** in nature to justify such liability.

## Decisions

Decisions are made by the **European Commission** against **Member States, corporations** or **individuals**. These are **binding** on those to whom the Decisions are directed. In the case of *Grad v Finanzamt Traunstein* (1970), the German Government was held to be in breach of a Decision relating to taxation when it imposed a transport tax on hauliers. The Decision was described as having **direct effect**.

The **European Commission** can also issue **Recommendations** and **Opinions**, but these have no binding force.

## CASE LAW OF THE ECJ

Judgments of the ECJ can **overrule** those of the national courts. As we have seen, **Member State courts** can **refer cases on points of EC law** to the **ECJ** under the **Art 234 procedure.** A Member State court should make such a reference where scope for a judicial remedy or appropriate appeal is unlikely within the Member State system. Where the validity of a piece of EC law is in question, the ECJ has recently ruled that a Member State court is under a duty to refer (*R (International Air Transport Association) v Department for Transport*, 2006, in the context of an EC Regulation on compensation schemes for air travellers who have suffered delays and cancellations, which the ECJ ultimately found to be valid).

The reference suspends court proceedings and can be a lengthy process (a practical point that needs to be borne in mind by judges for the benefit of the parties). The reference is *not*, technically, an appeal and the referring Member State court will apply the ruling once it has been given. The following examples demonstrate the importance of cases originating in the UK courts – including the landmark *Factortame* case, which you are advised to look at – involving the Art 234 procedure.

**Exercise 5.1: Recap on the European Institutions**

*There are four main institutions of the European Union: the European Commission; the European Parliament; the Council of Ministers; and the European Court of Justice.*

**Task 1: Geography of the institutions**
Which institution would you find in:

(a) Luxembourg?
(b) Brussels, Strasbourg and Luxembourg?
(c) Brussels?
(d) Brussels, but with rotating presidency held by Member States?

**Task 2: Powers of the institutions**
Which institution's powers include:

(a) The co-decision procedure?
(b) Proposing new EC secondary legislation?
(c) Responding to Art 234 References?
(d) Making decisions by Qualified Majority Voting (QMV)?

**Task 3: Composition of the institutions**
Which institution has:

(a) 25 appointed members, each with differing responsibilities?
(b) 735 elected members?
(c) A permanent staff, referred to as COREPER?
(d) Advocates-General?

**Task 4: Description of the institutions**
Which institution might be described as:

(a) the democratic voice of the European Union?
(b) the creator of a body of EC case law?
(c) the body that traditionally decides to approve new legislative proposals, though is often now involved in co-decision?
(d) the 'guardian of the Treaties'?

For Answers, please turn to pp 335–6.

## Let's look at cases: The use of Art 234 References

- *Bulmer v Bollinger* (1974). Bulmer, the drinks manufacturer, developed a new product and named it 'champagne cider'. Bollinger, an internationally famous champagne producer, took Bulmer to court, claiming under EC law that a product could be described as 'champagne' only if it were actually associated with the French Champagne region. The Court of Appeal found for Bulmer and dismissed Bollinger's request for an Art 234 Reference to clarify EC law. In this case, Lord Denning said that references should be made only in limited circumstances, drawing attention to the practical implications of bringing the case to the attention of the ECJ (see further below).
- *Macarthys Ltd v Smith* (1980). A man had been paid £60 per week to work in M Ltd's warehouse. He left and then, four months later, a female, S, was appointed to do effectively the same job. However, the pay she was offered was only £50 per week. She therefore claimed equal pay on the basis of comparison with the former employee. The claim raised a conflict between Art 119 (now Art 141) of the EC Treaty and the UK's Equal Pay Act 1970, and the Court of Appeal allowed an Art 234 Reference to resolve the issue. The ECJ ruled in favour of S. The right to equal pay in the Article of the Treaty prevailed over the more restrictive sections of the Equal Pay Act 1970.
- *Marshall v Southampton Health Authority* (1986). The dismissal of M, a woman, for reaching the State retirement age of 60 was a breach of the EC Equal Treatment Directive 76/207. This was because men did not have to retire until the age of 65. The ECJ ruled, on an Art 234 Reference, that where the national law (in this case the Sex Discrimination Act 1975) does not conform to the requirements of a Directive, the Directive could be relied upon against any State employer or any 'emanation of the State' (for example, the Health Authority).
- *R v Secretary of State for Transport ex p Factortame* (1991). The UK's Merchant Shipping Act 1988 restricted opportunities for foreign fishermen (particularly the Spanish) to register their ships in the UK, thus preventing them from fishing in UK waters. An Art 234 Reference was made, since this appeared to be in contravention of an Article of the EC Treaty. The ECJ ruled that the Merchant Shipping Act did not conform to EC law, and as such the House of Lords directed that the Act should be suspended. This marked the first time that national law was in clear breach of EC law, and so the House of Lords had to accept that, in such a situation, EC law would take precedence. The Factortame litigation, which went on to see the UK Government paying millions in compensation to the Spanish fishermen, gave the clearest indication that membership of the EC had, in practice, severely limited the principle of parliamentary sovereignty.
- *Arsenal Football Club plc v Reed* (2002). This concerned an action brought by Arsenal FC against a seller of football souvenirs for breach of its trademark. The case raised issues of EC law – an interpretation of the Trade Mark Directive – and was therefore referred, under Art 234, to the ECJ. However, the Court did not confine itself to a legal analysis of the case but actually made findings of fact that differed from the conclusions reached in the English court. The football club sought to enforce the ECJ's ruling with an application for an injunction, but the defendant argued that this should not be followed since it made new findings of fact. It was held, in the Chancery Division of the High Court, that the English courts would not be bound to follow the ruling because the ECJ had overstepped its power. Where references are made, and rulings given, the ECJ can only make determinations of law, not fact. The Court of Appeal subsequently approved this principle concerning the nature of the reference process, but nevertheless found for Arsenal on the breach of trademark issue.

The principles of making such a **reference** – and the extent to which a reference is of assistance to the **English courts** – were discussed by **Lord Denning** in *Bulmer v Bollinger* (1974). He said references could be made only where:

(a) such a reference would be **necessary to decide the case;**
(b) such a reference would be **conclusive;** and
(c) there had been **no previous ruling on the issue in hand.**

Lord Denning refused such a reference in this case.

There are other examples of the English courts choosing not to refer. These include *R v London Borough Transport Committee ex p Freight Transport Association* (1991) and *R v MAFF ex p Portman Agrochemicals Ltd* (1994), where, in the latter case, the parties did not want to refer since time was of the essence. However, Sir Thomas Bingham has made the point, both as a High Court judge and while Master of the Rolls (as the former in *Customs & Excise Commissioners v Samex* (1983) and as the latter in *R v International Stock Exchange ex p Else* (1993)), that since the **ECJ** has a great deal more knowledge and experience on matters of European law, the **English courts** *should* **adopt the *presumption* to make a reference,** unless the circumstances clearly indicate otherwise.

Some references have, in the past, been of great **constitutional significance.** As seen above, the *Factortame* case is one example where a reference was made, and an ECJ ruling given, which had then to be followed by the House of Lords, with the effect that the UK's Merchant Shipping Act 1988 was disregarded where it offended EC law.

## THE IMPACT OF EC LAW ON UK LAW

It is often argued that EC law has led to an **erosion** of **parliamentary sovereignty,** and that when the UK joined the European Community in 1973 it gave away many of the powers that enable it to determine its own affairs. This section examines this issue.

### Parliamentary sovereignty

As stated in Chapter 1, the doctrine of parliamentary sovereignty (supremacy) has great constitutional significance. The summary opposite provides a reminder of the main features of parliamentary sovereignty.

### Parliamentary sovereignty and EC law

It is declared in **Art 10** of the **EC Treaty** that '*Member States [are] to take all appropriate measures . . . to ensure **fulfilment of the obligations** arising out of this Treaty*'. Moreover, under the **European Communities Act 1972,** the UK agreed to follow all the provisions of the Treaty of Rome and the law made by the European institutions.

In **s 2(1)** of the **European Communities Act 1972** it is stated that provisions of EC law should be **directly applicable** where clear and precise – thus giving rise to the **direct effect** principle (*Van Gend en Loos*). Furthermore, in s 2(4) of the same Act, it is provided that UK Acts of Parliament (except for the European Communities Act 1972) will be subject to the provisions of the EC Treaty. The implication of this section is that any legislation passed will have to adhere to EC law. It does not provide scope for a later inconsistent Act, a point underlining the view that the 1972 Act is **entrenched** and therefore almost impossible to retreat from. Some commentators have optimistically interpreted s 2(4) as an 'escape clause': the UK could, in theory, repeal this section of the Act in later legislation to escape from its obligations in EC law. In practice, though, the extent to which the law has become entrenched renders the theory that the UK could leave the European Union (and thus avoid EC law) unrealistic in the face of political reality. It is perhaps correct to say that the UK's status as a Member State since 1973 has undermined UK sovereignty.

The **supremacy of EC law** and the **decline of parliamentary sovereignty** have been confirmed by a number of decisions made by the **ECJ**. In *Costa v ENEL* (1964) it was held that, in the event of a conflict between national law and EC law, **EC law prevails.** Moreover, in *Simmenthal* (1979), the ECJ went one stage further, by stating that any national court must apply EC law in its entirety, protect EC rights, and must accordingly **set aside any provisions of national law which conflict with EC law.** In the *Factortame* case considered at p 101 above, the UK's Merchant Shipping Act 1988 was actually **set aside** for EC law to take precedence. Therefore, the *Simmenthal* principle was applied directly in the *Factortame* case.

**SUMMARY BOX: PARLIAMENTARY SOVEREIGNTY**

- Parliament is the supreme law-making body in the British constitution and it can make any law it wants.
- An Act of Parliament cannot be dismissed, ignored, or even challenged by the courts, even though they may not agree with it.
- If there is a conflict between parliamentary law (that is, legislation) and other types of law (for example, common law), parliamentary law is the superior form of law and takes precedence. This doctrine is supported by traditional views adopted by constitutional writers in history. Blackstone, for example, said in the seventeenth century: '*What Parliament doth, no power on earth can undo.*' Dicey defined parliamentary sovereignty in the following terms: '*. . . Parliament . . . has, under the English constitution, the right to make or unmake any law whatever; and, further that no person or body is recognised by the law of England as having a right to override or set aside the legislation of Parliament.*'

However, it has become accepted that there are some *limitations* on the sovereignty of Parliament in English law:

- One Parliament cannot 'bind its successors', so law can, in theory, be changed by a later Parliament. Indeed, a later Act of Parliament that is inconsistent with an earlier Act impliedly repeals the earlier Act (under the doctrine of implied repeal).
- The power to make delegated legislation has been given to bodies such as local authorities and government Ministers. This falls largely outside the parliamentary law-making process. (See Chapter 2.)
- Devolution and independence. Where Parliament has transferred powers of governance and law-making from the centre (Westminster) to elected bodies in defined geographical areas, by way of Acts of Parliament, it is difficult to see how Parliament could reassert its powers, since the laws may have become entrenched.

As the *Factortame* case illustrates, EC law also places significant limitations on parliamentary sovereignty.

**Exercise 5.2: EC law cases and principles**

**Task 1: Identify the following cases from the facts given:**

(1) This case illustrates the sticky situation faced by The Netherlands when it imposed duties on importers of German glue products, in breach of EC law; and also develops a wider principle that gives rights to citizens.
(2) This case decided a crucial point: which prevails, a UK Act about the registration of fishing vessels or EC law?
(3) This case was about old people and sex (or to be more precise, retirement ages and discrimination on the grounds of gender).
(4) This case, arising in the context of Spanish company law, created an EC-friendly way of interpreting national legislation.
(5) Aside from its legal significance relating to EC legislation on the free movement of persons, this case revealed that the Church of Scientology's UK headquarters is in East Grinstead: I wonder whether Tom Cruise has ever visited?

**Case options:** (a) *Van Gend en Loos;* (b) *Factortame*; (c) *Van Duyn v Home Office*; (d) *Marshall v Southampton Area Health Authority;* (e) *Marleasing*.

**Task 2: Sources of EC law**

*Which sources of law are suggested by the following clues?*

(1) Directly applicable in national law, as *Re Tachographs* illustrates.
(2) These are binding on Member States, but discretion is allowed as to the method of implementation.
(3) Made by the European Commission and addressed to Member States, corporations or individuals.
(4) Art 141, for example, provides rights relating to equal pay for equal work.

**Sources of law options**: (a) EC Treaty; (b) Decisions; (c) Regulations; (d) Directives.

**Task 3: The principles of EC law**

*Insert the missing terms/phrases into the following statements:*

(1) The principle of _____ means that an individual can enforce certain EC rights against the State, or emanations of the State, in the national courts.
(2) The principle of _____ means that an individual can enforce certain EC rights against private enterprises in the national courts.
(3) As the cases of Simmenthal and Factortame illustrate, _____ has been undermined in certain respects by membership of the EC.
(4) Under the _____ principle, an individual can claim compensation from the State for failing to implement EC law.
(5) The European Communities Act 1972 is now so _____ that the likelihood, or practical ability, of the UK withdrawing from the European Union is in severe doubt.

For Answers, please turn to p 336.

Two quotes from UK sources also reveal the impact that EC law has had on the UK in terms of sovereignty. As the then Mr Justice Hoffmann commented in the case of *Stoke-on-Trent CC v B & Q plc* (1993): '[Subject to the theoretical right of withdrawal] ***Parliament surrendered its sovereign right to legislate*** contrary to the provisions of the Treaty on matters of social and economic policy that it regulated.' In addition, **De Smith and Brazier**, the constitutional writers, capture the tensions created by EU membership: '. . . the UK Government has seated Parliament on two horses, one straining towards the preservation of parliamentary sovereignty, the other galloping in the general direction of EC law supremacy.' The issues raised by these quotes assumed relevance in the case of *Thoburn* (2002), a Sunderland market trader who was prosecuted by Trading Standards officers for using imperial rather than metric measurements in breach of EC law requirements. Despite the attempts of Thoburn's counsel to invoke a strict view of parliamentary sovereignty, the courts swiftly confirmed the fact that where EC law requirements are in conflict with UK practice, it is **EC law that prevails.**

In the more recent case of *Commission of the European Communities v Council of the European Union* (2005) (see also Chapter 4 at p 81), the European Court of Justice seemed to take an extraordinary step in allowing the assertion of EC criminal law to ensure that rules on environmental protection were fully effective across the Member States. *The Times* newspaper declared that 'That this lamentable judgment **strikes at the heart of national sovereignty** and Britain's ability to decide the law for itself' (Leading article, 14/9/05). However, academics were not so surprised or angered by the judgment, pointing out that the European Court of Justice had explicitly recognised its general lack of competence in criminal law and that this was a proposal that had already been agreed at the institutional level. Whilst the implications of this decision for sovereignty beyond the area of environmental protection are less than certain, the European Commission announced a proposal in April 2006 for criminal sanctions to be applied in all Member States on organised counterfeiting, having reportedly identified seven areas of policy in which criminal law could be introduced.

Similar concerns about encroachment on national sovereignty were expressed about the draft **EU Constitution**, which you will recall has been rejected by a number of Member States and has yet to be ratified by the UK. This document includes a formal statement of the **primacy of EC law over the laws of the Member States**, though the temptation of controversy should be restrained, a little, by the thought that this merely reiterates, albeit more explicitly, the obligations set out in the *European Communities Act 1972*.

**HINTS AND TIPS**

**Three main areas** should be considered for revision:

- **The Institutions**. The general functions of the **European Commission, European Parliament** and the **Council of Ministers**, and their roles in the creation of European legislation; and the functions and composition of the **ECJ**, with particular regard to the Art 234 Reference procedure.
- The **primary** and **secondary sources** of **EC law**. To recognise the distinctions between the **primary source (the EC Treaty)**, the **secondary sources** (Regulations, Directives and Decisions) and the **case law** of the **ECJ**; and to show the relationship between EC law and Member State law, thus illustrating the way in which it takes effect.
- The **impact of EC law on English law**. The issue of **sovereignty**, explored with reference to the **relevant legislation** (the EC Treaty and the 1972 Act) and relevant cases (particularly *Factortame*).

Therefore, within these parameters, questions on European law can be reasonably **predictable**. This is interesting, since experience suggests that EC law questions are ones that students generally try to avoid. It is hoped that this conclusion will provide 'food for thought', to be borne in mind when planning for revision.

## Useful website addresses

| | |
|---|---|
| European Commission newsletter | www.cec.org.uk |
| European Court of Justice | www.europa.eu.int/cj/index.html |
| EU institutions (in general) | www.europa.eu.int |
| *Materials directly for AS studies:* | |
| John Deft (St Brendan's Sixth Form College) | www.stbrn.ac.uk/other/depts/law |
| Asif Tufal | www.a-level-law.com |

# The courts structure and civil and criminal processes

6

This topic enables you:

- To understand the courts structure for civil and criminal cases; the functions of the courts; and the relationships between courts in the appeal process.
- To recognise the difference between first instance and appellate courts.
- To appreciate how cases get to court, taking into account police powers in criminal law and the way in which claims are initiated in civil law.
- To identify the procedures for criminal and civil cases which determine their progress through the courts.

An understanding of the court structure is central to your legal studies, with links to the following:

- The areas of **statutory interpretation** and **judicial precedent** that find expression particularly in the appeal courts.
- The **judges** who staff the courts.
- The members of the **legal profession**, solicitors and barristers, who represent clients and undertake advocacy in the courts.
- The **lay persons** to be found in the courts, such as **lay magistrates** (who hear the vast majority of criminal cases and deal with some civil matters) and **juries** (who are charged with coming to a verdict in the most serious criminal cases and some civil matters).
- The methods of **funding legal claims** and other issues of **access to justice.**
- The **substantive areas of law**, particularly the **law of tort** which has developed largely through the medium of case law.
- The **alternative routes to dispute resolution**, such as tribunals, which provide an interesting contrast to the more formal courts.

When we think of law, one of the most common images is of a courtroom. It is the courts that often capture our imagination: this is where practical law takes place; where we can bring legal claims; and where cases work their way through the system on appeal to develop the great body of case law.

## INTRODUCING THE COURTS STRUCTURE

As we saw in Chapter 4 on Judicial Precedent, there is a clear hierarchy of courts established by the Judicature Acts 1873–75, as amended, in particular,

A judicial wig and a barrister's wig, two familiar sights in the courtroom

by the Courts Act 1971 and the Supreme Court Act 1981. In addition, it might be necessary for UK courts to request a ruling from the **European Court of Justice** to clarify an issue of EC law, under an **Art 234 (EC Treaty) reference:** the UK courts are obliged to follow these rulings, as the *Factortame* case in Chapter 5 vividly illustrates.

As the following example indicates, the system can prove to be an odyssey for some cases, given the potential for appeals to the higher courts and legal argument to ensue at all levels of the hierarchy.

**Talking point 6.1: introduction to the courts hierarchy**

*The case of Smedleys Ltd v Breed (1974) provides a memorable example. It began when a consumer bought a tin of Smedleys' peas, only to find that it contained a hawk moth caterpillar. The company was prosecuted for supplying food 'not of the substance demanded by the customer', a criminal offence now found under s 14 of the Food Safety Act 1990. This prosecution for a summary food safety offence was heard in the* magistrates' court. *There was then an appeal on a point of law to the* Divisional Court (Queen's Bench Division), *followed by a further appeal to the* House of Lords. *The company was arguing that the presence of the caterpillar could not have been prevented, since all reasonable steps had been taken to screen and check products prior to distribution, and that such occurrences, while very rare – the chances of the caterpillar's presence being 874,999 : 1 – were inevitable.*

*As you can see, this case – arising from one relatively minor incident, which caused no harm to the consumer – made its way through the courts structure to the highest appeal court in the land.* **Lord Hailsham** *famously opened his speech in the* **House of Lords** *with the following comments:*

> My Lords, on 25th February 1972 Mrs Voss, a Dorset housewife, entered a supermarket belonging to Tesco Stores Ltd and bought a tin of Smedleys' Peas . . . Unfortunately, and without any fault or negligence on the part of the management of either company, when Mrs Voss got home, she discovered that the tin, in addition to something more than 150 peas, contained a green caterpillar, the larva of one of the species of hawk moth. This innocent insect, thus deprived of its natural destiny, was in fact entirely harmless, since, prior to its entry into the tin, it had been subjected to a cooking process of 20 minutes duration at 250F and, had she cared to do so, Mrs Voss could have consumed the caterpillar without injury to herself, and even, perhaps, with benefit. She was not, however, to know this, and with commendable civic zeal, she felt it her duty to report the matter to the local authority, and in consequence, grinding slow, but exceeding small, the machinery of the law was set in inexorable motion.
>
> Thereafter, the caterpillar achieved a sort of posthumous apotheosis. From local authority to the Dorchester magistrates, from the Dorchester magistrates to a Divisional Court, presided over by the Lord Chief Justice of England to the House of Lords, the immolated insect has at length plodded its methodical way to the highest tribunal in the land. It now falls to me to deliver my opinion on its case . . .'

*The House of Lords upheld the conviction of Smedleys Ltd.*

## THE COURTS HIERARCHY

The following outline of the courts in the English legal system should be considered in relation to the illustrative Figures 6.1 and 6.2.

## The House of Lords

The Judicial Committee of the House of Lords is the senior appellate court in English law. It hears both civil and criminal appeals on matters of general public importance (from the Court of Appeal, the Divisional Court of the Queen's Bench Division and the High Court). The cases are heard by at least three (and often five) judges known as **Lords of Appeal in Ordinary**. In cases of great significance, a panel of seven (see, for example, the case of *Pinochet* (2000) in Chapter 8) or even a panel of nine (see, for example, *A v Secretary of State for the Home Department* (2004) in Chapter 1) will hear a case. There are 12 Lords of Appeal in Ordinary who staff the court. Government reforms in the **Constitutional Reform Act 2005** declare that the House of Lords will be replaced, in due course, by a **Supreme Court** which, unlike the current Lords, will be *independent* of the legislature.

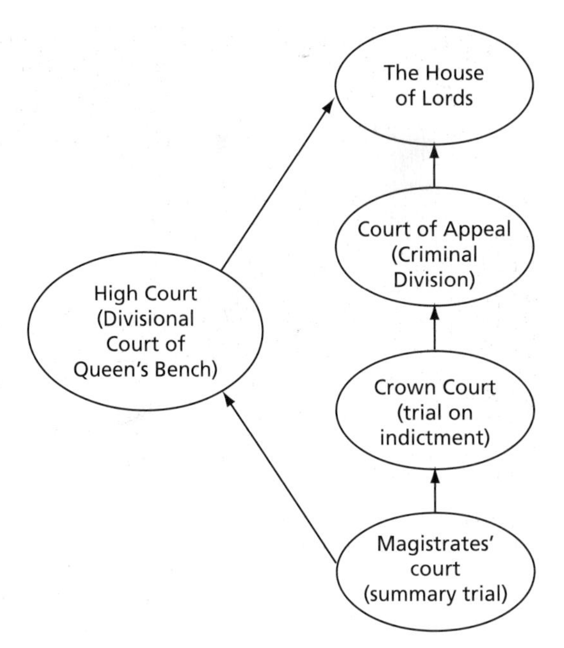


**Figure 6.1:** The criminal courts including appeal routes

## The Court of Appeal

The **Court of Appeal (Civil Division)** hears appeals from the lower first instance civil courts, the High Court and the county court (on law and facts), though following the **Access to Justice Act 1999** many such appeals are now heard at lower levels of the civil hierarchy. The cases are heard by a *minimum* of one **Lord Justice of Appeal (LJ)** and usually three.

The **Court of Appeal (Criminal Division)** hears appeals from the Crown Court (against sentence and conviction). The cases are heard by **Lord Justices of Appeal** and senior **High Court** judges, *usually* by benches of three.

The Royal Courts of Justice house the civil and criminal divisions of the Court of Appeal and the divisions of the High Court (see also, p 127, later in this chapter).

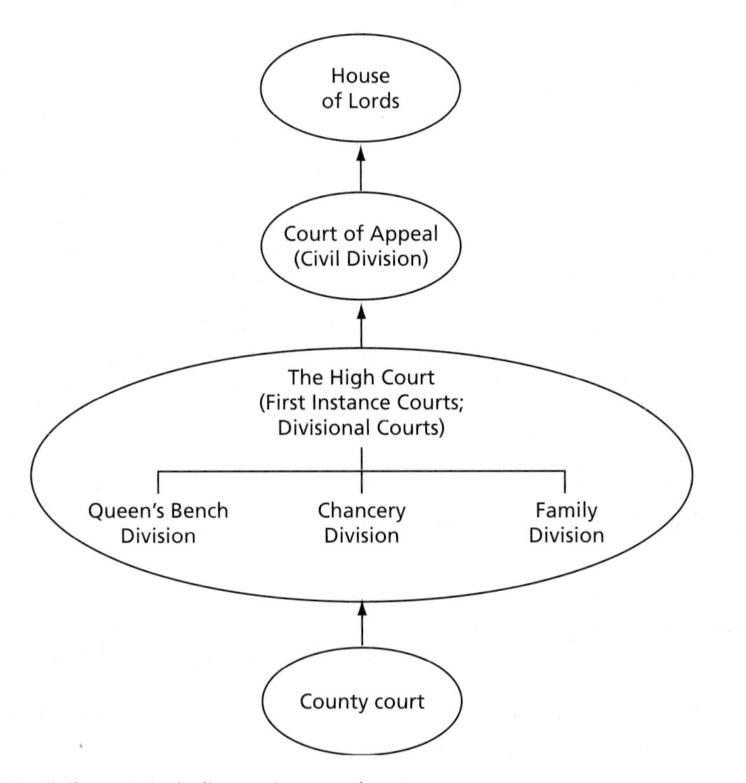


**Figure 6.2:** Civil courts including main appeal routes

## The Divisional Courts

The **Divisional Court of the Chancery Division** hears **civil appeals** in the area of bankruptcy. Cases are heard by **High Court judges.**

The **Divisional Court of the Family Division** hears **civil appeals** from magistrates' courts and county courts in matters of family law (such as custody proceedings). Cases are heard by High Court judges.

The **Divisional Court of the Queen's Bench Division (QBD)** hears **criminal appeals** *on a point of law* from magistrates' courts and Crown Courts (with reference to the Crown Court's appeal functions). Moreover, **judicial review claims** start here in a specially designated Administrative Court.

## High Court

The **Chancery Division of the High Court** hears **civil claims** on matters such as corporate law, property law, trusts, intellectual property and bankruptcy.

The **Family Division of the High Court** hears **civil family proceedings**, for example, cases relating to divorce and children.

The **Queen's Bench Division of the High Court** hears **civil claims** in contract, tort and commercial matters.

**IT'S A FACT!**

**Who says civil trials are dull?**

One of the trials to attract the greatest media coverage in 2006 was a civil trial in the Royal Courts of Justice (High Court: Chancery Division). In *Baigent and Leigh v Random House*, the authors of a book purporting to be non-fiction (*The Holy Blood and the Holy Grail*) sued their own publisher for releasing a work of fiction (Dan Brown's *Da Vinci Code*) which they claimed had plagiarised their main ideas and breached their copyright. The claim did not succeed, but the judge, Mr Justice Smith, ensured that the case stayed in the headlines by entering into the spirit of the proceedings and inserting a code into his own judgment!

## Crown Court

As an *appellate court*, the Crown Court hears **appeals** relating to conviction or sentence from the magistrates' courts. These are heard by a circuit judge or recorder together with at least two magistrates.

As a *first instance court*, the Crown Court hears **trials by jury** relating to criminal law indictable offences/either way offences. Depending on the seriousness of the offence, the case will be heard – in order of seniority – by High Court judges, circuit judges or recorders.

## Magistrates' court

Magistrates' courts have **criminal** *and* **civil** jurisdictions. By volume of cases, the magistrates' courts are the most important criminal courts. They hear first instance criminal trials involving summary or either way offences. These cases are mainly heard by a bench of three lay magistrates, or one district judge in the magistrates' court (ex-stipendiary magistrate). The magistrates' court is also the **criminal youth court.**

In their **civil jurisdiction**, the magistrates' courts hear **family cases** (relating to children) as well as **licensing** matters.

## County court

The county courts deal with *first instance* **civil claims** relating to contract, tort, divorce, bankruptcy, insolvency and property matters. They hear small claims cases up to £5,000, fast-track claims (between £5,000 and £15,000) and some multi-track claims according to their allocation (see section on civil procedure at pp 125–8 below). The cases are heard by circuit judges, district judges and recorders.

**Exercise 6.1: Identifying the courts**

**Use the following clues to identify the relevant courts:**

(1) Which court hears civil appeals relating to bankruptcy?
(2) Which court hears civil appeals on family law matters from the magistrates' courts and the county courts?
(3) Which court hears trials by jury for serious criminal offences?
(4) Although it will not exist in this form for much longer, which court hears civil and criminal appeals on matters of general public importance?
(5) Which court hears criminal appeals 'by case stated' from magistrates' courts?
(6) Which court hears trials for all minor criminal offences and is largely staffed by lay members?
(7) Which court hears civil appeals from the county court and High Court?
(8) Which court hears valuable civil claims in contract and tort?
(9) Which court hears first instance civil claims, particularly small claims and fast-track claims?
(10) To which court may references be made if a national court cannot resolve an issue in question?

**Court options:** (a) European Court of Justice; (b) House of Lords; (c) Court of Appeal (Civil); (d) Divisional Court of the Chancery Division; (e) Divisional Court of the Family Division; (f) Divisional Court of the Queen's Bench Division; (g) Queen's Bench Division of the High Court; (h) Crown Court; (i) county court; (j) magistrates' court

For Answers, please turn to pp 336–7.

## HOW CASES PROCEED WITHIN THE COURTS STRUCTURE: INTRODUCTION

The outline of the courts in the English legal system should provide you with an understanding that the work of some courts is either civil or criminal, or relates to both; and that courts generally have *first instance* (that is, where cases start) or *appellate* (that is, where appeals are heard) functions. This next section, taking criminal and civil law in turn, explores the way in which cases come to court and provides an overview of the legal processes and procedures that determine their progress.

## CRIMINAL PROCEDURE: POLICE POWERS

Since criminal procedure starts with an arrest and ends in the courts, this is the order in which this topic will be tackled.

### Police powers in the criminal process

The **Police and Criminal Evidence Act (PACE) 1984** covers the main powers that the police can exercise, subject to recent amendment in the **Serious Organised Crime and Police Act 2005**. The 1984 Act was introduced to safeguard the civil liberties of individuals at a time of increasing disquiet about police tactics and the treatment of suspects. PACE 1984 is *supported* by

**Home Office Codes of Practice**. The **Codes of Practice** have been *re-drafted* to take into account *human rights* considerations, the duty to be observed by police *not to discriminate* 'on the grounds of race, colour, or ethnic origin when using their powers' (**Race Relations (Amendment) Act 2000**), the Government's efforts in *tackling terrorism* and to complement the **Serious Organised Crime and Police Act 2005**.

## Powers of stop and search under PACE (the 'pre-arrest' situation)

Prior to arrest, a citizen is not obliged to answer police enquiries or attend a police station. The pre-arrest situation is, however, of significance, because police officers can exercise their powers of stop and search if they have reasonable grounds to suspect that a person is in possession of stolen or prohibited articles (PACE 1984, s 1). These powers may be exercised in a public place, which has been taken to include places, other than dwelling-houses and educational institutions, to which the public has access.

The key criterion determining a police officer's exercise of his or her statutory powers under PACE 1984, s 1, is that of **'reasonable grounds for suspecting'**. It is not enough for police officers merely to have a hunch that a person is probably engaged in criminal behaviour. **Code of Practice A** lays down the requirement that the **'reasonable grounds'** must have *some objective basis*. Officers are required particularly to avoid exercising their powers merely on the basis of personal characteristics – such as appearance, previous conduct or a stereotyped image – in the absence of any supporting information; a recent revision to the Code (2005) includes religion as a basis that will not be considered as 'reasonable grounds'. The problems presented by an officer exercising his discretion in such a situation were highlighted in the aftermath of the Stephen Lawrence Inquiry and the police force's acceptance of *'institutional racism'*. Personal characteristics can, however, be relied upon objectively where appropriate information has been received, for example, that a certain group or gang is in the practice of carrying prohibited weapons or articles and can be identified by a certain style or manner of dress. Therefore, the *revised* **Code A** emphasises the link between stopping a suspect and the intelligence or information that has been received by officers prior to doing so.

The 'reasonable grounds' must be evident *prior to* the stop and search. The stop and search should *not* be carried out in order to establish such grounds. The 'reasonable grounds' relate to a suspicion that stolen or prohibited articles (for example, offensive weapons; blades or other sharp objects; and articles associated with offences of theft, deception, burglary, or joyriding) are being carried. The police officer, acting on such grounds, can **stop, detain** and **search persons** (on foot) or **vehicles** (including occupants and contents), and **seize any articles** that have been found.

A police officer conducting a search must provide certain information to the person who has been stopped prior to carrying it out, including the purpose and grounds for the search and details of identification. Wherever practicable, a **written record** of the search should also be made (PACE 1984, s 3). The *revised* **Code A** suggests that the keeping of records will be necessary even where a request for a person to stop was not accompanied by a search.

Police officers can also exercise the power of demanding that a **person removes an item of headgear that covers the face** (such as a scarf or balaclava), where there are reasonable grounds to believe that the item is being worn to conceal the person's identity (Criminal Justice and Public Order Act 1994, s 60(AA)). Civil liberties commentators have complained that a refusal to remove the face covering is an offence, and a strict one at that, which does not allow defendants to offer justification for their behaviour. The penalty is up to one month's imprisonment!

**Police powers of search** are also available in respect of **premises** (PACE 1984, s 8 and **Code of Practice B**). The power is subject to the granting of a **warrant** by magistrates. The warrants available have been extended by **s 114** of the **Serious Organised Crime and Police Act 2005** to include warrants for a number of premises, warrants for all premises 'owned or occupied by' a person, and warrants that allow for repeated entry to certain premises.

A warrant is applied for where there are reasonable grounds for believing that a **serious offence** – such as murder and manslaughter, rape or other serious sexual offences, or, more broadly, any offence which is likely to lead to serious harm to the public at large or particular individuals – has been committed and that searching the premises would yield evidence relating to the commission of the offence. Any number of materials may be seized as a consequence of the search, and new provisions of the Criminal Justice and Police Act 2001 have influenced the revisions to Code B in that the search operation can involve both searching and sifting, that is, taking away materials to be sifted elsewhere that would not ordinarily be seized. Less dramatically, police powers of search may be exercised with the occupiers' consent. Further discussion of entry to premises is included below in relation to powers of arrest. If a person has been arrested, the police may search that person's premises where there are reasonable grounds for suspecting that relevant evidence could be obtained (PACE 1984, s 18).

In practical terms, police powers of stop and search extend *much further* than PACE 1984, since there is a great deal of specific legislation that enables officers to stop and search persons and vehicles in order to prevent the commission of particular offences: for example, in respect of controlled drugs (s 23 of the Misuse of Drugs Act 1971); road traffic matters (s 163(1) of the Road Traffic Act 1988); and firearms (s 47 of the Firearms Act 1968).

## Searches associated with arrest and detention

A suspect may also be searched upon arrest (PACE 1984, s 32) and upon being taken into custody (s 54). The criteria for both of these types of search are the same: that **reasonable grounds** exist to suggest that the suspect is carrying items that might cause danger to others or self-harm; or items that might be used as evidence in relation to the offence; or items that might be utilised in a bid to escape. If this process is carried out at the police station, a **detailed record** must be kept by the **custody officer**. Any items may be seized as a result of the search, though suspects are entitled to be given the reasons why such articles have been taken.

Generally, searches in public will require the removal only of coat, jacket and shoes, though there may be occasions when a more thorough examination of the suspect is required (a particular requirement in respect of drug-related offences). A **'strip-search'**, for example, must be authorised by a senior police officer. **Code of Practice C** states that:

> 'a strip-search may take place only if it is considered necessary to remove an article which a person would not be allowed to keep, and the officer reasonably considers that the person might have concealed such an article. Strip-searches shall not be carried out where there is no reason to consider that articles have been concealed.'

With regard to whether such a search is 'necessary', the suspect should be given a chance to volunteer anything that he or she feels might be relevant. Moreover, an **'intimate search'**, which looks for items concealed about the body, may be authorised if there is a reasonable belief that:

(a) the person has **Class A drugs** in his or her possession (for example, cocaine, heroin, etc); or
(b) the person has an **instrument** that he or she could use for the purpose of **self-harm**, or for the purpose of **harming others**.

It is a requirement that these searches be noted (including details as to the parts of the body included in the search and the reason for undertaking such a procedure). At least two people must be present when the search is being carried out. Searches for drugs *must* take place at a hospital or medical centre. Searches for other objects may be made at the police station. Any items found may be seized by the police. In the revised Codes, there is a presumption against authorising such searches, though if such a search has to be carried out it should be a medical or nursing practitioner, rather than a police officer, who undertakes the task.

## Police powers of arrest

A warrant to authorise an arrest may be granted – upon formal police application – by the magistrates' court. With a warrant, a police officer can also enter and search the suspect's property for the purposes of making the arrest. However, in many situations arrests are carried out *without* the support of a warrant.

Powers of arrest without the support of a warrant were governed under PACE 1984, ss 24 and 25, the former relating to 'arrestable offences' (any offences punishable by five years' imprisonment) and the latter to the general circumstances in which an arrest could be made even for 'non-arrestable offences'. However, under **s 110** of the **Serious Organised Crime and Police Act (SOCPA) 2005**, in effect from 1 January 2006, there is *no longer* any distinction between arrestable and non-arrestable offences and so, as a *Daily Telegraph* headline observed around the time of commencement, 'Now you can be arrested for any offence' (29/12/05). So how do the new powers of arrest work?

First of all, you should note that **SOCPA** *repeals* s 25 of PACE and creates a new s 24 (substituted into PACE). Second, the key to understanding the new s 24 is the **necessity test** it creates: an arrest can only be made under the section if the **constable** *reasonably believes* it is **necessary** to:

- establish the name of the suspect and/or their address;
- prevent the suspect from self-harm, physical injury or injury to others;
- prevent the suspect from causing loss or damage to property;
- prevent the suspect from committing an offence of public decency, where members of the public going about their business would not be able to avoid the suspect;
- prevent the suspect from committing an unlawful obstruction of the highway;
- protect a child or other vulnerable person from the suspect;
- allow for the prompt and effective investigation of the offence or conduct of the suspect;
- prevent the possibility of a prosecution being hindered by the disappearance of the suspect.

With the **necessity test** in mind, the three broad powers of arrest by a constable *without a warrant* are as follows, at the new PACE s 24, subsections (1) to (3) respectively:

- **Arrests prior to commission of an offence and during:** a constable may arrest anyone *about to* commit an offence, anyone *in the act of* committing an offence, anyone whom (s)he has reasonable grounds to suspect is *about to*, or is *in the act of*, committing an offence.
- **Arrests on reasonable grounds that an offence has been committed:** a constable with reasonable grounds for suspecting that an offence has been committed may arrest anyone whom (s)he has reasonable grounds to suspect of being guilty of it.
- **Arrests after an offence has been committed:** if an offence has been committed, a constable may arrest anyone guilty of it, or a person whom the constable has reasonable grounds for suspecting to be guilty of it.

The Government defended the changes to PACE, s 24, on the basis that the old distinction between 'arrestable' and 'non-arrestable' offences had become so complex as to be unworkable and that the new provisions simplify the position. However, civil liberties pressure groups, such as Liberty, have not welcomed the reforms, predicting that police interpretations of the necessity test will not always meet human rights standards and will thus require legal challenges in the courts. Liberty is also concerned about SOCPA's s 116 and its amendment of s 64A of PACE, giving the police **power to photograph suspects** *other than* at a police station, including at the **point of arrest.** Such a photograph can be taken with the appropriate consent or without consent if 'the appropriate consent is *withheld* or it is *not practicable* to obtain it'.

SOCPA also creates a new s 24A of PACE to replace the old provisions on **citizen's arrests.** Once again this power of arrest – made only where it appears not reasonably practicable for a constable to make an arrest instead – is subject to a **necessity test:** there must be reasonable grounds for the person making the arrest to believe that it is **necessary** to prevent the suspect from self-harm, physical injury or harm to others; causing loss or damage to property; or making off before a constable can assume responsibility for him (or her). A citizen may arrest a person *in the act of* committing an **indictable offence** (or where there are reasonable grounds for suspecting that such an offence is being committed), or where an **indictable offence** *has been committed* a citizen can arrest the guilty party or a person for whom there are reasonable grounds for suspecting guilt. The **Criminal Law Act 1967** remains relevant in this context, allowing citizens to assist the police using 'such force as is reasonable in the circumstances' in carrying out lawful arrests.

## The procedure for arrest

Under s 28 of PACE 1984, suspects are entitled to know that they have been formally arrested and the reasons for this, thus giving statutory effect to a common law rule established back in 1947 in *Christie v Leachinsky*. Police officers should choose the **most practicable time** to provide the suspect with the necessary information. For example, if the suspect is under the influence of alcohol at the time of the arrest then he or she may be informed at a more appropriate time (that is, when sober).

Every person who has been arrested should be given the formal caution, again when practicable. The caution is laid down in **Code of Practice C**, supplementing PACE 1984, at para 10.4, and should be recited by officers as follows:

> You do not have to say anything. But it may harm your defence if you do not mention when questioned something which you later rely on in court. Anything you do say may be given in evidence.

This is an *important* feature of the **arrest procedure**, setting out the rights of the individual but also recognising the powers of the police in carrying out their investigations.

When carrying out an arrest, the police can use **physical force** to restrain a person who is resisting arrest, but only in so far as this is **'reasonable'** (Criminal Law Act 1967, s 3; PACE 1984, s 117).

## Police powers of detention and treatment of suspects at the police station

Detention is carried out only if it is necessary, for example, to gain evidence through interviewing the suspect. Under s 36 of PACE 1984, the custody officer, or someone carrying out the role of a custody officer, is the person in charge of making sure the suspect is treated in the appropriate manner in the police station. A **custody record** must be made and kept: it is a record of what happens during this period.

The period of detention has to be kept *under review*, and the police should make efforts to charge the suspect as soon as possible following arrest. Generally, persons can be held without charge only for **up to 24 hours**, though longer periods may be applied for in respect of those accused of serious offences. The maximum period of detention, following police applications to the magistrates' court, is **96 hours**, though those accused of terrorist offences may be detained for longer periods. Once the time has elapsed, the police face the decision either to charge the suspect or to release him.

The period of detention indicates the *balance* that has to be achieved between **individual rights**, on the one hand, and **police powers of investigation**, on the other. The view is taken that the police investigation can be carried out effectively with certain safeguards in place to respect the liberty of the individual. Prior to PACE 1984, there were some high-profile examples where the police had taken advantage of suspects and the balance had tilted towards investigation at the expense of civil liberties, giving rise to **'miscarriages of justice'**. PACE 1984 remedied this situation with a set of rights that can be exercised by all those detained in a police station.

Two important rights are those that enable **suspects to consult with a solicitor** and **have a solicitor present during police questioning** (PACE 1984, s 58) and **allow a suspect to inform a third person** (usually family) that he or she is **being detained** following arrest (s 56). Where the focus of the investigation is a serious offence, these rights can be delayed for a period of up to **36 hours** in certain circumstances (such as concern that a detained person might use the right to contact other persons connected with the offence). The detained person can also exercise the **right to silence**, though this does not offer particularly strong safeguards, since adverse inferences might be drawn from this during a subsequent trial. The police caution, given upon arrest, makes this clear from the outset (see p 116 above). The revised **Code of Practice C**, however, attempts to strengthen the right to silence by ensuring that no adverse inferences will be drawn from a suspect's silence where legal advice has been requested but has yet to be received. This has the effect of cancelling out the initial caution, though a new caution will be given once legal advice has been obtained.

One of the main areas of concern at the time that PACE 1984 was being drafted was the issue of **confession evidence** that had been extracted from suspects using particularly oppressive means (with safeguards now found under ss 76 and 78 of PACE 1984, including the exclusion of confession evidence perceived to have been given under oppressive circumstances). Indeed, several high-profile 'miscarriage of justice' cases raised the issue of police officers 'beating confessions' out of suspects. *After* PACE 1984, **police questioning** is carried out under **strict conditions** and *all interviews* are **tape-recorded** (s 60).

In summary, the police powers in the criminal process are as follows:

- Main powers in the **Police and Criminal Evidence Act 1984 (PACE)**, though powers of arrest have been affected by the **Serious Organised Crime and Police Act 2005.**
- PACE powers supplemented by revised **Home Office Codes of Practice.**
- The extent of police powers in society is a political issue: there is a need to balance the requirements of crime investigation and prevention with the civil liberties of individuals. For further reading about police powers, see John Deft's article on the reforms to the powers of arrest in *A-level Law Review*, Vol 1, Issue 2, January 2006, at p 6; and my own piece in an earlier issue of that magazine on police powers as an 'issue' topic (*A-level Law Review*, Vol 1, Issue 1, September 2005 at p 20).

Table 6.1 Police powers in the criminal process

| *Police powers* | *Description* |
|---|---|
| Stop and search | • Must have reasonable grounds to suspect persons in possession of stolen or prohibited articles (PACE 1984, s 1).<br>• Code of Practice A: reasonable grounds must have an objective basis.<br>• Written record should, where practicable, be made.<br>• Powers of search available also in respect of premises (PACE 1984, s 8; SOCPA 2005, s 114; Code of Practice B) subject to granting of a warrant.<br>• New powers of searching and sifting in revised Code of Practice B.<br>• Additional rules in PACE 1984 relate to powers of search upon arrest and upon being taken into custody. |
| Arrest | • Straightforward powers of arrest where a warrant has been granted.<br>• Arrests without a warrant by a police officer governed by a new s 24 PACE (s 25 repealed) as substituted by s 110 SOCPA.<br>• Arrests without warrant subject to a 'necessity test'.<br>• Arrests without warrant can be made of anyone *about to* commit an offence, *in the act of* committing an offence or *who has* committed an offence. Will be sufficient for the police officer to have *reasonable grounds for suspecting* the person of being in one of the above situations.<br>• Citizens can also make arrests under a new s 24A, again substituted by SOCPA, but in more limited circumstances.<br>• The procedure for arrest is laid down in PACE 1984, s 28.<br>• The police caution (that is, 'you do not have to say anything . . .' etc) is in Code of Practice C. |
| Detention and treatments | • Custody record should be kept.<br>• Suspect can be held without charge for 24 hours, up to a general maximum of 96 hours upon approval by magistrates. Different rules apply to terrorist suspects.<br>• Right for suspect to have solicitor present.<br>• Right for suspect to inform a third person.<br>• Right for suspect to maintain silence.<br>• Police questioning tape-recorded.<br>• Confession evidence regulated by ss 76 and 78, PACE 1984. |

## Charging the suspect and bringing the case to trial

One of the key reforms in the **Criminal Justice Act 2003** is to take the responsibility for charging suspects with specific offences away from the police (save for 'routine offences') and to give this power to the **Crown Prosecution Service (CPS)**. It is thought that by closer working and co-operation between the police (as an investigative agency) and the CPS (as the State's prosecuting body), with the latter determining the charges brought against suspects, far fewer cases are likely to slip through the net and lead to discontinued prosecutions. It should be noted that the CPS determines whether to prosecute by considering two issues:

(a) is there enough evidence to support a **'realistic prospect of conviction'**; and
(b) would such a prosecution be in the **'public interest'**?

If affirmative responses can be given to both questions, the case will proceed to trial.

## PROCEDURES IN THE CRIMINAL COURTS

The court to which a case is tried will be **allocated** according to the **seriousness of the offence**. There are three types of criminal offences: summary, either way, and indictable. **Summary offences** are those of a minor nature. Examples include criminal damage, road traffic offences, and minor assault cases. These can be tried only by magistrates' courts. There is, however, a group of **'intermediate'** offences known as **'triable either way' cases** (including theft), in which the defendant can opt for jury trial. Therefore, these offences may be tried either by the magistrates' court, or by the Crown Court. **Indictable offences** are the more serious types of offences (such as murder, rape and armed robbery), and these are always tried by a judge and jury at Crown Court.

Even Crown Court cases begin in the **magistrates' court** for **preliminary examination**. This used to be a lengthy formal process for determining cases suitable for trial – known as 'committal' – but it is now little more than a 'paper exercise' where the defendant is **transferred directly to trial** (the procedure being governed by s 51 of the Crime and Disorder Act 1998, as amended by the Criminal Justice Act 2003).

The following sections provide an outline of criminal procedure within the courts structure in a step-by-step manner.

### The procedure relating to indictable offences

#### 1 To the magistrates' court (preliminary)

This is a **preliminary examination** – *not* a trial. It is heard by a bench of lay magistrates or a single district judge (magistrates' courts). The purpose of this stage of the procedure is to determine, and confirm, the charge as one of an indictable offence, and accordingly to **administer the transfer of the case** to the Crown Court. This hearing will also take into account any application for bail made by the defendant. Although the **Bail Act 1976** provides a **presumption in favour** of the granting of **bail**, this will *not* be given – save for in exceptional circumstances – for those charged with murder, attempted murder, rape, attempted rape and manslaughter (Criminal Justice and Public Order Act 1994). Bail might also be denied if there are strong reasons for believing that the defendant would misuse the freedom allowed – most obviously, for example, by failing to turn up for the next stage of proceedings, or by

The Lady of Justice atop the Central Criminal Court, known as the 'Old Bailey'

committing further offences whilst on bail. **Conditions** may be attached to the granting of bail to stem the likelihood of any problems, such as the placing of a defendant in a bail hostel, or the requirement of a financial surety from the defendant's family as a form of guarantee that the defendant will attend for trial.

If there is a dispute about the granting of bail to a defendant, the magistrates' court will hold a further hearing to resolve this. A defendant who has been **refused bail** is **remanded in custody**, and so has to be kept in prison until the next stage of proceedings. (For further reading on bail, see Chris Turner's revision summary of the topic in the *A-level Law Review*, Vol 1, Issue 3, April 2006.) Prisoners on remand make up a sizeable proportion of the prison population, an interesting point when it is considered that not all of these will be found guilty at the criminal trial.

### 2 First instance Crown Court trial

This is a **trial by judge and a jury of 12 lay persons**. The trial is often described as an *adversarial contest*, where barristers for the prosecution and the defence engage in a battle for the attention of the jury. It is the jury that will decide whether the defendant should be convicted or acquitted.

Every Crown Court trial is preceded by a **plea and directions hearing**, in which the defendant enters his or her plea to the offence or offences that have been charged (known as the arraignment). Where this is 'not guilty', prosecution and defence counsel in the case fix the trial date with the judge and make arrangements for the trial in respect of necessary witnesses, estimated trial length and other practical matters. If the defendant pleads 'guilty', however, the **judge** will take the opportunity to deliver **sentence**. This will take into account any *pleas for mitigation* offered by the defence (that is, factors to be taken into account on the defendant's behalf that might lessen the harshness of the sentence) and the requirement for any pre-sentencing reports. This pre-trial stage is also a point at which problems with the prosecution case may be exposed, either in terms of evidence or on legal grounds. The judge may, with reasons, order an **acquittal** *prior* to the investment of time, money and anxiety for the parties that the trial process represents.

The Crown Court trial will be familiar to many of you, since it is the image of law and legal procedure that is most often depicted on television (and this despite the fact that the Crown Court trial on indictment represents little more than 1 per cent of all criminal cases!). The order of the Crown Court trial is as set out below, though bearing in mind that trials may be interrupted by spells of legal argument in which the jury is asked to leave the court. Such issues may then be resolved confidentially by the prosecution and defence counsel in discussion with the judge.

- The **jury is sworn in**. The jurors are the **'masters of the facts'** in the case and must faithfully try the defendant on the evidence that they see and hear, thus providing a contrast to the **judge** who is the **'master of the law'** in the case (see also Chapter 9).
- With the judge managing the trial, the prosecution deliver an **opening speech** in which the facts of the case are outlined and the case against the defendant is broadly stated. The prosecution call witnesses to support its

case. Prosecution counsel will question each witness by a process of **examination-in-chief**, a method of questioning used to bring out all of the material evidence to the court without leading the witness. Each witness is then, in turn, **cross-examined** by counsel for the defence, where the questioning is instead aimed at exposing flaws in the evidence given, thereby raising doubts. It should be remembered, at this point, that the onus, or burden, of proving the case against the defendant lies with the prosecution to the standard of **'beyond reasonable doubt'**. Therefore, it is expressly *not* the role of the defence to prove that the defendant is innocent, but merely to raise doubts that call into question the prosecution's ability to prove their case.

- Once all of the prosecution witnesses have been heard and examined, it is then for the **defence** to outline the case for the defendant and to call witnesses accordingly. Whether the defendant gives evidence may be determined, in practice, by the counsel for the defence, who might advise, in the circumstances, that the defendant's right to silence be exercised. However, adverse inferences may be drawn from the exercise of this right in some situations. The defence will examine their witnesses in chief, and the prosecution will cross-examine them.
- When all of the evidence has been heard, counsel for the prosecution and defence are each allowed a **closing speech**. The prosecution go *first*. The defence have the last word, which has often led to some memorable appeals to the jury (see discussion of the **trials of Marshall Hall** in Chapter 10).
- Following the closing speeches, the **judge sums up** the legal and factual issues that have been raised in the case for the benefit of the jury. The judge's summing up should be balanced on the facts and the respective cases of the prosecution and defence, and contain clear legal advice to the jury. The jury is then led out of the court to begin its deliberations.
- Juries are sent out to try to achieve **unanimous verdicts** but, if this is not possible, **majority verdicts** (with no more than two in the jury in the minority) will be accepted by the court. If an acceptable majority cannot be reached then the situation is that of a **hung jury**. A hung jury may be sufficiently off-putting for the prosecution to halt proceedings against the defendant. However, a **retrial** can be requested in such circumstances.
- Once a verdict has been reached, the jury's job is done. If the jury finds the defendant 'not guilty' then he or she is **acquitted**, and released from the court. A person who is acquitted is protected against any appeals from the prosecution and the jury decision will stand, subject to the new rules on double jeopardy in the **Criminal Justice Act 2003** (see Chapter 9 on appeals against jury decisions). If, however, the jury finds the defendant 'guilty' then it is for the **judge to deliver sentence** (see Chapter 14).

### 3 Rights of appeal to the Court of Appeal (Criminal Division)

A defendant who has been found guilty of an indictable offence and sentenced can **appeal against conviction** on the **facts** or **points of law** (eg, to reduce a conviction of murder to one of manslaughter), and also against **sentence**, with the leave (or permission) of the Court of Appeal. The general grounds of appeal are that the **conviction is unsafe** (Criminal Appeal Act 1995, s 2(1)) or the **sentence too severe** (Criminal Appeal Act 1968, s 9). An independent body called the **Criminal Cases Review Commission** was established in 1997 to consider cases where 'miscarriages of justice' were alleged (with appeal routes in the legal system having been exhausted) and, where appropriate, to refer these cases to the Court of Appeal.

On the other hand, it is also open to the prosecution to ask the **Attorney-General** to *seek leave* from the **Court of Appeal** to consider an **unduly lenient sentence**. The Court of Appeal has the power to **increase a sentence accordingly** (Criminal Justice Act 1988, s 36). The Attorney General may refer a point of law to the Court of Appeal following prosecution concern about an acquittal: this is academic and technical in nature, seeking to settle a point of law for future cases, and does not practically affect the acquittal (Criminal Justice Act 1972, s 36). However, the prosecution may now seek to quash an acquittal so that a retrial is ordered, under the reforms to the 'double jeopardy' rule (Criminal Justice Act 2003, s 76: see further coverage in Chapter 9 at p 178).

### 4 Further appeal to the House of Lords

This is an option that can be exercised by the prosecution or defence only if the case presents a **legal issue of public importance**. Leave will therefore need to be given either by the Court of Appeal or by the House of Lords for this step to be made. Most criminal appeals are dealt with in the Court of Appeal and do not proceed to the House of Lords.

## The procedure relating to summary offences

### 1 To the magistrates' court (first instance trial)

The magistrates' court hears trials relating to summary offences, and as such is limited to the penalties it can impose. The vast majority (up to 95 per cent) of cases – encompassing trial, verdict and sentence – are dealt with by unpaid, volunteer lay magistrates (see, in general, Chapter 9).

The case is initiated by a **summons** to appear in court, though some matters – such as minor breaches of road traffic law – may be dealt with via correspondence where they are not contested. Most cases in which the defendant chooses to plead 'guilty' proceed straight to the sentence stage at the first appearance. For 'not guilty' pleas, an **early administrative hearing**, in which issues such as **legal representation** and **bail** are considered, will mark the defendant's first appearance in court.

The trial will follow shortly afterwards, and in some circumstances during the next court sitting (s 46 of the Crime and Disorder Act 1998). The trial takes a similar form to that of the Crown Court, though there is *no* jury. The order of proceedings is that the prosecution open and examine their witnesses in chief, followed by cross-examination by the defence. The defence will then bring their case in a similar manner. The burden of proof lies with the prosecution to a standard of 'beyond reasonable doubt'. The magistrates, usually **three lay members** guided by a **clerk** during the course of the trial, decide whether the standard of proof has been satisfied, and therefore make the decision whether to convict or acquit. A decision to convict means that the case will move – subject to adjournments – to the sentencing stage. An acquittal will mean that the defendant walks free from the court.

**2 Two appeal routes from the magistrates' court (first instance trial)**

There is a direct line of appeal to the Divisional Court of the Queen's Bench Division (High Court) in the form of an **appeal 'by case stated'** (that is, on a point of law). Both the prosecution and defence may decide to appeal in this way by requesting the justices' clerk to prepare a written account of the case, the reasoning adopted in arriving at a decision, and the legal point at issue. The Divisional Court has a number of options at its disposal, including reversing or confirming the magistrates' decision and remitting the case back to the magistrates' court with a direction to acquit or convict the defendant.

The defendant can also **appeal against conviction or sentence to the Crown Court**. This is a rehearing of the case. Such appeals from the magistrates' court can also be referred to the Crown Court by the Criminal Cases Review Commission.

**3 Further appeals**

Following an unsuccessful Crown Court appeal, the only avenue for the defendant is an **appeal 'by case stated'** to the **Divisional Court of the Queen's Bench Division (High Court)**. There is no further appeal on the facts, only on the law. To appeal further to the House of Lords there must be a **point of law of public importance**.

## The procedure relating to triable either way offences

Since a triable either way offence may be tried *either* as a summary offence before the magistrates' court, *or* as an indictable offence before the Crown Court, the appropriate **'mode of trial'** has to be determined. In the absence of a direction that the case be tried on indictment, the mechanism for determining the 'mode of trial' is the **plea**: if the defendant pleads 'guilty' then the matter is dispensed with summarily; if, however, the defendant pleads 'not guilty' then he or she has the right to opt for jury trial (Criminal Procedure and Investigations Act 1996, s 49). Opting for that right necessitates that the case is formally transferred to the Crown Court. In practice, however, jury trial is *not* the preferred mode of trial for many defendants and amendments to the 'plea before venue' process – in which the mode of trial is determined for either way offences – in the Criminal Justice Act 2003, provide further encouragement to defendants to have their cases tried summarily. Once the mode of trial decision has been taken, the processes outlined above for indictable and summary offences apply.

Table 6.2 (see p 124) summarises criminal procedure according to the nature of the offence.

# CIVIL PROCEDURE

## Introducing civil procedure

The civil justice system has been subject to a great deal of reform in recent years. The reforms were a response to dissatisfaction with the civil courts and

Table 6.2 Criminal procedure according to offence

| *Indictable offences (serious)* | *Summary offences (minor)* | *Triable either way offences (intermediate)* |
|---|---|---|
| • Magistrates' court (preliminary examination).<br>• Crown Court trial (judge + jury).<br>• Right of appeal to the Court of Appeal (Criminal Division).<br>• Further appeal to the House of Lords. | • Magistrates' court trial before bench of lay magistrates or district judge (magistrates' court).<br>• Appeal on a point of law to the Divisional Court of the Queen's Bench Division.<br>• Appeal against conviction or against sentence to the Crown Court.<br>• Further appeal to the House of Lords only on points of law of public importance. | Here the determination of the *mode of trial* is the *plea*.<br>If the defendant pleads guilty then summary trial process.<br>If the defendant pleads not guilty then can opt for either:<br>• summary trial process; *or*<br>• indictable trial process. |

their procedures based on three major criticisms that have dogged civil justice at various times of its history. First, that the progress of litigation was, at times, **too slow**; second, that the procedures were **too complex**; and third, that the courts had become both **intimidating** and **out of date**. The Lord Chancellor therefore set up the **Woolf Inquiry in 1994** in order to effect 'far-reaching consequences' for the civil justice system. In the words of Lord Woolf himself, to set forth a 'new landscape' for lawyers, judges and court users in bringing greater efficiency and modernising the process of civil justice.

Lord Woolf's recommendations have led to major changes to the system. These largely came into effect in April 1999. Slapper and Kelly (2003, p 264) quote David Gladwell, of the then Lord Chancellor's Department, who said that the reforms represented the 'greatest change the civil courts have seen in over a century'. The authority for the changes lay in the **Civil Procedure Act 1997**, the **Access to Justice Act 1999** and the **Civil Procedure Rules (CPR)**.

There are four principal features of the civil justice reforms.

- **Simplified procedures.** These have been applied in all county courts and High Courts. The main aim of the reforms is to ensure that cases are dealt with 'justly'. These procedures have been accompanied by the introduction of simpler court forms and language. Perhaps the most significant aspect of the reforms has been the creation of a **tracking system for civil claims.** There are now three tracks of claim:
  - *small claims*: for civil claims up to the value of £5,000
  - *fast-track*: for civil claims between £5,000 and £15,000
  - *multi-track*: for civil claims over £15,000.
- **Judicial case-management.** Judges become 'case managers' under the reforms. This means that cases follow a timetable set by the court and

judges take a more 'hands on' role in managing the case towards its settlement or conclusion.

- **Pre-action protocols.** These enable the courts to control the 'pre-action' activities of lawyers, to stop them dragging out the exchange of pre-action information, and to put the parties in the position of settling the case fairly and at an early stage. The **General Pre-action Protocol Practice Direction 2003** requires that the parties to a civil claim 'act reasonably in exchanging information and documents relevant to the claim and generally in trying to avoid the necessity for proceedings', and lays down a pre-action process accordingly.
- **Encouragement of alternatives to court action.** Courts are required to facilitate the use of **alternative dispute resolution (ADR)** where this is perceived to be in the parties' interests. The decision in *Dunnett v Railtrack plc* (2002) reinforces this point (see further Chapter 7).

## The civil claims procedure

Civil claims (that is, those initiated by individuals or companies in respect of private legal interests) begin with the issue of a written claim on the defendant. The **claim form** contains the **particulars of claim** that describe the nature of the civil matter at issue and the remedies being sought. The defendant is given 14 days to reply. This section examines what happens when the defendant responds to the claim with a **defence**, thereby indicating that the **civil matter will be contested** through the courts. (Many such matters are not contested and therefore judgments are issued automatically – if no defence has been made – to reflect the fact that the defendant is in default.)

One of the most important parts of the pre-trial process is **allocation.** Upon receipt of a defence, and the completion of allocation questionnaires by all of the parties to a case, the court in which the claim has been initiated makes a decision to allocate the case to one of three tracks:

- **Small claims track.** Cases allocated to this track are heard in the county court. The value of claims for this track is up to £5,000, though notably the limit is £1,000 for personal injury claims. These cases are heard and managed by district judges, and are usually conducted in the judges' chambers rather than in open court. The small claims procedure is a relatively informal process and many litigants continue to take their claims to this court in person, rather than being represented by a lawyer. Small claims usually relate to consumer claims, such as defective goods and the unsatisfactory delivery of services. This is also the procedure used to pursue small debts. A frustrating aspect of the small claims process, however, is that while judgments of the court might be given in favour of the claimants, the amounts awarded have proved difficult to enforce against defendants.
- **Fast-track claims.** Cases allocated to this track are heard in the county court. The value of claims for this track is over £5,000 and up to £15,000, plus personal injury cases valued at between £1,000 and £15,000. The aim is for fast-track claims to be tried within one day,

based on a limited timetable for the giving of evidence, and heard within 30 weeks of allocation. The fast-track is a formal process, in open court, and legal representation is more appropriate given the need for evidence to be presented and witnesses examined.

- **Multi-track claims.** Cases allocated to this track are heard in the county court or High Court, depending on which court the claim was started in and the value of the claim. As a *general* rule, personal injury cases with a likely claim value of over £50,000 will be heard in the High Court along with other civil cases over £15,000 in value. Once again, these types of claim will be formally heard, though before a circuit judge or a High Court judge, and **legal representation** is the norm. The Queen's Bench Division of the High Court will hear the larger value claims in tort (such as defamation, and personal injury and nervous shock cases) and in contract law. The Chancery Division of the High Court will deal with matters relating to property, taxation, bankruptcy and insolvency, wills, probate and trusts.

Civil cases are heard before a **judge**: *juries* will be present in respect of only four civil areas: fraud (tort of deceit); defamation (libel/slander); malicious prosecution; and false imprisonment. The jury will have a high-profile role – though declining, in practice – in defamation cases heard before the Queen's Bench Division of the High Court.

The county court, High Court and magistrates' court all have some jurisdiction over family proceedings. The common practice area of divorce, for example, starts its proceedings in the county court, with some transfers to the High Court. Trials in civil law are an *adversarial process* between counsel for the claimant and counsel for the defendant (though the judge plays a more interventionist role in proceedings following the Woolf reforms). The standard of proof differs from that of criminal law: here the claimant must prove the case **'on the balance of probabilities'**.

**IT'S A FACT!**

**6.1: A significant civil trial in English legal history**

The so-called **'McLibel' case** (*McDonald's v Steel and Morris*), brought as a defamation action by fast-food chain McDonald's against two animal rights protestors (Helen Steel and Dave Morris) who had been distributing protest leaflets outside one of its stores, was identified by the media as 'the longest civil trial in English legal history'. Beginning in June 1994 and ending in December 1996, the trial, presided over by Mr Justice Bell, lasted 313 days and involved 130 witnesses.

This High Court case was heard without a jury (see Chapter 9) and Morris and Steel, who were not eligible for legal aid, represented themselves in court. Mr Justice Bell found for McDonald's, awarding them £40,000 in damages, a sum that Morris and Steel steadfastly refused to pay. Instead they took their case to the European Court of Human Rights, alleging a breach of ECHR Art 6 (right to a fair trial).

In 2005, over ten years on, the European Court of Human Rights found in *their* favour and agreed that a denial of legal aid for defamation within the English legal system had meant that their Art 6 right had been violated (*Steel and Morris v UK*: see also Chapter 1). The original case was a huge own-goal for McDonald's, bringing greater public attention to the animal rights allegations against it and allowing itself to be portrayed as the corporate bully in a trial often described by the press in David and Goliath terms.

Table 6.3 summarises the tracking process for civil claims.

Table 6.3 Civil claim tracking procedure

| *Small claims track* | *Fast-track claims track* | *Multi-track claims track* |
|---|---|---|
| • Claims heard in the county court.<br>• Hears claims up to the value of £5,000.<br>• Hears personal injury claims up to the value of £1,000. | • Claims heard in the county court.<br>• Hears claims valued at between £5,000 and £15,000.<br>• Hears personal injury claims valued at between £1,000 and £15,000. | • Claims heard in the county court or the High Court.<br>• Claims valued at over £50,000 will be heard in the High Court. |

## Appeals in the Civil Justice System

In line with the reviews of the system initiated by the Woolf reforms to civil justice, changes have also been effected to the civil appeals process. The key authority for these changes is the **Access to Justice Act 1999**, and it ensures compatibility with the **Civil Procedure Rules** approach to 'tracking civil cases'. These reforms had been prompted by concerns about the slow progress of cases, and cases being inappropriately dealt with in the system. Thus, permission ('leave') for appeals is now to be required at all levels in the civil justice system; and this requirement is supported by a set of measures to ensure that appeals are heard at the right level and dealt with according to their weight and complexity. Often, therefore, appeals will be heard by *more senior judges* in the judicial hierarchy, rather than automatically by the next highest court. For example, appeals relating to small claims heard by a district

### Talking from experience
### Royal Courts of Justice, The Strand, London

The Royal Courts of Justice on the Strand comprise the High Court (Chancery, Family, Queen's Bench Division), the Divisional Courts and the Courts of Appeal (Civil and Criminal). Therefore, the Royal Courts are a mixture of first instance and appellate courts, and so a great deal of legal business is dealt with each day. It is the most prominent High Court complex in England, though there are regional High Court centres in 26 locations, mainly the larger towns and cities, across the country. You are encouraged to visit the Royal Courts of Justice on the Strand. (It is open to members of the public Monday–Friday between 10.00 am and 4.30 pm.) This is a lively place which will provide you with a flavour of both branches of the profession, since solicitors and barristers can be seen both in and out of the courts engaged in their work.

However, it should be remembered that behind the scenes there are many Court Service administrators at the Royal Courts of Justice. Take, for example, the cashiers in the Supreme Court Fees Office. They deal every day with barristers' clerks and members of the public. Their work involves the processing of court fees using a computerised cash system and dealing with applications for court fee refunds. This is a practical side of the law that members of the public rarely see.

judge in the county court can be heard by a circuit judge. However, there are a number of established appeal routes between courts that can still be identified in the civil justice system and these are as follows:

- From the **county court** to the **Divisional Courts of the High Court.** Family proceedings relating to children that begin in the county court, and in some cases from the magistrates' court exercising its civil family jurisdiction, have grounds of appeal that can be activated in the Family Divisional Court of the High Court. Proceedings in bankruptcy and insolvency in the county court can be appealed to the Chancery Divisional Court of the High Court.
- From the **county court to the Court of Appeal (Civil).** The Court of Appeal (Civil Division) will still hear some appeals from the county court, particularly those relating to multi-track claims, on factual and legal grounds.
- From the **High Court (first instance jurisdiction) to the Court of Appeal.** The Court of Appeal (Civil Division) will hear appeals from the three divisions of the High Court on factual and legal grounds.
- From the **High Court straight to the House of Lords.** This procedure, known as the **'leapfrog appeal'**, can be activated only if the case raises a legal matter of **'general public importance'** and it receives the approval of both the courts and the parties (under the **Administration of Justice Act 1969**).
- From the **Court of Appeal to the House of Lords.** Cases that raise matters of general public importance – such as important matters of **precedent** in contract or tort; or troubling, but significant, matters of **statutory interpretation** – can be appealed to the House of Lords to settle the issue of law.

The UK's membership of the European Community since January 1973 has meant that any cases involving a *potential conflict* of UK law and EC law should be referred to the **European Court of Justice** under the Art 234 procedure for a ruling. This is *not* an appeal, since the case will be returned to the UK court so that the ruling can be applied (see Chapter 5).

Table 6.4 Civil appeals

| *From the county court* | *From the High Court* |
|---|---|
| Either: | Either: |
| • to the Divisional Courts on specific matters; *or* | • to the Court of Appeal on facts or law for general matters; *or* |
| • to the Court of Appeal on facts or law for general matters. | • to the House of Lords via the 'leapfrog' procedure. |

*Notes*

- Appeals may proceed from the Court of Appeal to the House of Lords, subject to importance and 'leave' being granted.
- Courts are entitled to make references, under the Art 234 procedure, to the ECJ where matters of conflict between EC law and UK law arise.

**HINTS AND TIPS**

Experience of past examination papers suggests that the courts structure is one of those topics that can be conveniently mixed with other areas. Knowledge of the courts is often assessed as a *contrast* to **tribunals** and **alternative methods of dispute resolution**, or as part of an **access to justice** (that is, legal funding, advice and representation) question.

For *descriptive/explanatory* questions, it is likely you will be asked to give advice as to the courts to be encountered in certain types of case, and to detail the processes associated with them. Look out for **'signposting'** here. If you are asked to advise a person with a **'very valuable claim'** as to the civil process, for example, this will point you in the direction of multi-track claims. Moreover, in a criminal law question, the **seriousness of the offence** will determine the advice that you give, bearing in mind the differing procedures for indictable and summary offences.

*Evaluative questions* about the courts structure and civil and criminal procedures are less common, though remember the earlier point that this topic mixes so well with others. Do not be surprised, for example, if a *descriptive* question about the **criminal courts** leads to an *evaluation* of **juries or lay magistrates**; or if a question requiring you to outline the functions and processes of a civil court leads to a question about the contrasting merits of alternative dispute resolution for civil matters.

Although the topic of **police powers** does not feature in all law courses, it is one component which lends itself to self-contained *descriptive* and *analytical* questions. You might be asked, for example, to detail procedures relating to stop and search, arrest or detention, and then to assess the extent to which police powers are balanced with individual liberties. The latter question is increasingly in the news, given the impact of the Human Rights Act 1998, on the one hand, and rising concern about violent crime and the threat of terrorism, on the other. It is certainly worth keeping an eye on coverage of policing in the media.

## Useful website addresses

| | |
|---|---|
| Department for Constitutional Affairs | www.dca.gov.uk |
| Courts Service | www.hmcourts-service.gov.uk |
| *Materials directly for AS studies:* | |
| John Deft (St Brendan's Sixth Form College) | www.stbrn.ac.uk/other/depts/law |
| Asif Tufal | www.a-level-law.com |

# Alternatives to courts

This topic enables you:

- To develop an awareness of the range of options members of the public may have for resolving disputes.
- To understand the tribunal system, which hears more cases each year than the civil justice system and allows for the enforcement of important public rights.
- To consider, through evaluation, the best dispute resolution option for members of the public to use in differing circumstances.
- To acquire useful, practical knowledge which may be of benefit for the future.

## INTRODUCTION: TRIBUNALS AND ALTERNATIVE DISPUTE RESOLUTION

When a dispute occurs, the parties can settle it in a number of ways. The majority of disputes will be settled by simple negotiation and will not get near the courts. For example, disputes over individual goods in shops will usually be dealt with informally at the customer service desk. However, some disputes require a much more formal mechanism, and for these the courts are the natural next step. In the gap between negotiation and the courts lies a wide range of **alternatives for resolving disputes**, and it is these on which this chapter will focus.

There are two significant avenues for resolving disputes that are recognised within the legal system but fall outside the courts system. The first is through **tribunals**, established by statute to allow citizens to assert their social and welfare rights. The second relates to the alternative methods of resolving disputes to avoid the cost, formality and intimidating nature of court cases (referred to as **alternative dispute resolution (ADR)**). Furthermore, opportunities for members of the public to complain about the services they have received are also provided by **ombudsman schemes**.

## TRIBUNALS

Tribunals developed in the post-war period to provide members of the public with a way of enforcing certain rights. Many of these rights were associated with the **'welfare state'** (the provision of social security and welfare benefits by the State) but statute law has broadened the number of areas in which tribunals are now used in preference to courts to settle certain disputes:

- The Lands Tribunal Act 1949 created the Lands Tribunal.
- The Mental Health Act 1983 created the Mental Health Review Tribunal.
- The Child Support Act 1993 created the Child Support Appeals Tribunal (now joined with other appeal tribunals as part of the Appeals Service, which was itself created by the Social Security Act 1998).
- The Employment Tribunals Act 1996 created employment tribunals (following earlier legislation on 'industrial tribunals').

The **Franks Committee on Tribunals (1957)** stated that tribunals should offer some of the following advantages:

- independence;
- accessibility;
- promptness in dealing with cases;
- informality;
- low cost for the complainant.

As a result of this Committee's Report, Parliament legislated to bring tribunals under the supervision of a **Council on Tribunals.**

The Council does not control tribunals but monitors their operation through visits and by responding to complaints about the tribunals system. It can only encourage reforms and improvements to tribunals through publicising

**IT'S A FACT!**

**7.1: Tribunals in a nutshell**

- There are 70 different types of administrative tribunal in England and Wales, some with a number of centres around the country.
- They have a greater case load than the civil courts system.
- There are three different types of tribunal: administrative (dealing with rights arising from public/social welfare legislation); employment; and domestic (that is, internal disciplinary tribunals within private bodies, such as those to resolve disputes about the competence of a member of the medical profession).

Moreover, tribunals resolve disputes between a number of competing interests, such as employer and employee (employment tribunals, see p 133 below); landlord and tenant (rent assessment tribunals); and parents and school (Admission Appeals Panels). Clearly, the workloads of different types of tribunals will vary. The Plant Varieties and Seeds Tribunal will rarely hear any cases at all, whereas employment tribunals are presented with around 100,000 claims per year.

The unified **Tribunals Service** brings together the largest existing tribunals and tribunal groupings – the Immigration Appellate Authority; the Social Security and Child Support Commissioners; the Tax Appeals Tribunals; the Pensions Appeal Tribunal; the Lands Tribunal; the Employment Tribunals Service; the Mental Health Review Tribunal; the Special Educational Needs and Disability Tribunal; the Criminal Injuries Compensation Appeals Panel; and the Appeals Service – under a common administrative structure allied to the Department for Constitutional Affairs, with the Lord Chancellor taking accountability for this 'distinct part of the justice system' (see Lord Chancellor's announcement of the Tribunals Service and comments:

www.dca.gov.uk/civil/tribsann.htm; and
www.dca.gov.uk/speeches/2006/sp060403.htm; and visit the Tribunals Service website at www.tribunals.gov.uk)

Within the main groupings identified above there are actually 22 functioning tribunals and the Tribunals Service is expected to accommodate other tribunals in due course.

the conclusions and recommendations that are contained in its annual reports to Parliament. In 2003, following a **Review of Tribunals** commissioned by the Government and known as the **Leggatt Committee (2001)**, it was announced that the tribunal service would, like the Court Service, become unified, thus bringing together the main tribunals under one administrative system: a unified **Tribunals Service**, effective from April 2006. The Council on Tribunals has welcomed this proposal, recognising the need for clear and coherent first instance and appellate procedures.

## Developing the subject 7.1: Focus on employment tribunals

An employment tribunal comprises a legally qualified chairperson, flanked by two lay persons. The chairperson must be a barrister or solicitor of at least seven years' experience. The lay persons represent, on the one side, employer interests (perhaps with experience of management or membership of a business association) and, on the other side, employee interests (through shop floor or trade union experience).

Employment tribunals hear cases regarding:

- discrimination claims against employers;
- unfair dismissal claims against employers and claims for redundancy pay; and
- contractual rights claims, relating to terms and conditions and other statutory entitlements.

It is reasonably easy for a complainant to have his or her claim heard by an employment tribunal. The stages are as follows. First, the applicant completes a claim form and submits it to the tribunal. It is forwarded to the employer, who then has 14 days to reply. The Advisory Conciliation and Arbitration Service (ACAS), an ADR body involved in settling employment disputes, receives copies of both completed forms and encourages the parties to settle. If this does not work, the case goes to the tribunal for a preliminary investigation and hearing. The claim may then proceed to a full tribunal hearing.

A full tribunal hearing is similar to a court hearing, though there are some important differences. There will be no legal aid for claimants and so costs awards are rare. The rules of evidence are also more relaxed than in the civil courts. Moreover, the panel hearing the case will interrupt the proceedings often to ask questions, thus making the proceedings as much inquisitorial (that is, investigatory) as adversarial (a battle between the parties). The hearing will take place in a room rather than a formal 'court', and proceedings may be held in public or private. The remedies available to the tribunal are laid down in statute: in unfair dismissal claims, for example, the tribunal can award compensation and order either reinstatement (the return of the employee to his old position), or re-engagement (where the employee is offered a position of equivalent worth within the company). In 2004, employment tribunals awarded £6.2 million in compensation overall, marking a significant increase on the previous year's figures (£4.3 million) and revealing some substantial awards in disability discrimination cases (statistics taken from a report in *The Daily Telegraph*, 8/8/05).

Any appeals from an employment tribunal are made to the Employment Appeal Tribunal (EAT). Further appeals from the EAT enter the civil courts system, to the Court of Appeal, and, from time to time, to the House of Lords. Some other tribunals exhibit this feature of an appeal route to a specialist appeal tribunal and then to the Court of Appeal and so on: for example, the Immigration Appeal Tribunal.

**Exercise**

(1) Describe the three types of person to be found on the panels that hear claims in employment tribunals. What is the justification for this approach to hearing employment claims?

(2) Provide an example of a typical employment tribunal claim. (See whether you can find good recent examples from newspapers, or via the employment law links on websites such as www.venables.co.uk/sitesd.htm.)
(3) What is ACAS? Describe the role that it plays in employment disputes. (You may also wish to refer to www.acas.org.uk.)
(4) How do hearings in employment tribunals differ from those in the civil courts?

Tribunals as administrative institutions are subject to claims for **judicial review** by complainants who believe that their procedural or substantive rights have been undermined during the course of proceedings; for example, if one party feels that their side of the story has not been heard. Judicial review may lead to the tribunal's decision being declared invalid (referred to as the decision being **quashed**).

## Evaluating tribunals

Tribunals are *less* costly than civil court hearings because representation by lawyers is discouraged. As the **Leggatt Committee (2001)** noted, 'Every effort should be made to reduce the number of cases in which legal representation is needed'. For this reason, an 'order for costs' will only rarely be made against the losing party in the case.

An aim of tribunals is to deal with cases **quickly** and **efficiently**, but some tribunals with a large volume of work – such as the employment tribunals – experience delays in a similar manner to the courts. The **Leggatt Committee (2001)** points out that each case in a tribunal should be dealt with 'economically, proportionately, expeditiously and fairly', though 'speed should not be an end in itself. It should follow from obedience to the watchwords which should inform every tribunal: informality, simplicity, efficiency, and proportionality.' In its review of current practices in tribunals, however, the same report went on to note ***'serious problems of delay'*** in **Mental Health Review Tribunals** and problems relating to **Leasehold Valuation Tribunals** that meant cases could 'wait between 30 and 40 weeks for a hearing'.

Other than employment tribunals, most tribunal cases are heard in **private**. Some tribunals – such as the **Criminal Injuries Compensation Appeals Panel** – are often private by necessity, with hearings across the country taking place in hired rooms rather than dedicated buildings.

Each tribunal has its own **appeals structure** – or in some instances, such as the **Mental Health Review Tribunal** and the **Pensions Appeal Tribunal**, a lack of one: the only option for those dissatisfied with the findings of these tribunals is a claim for **judicial review**. Certain tribunals – such as the **VAT and Duties Tribunal** – have made a number of **Art 234 References to the ECJ** (see Chapter 5).

Tribunal hearings are *more* **informal** than court hearings, including flexible procedures, without strict rules of evidence. As we have seen above, employment tribunals are more formal, but still lack strict rules of evidence and mix the adversarial approach with an inquisitorial approach from the panel. A particular exception to the rule is the **Lands Tribunal**, which the **Leggatt Committee (2001)** described as 'comparatively formal and adversarial' with cases of a 'legally and factually complex' nature.

Generally applicants will not be legally represented in tribunals. However, lawyers are sometimes used in those tribunals that deal with difficult legal problems, such as the **Lands Tribunal** mentioned above; and in tribunals such as the **Mental Health Review Tribunal** and the **Immigration Appeal Tribunal,** where public funding is available to make progress with cases. While tribunals encourage the taking of cases without legal representation, it is unfortunately the case that applicants without representation facing parties who do have legal representation are often put at a considerable disadvantage. The **Bar's Free Representation Unit** will take on cases for disadvantaged applicants, and has made a particular impact on access to justice in appeals to the **Social Security** and **Child Support Commissioners.** Public funding is available for cases before the Mental Health Review Tribunal, the EAT, the Immigration Appeal Tribunal and the Tax Tribunals (VAT and Income Tax).

## The general advantages of tribunals

- Tribunals are created by statute for citizens to enforce rights granted through social and welfare legislation. Each tribunal is tailored to deal with *specific disputes* that might arise where rights and duties have been created.
- Tribunals can be a *cheaper option* than going to court as the parties are generally encouraged not to have legal representation. However, statistics gathered in the 1990s showed that people who had a lawyer to represent them were more likely to be successful than those without. So what is this telling us?
- Generally tribunals process claims *more quickly* than the civil courts, though some have now to contend with such a volume of cases that this advantage is being lost.
- As proceedings in tribunals are *informal*, they are much less intimidating than courts. Also tribunal panels play a more interventionist role, thus guiding claimants through the hearing rather than leaving procedure in the hands of lawyers.
- Tribunals deal with almost one million cases a year – they therefore *reduce* the workload for courts, which could in fact have become unsustainable.

## The main disadvantages associated with tribunals

- Poor decisions may be made by tribunals because of the speed, informality and, at times, inconsistency of the proceedings. For example, the **Leggatt Committee** (2001) observed the following in the **Pensions Appeal Tribunal:** 'There was little consistency . . . the assessment hearing was poorly managed and there were a number of procedural mistakes.' However, a check is kept on tribunal proceedings through judicial review and by the **Council of Tribunals.** A unified **Tribunals Service** should also ensure a greater degree of consistency in the procedures adopted by tribunals, though it is limited to the largest tribunals at present.
- Applicants are encouraged not to use legal representation, but it is clear that represented applicants are *more likely* to be successful. This is a considerable disadvantage to those who should benefit most from the tribunal process – members of the public seeking to assert their rights.

- Tribunals rarely operate a system of precedent, so safeguards that are present in the civil process – such as that like cases are dealt with alike – will not always operate in the tribunals system.
- There is concern, at times, that the legally qualified chairperson may perhaps *lack impartiality* and may therefore influence the lay members in their appreciation of the disputes before them. Another potential for bias was identified in the case of *Lawal v Northern Spirit* (2003), when the House of Lords, reversing the decision of the Court of Appeal, found that a lawyer who was a part-time tribunal chairperson and knew the local lay members should not be permitted to appear as an advocate in that tribunal, since this would undermine public confidence in the administration of justice.

## METHODS OF ALTERNATIVE DISPUTE RESOLUTION (ADR)

ADR is an umbrella term for ways of settling disputes that avoid the potentially costly, time-consuming and adversarial nature of the legal process.

In brief, the main methods are negotiation; mediation; conciliation and arbitration. Table 7.1, opposite, details their differing characteristics.

There has been recent judicial emphasis on the importance of ADR in resolving civil disputes, to the extent that in *Dunnett v Railtrack plc* (2002) a winning party who had unnecessarily obstructed the use of alternative methods of settlement was denied an award of costs. This costs penalty for unco-operative parties to legal disputes has been confirmed by the Court of Appeal in the cases of *McMillan Williams v Range* (2004), *Halsey v Milton Keynes NHS Trust* (2004) (though subject to the human rights consideration that parties should *not* be forced into ADR, leaving a refusal to be assessed on its reasonablenes) and *Burchell v Bullard and Others* (2005). Moreover, in *Cable & Wireless plc v IBM UK Ltd* (2002), judicial approval was given to clauses in commercial contracts which refer the parties to alternative methods of resolving disputes. These indicate the importance of ADR for achieving settlement of civil claims and provide some measure of the impact of the *post*-**Woolf civil justice reforms** (see Chapter 6). As Lord Justice Ward put it in the *Halsey* case mentioned above, lawyers' discussions with clients about the merits of ADR should now occur 'routinely'.

**IT'S A FACT!**

**7.2: Summarising some important points about tribunals**

- Tribunals have been established by statute.
- They hear cases concerning the statutory rights of citizens, in the main, and are designed to offer advantages of speed, efficiency and informality in contrast to the ordinary courts.
- There is a Council of Tribunals to keep tribunals under review, and a unified Tribunals Service bringing together some of the largest tribunals which came into effect in April 2006.
- Tribunals involve lay persons in the making of legal decisions: for example, cases in the employment tribunal are heard by a legally qualified chairperson and two lay members.
- The appeals from some tribunals may be heard in appeal tribunals, and in some cases may then be heard by the higher appeal courts.

There has been a lot of coverage in the legal press about further forms of dispute resolution, referred to under the collective name **online dispute resolution (ODR)**. This describes arbitration and mediation services that are offered online to deal with disputes between companies, particularly those engaged in e-commerce. You are advised to keep abreast of legal developments in this area

Table 7.1 The main methods of ADR

| *Negotiation* | *Mediation* | *Conciliation* |
|---|---|---|
| The parties themselves resolve the dispute, with or without the aid of a lawyer | The parties resolve the dispute with the help of a neutral third party. The emphasis is on getting the parties to reach a compromise. The mediator will consult each party and look for common ground. | Similar to mediation, but the third party plays a more active part in suggesting a solution. The conciliator will suggest grounds for compromise and the possible basis for a settlement. |

| *Arbitration* |
|---|
| The parties agree to let an independent person (the arbitrator) make a binding decision. Many contracts include a clause that in the event of a dispute, the matter will be settled by arbitration. Many trade organisations, eg in the travel industry, have their own arbitration scheme for dissatisfied customers. |

in order to complement your understanding of ADR and its increasing role in civil disputes.

## Arbitration

Here, parties refer the issue in dispute to a **third party** for judgment, rather than taking the case to the courts. This is common in commercial contracts between businesses: indeed, there may be an express clause in such a contract to the effect that any dispute should be resolved by arbitration. These clauses have been referred to by lawyers as *Scott v Avery* clauses ever since a case of that name in 1856. The **Arbitration Act 1996** sets out the law relating to private arbitration.

**IT'S A FACT!**

**7.3: Key principles of the Arbitration Act 1996**

The main statutory requirements of arbitration:

- The choice of dispute resolution is left to the parties (which respects freedom of contract).
- The agreements to refer to arbitration must be in writing.
- Arbitration of a dispute must be fairly resolved without unnecessary delay or expense.

There is an **Institute of Arbitrators,** which provides trained arbitrators, though commercial contracts may refer a dispute to an arbitrator appointed by a relevant trade association. A number of these associations also offer **voluntary arbitration schemes** for general consumers pursuing complaints. Examples of trade associations which offer such services include the **Retail Motor Industry Federation,** the **Motorcycle Retailers Association** and the **Mail Order Traders Association.** Parties may require a **single arbitrator** or a **panel of arbitrators** in seeking to resolve a dispute.

Arbitrator decisions are called '**awards**'. Parties to a commercial contract will generally have agreed that these shall have binding effect. In such circumstances, a court will enforce an arbitration award, should a further dispute arise.

### Evaluating arbitration

Referring a case to arbitration is generally *less expensive* than going to court. This is because the parties are usually paying only for the services of an arbitrator. However, parties to arbitration may have legal representation if they wish, unless the agreement to refer disputes to arbitration states otherwise (s 36 of the **Arbitration Act 1996**). The services of a professional arbitrator will be costly, but not in comparison with taking a dispute through the courts.

A dispute referred to arbitration should take *less time* to settle as compared to a court hearing, though legal representation might delay matters for the parties. It is also the case that the arbitrator has the discretion to impose strict rules of evidence and formal procedures where these are perceived to be appropriate. However, as we have seen, the arbitrator is required by statute to avoid unnecessary delay and expense (s 3 of the **Arbitration Act 1996**).

Matters subject to arbitration will generally be dealt with *confidentially*, although trade disputes, accompanied by industrial action, may attract the attention of the press. A dispute relating to the pay and conditions of firefighters in 2002/03, which was contested strongly by the Fire Brigades Union, is one such example.

An **arbitrator's award** may be *enforced* in the **High Court** if the parties do not stick to their agreement. However, the award may be challenged on procedural/legal grounds under ss 68 and 69 of the **Arbitration Act 1996**, and if it is found that the arbitrator did not conduct the arbitration process reasonably or appropriately, the award may be set aside. If the court chooses not to set aside the award, but instead to have it reconsidered, then a High Court judge will be appointed to act as a new arbitrator between the parties. If the decision of the judge is also challenged then a further appeal lies to the Court of Appeal.

The *formality* of the arbitration depends on the choice of the parties in framing their agreement to refer the matter to arbitration, and then on the choice of the arbitrator as to how the process should be conducted, bearing in mind the statutory framework of the **Arbitration Act 1996**. Arbitration hearings can either be very formal (with witnesses and legal representation), or informal and flexible to suit the needs of the parties.

Parties *without* legal representation are at a disadvantage in the arbitration process against businesses, for example, since these will often be legally represented. Nevertheless, the aforementioned s 3 of the **Arbitration Act 1996** requires arbitrators to be fair, impartial and allow both sides of the argument to be clearly stated. Public funding is not available for arbitration hearings. However, since the parties – by and large – make their own arbitration agreements, these can be as accessible as the parties wish.

It is common for commercial contracts between businesses to *refer* disputes to arbitration. Moreover, *optional arbitration clauses* have been introduced to some types of consumer contracts. Such a clause, signed by the consumer, enables businesses to settle disputes quietly and effectively 'in-house', without attracting the sort of media attention that would follow a court case.

### The advantages of arbitration

- The parties in commercial situations have discretion as to the *choice of arbitrator*. The existence of an **Institute of Arbitrators** at least ensures that there are people with a recognised qualification who can call themselves 'arbitrators'.
- The arbitration arrangement is an *informal one* between the parties – in fact the parties can determine the location, level of formality and time-scale for the dispute to be resolved.
- There is *rarely any publicity* with arbitration, although industrial disputes that are referred to arbitration tend to attract the glare of media publicity.
- The arbitrator's award may be *enforced* by the **High Court** where the parties agreed, at the outset, to accept the arbitrator's judgment.

### Significant disadvantages of arbitration

- Public funding is *not* available, so one party may have an advantage from the outset. If a professional arbitrator and legal representation are used then the process may become *costly*.
- Appeals are *restricted* in the arbitration process, though awards may be enforced through the courts where the parties agree that they will consider the arbitrator's decision to be binding.

## Mediation

This is an example of a form of **assisted settlement**: the third party assists the disputed parties in reaching a mutually agreed settlement. Mediators *encourage* progress in the negotiations. They tend *not* to offer an opinion about the dispute in question. Thus, in theory, mediation places the onus on the parties to reach a solution. If the parties are totally at loggerheads, mediation is unlikely to be successful: both sides must have room for manoeuvre and be willing to give and take in the course of the process. If the mediation results in a **written agreement** then it can form a **legally binding contract** that may be capable of *enforcement* in the courts.

Often businesses in dispute will try to give the mediation some structure through formal '**settlement conferences**' which might, in some respects, mirror aspects of a court trial. However, the purpose of these is to discover all of the issues in dispute in order that progress can be made in resolving them.

Mediation is used in a number of contexts: it has been applied to trust and probate cases to resolve conflicts within families; to divorce cases to settle the end of the relationship amicably; to commercial disputes; and to arguments between neighbours. In *IDA Ltd v Southampton University* (2006), Lord Justice Jacob identified that disputes relating to patents (ie, rights to an invention) were 'apt for early mediation', given that fighting such disputes in court could be 'protracted, very expensive and emotionally draining'. Moreover, Lord Justice Longmore, in *Validi v Fairstead House School Trust Ltd* (2005), a negligence case concerning work-related stress, expressed regret that there had been no mediation prior to the trial and 'shuddered at the costs of the trial and of the appeal'.

**IT'S A FACT!**

**7.4: Promoting mediation**

There was a National Mediation Awareness week in October 2005, building on other initiatives such as the Department for Constitutional Affairs' National Mediation Helpline (launched the previous year: see www.nationalmediationhelpline.com). One successful user of the helpline, Mark Tennent, told *The Times* (Law, 25/10/05) that his use of mediation in a dispute with a builder achieved 'everything you don't expect from lawyers – (it was) cheap, quick and informal'. The costs of mediation tend to range between £100 and £300 per party for small and fast-track civil claims (with reductions for those using the helpline), rising to £1,000 for complex, valuable claims. However, law firms have generally been slow to embrace mediation, perhaps taking the view of the barrister and author Paul Randolph, also expressed in *The Times* (Law, as above) that some lawyers read the term ADR not just as Alternative Dispute Resolution but also as 'A Drop in Revenue'! Such attitudes are unlikely to last long when judges, following the lead in *Dunnett v Railtrack*, have punished lawyers – by denying costs awards – for failing to encourage their clients to engage in ADR.

A recent scheme, part-funded by the **Legal Services Commission**, aims to bring claimants and defendants together to settle clinical negligence claims. The Chief Executive of the Action for Victims of Medical Accidents (AVMA) group, which is, in conjunction with the Centre for Effective Dispute Resolution and the NHS, developing the clinical negligence scheme, told the *New Law Journal* (2002) that 'mediation adapted to the needs of clinical disputes could benefit patients, trust managers and health care professionals alike because it avoids the stress, delay, cost and risks of litigation and provides a forum where all issues can be effectively, sensitively and confidentially addressed'.

## Evaluating mediation

Mediation is *private* as it takes place between the parties: it is a *confidential* process, *voluntarily entered into* by the parties seeking resolution of their dispute. Even where formal settlement conferences have been arranged, these will be *less* formal than court procedures. The parties may or may not be legally represented. In commercial, industrial and clinical negligence disputes, the parties will probably have legal representatives in their negotiating teams, though this is much less likely, for example, in mediation sessions relating to neighbour disputes.

In terms of cost, mediation is far more accessible than litigation. Michael Lind, a member of the ADR Group, a provider of mediation services that claims a dispute settlement rate of 80 per cent, told the *New Law Journal* in 2002 that:

> The benefits of mediation are clear. It offers parties a *quick* and *cost-effective* forum in which they (the parties) *retain control* of their dispute in reaching a sensible solution whilst *preserving their existing relationship*. Mediation is a voluntary, without prejudice and *confidential* process. Those elements are central to the process of assisted negotiation. Creativity and flexibility are core features . . . In mediation, there is no decision-maker other than the parties themselves. (emphasis added)

What is not mentioned here is that if the dispute is not resolved then court proceedings might ensue anyway. Nevertheless, mediation will often have *identified* the key areas of dispute and will therefore *reduce* the time required to resolve the matter by other means.

Aside from its role in commercial disputes, mediation is particularly useful in divorce cases, though it is encouraged rather than being compulsory. The parties should control the discussion, not the mediator. Research by **Hazel Genn**, however, suggested that mediators do sometimes *overstep* the mark and take control of the discussion, thus undermining the principle that the parties determine the pace, direction and outcome of the mediation. Genn further reported in 2002 that the voluntary take-up of mediation in civil cases had been 'modest', and that the legal profession relatively 'cautious' about its use as a method of ADR. However, more recent Court of Appeal judgments, such as *Burchell v Bullard and Others* (2005), have made it clear that 'the (legal) profession can no longer with impunity shrug aside reasonable requests to mediate' (Lord Justice Ward) and it would be surprising if lawyers did not heed this warning, given the danger – post-*Dunnett v Railtrack Plc* (2002) – of costs penalties being imposed on unco-operative parties.

## Conciliation

Here the third party takes an *interventionist* role in the discussions between the parties in order to push them in the direction of a settlement. A body that acts as the third party in industrial disputes, and therefore has a high-profile conciliation role, is the **Advisory, Conciliation and Arbitration Service (ACAS)**. Most trade associations will also offer conciliation services, and this includes those already mentioned under 'Arbitration' at p 137 above. However, some trade associations offer conciliation services but not arbitration, and examples include the **Textile Services Association** and the **Radio, Electrical and Television Retailers Association.**

### Evaluating conciliation

This is a *cheaper* option than civil litigation but, as with other methods of ADR, if the dispute is not resolved, then court proceedings might ensue. Resolving the dispute successfully will often depend on the skill of the conciliator and the willingness of the parties to co-operate. Again, however, conciliation has the advantage of *identifying*, and *clarifying*, the main issues in the dispute.

The process of conciliation is *private* as it takes place between the parties. It is as formal or informal as the parties and the conciliator wish. In commercial and industrial disputes, the parties will probably include legal representatives in their negotiating teams. It is generally a *more accessible* method than litigation, though accessibility will depend, in practice, on the time taken in working towards a settlement and whether the issue is finally resolved. Conciliation is particularly appropriate for major industrial or commercial disputes; for example, the role of **ACAS** in seeking to settle major employment disputes where industrial action is threatened.

## Negotiation

As Lord Justice Dyson acknowledged in the recent case of *Daniels v Commissioner of Police of the Metropolis* (2005), the 'definition of alternative dispute resolution, as a collective description of methods of resolving disputes otherwise than through the normal trial process' also included '*any kind of negotiation between the parties, whether direct or indirect*'. Indeed, negotiation, can be a very *quick, confidential* and *cost-effective way* of settling a dispute, particularly for small-scale local matters as between neighbours, or between consumers and shopkeepers. A problem arises, however, if the matter is proving difficult to resolve and the parties resort to engaging solicitors to act on their behalf. This has the potential to escalate both the time-scale of the negotiations and the expenses incurred, and might undermine some of the main benefits of the negotiation process.

### Evaluating negotiation

The costs of negotiation will depend on the circumstances: it is the *cheapest* option if the bargaining takes place between the parties, but it can swiftly become costly if lawyers get involved to negotiate an *'out of court' settlement*. The speed of the process will depend on the circumstances: as a general rule, negotiation can be very quick if face-to-face between parties, but may become long and drawn-out if lawyers are involved.

Negotiation can be undertaken in a completely *private* and *confidential* manner. If this takes place during legal proceedings, the relevant court should be kept informed so that judicial time is not wasted (*Gurney Consulting Engineers v Gleeds Health and Safety Ltd*, 2006). Typically parties are not legally represented and much negotiation may therefore be informal. If solicitors are involved, they will formalise the process and charge clients for letters written and meetings arranged in the dispute resolution process. Very often cases are settled '*out of court*', thus suiting parties who might wish to avoid any unwelcome publicity, though in high-profile instances the media will speculate about the size of privately-agreed settlements. Sometimes, the likely target of legal claims arising from a public accident will offer victims a settlement process to avoid the prospect of costly and damaging law-suits going through the courts. For example, the drugs manufacturer, TeGenero, was reported in April 2006 to have offered the victims of a drugs trial that had gone wrong an interim payment of £5000 each, and further compensation awarded by arbitration, subject to an agreement that the victims would not sue the company. If negotiation does not result in a settlement, then legal action may of course ensue. Although, as we have seen, parties are expected to act reasonably when considering offers to enter into alternative dispute resolution, public bodies 'routinely facing unfounded claims' might not be considered unreasonable if they refuse to negotiate. Courts, accordingly, should be reticent to apply costs penalties in these circumstances (*Daniels v Commissioner of Police of the Metropolis* 2005).

Table 7.2, opposite, recaps the main methods of ADR.

## OMBUDSMEN

Ombudsmen can be found in the public and private sectors. The **public sector ombudsmen** provide a remedy for **maladministration**, that being the poor governance of national and local public services as evidenced by factors such as administrative delay, incompetence and lack of impartiality in handling local affairs. The **Parliamentary Commissioner Act 1967** and the **Local Government Act 1974** are two statutes that gave powers of investigation and reporting to Commissioners: the **Parliamentary Commissioner for Administration** (dealing with complaints relating to Government departments and other executive agencies) and the **Commissioner for Local Administration** (dealing with complaints relating to local government). There are also **public sector ombudsmen** in areas such as the **National Health Service**, to deal with complaints from members of the public about treatment received, waiting times, and so forth.

In the **private sector**, there are ombudsman schemes relating to a range of service providers, from financial services (banks, building societies, insurance,

Table 7.2 Methods of alternative dispute resolution

| *Methods of ADR* | *Brief description* |
|---|---|
| Arbitration | • Dispute referred to third party, known as arbitrator.<br>• Clauses often found in commercial contracts referring parties to arbitration.<br>• Arbitrators can make awards that may be enforced in the courts. |
| Mediation | • A form of 'assisted settlement': a third party helps the parties in dispute towards a settlement.<br>• Formal settlement conferences might be used to further the progress of the parties.<br>• Seen as especially useful in divorce cases, but also used in commercial and other contexts. |
| Conciliation | • The third party actively suggests ways of settling the dispute.<br>• Example of an important conciliation body: ACAS.<br>• Used for commercial and industrial disputes. |
| Negotiation | • This is settling a dispute through bargaining between the parties.<br>• Generally informal, but may be conducted formally through solicitors. |

personal investment and pensions) through to funerals. As discussed in Chapter 10, there is also a **Legal Services Ombudsman** to oversee complaints-handling with regard to the legal profession. Some private sector ombudsmen have the power to make large awards against businesses; for example, up to £50,000 compensation that may be awarded against service providers by the **Funeral Services Ombudsman**, and up to £100,000 compensation that may be awarded against banks by the **Banking Ombudsman**.

## Evaluating the ombudsmen

The ombudsman is a *free*, non-court method of raising complaints about services or treatment received from public or private bodies.

Ombudsmen have the power to assess what is '*fair and reasonable*' in the circumstances. For voluntary ombudsman schemes, this power is given more weight by the fact that the courts have preferred not to subject ombudsman decisions to judicial review.

### Strengths of the ombudsman system

- Proceedings and investigations undertaken by the ombudsmen are generally conducted *in private*.
- Ombudsmen can be very persuasive in the reports that they prepare, thereby providing the potential for *some redress*.
- The investigations made by ombudsmen are *very thorough*.

### Weaknesses of the ombudsman system

- The ombudsman can take a *long time* to deal with complaints.
- Private sector ombudsmen are largely *unregulated*.
- Public sector ombudsmen can *make recommendations only*, so the powers of the ombudsmen to effect change can be very limited.
- There is a *lack of advertising* regarding the services of the ombudsmen – in fact many people do not even know that they exist.
- The jurisdiction of the ombudsmen is limited to *specific areas* only.

**Exercise 7.1: Recap on ADR and tribunals**

(1) Identify the methods of ADR from the following definitions:

(a) Dispute referred, by mutual consent, to a third party for resolution.
(b) In effect, bargaining between the parties.
(c) A third party plays an active role in moving the parties towards a settlement.
(d) A third party assists the parties but it is the parties who are in control of the process in moving towards a settlement.

(2) With which methods of ADR would you associate the following:

(a) Formal 'settlement conferences'.
(b) *Scott v Avery* clauses.
(c) ACAS.
(d) Awards.

(3) Although they have not made ADR mandatory for litigants (since this would breach Art 6 ECHR with regard to a fair trial: *Halsey v Milton Keynes NHS Trust* (2004)), the courts have nevertheless given clear direction to parties that they should not unreasonably refuse requests for ADR. How have they done this and name one case to illustrate your point.

(4) Name:

(a) Three tribunals originating from Acts of Parliament.
(b) Three types of claim heard by Employment Tribunals.
(c) One tribunal that hears lots of cases each year and one that hears very few.
(d) The full title of ACAS.

(5) With which alternatives to courts would you associate:

(a) Maladministration.
(b) Reinstatement or re-engagement.

(6) List three general advantages and three disadvantages of ADR by comparison with going to court.

For Answers, please turn to pp 337–8.

## Useful website addresses

| | |
|---|---|
| ADR Group | www.adrgroup.co.uk |
| Advisory, Conciliation and Arbitration Service | www.acas.org.uk |
| Centre for Effective Dispute Resolution | www.cedr.co.uk |
| Council on Tribunals | www.council-on-tribunals.gov.uk |
| Employment tribunals | www.employmenttribunals.gov.uk |
| Leggatt Review of Tribunals 2001 | www.tribunals-reviews.org.uk |
| Tribunals Service | www.tribunals.gov.uk |

*Materials directly for AS studies:*

| | |
|---|---|
| John Deft (St Brendan's Sixth Form College) | www.stbrn.ac.uk/other/depts/law |
| Asif Tufal | www.a-level-law.com |

## HINTS AND TIPS

Examination questions on this topic often require an **outline** of the alternative methods of resolving disputes, together with some **evaluation** of these methods as compared *either* with **each other**, *or* with the **civil courts**.

In **outlining** the options, knowledge of the main alternatives to the courts – tribunals, arbitration, mediation, conciliation, negotiation and the ombudsmen – is clearly required. You need to demonstrate an understanding of how these methods seek to resolve disputes, using examples (such as **employment tribunals**), explaining basic procedures (such as **settlement conferences in mediation**) and identifying the bodies involved (such as **ACAS in conciliation**).

As you may have found in reading this chapter, **evaluating** each method in turn can actually be very repetitive, and so it is better to talk about advantages and disadvantages *in general*. (We have focused on the advantages and disadvantages of tribunals and arbitration only, though in our coverage of other areas of comparison there are some useful points particular to each of the given methods.) Key points on **alternative dispute resolution** and **tribunals** might include that these are *cheaper, less* formal, more *private*, less procedural and therefore more *user-friendly* than the courts. However, it should be noted that the courts have some advantages over the alternatives, such as clearer rights of appeal, a more accountable set of judges and a more formal, and arguably more structured, approach to bringing the dispute to a close.

For the purposes of **evaluating dispute resolution** options as against each other, a table format is recommended for revision, thus allowing for quick comparison of the methods in relation to key variables such as cost, speed, formality, legal representation, suitability, and so on.

# Judges

8

This topic enables you:

- To broaden your knowledge of the courts and how they work.
- To identify the different types of judges in the courts, their respective roles and how they are selected, appointed, trained and removed, taking into account recent changes in the Constitutional Reform Act 2005.
- To recognise the two branches of the legal profession and the traditional bias in judicial appointments towards barristers (a position that is now changing).
- To understand the theory of the 'separation of powers' and the relationship of the judiciary to the other constitutional powers in practice.
- To supplement earlier knowledge of the doctrine of judicial precedent and the process of statutory interpretation, taking into account the potential for judicial law-making.

The **judge** is perhaps the most *visible* expression of law in the English legal system. In their wigs and gowns for ceremonial occasions or at the head of the court, judges are often depicted as representing the full majesty of the law. As **Berlins and Dyer** (2000) have commented: '*The English judge . . . is, to some people, the awesome embodiment of wisdom, independence and impartiality in a free society. To others he is an elderly, remote, crusty figure wearing ridiculous fancy dress, speaking strange jargon and holding views more appropriate to the nineteenth century*'. The latter view reflects the suspicion that the background of the judges means that they are, in some senses, 'out of touch' with society. Nevertheless, there have been many famous, and many great, judges and, as this chapter indicates, some have had a profound influence on the law.

## THE ROLE OF THE JUDGE

The role of the judge *differs* according to the type of case being tried or appeal being heard. In general, the judge's role is to manage the case and ensure that the evidence is properly admitted and the legal arguments heard.

### Criminal trials

In **Crown Court** trials, the role of the judge is to manage the trial, determine the admissibility of evidence and sum up the evidence and the law for the jury. In such situations, the judge assumes the role of **'master of the law'** and the jury adopts the role of 'master of the facts'. Therefore, it is the jury that determines whether the defendant is to be found 'guilty' or 'not guilty' on the evidence that the jurors have heard. The role of the judge is then to release or

**sentence** the defendant according to whether the jury has decided to acquit or convict. In the **magistrates' courts** the criminal trials have no juries, and so the role of the **district judge (magistrates' court)** is to manage *both* the **facts** and the **law** in order to either acquit or convict. If a decision is made to convict, the district judge (magistrates' court) must then also **sentence** the defendant. (It should be noted that **benches of lay magistrates** hear the *majority* of trials in the magistrates' courts and *also* carry out these roles: see Chapter 9.)

## Civil trials

The ultimate role of the judge in civil trials is to come to a **decision on the dispute:** the judge will determine whether the claimant has proved his or her case and the appropriate remedies to be awarded. Since juries are used in civil trials in a limited number of areas only (see Chapter 9, pp 172–3), the judge generally has to make a decision as to the **amount of damages** to be paid to the injured party and/or to consider whether **equitable remedies** would be appropriate in the circumstances (such as to award an injunction). Remember that civil trials might also involve divorce, or disputes over child custody, or disputes about the distribution of monies from wills, or claims concerning the interpretation of commercial contracts. In all such cases, it is the **judge** who has to decide which of the parties in dispute wins and which one loses.

As Chapter 6 on the court structure illustrates, the role of the civil trial judge has become much *more* **managerial** and **interventionist** following the **reforms to civil justice.** In effect, civil trial judges are now **trial managers** and have much *more* **responsibility** for the **time management** of the case.

## Appeals in civil and criminal cases

With regard to **civil** and **criminal appeals**, consider the coverage that follows in this chapter and also in Chapter 6. It is in the performance of the appellate function that judges engage in **statutory interpretation** and **judicial precedent,** thus contributing to the law-making process (see earlier coverage in Chapters 3 and 4 respectively).

## WHO ARE THE JUDGES?

As with the courts, there is a hierarchy of judges:

- The **Lord Chief Justice** (*replacing* the Lord Chancellor as head of the judiciary under the Constitutional Reform Act 2005 from **April 2006,** with the title of **President of the Courts of England and Wales**).
- **The Lords of Appeal in Ordinary** (to become **Justices of the Supreme Court** when the Constitutional Reform Act 2005 comes into effect: **October 2008** anticipated).
- The **Heads of Division**
- The **Lords Justices of Appeal**
- **High Court judges**
- **Circuit judges**

- Recorders
- District judges
- District judges (magistrates' courts)

## The Constitutional Reform Act 2005: the changing role of the Lord Chancellor and the elevation of the Lord Chief Justice to head of the judiciary

Prior to the Constitutional Reform Act 2005, the Lord Chancellor occupied a somewhat unusual position in the British constitution. This is because the Lord Chancellor's role indicated that the **'separation of powers'** constitutional theory existed in theory and *not* in practice, with the Lord Chancellor having a role in all three constitutional bodies, as a Government Cabinet Minister (**executive**), Speaker of the House of Lords (**legislature**) and head of the judiciary (**judiciary**).

The post of Lord Chancellor had begun to attract a great deal of scrutiny, and criticism, arising from the breach of the separation of powers doctrine. A Bar Council Working Party observed, in 2003, that the prospect of judges being selected by a Cabinet Minister was not politically acceptable, since it might be seen to compromise the independence of judges when hearing cases brought against the Government and other public authorities. The Government therefore announced reforms, in 2003, to take account of such criticism, heralding first the abolition of the Lord Chancellor's post (after 1400 years of history, as most newspapers pointed out) and paving the way for judicial appointments to be made by an independent appointments commission. However, the Government needed first to consult Parliament – something it had neglected to do when announcing its reforms in 2003 – and so plans for the Lord Chancellor proved premature, with the House of Lords, in particular, showing strong resistance to them: indeed, the office of the Lord Chancellor has survived Government attempts at abolition, though the 2005 Act changes the role significantly.

The **Constitutional Reform Act 2005**, at Part 2, leaves the Lord Chancellor with ministerial significance in the **executive**, but transfers the other constitutional roles elsewhere: thus, the Lord Chancellor is *no longer* Speaker of the House of Lords (being replaced by another form of presiding officer) and is *no longer* head of the judiciary. The latter role is now carried out by the **Lord Chief Justice**.

The division of roles between the Lord Chancellor and the Lord Chief Justice observes a **'Concordat'** that had been drawn up by the two offices prior to the 2005 Act. Therefore, the roles divided after April 2006 as Table 8.1 (on p 150) illustrates.

For further reading on the background to the Constitutional Reform Act 2005, see Graham Arnold's article in Cavendish's *Student Law Review*, Autumn 2005, at p 16.

## The Lords of Appeal in Ordinary

As at June 2006, the 12 Lords of Appeal in Ordinary (referred to in the press as the 'Law Lords') were, in order of seniority, as follows:

- Lord Bingham of Cornhill
- Lord Nicholls of Birkenhead
- Lord Hoffmann
- Lord Hope of Craighead
- Lord Saville of Newdigate
- Lord Scott of Foscote
- Lord Rodger of Earlsferry
- Lord Walker of Gestingthorpe
- Lady Hale of Richmond
- Lord Carswell
- Lord Brown of Eaton-under-Heywood
- Lord Mance

Table 8.1 The respective roles of the Lord chancellor and the Lord Chief Justice from April 2006

| *Lord Chancellor* | *Lord Chief Justice* | *Joint responsibility* |
|---|---|---|
| **Ministerial post** – no longer a sitting judge | **Head of the judiciary** – no political role, but expected to represent the judiciary's interests to Government | Establishing a system of **complaints-handling and disciplinary procedures** for the judiciary |
| Duty to ensure the **efficient and effective administration of the courts** | Responsible for **judicial training and deployment** | Consulting on appointments guidance to the **Judicial Appointments Commission** |
| Provision of **resources for the administration of justice** | Responsible for witnessing oaths taken by judges | |

The Lords of Appeal in Ordinary, sitting on the **Appellate (or Judicial) Committee of the House of Lords,** hear the most important civil and criminal legal appeals in the English legal system. They also hear appeals from appeal courts in Scotland and Northern Ireland, and courts-martial appeals relating to the armed forces. As the **senior appeal court** in the English legal system, the House of Lords has to resolve very significant issues of **statutory interpretation** (see Chapter 3) and **establish precedents** (see Chapter 4) for the lower courts to follow, occasionally exercising its discretion to make important new law.

The Lords of Appeal in Ordinary, as Life Peers of the House of Lords in its legislative capacity, might also contribute to debates, though, by convention, their Lordships rarely exercise their rights in areas unrelated to technical law reform. Nevertheless, the issue of senior judges also being members of the legislature caused sufficient concern to have been addressed in the Government's **Constitutional Reform Act 2005**. It is estimated that by October 2008, the House of Lords will *no longer* have any connection with the legislature and be constituted, independently, as a **Supreme Court**. The 12 Lords of Appeal in Ordinary will transfer to the Supreme Court as **Justices of the Supreme Court.**

The Supreme Court's jurisdiction will mirror that of the House of Lords – so the same sorts of appeal will be heard – but in addition, the Supreme Court will take over the role of the Privy Council in hearing cases relating to the UK's devolution arrangements (that is, the devolution of powers to Scotland, Wales and Northern Ireland).

Under the existing arrangements, the Lords of Appeal in Ordinary wear suits, rather than wigs and gowns, in court: however, full judicial dress is worn on ceremonial occasions. Looking at the Law Lords, all 12 are white, eleven of them male (with Lady Hale, the notable exception), all with associations to Oxford or Cambridge universities and, as barristers originally, all having **taken silk** (that is, having been accorded the status of **Queen's Counsel (QC)**).

Some of the Lords of Appeal in Ordinary have held other senior legal posts or headed high-profile legal inquiries. **Lord Bingham of Cornhill**, for example, has held the high judicial posts of Master of the Rolls (1992–96) and Lord Chief Justice of England and Wales (1996–2000). **Lord Scott of Foscote** came to dominate the front pages of newspapers when he headed the controversial inquiry into the 'Arms to Iraq' scandal. This concerned allegations that the then Conservative Government had colluded with the British defence industry to send arms to Iraq, in breach of its own exporting rules (1992–96).

**IT'S A FACT!**

**8.1: Top jobs!**

At the time of writing, Lord Falconer of Thoroton is carrying out the Lord Chancellor's duties alongside the post of Secretary of State for Constitutional Affairs. Lord Falconer studied at Queens' College, Cambridge. He became a barrister in 1974, as a member of Inner Temple, and achieved the status of QC in 1991 at the age of 40. Since 1997, he has held three Cabinet posts and acted as Solicitor-General to the Government prior to assuming the Constitutional Affairs role. He has been a close friend of Tony Blair since schooldays and even shared a flat with him in the 1970s. For this office, he is entitled to claim a salary of £213,899, but sensitive to the claims of extravagance that attached to Lord Irvine in particular when he was Lord Chancellor, Lord Falconer has opted to receive the standard salary for a Cabinet Minister in the House of Lords: £136,677. (The Prime Minister's salary is currently £187,610.)

The current Lord Chief Justice is Lord Phillips of Worth Matravers, who replaced Lord Woolf in October 2005. Lord Phillips studied at King's College, Cambridge. He became a barrister in 1962, establishing success in the commercial law field and attained the status of QC in 1978. His judicial career developed as follows: Recorder (1982–87); High Court Judge (QBD: 1987–1995); Lord Justice of Appeal (Court of Appeal: 1995–99); Lord of Appeal in Ordinary (House of Lords: 1999–2000); and Master of the Rolls (2000–2005). He handled a Judicial Inquiry into the BSE Crisis, published in 2000, which was widely praised for its thorough approach to the issues. Lord Phillips is entitled to a salary of £225,000.

The salary figures reflect pay rises awarded in April 2006: see *The Times*, 31 March 2006, at p 26.

## The Heads of Division

The Heads of Division roles are as follows:

- Prior to the Constitutional Reform Act 2005, the Lord Chief Justice was head both of the Court of Appeal (Criminal) and the Queen's Bench Division: he remains head, or **President, of the Court of Appeal (Criminal)**; a **President of the Queen's Bench Division** (currently Lord Justice Judge) now holds the latter post.
- The **Master of the Rolls** (Head of the Civil Court of Appeal). The 2005 Act also provides for the posts of **Head** and **Deputy Head of Civil Justice**, roles that may be held by the Master of the Rolls and the Chancellor of the High Court respectively (see below).
- The **Chancellor of the High Court** (Head of the Chancery Division of the High Court, referred to as Vice Chancellor prior to the 2005 Act).
- The **Head of Family Justice** (Head of the Family Division of the High Court, also referred to as President of the Family Division).

At the time of writing the main Heads of Division posts are represented by the following four individuals:

- The Lord Chief Justice: Lord Phillips of Worth Matravers.
- The Master of the Rolls: Lord Justice Clarke.
- The Chancellor of the High Court: Sir Andrew Morritt.
- Head of Family Justice: Sir Mark Potter.

The significance of the Heads of Division is that they have a strong influence in shaping the direction and pace of legal and policy growth in their respective areas.

## Profile 8.1: Lord Denning: a famous Master of the Rolls

Alfred Thompson (or more commonly 'Tom') Denning was born in 1899 in Whitchurch, Hampshire. His father was a draper with a shop in Whitchurch, and his mother a school-teacher by training. Denning's family life was comfortable because of the wealth that a grandfather had amassed as a coal merchant in Lincoln. Denning's education, and home life, was greatly affected by World War I. He saw active service in France and lost two of his four brothers.

Denning was educated at Andover Grammar School and then Magdalen College, Oxford, where he achieved academic excellence in Mathematics and Jurisprudence (Legal Philosophy). He won prizes for his performance in Bar examinations and was called to the Bar, by Lincoln's Inn, in 1923. He took silk, as an established common law barrister in commercial matters, 15 years later.

Denning's judicial career began as a **High Court Judge** in 1944. His promise was revealed as early as 1947 with an outstanding judgment in *Central London Property Trust Ltd v High Trees House Ltd* (1947) on the equitable remedy of estoppel (which prevented a party seeking to enforce strict contractual rights when that party had given the impression that he or she would not do so – see Chapter 4).

In 1948, Denning became a **Lord Justice of Appeal** in the **Court of Appeal** where he remained until 1957; and then a **Lord of Appeal in Ordinary** between 1957 until 1962. However, the position in which he made perhaps the greatest impact was as **Master of the Rolls** between the years 1962–82. Although it was in this role that he came into conflict with the House of Lords on a number of issues, he maintained his interest in developing a 'new equity' in civil law that brought fairness where a strict application of common law might have led to injustice. He identified some of the landmark cases of his period as Master of the Rolls as including:

- *Hinz v Berry* (1970), which allowed a tort claim for nervous shock made by a widow who had seen her husband killed and children injured in an accident;
- *Lloyds Bank v Bundy* (1975), in which a bank was prevented from misusing its greater bargaining power by taking possession over a man's property when he had mortgaged it for the benefit of his son: a key case in the development of the equitable doctrine of 'undue influence'.

Denning clearly enjoyed his time as Master of the Rolls and took a great interest in the post. Here is his description of it from *Lord Denning: The Family Story* (1981):

> *There have been Masters of the Rolls ever since the year 1290 – there are records to prove it – and probably before that. He has always been one of the great officers of State. He was the Keeper of the Rolls or Records of the Chancery of England. The Rolls were the old rolls of parchment which contained the records of the proceedings of the Court of Chancery . . . the Master of the Rolls is still one of the most coveted posts in the land. He presides in the Court of Appeal on the civil side: where he has much influence on the development of the law . . . He has, by statute, a fatherly eye on the Roll of Solicitors. He is a Jack-of-all-trades and Master of One – the master as he is affectionately known in the profession.*

Denning's willingness to speak his mind, both in and out of court, got him into a great deal of trouble at times. Thus his comments about the racial balance of a jury (which had to be deleted from his 1982 book *What Next in the Law?*) were picked up on by the media as 'racist'. This was a disappointment to Denning after years of work (between 1954 and 1977) addressing students across the Commonwealth on legal matters. Furthermore, an interview with *The Spectator* caught Denning, at the age of 92, speaking his mind about miscarriages of justice, in which he appeared to suggest that the death penalty would have saved the legal system from many embarrassments. He complained about the coverage, but the damage had been done. Still, while commentators take account of such indiscretions, they are outweighed by Denning's huge contribution to English law from a judicial career spanning 38 years.

Lord Denning died in Winchester, Hampshire on 5 March 1999. It is fitting to end with this passage, taken from Denning's obituary in *The Independent* newspaper:

> *Lord Denning was one of the greatest judges of the twentieth century. His name will always be associated with doing justice to the parties before him, come what may. He was a judge for 38 years and had time to leave his imprint on the law of the post-war period . . . Denning put justice first and precedent came lower down in the scale of importance. Justice was achieved by applying the principles of equity, where necessary, and adapting the law to modern conditions. His attitude to the law was positive and he exercised all the powers of a judge to do right.*

## The Lords Justices of Appeal

The Lords Justices of Appeal hear appeal cases in the **Civil** and **Criminal Divisions** of the **Court of Appeal.**

The Court of Appeal in the Criminal Division does *not* rehear cases from the Crown Court; it reviews whether a jury decision can stand on the basis of the fresh evidence brought before it.

Civil appeals, on the other hand, can involve a **rehearing of cases** where necessary. They come to the Court of Appeal from the county court and the High Court and concern matters of fact and law.

Court of Appeal judges wear wigs and plain black gowns and, like Lords of Appeal in Ordinary, have very elaborate ceremonial dress. Of the 37 Lords Justices of Appeal, there are three female judges (Lady Justice Mary Arden, Lady Justice Janet Smith and Lady Justice Heather Hallett), *no* ethnic minority judges and *no* judges representing the solicitors' branch of the profession. All of the Heads of Division are also *ex officio* judges of the Court of Appeal (that is, they can also hear cases in the Court of Appeal from time to time owing to their judicial status).

## High Court judges

High Court judges (sometimes referred to as *puisne judges*) hear both first instance and appeal cases in the three Divisions of the **High Court** (Chancery, Family, and Queen's Bench), and hear some criminal **Crown Court** trials (where they will be recognised by their distinctive scarlet robes). They are supported by part-time deputy High Court judges. There is also a set of specialists who deal with procedural and costs management issues at the pre-trial stage in High Court cases, known as Masters and Registrars of the Supreme Court. High Court judges are addressed in court as 'My Lord/My Lady' as with the other senior judges we have encountered thus far. Of the 108 High Court judges, there are just 11 female judges (one of whom, Mrs Justice Linda Dobbs, is the only ethnic minority judge) and three judges representing the solicitors' profession.

## Circuit judges

Circuit judges hear *criminal cases* in the **Crown Court** and *civil cases* in the **county court**. Circuit judges may be recognised in the courts by their violet robes: in civil cases they will wear a sash (or tippet) of lilac; in criminal cases this will be red. Circuit judges are referred to in court as 'Your Honour', though for historical reasons circuit judges conducting criminal trials at London's Central Criminal Court, known as 'The Old Bailey', retain the title My Lord/My Lady. There are 626 circuit judges, of whom there are 72 female judges, 83 judges from the solicitors' profession and seven ethnic minority judges.

## Recorders

Recorders are **part-time judges** who hear either *criminal cases* in the **Crown Court**, or *civil cases* in the **county court**, or in some instances both. The work that they undertake will generally be of a less serious or important nature than that carried out by circuit judges. They are referred to in court as 'Your Honour'. There are 1,380 recorders, of whom there are 194 female judges, 56 ethnic minority judges and 125 from the solicitors' profession.

## District judges

District judges form the *lowest tier* of the judicial hierarchy and yet they adjudicate on the great majority of **civil law disputes** (including personal injury cases, consumer claims, divorces, possession of property and bankrupcy proceedings) in the English legal system. They hear cases in the **county court**. There are 450 district judges, of whom there are 86 female judges, 13 ethnic minority judges and 418 from the solicitors' profession.

## District judges (magistrates' court)

Full-time, legally qualified magistrates, once referred to as stipendiary magistrates and now called district judges (magistrates' court), adjudicate on the more serious criminal and civil matters dealt with by magistrates' courts. There are 137 district judges (magistrates' court), of whom 32 are female judges, five ethnic minority judges and 90 from the solicitors' profession.

All judicial statistics were taken from www.judiciarg.gov.uk/keyfacts/statistics/index.htm, as at June 2006.

Table 8.2, opposite, summarises the judicial hierarchy.

## Conclusions on the composition of the judicial profession

The judiciary has often been attacked for being out of touch with society and comprising a white, male, middle-class elite. The findings of JAG Griffith in his book *The Politics of the Judiciary* confirm this view: the judges, he points out, are largely homogeneous in background and attitude, and therefore

Table 8.2 The judicial hierarchy (post-Constitutional Reform Act 2005)

| *Type of judge* | *Relevant courts* |
|---|---|
| Lord Chief Justice | • Head of an independent judiciary (President of the Courts of England and Wales), replacing the Lord Chancellor, whose role becomes limited to executive functions |
| The Lords of Appeal in Ordinary | • Hear the most important civil and criminal appeals in the English legal system as judges of the House of Lords (subject to replacement by a **Supreme Court** in 2008, in which existing Lords of Appeal in Ordinary will become Justices of the Supreme Court) |
| The Heads of Division | • Court of Appeal (Civil): Master of the Rolls<br>• Court of Appeal (Criminal): President of the Criminal Division (Lord Chief Justice)<br>• President of the Queen's Bench Division<br>• Chancery Division of the High Court: Chancellor of the High Court<br>• Family Division of the High Court: President of the Family Division (Head of Family Justice) |
| The Lords Justices of Appeal | • Civil and Criminal Divisions of the Court of Appeal |
| High Court judges | • First instance High Court matters<br>• Appellate High Court matters (Divisional Courts)<br>• Criminal cases in the Crown Court |
| Circuit judges | • Criminal cases in the Crown Court<br>• Civil cases in the county court |
| Recorders | • Criminal cases in the Crown Court<br>• Civil cases in the county court |
| District judges | • Civil cases in the county court |
| District judges (magistrates' courts) | • Criminal and civil matters dealt with by the magistrates' court (bulk of work is undertaken by voluntary lay magistrates) |

perpetuate a conservative attitude that can best be described as 'corporate prejudice'. It is certainly true, as we can see from the statistical information provided above, that judges are predominantly **white males** and drawn from the **barristers' profession**. It is also true to say that the senior members of the judiciary have certain common traits, such as an **Oxbridge education**, that might also account for a perceived judicial mindset that places certain conservative values above other factors. Research undertaken by the **Labour Research Department** in 2002 confirms that a public school and Oxbridge bias in appointments remains. It is submitted, however, that at times criticism should be reserved for *what the judges do*, rather than what they represent.

Professor Gary Slapper has argued in the *Student Law Review* that Griffith's position has relevance only if it can be used to show either that: (a) the judges are delivering defective judgments because of such a background; or (b) that such a background reduces 'public confidence' in the administration of justice. Otherwise, to attack the judges just because they represent a privileged elite is meaningless, because the outcome, in legal terms, is unimpaired.

As to the representation of women and ethnic minorities in the judiciary, it is clear from the statistics, as Darbyshire (2002) points out, that '. . . women, solicitors and members of the ethnic minorities are not reflected in the judiciary in the proportions in which they populate the legal profession'. However, Lord Irvine argued that the proper measure is not of the number of women in the profession today compared with the number appointed to judicial posts. Instead, he suggested, it is the number of women in the profession 20 years ago compared to the number of women in judicial posts today. This does seem a more relevant measure, because it considers the number of women in the profession who would have become eligible for judicial office.

Furthermore, it seems that women and ethnic minority applicants for judicial posts are **on the increase** at the base of the judicial hierarchy (as illustrated by the recent Judicial Appointments Annual Reports). Slapper has welcomed this trend as indicative that the 'social composition of the judiciary is beginning to change'.

Whether the judges should more accurately reflect the social mix of the wider community is a question that continues to provoke considerable debate. Lord MacKay, Lord Irvine's predecessor, took the view that the judiciary was distinct from the legislature and therefore did not have to reflect a democratic and representative social group, a view that Griffith deplored. Slapper has provided an interesting example to illustrate the problems with the sort of position adopted by Lord MacKay:

> . . . during the last millennium right up to 1992 (the case of *R v R*) it was not a crime for a man to rape a woman if she was his wife. The people who fabricated this rule and perpetuated it for centuries were all judges (not MPs) and they were all men, many of whom regarded women as inferior beings.

However, this point loses its impact when it is considered that the judges who reversed this rule, and did so without waiting for Parliament, were also white men from a shared cultural, economic and academic background. That judges, from such a narrow background, were capable of **radical law-making** suggests that perhaps more emphasis needs to be placed on the judicial role of objective decision-making.

The current Lord Chancellor, Lord Falconer, has shown strong support for the view set by his predecessor Lord Irvine that judicial appointments should be **merit-based** above all, though welcoming eligible candidates from both sexes and all ethnic and social backgrounds. This is complemented by the prevailing opinion, supported by the Bar Council in particular, that the legal profession as a whole should be more representative of wider society. The Government has responded by seeking to widen the pool of applicants to the judiciary, including other branches of the profession such as **legal executives**, though this statement of intent has had a cautious welcome (characterised by the headline in *The Times*, July 2005, 'Four GCSEs? Then you can be a judge'). While such approaches are not going to bring about change quickly, they arguably lay the foundations for the long-term development,

**IT'S A FACT!**

**8.1: Oxbridge and the judiciary**

The Sutton Trust released figures to the media in 2005 suggesting that 81 per cent of judges were educated at Oxford or Cambridge, along with 82 per cent of barristers under the age of 39: both of these percentages, however, represented a decline from statistics in previous years. In addition, the Commission for Judicial Appointments seemed to imply that the Lord Chancellor had shown an apparent bias towards Oxbridge candidates in appointments, a point hotly denied by Lord Falconer.

and improvement, of the judiciary. The **Constitutional Reform Act 2005** should assist in this process, as the next section indicates.

## SELECTION AND APPOINTMENT OF JUDGES

Judicial selection has been one of the most criticised aspects of the English legal system, with the main area of controversy being the traditional lack of application process for senior members of the judiciary, with appointments made on the basis of '**secret soundings**'. Given the narrow social background of the senior judges, in particular, 'secret soundings' gave rise to the fear that an 'old boy network' was merely being perpetuated, with judges being selected on grounds *other than* merit.

In responding to criticisms levelled at the system, the Labour Government established a Commission for Judicial Appointments in 2001 to review the appointments made following the **Peach Review of the Appointment Processes of Judges and Queen's Counsel in England and Wales (1999)**. The Commission was not, however, set up as an *appointing* body and yet it soon became clear that a body with this sort of power would be necessary to create an open appointments process and boost public confidence: hence, the creation of an independent **Judicial Appointments Commission** in Part 4 of the Constitutional Reform Act 2005.

In operation from April 2006, the **Judicial Appointments Commission's** role is to select candidates for judicial appointments, based on transparent methods of application and assessment. Competitions, or new rounds of appointment, will be announced so that those seeking judicial appointment can formally apply. The Commission has a balanced composition: the Commissioners represent lay persons (six members), judges (five members), lawyers (one solicitor and one barrister), one tribunal member and one lay justice, with the Chairman being one of the lay members. A smaller selection panel will consider **senior judicial appointments** (Lord Chief Justice and the Heads of Division). Lords of Appeal in Ordinary and Lords Justices of Appeal will be selected by the Judicial Appointments Commission and recommended to the Lord Chancellor, though formal appointment by the Queen 'on the advice of the Prime Minister' will be retained. The Supreme Court, when implemented, will have its own **Selection Commissions** for the appointment of new Justices of the Supreme Court.

Although aspects of the procedures differ according to the types of judge being appointed, the basic position is that the **Judicial Appointments Commission** will select a candidate and recommend that person to the Lord Chancellor. If the Lord Chancellor *accepts* the selection, then the process can move to formal appointment by the Queen. However, the Lord Chancellor does have the option of *rejecting* a candidate or asking the Commission to *reconsider* its choice; the *rejection* option may only be exercised once, whether at the outset or following a request for reconsideration. Even then, the power of rejection is limited, since only the next preferred candidate, or the original one, will be entitled to appointment.

The 2005 Act places the stated intentions of recent Lord Chancellors on a statutory footing, by requiring that selections must be made on the basis of '**merit**' and '**good character**' (s 63: see discussion above), subject to which the **Judicial Appointments Commission** 'must have regard to the need to **encourage diversity** in the range of persons available for selection for appointments' (s 64). The Lord Chancellor, and all Ministers, must '**uphold**' the principle of judicial independence, with the Lord Chancellor further required to '**defend**' it: these provisions represent two safeguards against executive pressure in the appointments process.

## Selection and appointment of senior judges

The most senior judges, Lords of Appeal in Ordinary and Lords Justices of Appeal, are formally appointed by the Queen 'on the advice of the Prime Minister', but it is the Lord Chancellor's acceptance of the **Judicial Appointments Commission's** selection that seals the appointment. Prior to the 2005 Act, candidates were invited to join the senior judiciary, subject to 'secret soundings' about the suitability of the applicant: they did not have to apply. Such a lack of transparency, over so many years, made reform inevitable.

The qualifications required for candidates to the most senior judicial posts are as follows:

To be considered as a candidate to be a **Lord (Lady) of Appeal in Ordinary**, a person would need to have:

(**a**) held high judicial office for at least two years (most being promoted from the Court of Appeal); or
(**b**) held Supreme Court rights of audience (that is, advocacy rights in the higher courts) for 15 years.

To be considered as a candidate to be a **Lord (or Lady) Justice of Appeal**, a person would need to have:

(**a**) held judicial office as a High Court judge; or
(**b**) held Supreme Court rights of audience for ten years.

**Lords Justices of Appeal** are eligible to apply for the **Heads of Division** posts.

**High Court judges** are formally appointed by the Queen, having been selected by the **Judicial Appointments Commission**. To be considered as a candidate to be a High Court judge, a person would need to have:

(**a**) held a post as a circuit judge for at least two years; or
(**b**) held High Court rights of audience for at least ten years.

Solicitor-Advocates are now able to seek appointment to this judicial office, which prior to 1990, would have been available only to barristers.

## Selection and appointment of less senior judges

Less senior judges (that is, circuit judges, recorders and district judges) are formally appointed by the Queen, having been selected by the **Judicial Appointments Commission**. The general requirement for these judicial posts is to have held possession of Crown Court or county court rights of audience for at least ten years, or seven years in respect of district judges. For district judges (magistrates' courts) see Chapter 9 at p 186.

## TRAINING JUDGES

The training of judges is undertaken by the **Judicial Studies Board** (JSB, established in 1979) and, following the 2005 Act, is the overall responsibility of the **Lord Chief Justice.**

The JSB functions through a main Board and a number of committees, which specialise in training for specific areas such as criminal, civil, family, etc. These committees are staffed by judges, ranging from Lords Justices of Appeal through to district judges; heads of tribunals; academics (university scholars in law); and civil servants representing both the Home Office and the Department for Constitutional Affairs. The Judicial Studies Board is a product of, but distinct from, the Department for Constitutional Affairs and prides itself on a degree of independence. It describes itself as follows:

> *The Judicial Studies Board (JSB) was set up . . . following the Bridge Report which identified the most important objective of judicial training as being 'To convey in a condensed form the lessons which experienced judges have acquired from their experience' . . . The activities of the JSB range from advising on and producing materials for the training of magistrates and judicial officers in tribunals to training of members of the full and part-time judiciary (in exercise of their Civil, Criminal and Family Law jurisdictions) on appointment, and on specific changes in law and procedure which directly affect the management and conduct of cases.*

Judicial training generally takes place at the lower ends of the judicial scale and is not therefore relevant for the senior judges.

### Criminal law training for judges

The training regime for assistant recorders and recorders (known as the **Criminal Law Induction Course**) lays down the requirement that **recorders** should undertake a **four-day residential course** before sitting in a Crown Court. The course includes lectures; sentencing and summing-up exercises; mock trials; and equal treatment training. Visits to penal institutions (such as prisons), the opportunity to observe serving judges and meetings with probation officers will also be provided to supplement the training. Further training is given in the form of a one-day Criminal Conference 18 months later. **Criminal Continuation Seminars**, representing short courses for judiciary in the Crown Court (new High Court judges, circuit judges and recorders), also take place on a residential basis and should be attended once every three years. Continuation seminars include topics such as 'Vulnerable and Intimidated Witnesses', 'Mentally Disordered Offenders' and 'The Drug Using Offender'.

### Civil law training for judges

The civil law training regime for recorders, assistant recorders and district judges (**Civil Law Induction Course**) lays down the requirement for a four-day residential course prior to sitting in a county court. The training includes lectures and sessions on equality and poverty. Before practising, trainees are required to sit with existing judges (circuit judges and district judges). Other relevant Conferences and **Civil Continuation Seminars** are held annually and should be attended once every three years by circuit judges, recorders, assistant recorders and district judges. Continuation seminars include topics such as 'Access to Justice', 'Compromise and Settlement', 'Damages', 'Costs' and the 'Medical Aspects of Personal Injury Cases'. The Judicial Studies Board offers special training on aspects of family law.

## *Ad hoc* training for judges

Sometimes judicial training is *ad hoc* (as and when) for certain aspects. For example, all civil judges have had to undertake training on the civil justice reforms and on alternative dispute resolution (ADR). Moreover, on enactment of the **Human Rights Act 1998**, both civil and criminal judges were required to undertake a great deal of training offered by the Judicial Studies Board. All judges were issued with an **Equal Treatment Bench Book** in 1999.

## Evaluation of training for judges

If you are required to evaluate the training regime for judges, the two most striking points are surely that: (a) there is **so little of it in practice**; and (b) the focus of the training is largely on the **less senior members of the judiciary**. The latter suggests that senior judges no longer require training and guidance sessions to update them. As to the former, the point has often been made that four days' induction to Crown Court work, for example, is simply *insufficient* when a judge will be expected to make sentencing decisions that will affect the liberty of offenders. Moreover, the assumption that skills of advocacy will translate to skills of adjudication is not always sound. Some advocates are placed in the position of having to undertake judicial work with which they are unfamiliar because they did not practise in that area. There have been a number of calls for reform, including:

- The establishment of a **Judicial Training College**.
- The extension of **judicial performance appraisal** to monitor the progress, and performance, of recently appointed judges.
- The development of a **career judiciary** (as in France, where judicial training is a university option and lawyers specialise in this aspect from the outset).

# REMOVAL AND RETIREMENT OF JUDGES

A point that emphasises the independence of the judiciary is that the Government cannot remove judges, since this would subject them to political interference and undermine their independence in the English constitution. We have seen already, in Chapters 1 and 2, that judges can keep a check on the executive through the mechanism of **judicial review**. Such a power would clearly be compromised if the Government had the power to remove judges who proved to be 'difficult' in obstructing their business.

## The security of tenure of the senior judges

Senior judges are remarkably difficult to get rid of: they enjoy a very great 'security of tenure'. Senior judges hold office '*while of good behaviour*', though in practice they retain that office even if standards fall short of this. The 'security of tenure' is based on the Act of Settlement 1700. This states that both Houses of Parliament may remove senior judges only following a motion to that effect to the monarch. The procedure has never been applied to an English judge, though in 1830, Sir Jonah Barrington, an Irish judge, was removed after a financial scandal relating to missing court funds.

The Act of Settlement is applied for Lords of Appeal in Ordinary under the Appellate Jurisdiction Act 1876; and for Lords Justices of Appeal and High Court judges under the Supreme Court Act 1981.

## Security of tenure of the less senior judges

The Courts Act 1971 provides that the Lord Chancellor 'may, if he thinks fit, remove a circuit judge from office on the grounds of incapacity or misbehaviour', subject to a requirement in Part 4 of the Constitutional Reform Act 2005 that he has followed a set of 'prescribed procedures' agreed by the Lord Chancellor and the Lord Chief Justice. The categories of '**misbehaviour**' range from discourtesy through to dishonesty. However, it is clear that drink-driving will not be tolerated, since convictions for this offence have prompted a number of judicial resignations.

**IT'S A FACT!**

**8.2: Judges in the news, but for all the wrong reasons . . .**

In July 2004, it was reported that Major-General David Selwood, QC, had been forced to resign from Portsmouth Crown Court owing to convictions for possessing indecent images of children on his computer. After what was described as an exemplary record in the armed forces and the law, he was placed on the sex offenders register for five years.

In March 2005, the Court of Appeal had to deal with an allegation of judicial bias in the conspiracy to defraud case of *R v Odewale and another* (2005). Comments had been made at the sentencing stage by Judge Ball, QC, at Chelmsford Crown Court that Mr Odewale was a deeply dishonest man who would 'not recognise the truth if it stood up and bit him'. The Court of Appeal found that this had overstepped the mark so as to give an impression of bias and allowed the appeals.

In April 2005, Mrs Justice Rafferty, a High Court judge, got into trouble over an 'outrageous' after dinner speech she had given for the Association of Chief Police Officers. The speech had apparently included some rather dubious jokes about regional stereotypes.

In July 2005, Judge Medawar, QC, a judge hearing cases at Snaresbrook Crown Court gained a great deal of press coverage for his apparent rudeness to counsel while hearing cases. The Court of Appeal was reported to have quashed three convictions in succession from trials over which Judge Medawar had presided. However, it was also noted in the press that Justice Medawar had reached the compulsory age of retirement.

And finally, a civil judge in trouble: in November 2005, it was reported that in a case relating to injuries from a wheelie bin sustained by a council dust-cart worker heard at Southend county court (*Baird v Thurrock BC*), Judge Yelton gave such a short judgment that the reasons for his decision in favour of the worker were not sufficiently explained. The Court of Appeal therefore, with regret, allowed the council's appeal and remitted the case to be reheard.

## General disciplinary action for judges, falling short of removal

The Constitutional Reform Act 2005 gives the Lord Chief Justice, with the *agreement* of the Lord Chancellor, powers to **discipline judges** in the following manner:

- To give **formal advice, warning** or **reprimand** (not applicable to Justices of the Supreme Court).
- To **suspend** any person subject to criminal proceedings, a sentence or in certain cases, a conviction, from judicial office.
- To **suspend** any senior judge if Parliament is in the process of seeking to remove that person; the same may be applied to any judge who is under investigation for an offence.

A judge who has been **suspended** is not allowed to carry out any functions of the judicial office.

A new opportunity for court users to complain about rude or inappropriate judicial conduct, associated with the 2005 Act, is provided by the creation of an **Office for Judicial Complaints**. The way in which public complaints are handled by this agency, and also the investigation of complaints about the judicial appointments process, is overseen, from April 2006, by a **Judicial Appointments and Conduct Ombudsman**. Lord Falconer, in announcing the latter initiative in 2005, said:

> *This new office, created as part of a wider constitutional reform package, will have a vital role to play in ensuring the integrity and transparency of the new framework for judicial appointments and the judicial system as a whole.*

## Judicial retirement

Judges must now retire at 70, though in limited circumstances they can continue beyond that age under provisions in the **Judicial Pensions and Retirement Act 1993**. For example, some retired senior judges hear cases on a part-time basis, though when they reach the age of 75 they become ineligible to carry out further judicial duties. The issue of judicial pensions raised controversy in 2005 because of Government plans to place limits on the tax relief allowed on pensions, with some judges threatening to stand down unless concessions are made. The real reason for this disquiet is that a judicial career – whilst attractive – can be far less lucrative than the Bar, so judges are basically asking to be treated well in retirement for the financial sacrifices they have already made. They also point out that a disadvantageous pension, in addition to a probable cut in salary at the time of entering the profession, might start to put barristers off joining the judiciary. (Be aware, however, that the limit on tax relief the judges are complaining about will be £1.5 million!)

**Exercise 8.1: Recap on judges**

(1) Identify the following judges or judicial titles:

(a) Most senior judge in the English legal system.
(b) Head of the Chancery Division of the High Court.
(c) Lowest tier of the judicial hierarchy, hearing cases in the county court.
(d) Head of the Civil Court of Appeal.
(e) Part-time judges in the Crown Court and county court.
(f) Judges of the House of Lords.
(g) Judges of the Court of Appeal.

(2) With which aspects of the judiciary topic would you associate:

(a) The Judicial Studies Board.
(b) Rights of audience.
(c) Security of tenure.
(d) Misbehaviour.

(3) Provide the following facts:

(a) Age of judicial retirement.
(b) Rights of audience requirements for judges in the House of Lords and, by contrast, of judges below the High Court level.
(c) Name of the Act that allows judges to be suspended, in certain circumstances.
(d) Difference between the Commission for Judicial Appointments and the Judicial Appointments Commission.
(e) Name of the action, brought by aggrieved citizens, which enables judges to maintain a check over executive power.

For Answers, please turn to p 338.

## INDEPENDENCE OF THE JUDICIARY

As we have seen in Chapter 1, Parliament is perceived as the supreme law-making power in the constitution and judges merely play a '*declaratory role*' in the courts. However, the accuracy of this theoretical position, in practice, is open to question (a point illustrated by the judicial law-making discussed in Chapters 3 and 4). The **independence of the judiciary** is clearly established in practice, and this puts the judicial role in a powerful position in the 'separation of powers'. Moreover, the Government has legislated to this effect in the Constitutional Reform Act 2005: according to s 3, titled 'Guarantee of continued judicial independence', there is a duty on 'all with responsibility for matters relating to the judiciary or otherwise to the administration of justice' – and explicitly the Lord Chancellor and Government Ministers – to **uphold** the 'continued independence of the judiciary'. The Lord Chancellor is also required to take into account the need to defend judicial independence. The provisions are significant because they recognise the changing relationship between executive and judiciary in the constitutional reform process and use statute law to re-state an old principle.

The relationship between the judges and the other powers is illustrated by the following:

- The judges are paid their salaries out of a **Consolidated Fund,** which is administered independently of Parliament.
- The judges keep a check on the executive through the mechanism of **judicial review.**

**IT'S A FACT!**

**8.3: Government and judiciary clash over independence of the judiciary**

Relations between the Government and the judiciary almost reached a constitutional crisis point in 2006, with senior Government figures attacking the decisions of judges in judicial review and human rights cases before the courts. The following examples illustrate the fractious relationship between the Government and the judiciary in recent times.

- The Prime Minister and the Home Secretary attacking a decision by a High Court Judge, Mr Justice Sullivan, when he allowed nine Afghan asylum-seekers who had hijacked a plane to stay in the country: the ruling was described by the Prime Minister as 'an abuse of common sense' and by Mr Reid, the Home Secretary, as 'inexplicable or bizarre to the general public'. The Government also responded fiercely to another recent decision by Mr Justice Sullivan which found the Government's 'control orders' for terrorist suspects in breach of Art 5 of the European Convention on Human Rights (June 2006).
- The Home Secretary, backed by the Prime Minister, attacked 'soft sentencing' in two high-profile cases relating to child sex offenders (see also coverage in Chapter 14). The Prime Minister was reported as saying that the public's 'common sense view of right and wrong' had become disconnected from the values 'reflected in judicial decisions'. The Lord Chancellor acted as a mediator, interpreting the Prime Minister's words not as an attack on judges but as recognition that in certain areas, such as sentencing and the release of potentially dangerous prisoners, 'public safety comes first'.
- The Prime Minister called for a 're-balancing' of rights and responsibilities, in May 2006, so that public safety would have to be given greater weight over concerns about civil liberties. In an implicit criticism of the way in which judges have been applying the Human Rights Act 1998 (one of the most radical pieces of legislation associated with the Prime Minister's 'New Labour' project) he said that 'We (the Government) should not have to fight continual legal battles to deport people committing serious crimes or inciting terrorism'.

These arguments also raged in the media, with the tabloids, in particular, lining up to condemn the judges on sentencing and the broadsheets in profound disagreement about the merits of the Human Rights Act 1998 (contrast *The Independent*, 27/6/06, in favour, with *The Sunday Telegraph*, 14/5/06, strongly against). Lord Woolf, a former Lord Chief Justice, criticised the Government for making comments that were 'ill-informed', undermined public confidence in the judiciary and, indeed, damaged the independence of the judiciary.

However, two commentators, both highly respected legal academics, made perhaps the most telling observations on these events. Vernon Bogdanor, Gresham Professor of Law at Oxford University, told *The Times* (31/5/06) that 'There is a clash between two conflicting constitutional principles – the principle of the **sovereignty of Parliament** and the principle of the **rule of law** . . . The Government believes that issues of human rights should be settled by Parliament. The judges that they should be settled by the courts.' He believes that the outcome of this clash will be a new constitutional settlement, though whether the Human Rights Act 1998 will survive this process remains to be seen, and is perhaps unlikely. Jeffrey Jowell, Professor of Public Law at University College, London, in a letter to *The Times* (16/5/06) pointed out the irony of the Government's combative stance towards the judiciary, given its very recent commitment, in the Constitutional Reform Act 2005, that all ministers of the Crown should 'uphold the continued independence of the judiciary'.

What do you think about this issue? Should Government Ministers be attacking the judges in this way? Are they justified in doing so? What does this issue tell you about constitutional principles such as the 'separation of powers'? Are they working? How have claims relating to the Human Rights Act 1998 provoked a clash between parliamentary sovereignty and the rule of law? What do these constitutional terms mean? (Refer back to Chapter 1 for a reminder.)

How important is the principle of the 'independence of the judiciary' in a modern democracy?

- The judges apply the intentions of Parliament in the courts through the process of **statutory interpretation**. This is the traditional position. More recently, however, the judges have tended to look to the purpose of the legislation rather than the strict wording of the statute.

Indeed, the relationship between the courts and Parliament is now very different to its traditional roots. This is largely because of two important factors: judges will now acknowledge that they do, *in fact*, **make and change the law** through **judicial precedent** and **statutory interpretation**; and judges now have the power, under the **Human Rights Act 1998**, to *declare* **Acts of Parliament 'incompatible' with the European Convention on Human Rights.**

Some writers are uncomfortable with the judges having *too much* law-making power, given that they are **appointed** and *not* elected. Moreover, as Griffith observed (see p 154 above), their shared backgrounds, education and networks mean that they might, at times, exhibit common prejudices.

Four further points need to be made about the judges in relation to their independence and its consequences:

- Judges can **speak out in public**. This exposes them to the full glare of media publicity and is a judicial freedom that must be exercised with a great deal of care.
- If judges do impede the course of justice (for example, if they fall asleep, as occasionally happens!) then the **appeal process** will assist complainants.
- Judges enjoy **immunity from suits for defamation**: they cannot be sued for anything they say in court, though clearly they have to be mindful of the response of the press if they do make controversial comments.
- Judges will be **disqualified** from hearing cases in which they have a personal interest. Any judicial bias would lead the courts to be in **breach** of **Art 6** of the **European Convention on Human Rights.**

*Dimes v Grand Junction Canal* (1852), where a judge presided over a case involving a company in which he held shares, when he should clearly have declared his interest in the case, was an early common law statement that judicial bias would not be tolerated. After the *Pinochet* case (2000), judges will also be disqualified from cases in which the judge has a personal interest, such as a commitment to a certain political viewpoint.

The *Pinochet* case concerned the arrest of the former Chilean dictator, **General Pinochet**, while he was receiving medical treatment in England, and the subsequent proceedings for extradition to Spain on the basis of crimes of murder and torture allegedly committed by Pinochet during his time as the Chilean leader. Extradition is, in simple terms, the handing over of a person accused of committing crimes to the State that wishes to put that person on trial. Pinochet argued that he could not be extradited since he enjoyed 'diplomatic immunity' as a former head of State.

The House of Lords held, with Lord Hoffmann supporting the majority view, that he should be extradited. However, it later emerged that Lord Hoffmann was an unpaid director of Amnesty International, a human rights and civil liberties pressure group that had made representations to the court during the case to have Pinochet extradited. Thus, Pinochet's lawyers seized on the *conflict of interest*, and a second seven-member House of Lords Committee was assembled to rehear the case and consider the impact of Lord Hoffmann's failure to reveal his interest. The outcome was that by neglecting to withdraw from the case, Lord Hoffmann created a conflict of interest, and such a conflict would disqualify the original judgment. However, while the rehearing supported the original House of Lords' decision to extradite Pinochet, it did so on narrower grounds.

There was no finding of judicial bias, by contrast, in *Hart v Relentless Records Ltd* (2002). Here, the judge had held informal discussions with counsel in the 'judge's corridor' and the claimants believed that this had prevented them from having a fair trial. However, it was held, by the Chancery Division, that such informal discussion was valuable and within the spirit of the Civil Procedure Rules in helping the parties towards a settlement.

**HINTS AND TIPS**

The topic of judges encourages both **factual recall** and a **critical, questioning approach** to the law. It is clearly useful to understand which judges sit in which courts and how their roles differ, based on whether they are trial or appellate judges and whether the law is civil or criminal. I thoroughly recommend the **Judiciary of England and Wales website** provided *below* as an aid to learning more about the judges, what they look like, what they wear and what they do; it is also a fun, interactive site with plenty of exercises.

Examiners often focus on the aspects of the topic set out in Table 8.3 (on p 167: **appointments** and **training**) for **descriptive questions**, though note that each of these areas might also lead to **evaluative** discussion (on background and diversity of the judiciary, for example). The creation of the **Judicial Appointments Commission (JAC)** has brought both *consistency* and *transparency* to the appointments process, though note that differences remain in the *formal appointment* of judicial posts once the JAC has made a recommendation that the Lord Chancellor has accepted (Lords Justices and above: by the Queen 'on the advice of the Prime Minister'; High Court judges, Circuit judges, recorders and district judges by the Queen); you should also *revise* the **qualifications** required for appointment to the main judicial posts.

The other popular area of **descriptive questioning** relates to the **removal of judges** and the level of **security of tenure** that the judges enjoy. In answering questions in this area, you must *distinguish* the **senior judges** (High Court judges and above), who have *strong* security of tenure, from the less senior judges.

As we have seen, there are a number of areas of critical evaluation that could be developed in this topic, such as the **background of the judges** and the **independence of the judiciary**. You should take account of the *constitutional background* (such as separation of powers theory and parliamentary sovereignty) in tackling both. The following factors would be relevant in discussing judicial independence, for example:

- The ability of the judiciary to challenge executive decisions through the mechanism of **judicial review**.
- The significance of s 3 of the **Constitutional Reform Act 2005**.
- The **security of tenure** of the **senior judges**.
- The fact that the judiciary are paid out of the **Consolidated Fund** and are not therefore subject to parliamentary control in this area.
- The capacity for judges to *develop areas of law* through **judicial precedent** and **statutory interpretation**, rather than rely on Parliament.
- The importance of judges declaring any *conflicts of interest* (consider the ***Pinochet*** case).
- The new power to *declare* **Acts of Parliament incompatible with the European Convention on Human Rights under the Human Rights Act 1998**.
- The point that judges are appointed and *represent* a **narrow social/academic background**.

**Judicial independence** is clearly important for judges to carry out their roles effectively. Judges could not undertake effective **judicial review**, for example, if the executive could seek to punish 'difficult judges'; neither could they function with any confidence if they were subject to the whims of Parliament on the payment of salaries and less favourable rules on security of tenure.

## Useful website addresses

| | |
|---|---|
| Commission for Judicial Appointments | www.cja.gov.uk |
| Department for Constitutional Affairs | www.dca.gov.uk |
| Judicial Studies Board | www.jsboard.co.uk |
| Judiciary of England and Wales | www.judiciary.gov.uk |
| *Materials directly for AS studies:* | |
| John Deft (St Brendan's Sixth Form College) | www.stbrn.ac.uk/other/depts/law |
| Asif Tufal | www.a-level-law.com |

Table 8.3 Judges: examples for descriptive questions

*Context of constitutional reforms: creation of Department for Constitutional Affairs, Lord Chief Justice replaces the Lord Chancellor as head of an independent judiciary, creation of an independent Judicial Appointments Commission and a new Supreme Court planned for 2008/9 (Constitutional Reform Act 2005).*

| *Selection and appointment* | *Training* |
|---|---|
| Lack of transparency in the existing selection methods – such as the 'secret soundings' approach for senior judges – leads to calls for reform. | Training undertaken by the Judicial Studies Board. |
| Government responds with proposal for a Judicial Appointments Commission: Parliament approves – Constitutional Reform Act 2005. | Relates largely to the less senior judges. |
| Judicial Appointments Commission begins work in April 2006: has balanced membership and a lay chairman. | Induction courses provided for Recorders (Criminal Law Induction Course), together with Criminal Continuation Seminars for Crown Court practitioners. |
| Special selection arrangements made for senior judges and Justices of the Supreme Court. | Induction courses provided for recorders and district judges (Civil Law Induction Course). Civil Continuation Seminars and special Family law seminars held annually. |
| Judicial Appointments Commission selects; Lord Chancellor can accept, reject (once) or request that a candidate be reconsidered. (Powers of rejection limited.) | *Ad hoc* training on human rights, civil justice reforms and equal opportunities. |
| Formal appointment by Queen (on the 'advice of the Prime Minister' for very senior judges). Formal appointment by the Queen for High Court judges and below in the judicial hierarchy. | Involvement of judges, academics and Home Office and Department of Constitutional Affairs civil servants in judicial training. |
| Note qualifications required for each judicial post (for example, the need to have held a judicial office for a set period, or 'rights of audience' for set periods of time). | |

# Lay persons in the English legal system

This topic enables you:

- To appreciate the contribution of the general public to the systems of criminal and civil justice.
- To understand the respective roles of jurors and lay magistrates, and recognise the differences in selection that characterise these lay persons.
- To develop knowledge of how jurors and lay magistrates carry out their roles in practice.
- To form opinions on the future for jurors and lay magistrates, based on an examination of their value to the English legal system.
- To broaden your understanding of the courts structure in criminal and civil law.
- To underline the differences between criminal offences – summary, triable either way, and indictable.
- To identify the process of law reform as it applies to this topic.

Lay people – persons neither legally qualified nor paid for carrying out legal services – play a far larger role in the criminal justice system than is perhaps credited in the media. The vast majority of criminal trials in this country are actually presided over by **lay magistrates**. For the most serious criminal offences, defendants are tried before a judge *and* a **lay jury** of 12 members in the **Crown Court**. There are over 28,000 lay magistrates in the English legal system and around 200,000 jurors hearing cases every year.

While this chapter focuses on lay magistrates and juries, there are other examples of lay involvement in the legal system. **Lay tribunal members**, for example, accompany a legally qualified chairperson to decide tribunal cases. These lay persons can generally offer specialist skills and knowledge, which will be of benefit to the tribunal in determining the cases that come before it (see Chapter 7).

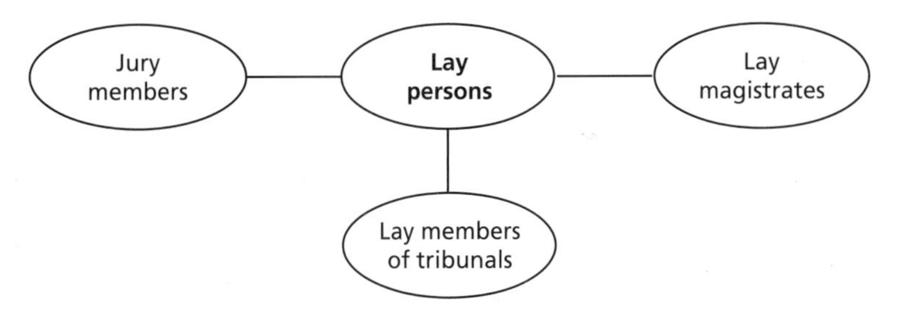


## JURIES

Trial of criminals by jury emerged in the thirteenth century to replace 'trial by ordeal' and other rather cruel forms of determining guilt. Juries were initially chosen for their local knowledge and as '**witnesses to the justice process**'. The role changed, in time, so that jurors became **judges of fact**.

*Bushell's Case* (1670) established that jurors were not to be punished for acquitting a person even where judges recommended conviction. In *Bushell's Case*, the jurors had been sent to prison for acquitting William Penn, a Quaker, of riotous assembly. Such a decision went against the express wishes of the trial judge, but the jurors were later released by the Lord Chancellor. This marked the beginnings of the principle of **jury equity**, which established the independence of the jury in coming to decisions. This has meant, in more recent times, that juries have decided cases in ways that would not conform strictly to the law.

Table 9.1 indicates the way in which trial by jury has developed in civil and criminal cases to the present day.

Table 9.1 The development and progress of jury trials

| *Civil law* | *Criminal law* |
|---|---|
| • Before 1854, juries were used in all civil cases. However, law reform in the nineteenth century, followed by the **Administration of Justice (Miscellaneous Provisions) Act 1933**, abolished civil juries in most cases.<br>• Under s 69 of the **Supreme Court Act 1981**, the right to a jury trial is effectively limited to four main civil areas:<br>  • fraud<br>  • defamation (libel and slander)<br>  • malicious prosecution<br>  • tort of false imprisonment.<br>• Generally civil juries will consist of 12 members, though on rare occasions civil juries of eight may be used in cases of malicious prosecution and false imprisonment. | • 'Trial by jury' has become essential to the role of the Crown Court, but very few criminal cases are actually tried by jury. It has been estimated that 85 per cent are summary (tried by magistrates); 12 per cent are either way and tried by magistrates; 2 per cent are guilty pleas/acquittals in Crown Court; only about 1 per cent are, in practice, tried by jury.<br>• Since 1973, the right to jury trial has been removed in certain cases (especially terrorism cases) in Northern Ireland. This was done in response to the intimidation of jurors. Such trials take place in Diplock courts.<br>• **The Criminal Justice Act 2003** has reformed the criteria for jury selection, provided for trial by judge alone where there is a 'real and present danger' of jury intimidation and set the foundation for the use of juries in serious fraud trials to be reviewed. The Government's further attempts to restrict trial by jury at the Bill stage of this legislation – such as by allowing defendants to opt for trial by judge alone – were met both in Parliament, and in the media, with firm resistance.<br>• At the time of writing, the Government has signalled its readiness to remove trial by jury from serious fraud trials, though this will be strongly challenged in Parliament. |

Investigation into the usefulness of juries in fraud trials, particularly criminal serious fraud trials, was undertaken by the **Roskill Committee on Fraud Trials (1986)**. It recommended the abolition of trial by jury in these cases, a point that was supported by the **Auld Review (2001)** and which the Government managed to include, despite much controversy, in the **Criminal Justice Act 2003**, at s 43, subject to a guarantee from the Government that the change would not be made without further consultation as to the alternatives to jury trial.

The use of juries in the area of civil law referred to as defamation has also been brought into question by the **Faulks Committee on Defamation** (1975). While there has been no legislation in this area, the courts have begun to restrict juries in these trials (see coverage of civil juries at pp 172–3).

## Let's look at cases: A modern reminder of the role and independence of juries (*R v Wang* (2005) )

Bringing to mind *Bushell's Case* (1670), the House of Lords recently upheld the position that a judge can never tell a jury to convict. The defendant, Mr Wang, was a Buddhist and practised Shaolin, a martial art, which required, within its training and progression regime, mastery in the use of up to 18 weapons. He was charged with a breach of s 139(1) of the **Criminal Justice Act 1988**, that is having an article with a blade or point in a public place, when found to be carrying a curved sword and a Gurkha-style knife (a 'willow leaf knife') in a bag at a seaside railway station. (The bag had been stolen by a thief and then recovered by police, who were shocked when they discovered its contents.) His defence was that, under s 139(4) and (5), he could prove good reasons, supported by his religious beliefs, to be carrying these articles. Informing counsel that he could see no defence to the charge, despite protests from Mr Wang's counsel, Judge Pearson directed the jury to convict him as a matter of law; the matter of the lawful defence under s 139(4) and (5) was not put to the jury. In accordance with this, the jury convicted and Mr Wang was sentenced, being conditionally discharged for 12 months with forfeiture orders made.

The Court of Appeal had upheld the decision on the basis that this was a situation where the defendant had been unable to discharge the burden of proving the 'lawful defence'. However, the **House of Lords disagreed**. The view was unanimously taken on a **point of law of general public importance** that 'there are no circumstances in which a judge is entitled to direct a jury to return a verdict of guilty'. Even if a judge would consider any other conclusion than his own to be perverse, he must leave any such matters of evidence to be determined by the jury. Mr Wang's conviction was accordingly quashed.

## The role of juries

We have noted, above, that juries assumed the role of **judges of the facts** over the course of time. This role consists of listening carefully to the evidence presented and to the directions of the judge in the case. The **judge** is, by contrast, the **master of law** and will ensure that the jury's task is clear by *summing up* the case in legal terms when all of the evidence has been heard. It is then for the jury to discuss the case, in **secret**, and come to a decision about it that all or, if discussions are lengthy, a specified majority, can agree upon.

In criminal cases, this decision is the **verdict**. The jury decides whether the defendant should be found **guilty** *or* **not guilty** of the crime with which he or she has been charged. A verdict of **guilty** secures a *conviction* for the **prosecution**, whereas a verdict of **not guilty** leads to the defendant's *acquittal* (that is, release). In the event of a conviction, it is the role of the **judge** alone to determine the **sentence** to be served by the offender.

In **civil cases**, the role of the jury is different. Here, the jury decides the **defendant's liability** and the **amount of damages to be awarded** (see pp 172–3 below).

## Juries in civil law

Juries in civil cases have declined to the extent that they are used in *less* than 1 per cent of cases. The right to a jury trial in civil law is restricted generally to four areas: defamation; fraud; malicious prosecution; and false imprisonment. Today, **defamation (especially libel) cases** constitute the majority of civil jury cases. However, the discretion to have a jury has been exercised very occasionally in personal injury cases.

After the **Faulks Committee on Defamation 1975** recommended that judges should decide whether a jury is appropriate in civil cases, and the conditions for granting a jury trial were laid down in **s 69** of the **Supreme Court Act 1981**, claimants have been active in trying to limit the use of the jury. The prevailing view was set in the case of *Goldsmith v Pressdram Ltd* (1988), where it was suggested that the emphasis should be *against* trial by jury in defamation cases. In the so-called McLibel case (*McDonald's Corporation v Steel and Morris* (1997)), where McDonald's won a legal battle to have their libel action against two animal rights activists heard by the judge rather than a jury, the case was considered to be too complex for a jury trial. However, concerns about the equality of the parties in this case, and the lack of procedural fairness to the defendants, have been highlighted in a European Court of Human Rights decision in the defendants' favour, thus perhaps casting doubt on the approach to such cases in the UK courts (*Steel and Morris v UK* (2005)).

A key area of concern about juries in defamation cases is their enthusiasm to award huge amounts of damages. In *Sutcliffe v Pressdram Ltd* (1990), for example, the initial award was £600,000 to Sonia Sutcliffe, wife of the Yorkshire Ripper, who had been libelled by the satirical magazine Private Eye (with the amount later reduced on appeal). The law is, however, responding to these concerns: the **Courts and Legal Services Act 1990** gave power to the Court of Appeal to change the amount of damages awarded, if excessive. This occurred in *Rantzen v Mirror Group Newspapers* (1993), where an award in favour of Esther Rantzen, the TV presenter, amounting to £250,000, was reduced to £110,000. An 'excessive sum' is one that is larger than 'necessary'.

The **Defamation Act 1996** retained the role of the jury to assess damages, but a judge may now guide a jury as to the amount of damages. Common law support for this position can be found in the earlier case of *Elton John v Mirror Group Newspapers* (1995), relating to allegations that Elton John had an eating disorder: damages were accordingly reduced by the Court of Appeal from £350,000 to £75,000, with the view expressed that judges should be allowed to assist juries with their deliberations as to the appropriate amount of damages to award.

The Court of Appeal's unusual decision to set aside a jury verdict in the *Grobbelaar v News Group Newspapers Ltd* libel trial (2001) once again raised concerns about the suitability of juries to hear libel cases. The trial, concerning whether the former Liverpool goalkeeper, Bruce Grobbelaar, had accepted money to influence the results of games, led to a jury verdict that was considered perverse in the circumstances (finding in favour of Grobbelaar as against compelling evidence that had been amassed by the defendant newspaper, *The Sun*). The Court of Appeal therefore exercised its right to set aside a civil jury verdict on the grounds of a *perverse* decision (an option that is not available in criminal law, despite proposals in the **Auld Review 2001**). However, in a further twist to this case, the House of Lords (2002) subsequently restored the jury's verdict, with an accompanying award to Grobbelaar of just £1 in damages!

## Jury selection

Jurors are selected at random from the **electoral register**. This is the responsibility of a **Central Jury Summoning Bureau (CJSB)**, and names are generated by **computer**. More than 12 jurors are called by the Summoning Officers of the court to be selected as a **'panel'** for each case, because some may be disqualified or excused for certain reasons. There are some members of the community who will not form part of the selection process. Those who are not registered as voters and those who are homeless will not therefore have a chance to be jurors.

The **Criminal Justice Act 2003** has reformed the rules on jury selection at s 321, referring to Schedule 33 of the Act, and amends the **Juries Act 1974, s 1**. Jury service is available for persons aged 18–70 whose names appear on the electoral register. Moreover, such persons must have been a UK resident for at least five years (from the age of 13). **'Every person'** who meets these general criteria is qualified to serve as a juror in the Crown Court for criminal cases and the High Court and county court for civil cases, *unless* they are a **mentally disordered person** or **disqualified**, generally by virtue of **conduct**.

A **mentally disordered person** is a person suffering from mental illness, psychopathic disorder or mental handicap and accordingly is either a resident in a hospital or institution, or attends a medical practitioner for treatment. The definition also includes persons identified as mentally disordered by reference to criteria in the **Mental Health Act 1983**.

A person will be **disqualified** from jury service if they:

- are on **bail** in criminal proceedings;
- have *at any time* been sentenced to a **custodial term** (imprisonment/detention) for a period of **five years or more;**
- have, *in the last ten years*, been subject to a **custodial term,** a **suspended sentence** or a specified **community sentence;**
- have been convicted under a **court-martial** and sentenced to a period of **detention.**

Although jury service can also be **deferred** for various reasons – such as the observance of religious holidays and the taking of examinations – and also **excused** – where a person can show it would be unreasonable for them to carry out the service within the following 12 months – the reforms effected by the Criminal Justice Act 2003 have considerably widened the pool of potential jurors. Prior to this Act, many middle-class professionals could avoid jury service either through being part of a profession deemed ineligible (such as lawyers and judges), or owing to excusals 'as of right' (such as MPs and medical practitioners): today, **all** may be called for jury service. The Lord Chancellor, under s 9 of the Juries Act 1974, has issued guidelines for summoning officers on deferrals and excusals under the new regime; and Lord

Woolf, as the then Lord Chief Justice, issued guidance to judges on 'dealing sensitively and sympathetically' with jurors whose 'professional' and 'public service' commitments impacted on their ability to fulfil jury service duties (Practice Direction, Jury Service: Excusal, 2005).

Under s 10 of the Juries Act 1974, the judge has the power to discharge members of the jury if it is clear that a juror cannot effectively perform the duty, for example, because of difficulties with language. It is an offence for any person to undertake jury service on behalf of another by assuming the other's name: this is known as **jury personation.** In addition, under s 12 of the Juries Act 1974, the parties to proceedings have the right to challenge the whole panel by claiming that the summoning officer has acted unfairly in the selection process.

## Developing the subject 9.1: Some implications of changes to the jury selection rules

The **Criminal Justice Act 2003** reformed the rules on jury selection, substituting a new s 1 into the **Juries Act 1974** so that groups previously considered ineligible because of their involvement in the administration of justice – such as police officers, lawyers and judges – could now be selected for jury service. The cases of *R v Abdroikov* (2005) and *R v Green* (2005) involved appeals by the defendants complaining that the composition of the jury in both cases included a **serving police officer** and that this gave rise to concerns about *bias*. In a third case, *R v Williamson* (2005) (as above), the defendant complained that a **solicitor employed by the Crown Prosecution Service** on the jury led to the concern of *bias*.

The leading judgment for the three cases heard together was delivered by the Lord Chief Justice (then Lord Woolf) in the Court of Appeal. The defendants had relied on the **right to a fair trial in Art 6** of the ECHR, arguing that any *actual, or apparent, bias* would infringe that right. The Crown, on the other hand, pointed out that the 2003 Act was the product of the **democratically elected legislature (Parliament)** and had the **legitimate purpose of maximising the pool of people available to perform jury service**.

Lord Woolf rejected the defendants' submissions that membership of law enforcement or legal professions should disqualify individuals from jury service. On the facts, there was no question of the three jurors actually showing any partiality. Lord Woolf stated: 'When they became members of the jury, they were not becoming members of the jury in their capacity as policemen or prosecuting solicitors. Having been randomly selected, they served on the jury in the same way as any other members of the public in their capacity as citizens eligible for jury service'. The parameters within which juries operated, including the **jury oath** and **instructions from the judge and court staff**, prevented the possibility of bias. Whilst jurors with prejudices did pose dangers, the majority verdict system was a useful safeguard against them. Jury domination by one individual on the basis of his/her profession was perceived as unlikely. Where a juror had any special knowledge of the case, or individuals involved in it, the onus was on that juror to disclose the fact to the judge. It was not desirable for those involved in the administration of justice to be summoned for jury service to courts where the likelihood of special knowledge was especially great. Lord Woolf concluded that a 'fair-minded and informed observer' would not identify a 'real possibility' that a juror was biased just because of their profession.

**Discussion points:**

- Do you agree with the decision in this case? Should jury selection have been reformed?
- Has the Government, by reforming jury selection, solved one problem (that of maximising the pool) but created another (the apparent potential for bias)?

**Exercise 9.1: Quick quiz on jury selection**

**Advise the following individuals whether they will have to undertake jury service:**

(1) An MP.
(2) A police officer.
(3) A person with severe clinical depression.
(4) A 75 year-old pensioner.
(5) A 17 year-old student due to take her AS examinations.
(6) An 18 year-old student due to take his A2 examinations.
(7) A 25 year-old asylum seeker.
(8) A person with a recent conviction for assault occasioning actual bodily harm.
(9) A member of the clergy.
(10) A person currently on bail.

For Answer, please turn to p 339.

On a final practical note, you will recall that members of the public generally become eligible to undertake jury service when they reach the age of 18. If this applies to you, just think – you could be the next person to be selected!

## Practical aspects of juries in criminal cases

### Challenging jurors

Once a panel of jurors has been assembled (referred to as the **empanelling** of the jury), it might be the case that the parties wish to challenge certain jurors and thereby have them removed from the trial prior to the process of being sworn in. In a criminal Crown Court trial, for example, the **prosecution can challenge any number of jurors** (a process in which the juror is asked to **'stand by for the Crown'**). The defence can only **'challenge for cause'**, for example, because a juror knows one of the parties, or there is reason to think that the appropriate qualifying criteria for jury selection have not been met.

## Jury vetting

This is when members of the jury are **checked** to see if they are appropriate for the case being tried. Checks can be made on jurors to see, for example, whether they have a criminal record (*R v Mason* (1980)), since there might be instances where such information has not been brought to the attention of the Summoning Bureau. However, political vetting of the juries by the intelligence services is more controversial. In *R v Ponting* (1985), a case involving national security, many jurors were 'vetted' for political reasons. This case is explained in 'Let's look at cases' on p 176.

## Nature of the verdicts in criminal trials

Juries must try to reach a **unanimous verdict** for **two hours and ten minutes** at least, though beyond this time the judge has the discretion to ask for a majority verdict (and this can, in practice, be much longer than two hours and ten minutes). Juries may only then return a **majority verdict**, which amounts to no fewer than ten members of a jury of 11 or 12. Ronald Thwaites QC has argued in the *Times Law Supplement* (2001) that this area should be

## Let's look at cases: Jury equity and *R v Ponting* (1985)

The Ponting case related to the **Falklands War of 1982**, which was fought between **Britain** and **Argentina** over control of the Falkland Islands: Britain was successful in protecting its Crown colony. During the hostilities, a British naval vessel sank an enemy ship called the *General Belgrano*, causing the deaths of 323 members of its crew. However, the ship was attacked when it was not posing any danger; it was actually moving away from the 'zone of exclusion' that the British Navy was seeking to enforce. Ponting, a civil servant, leaked information to the press that the ship had posed no military threat when it had been attacked (a claim that has been subsequently questioned by historians). Ponting was prosecuted for a breach of the **Official Secrets Act 1911**. The role of the jury was controversial in this case, and jury vetting was undertaken to ensure that jurors had no political leanings that could affect their deliberations. Even so, the jury *refused* to convict Ponting, even though he had committed a technical *breach* of the **official secrets legislation**. This is a striking example of **jury equity**: in other words, the jury, as the masters of the facts, were prepared to acquit a defendant who would have been found guilty under a strict application of the law. As Brain Redmond, Ponting's solicitor, reportedly said at the time, 'The Government have been hijacked by a gang of 12'.

**Discussion points:**

- If you were a member of the jury on this case – and clearly you are working here with just a tiny amount of information, rather than the evidence in the case – what position would you recommend to the jury foreman: guilty or not guilty?
- Is this case about the distinction between law and conscience, or a more complex mixture of the two?
- Does *R v Ponting* support the case of those who argue that juries should give reasons for their decisions?
- Should judges ever be able to overturn 'perverse jury verdicts' on appeal in criminal cases (as has occurred in civil cases)?

reformed. He believes that the system should be changed so that majority verdicts can be delivered as soon as the jury is ready, rather than having to wait for the judge to allow them: to maintain the present system is to perpetuate wasted time and expense.

If more than two people drop out of a jury there should be a **retrial**. Eleven members will be acceptable if, for example, one juror falls ill during the trial. This was the case in the high-profile criminal trial of Barry George, accused and convicted of murdering the BBC presenter, Jill Dando.

## Contempt of court

The deliberations of the jury should be **secret**. It is a contempt of court to reveal jury secrets (**Contempt of Court Act 1981, s 8**). This can result in a prison sentence or fine. However, on occasions, jury secrets have been revealed in the interests of justice. In the case of *Vaise v Delavat* (1785) it was discovered, for example, that a jury had decided a criminal case by tossing a coin! (See 'Let's look at cases' opposite for a more modern example of this.) Moreover, in *R v Young* (1995), the jurors were taken to a hotel and a group of jurors, in the course of their deliberations, tried to 'contact' the deceased murder victim using a 'ouija board' (a device used by spiritualists to contact the dead, consisting of a ring of numbers and letters of the alphabet). The board apparently spelled out the following – 'STEPHEN YOUNG DONE IT'. When the court found out about this a retrial was ordered. However, it was suggested that if this had happened in the jury room, rather than a hotel, the verdict would probably have remained as it was.

It has been suggested that two reforms – that a jury should give reasons for its decision and that research into jury deliberations should be allowed – would resolve the sort of problems outlined above. On the first point, the **Auld Review 2001** has suggested some reform. However, it did not go as far as to suggest that the Contempt of Court Act 1981 be amended to allow general research into juries, though it did contemplate inquiries into the jury's deliberations where alleged 'improprieties' had taken place. The Government has yet to be persuaded of these reforms.

## Let's look at cases: Recent cases relating to jury secrecy

- *R v Mirza*/*R v Connor and Rollock* (2004), concerned jointly-heard appeals where complaints had been made about conduct in the jury room: in *Mirza*, an indecent assault case, the trial judge received concerns from a juror of **'racial bias'** in the jury room; in *Connor and Rollock*, a juror complained that other members of the panel had been prepared to **'toss a coin'** to determine the verdict (this is a modern example of the *Vaise v Delavat* phenomenon: see p 176). The House of Lords dismissed the appeals, which had been brought under Art 6 ECHR (right to a fair trial), defending the principle of jury confidentiality and the ability of jurors to discuss cases in a full and frank manner without judicial interference. However, Lord Hope stressed the need for jurors to receive clear information on reporting irregularities in the jury room and for trial courts to inform appeal courts if such allegations had been made.
- *R v Smith*/*R v Mercieca* (2005), concerned appeals against convictions for a number of serious offences of violence and the House of Lords had to consider the response of a trial judge to allegations of **misbehaviour in the jury room**. At trial, a juror handed a note to the judge alleging that 'jurors are being badgered, coerced and intimidated into changing their verdict to that which a certain group of jurors deem to be the right verdict regardless of what the evidence shows' and that, as a result of a bargain being struck by some jurors as to certain counts of the indictment, the verdict would not truly represent what all jurors believed. The House of Lords, following *R v Mirza*, decided that trial judges had to deal with this *not* by encroaching on jury secrecy, but by **providing clear guidelines to the jury** in response to the allegations. In this instance, the trial judge had proceeded correctly, but his guidance was insufficient. The convictions were quashed and the case was remitted to the Court of Appeal to consider whether a retrial should be ordered.

  This case prompted a former senior judge of Northern Ireland, Donald Murray, to write to *The Times* newspaper with the view that justice demanded the need for juries to justify their decisions: 'These cases (ie, *R v Smith*/*R v Mercieca*) expose once again **one of the main weaknesses of jury trial**, namely, that no reasons are, or can be, given for the jury's verdict, and so no one knows how or why they arrived at their verdict.' (*The Times*, 15/4/05.) Further support for this view was provided by the **Michael Jackson trial**, where jurors had appeared on television afterwards to explain their decision, an example some journalists thought the UK could do with adopting.
- In *R v Karakaya* (2005), at the conclusion of a trial relating to sexual offences, a jury bailiff found evidence of information from the internet that had been introduced by a juror to the jury room. This breached an important rule of procedure: no new evidence can be admitted to assist jury deliberations. For these reasons, the convictions were not safe.

*NB: The Lord Chancellor launched a consultation on jury secrecy in 2004.*

## Appeals against jury decisions

In very broad terms, it might be said that there can be no challenge to an **acquittal by jury**. However, the position is no longer so clear-cut.

On technical grounds, the Attorney-General, a senior legal officer of the Government, has the right to appeal on behalf of the prosecution against the procedures relating to an acquittal. This has no impact on the verdict (but only future procedures). The **Auld Review 2001** suggested that an appeal procedure by the prosecution against *perverse decisions* of the jury should be allowed – as it is in civil jury trials (see p 172 above) – though this seems to undermine the principle of **'jury equity'**. The 2002 Government White Paper on the criminal justice system, 'Justice for All', has not supported this view. However, the position on the **'double jeopardy' rule** – that a person cannot be tried for the same offence twice – has changed. Under s 76 of the **Criminal Justice Act 2003**, the prosecution can now apply for an order quashing a person's acquittal by jury and an order for that person to be retried for the same offence. The Court of Appeal's power to make these orders is subject to two significant safeguards:

- Is there **new and compelling evidence** to support a retrial?
- In all the circumstances, is the **order for a retrial in the interests of justice?**

**IT'S A FACT!**

**Double jeopardy**

Cleveland Police have taken advantage of changes to the position on double jeopardy and submitted new evidence to the Court of Appeal in the case of Billy Dunlop, 42, who will be re-tried for the murder of Julie Hogg, 22. Dunlop has already been tried, and acquitted, of her murder. Announced in November 2005, this is the first trial initiated following changes to the rules on double jeopardy.

A retrial can be ordered for all of the following offences in Schedule 5 of the Criminal Justice Act 2003: murder, rape, manslaughter, kidnapping, a range of serious sexual offences, serious drug offences, serious criminal damage offences, war crimes and terrorist offences, and conspiracy offences related to other offences in the list. As a concession to opponents of the Act at Bill stage, the Government did not seek to include some offences, which explains the absence of serious offences such as grievous bodily harm.

If the **jury convicts**, the position on **appeals** is more straightforward. Here, the defendant can appeal to the Court of Appeal against conviction on grounds of law or fact. For fuller coverage of appeals against conviction please see Chapter 6 at pp 121–2.

## Talking from experience: Observing jury trials

An insight that may be gained from observing jury trials in the Crown Court is that juries are sometimes willing to pass notes to the judge when they do not understand a point, or are seeking clarification of the issues. This also occurs when the jury deliberates on its decision: the jurors can, once again, seek clarification of any points that arise.

You might also notice that when counsel for the prosecution or defence raise issues of law, the jury is asked to leave the court. Often, for example, the debate between barristers might involve the admissibility of evidence according to the rules of evidence. This procedure is known in criminal law and evidence as a *voir dire*, or a trial within a trial.

## EVALUATING JURIES

In evaluating juries, the following quotes might provide supporting evidence, inspiration, or open up new ways of looking at the topic (see 'Talking Points' below).

**Talking points . . .**

In favour of trial by jury:

- *'[W]hen a man is on trial for a serious crime . . . then trial by jury has no equal.'* (Lord Denning)
- *'The jury is more than an instrument of justice . . . it is the lamp that shows that freedom lives.'* (Lord Devlin)
- *'Were a dictator to seize power . . . he would abolish or restrict trial by jury. This is because no dictator could afford to leave a person's freedom in the hands of his countrymen.'* (Robert Rhodes QC)

And criticism . . .

- *'Society appears to have an attachment to jury trial which is emotional or sentimental rather than logical.'* (Roskill Committee on Fraud Trials, 1986).
- *'Like motherhood and apple pie, everyone loves democracy and jury trial. But the closer you look at these favourites, the more you see how flawed they are . . . Like democracy, jury trial is worth fighting for. But this support of the process will be wasted if we pretend that its difficulties do not exist.'* (Ian Francis, *New Law Journal*, 2001)
- *'Jury trial has outlived its usefulness. To pretend that it delivers justice is absurd. This archaic theme park democracy is expensive, a waste of time and adds nothing to fair trial. Abolish it.'* (Simon Jenkins, *The Sunday Times*, 12/2/06)

Consider, also, the amusing comments of Trevor Grove in *The Juryman's Tale*:

- *'No one would claim that the jury is a precision instrument for discovering the truth . . . Juries are clumsy, expensive, fallible and slow. But the jury is not only an administrative device. It also has a symbolic and political function. It is Lord Devlin's "lamp that shows that freedom lives". It is Sir William Blackstone's "sacred bulwark of the nation". It is de Tocqueville's "peerless teacher of citizenship". It is Lord Bingham's "safety valve". It is the rope by which the great hot-air balloon of the law is tethered to terra firma. It is a prodigious breeder of metaphors.'*

## Advantages of juries

The main points in favour of juries have been divided into three categories. The coverage of juries in this chapter should provide the necessary elaboration for these main points.

### Trust and confidence of the public in the legal system

- Jury trials are an important part of English legal history. The principle of 'trial by peers' stretches back to **1215 (Magna Carta)**, and *Bushell's Case* (1670) shows that by the seventeenth century, the role of a jury as **'masters of the facts'** had become established.
- A jury trial delivers transparent justice (*'justice is seen to be done'*) since the public plays an important role in the criminal justice process. As David Bean QC, the then Chairman of the Bar Council, was reported as saying in February 2002, 'the evidence is clear: **people trust juries**'.
- Juries provide a panel that, through **random selection**, may be representative of 'all walks of life', whereas a single judge represents only a certain narrow perspective. Therefore it is often argued that 12 persons, with differing perspectives, have a greater chance of achieving justice in a case than one person with a more limited, technical approach.

### The 'lamp that shows that freedom lives': juries as an expression of liberty

- *Ponting's Case* (1984) and *Bushell's Case* (1670) provide clear examples of **jury equity**, where the jury expresses its independence and makes a finding that arguably favours justice over the strict application of law.
- It has been argued that juries are essentially **democratic** and that no dictator would be prepared to allow the freedoms provided by an independent jury system.

### Benefits of juries compared to 'case-hardened' judges

- There is a better chance of acquittal by juries: broadly speaking, 40 per cent acquittals in the Crown Court, in contrast to 25 per cent in the magistrates' courts (Liberty, 2000: see also Vennard, 1985). It might be argued, therefore, that juries do take the **standard of proof** – 'beyond reasonable doubt' – very seriously, and that they will not convict if they are unsure. This also supports the view that it is better for juries to make occasional mistakes by allowing guilty men to go free, than to subject innocent persons to a term of imprisonment. However, the statistics have to be treated with some caution as they conceal more specific information, such as the fact that juries acquit defendants on *all counts* relatively rarely (8.9 per cent in 2001, according to judicial statistics cited in Ward and Wragg, 2005).
- Jury decisions are **collective**, rather than individual: therefore, a range of opinions on the evidence informs a decision and no individual is accountable for taking such a decision alone. It is also beneficial that the jury comes to the courts fresh, often without any preconceptions, whereas an experienced judge in the criminal courts might have developed certain views and prejudices about the sort of offences, and offenders, he or she sees every day. This is why judges are often perceived as 'case-hardened'.

## Disadvantages of juries

Once again, the main evaluative points have been divided into categories. You are encouraged to draw upon earlier coverage to develop these points.

### Inability to comprehend the issues in a case

- Although research into juries is restricted by the rules on jury secrecy (under s 8 of the **Contempt of Court Act 1981**) – a disadvantage in itself – anecdotal evidence suggests that some jury members not only fail to understand the evidence, but also disregard it when forming their views on a case. There is also the juror stereotype – as included in the great law film, **'Twelve Angry Men'** (see Chapter 15) – of the person who votes with the majority merely to bring the jury service to an end, rather than because he has taken a firm view of the issues in the case. Moreover, because a jury decision does not have to be justified, there is actually no need for jurors to have a firm grasp of the facts of the case.

**IT'S A FACT!**

**A favourable – and rare – example of jury research**

The Lord Chancellor allowed academics at Middlesex University's Centre for Criminology to interview 361 jurors for a research project in 2004. Almost two-thirds of the jurors had a positive view of the criminal justice system after serving on a jury, though just over a third felt intimidated by the prospect of meeting the defendant or their family.

- Eligibility for jury service begins at the age of 18, and it might be thought that this is *too young* to start making decisions about the liberty of an offender, or indeed to accept the responsibility of doing so. What do you think?
- There are some legal areas that are seen as especially difficult for lay juries to get to grips with. It is suggested, for example, that juries are not suitable for complex fraud trials (**Roskill Committee**), and the Government is committed to reforming the law accordingly. Moreover, the Court of Appeal, Criminal Division, has recently held that the defence of necessity is not available to those charged with possession of cannabis and a trial judge is entitled to hold, as a matter of law, that this should not be argued before a jury (*R v Altham*, 2006).

  Juries have also revealed difficulties, in civil law, in setting the amount of damages appropriately in defamation cases, and legislation has had to be passed to provide safeguards against excessive awards.
- While there are many advantages in allowing ordinary members of the public the chance to enter the courts and participate in the justice process, it would not be surprising if some were swayed by the speeches of the experienced professionals in court rather than by the evidence itself. A glance at the powerful oratory of **Marshall Hall** (see Chapter 10), directed entirely at the jury, shows how such performances might be difficult to resist.

### Juries might not be truly representative of the wider society

Jury selection is random, but this can mean, for example, that the racial composition of juries generated from this process might lead to a suspicion of bias. This issue was raised directly in *R v Smith* (2003), but there was held to be no breach of the defendant's right to a fair trial. However, this right will be breached if it is clear that racist views on a jury might unfairly influence the outcome of a trial, and the judge, having knowledge of these views, does nothing about the situation (*Sanders v UK* (2000)). The Government does not advocate reforms in this area – a defence of the principle of random selection – despite recommendations in the **Auld Review** (2001).

### Practical objections to jury trials

- **Crown Court trials** take *longer* than those in the **magistrates' courts** and *cost more*. Whilst estimates vary, recent 'regulatory impact assessments' on new legislation suggest an average of £14,000 for a Crown Court trial (about £3,700 per day) compared with £2,500 in total for a contested trial in the magistrates' courts. However, it has been argued – for example, by Liberal Democrat Peer, Lord Thomas of Gresford, during a parliamentary debate in 2000 – that this is *not* a fair comparison, given the differences in the type and nature of the cases heard in the two courts.
- Jury service is **compulsory**, and this will mean that a juror will miss two weeks, or sometimes longer, from work. The lost opportunities presented

by this situation for certain types of workers mean that jury service can be very costly, since the expenses for undertaking the service will not provide an equivalent sum.

## Risk of jury intimidation

This refers to **intimidation of jurors** by outsiders seeking to manipulate their decisions (also referred to as **'jury nobbling'**). The Government has sought to tackle this problem in s 44 of the Criminal Justice Act 2003, with the option being trial by judge alone where the circumstances warrant it.

# ALTERNATIVES TO JURY TRIAL

You might wish to consider whether the following alternatives to jury trial are satisfactory. This will add to any evaluation of juries.

## Single judge

This is the situation in **civil cases**, where the judge tries both fact and law; district judges (magistrates' courts) have the same function. This method of hearing cases is also employed in **Diplock courts** in Northern Ireland. The Government sought to allow defendants to **opt for trial by judge alone** at the Bill stage of the **Criminal Justice Act 2003**, but withdrew the proposal after strong resistance in Parliament. Trial by judge alone will, however, take place if there is a 'real and present danger that jury tampering would take place' (s 44 of the **Criminal Justice Act 2003**, relating to **jury intimidation**).

A single judge has a number of *advantages*, such as the adoption of a more legal approach to cases, with, as a consequence, time and money more likely to be saved. There are, however, some *drawbacks*: a single judge undermines the great historic principle of 'trial by peers', and there might therefore be a loss of public confidence. Moreover, a single judge can arguably become 'case-hardened' through experience of the criminal justice process.

## Bench of judges

Apart from the huge **cost** of a bench of three to five judges, public confidence may be lost in decision-making by **'case-hardened' professionals.** In the example of *Grobbelaar* (2001), in which three judges in the Court of Appeal overturned the verdict of a civil jury in a libel trial, a correspondent to *The Times* newspaper asked 'how can three judges who live a sheltered existence and have not heard the evidence, have the right to say that the jury's decision is perverse?'. However, the House of Lords – a further panel of judges, for whom similar comments could apply – subsequently reversed the Court of Appeal's decision.

## Professional or special jury

Professional jurors are a panel chosen from an **established body of non-legal experts.** A professional jury might not be representative of the wider society and might not therefore carry public confidence. It is also the case that such a jury would be useful only for certain types of cases. It could not be proposed, for example, that professional juries be set up for each branch of criminal law, though the Government has suggested this approach as a possible alternative to the use of juries in serious fraud trials.

## Composite tribunal

Here, **lay persons**, trained for the task, or **experts**, sit on **special tribunals led by a judge**. This sort of tribunal was suggested both by the **Roskill Committee** and the **Auld Review** for serious fraud trials, though the Government in its 'Justice for All' White Paper (2002) placed greater emphasis on trial by judge alone. It did so because the composite tribunal option gave rise to the 'considerable difficulties' of 'identifying and recruiting suitable people (. . .), not least because this would represent a substantial commitment over a long period of time'. However, the Government's experience of having to withdraw trial by judge alone provisions from the Criminal Justice Bill, save in cases of jury intimidation, might have changed its mind. Indeed, in seeking to take forward its plans to remove juries from serious fraud trials, the options for consultation in 2005 included a single judge with two expert assessors (with experience of finance and industry), a single judge with two magistrates or a panel of three judges. The composite tribunal also exhibits the potential problem that the judge may exert too much influence in the decision-making process, especially where lay people represent the other members of the panel.

## Conclusion

The Government's problems in getting the **Criminal Justice Act 2003** through Parliament, and having to sacrifice key elements at the Bill stage, illustrate the fact that attempts to restrict trial by jury rarely carry a great deal of favour. For the time being, it is highly unlikely that the jury system will be replaced, though it is clearly an area that is under scrutiny and subject to ongoing reform.

# LAY MAGISTRATES

## Introduction to lay magistrates

One of the most astonishing facts about the English legal system is that the vast majority of the criminal trials that take place are heard by **non-lawyers**, not judges, and the prison population in the UK owes part of its size to some of the sentences passed by these unpaid, unqualified and part-time officials. These are the **lay magistrates**, of whom there are about 28,000 administering justice in the English legal system compared with only 137 legally qualified, paid and full-time magistrates referred to as **district judges (magistrates' courts)**. Both types of magistrates are also referred to by the historical title of justice of the peace (JP). In a Foreword to the *Magistrates Bench Handbook: A Manual for Lay Magistrates,* Lord Irvine (when he was in the role of Lord Chancellor) made the following introductory comments:

> A major objective of government policy is the *promotion of volunteering*. The lay magistracy are volunteers who give their time to the community they serve for no financial reward. They play a key role in our criminal justice system. At least 95 per cent of the criminal business of the courts begins and ends with them. (emphasis added)

## Selection and appointment of lay magistrates

Traditionally, to serve as a lay magistrate a person had to be at least 21 and would not generally be appointed until the age of 27. However, times and attitudes have changed and the Government recognised that to maintain these age barriers would be to breach EC legislation on age discrimination. Therefore, since 2005, when the policy decision was taken, lay magistrates can be appointed between the ages of 18 and 65, and can serve until the age of 70.

**IT'S A FACT!**

**Increasing diversity in appointments to the magistracy**

A 20-year-old man, described in the press as an 'Asian DJ' amid much speculative reportage, became 'Britain's youngest magistrate' when he was appointed to the North Sussex bench in September 2005.

Serving as a lay magistrate is a voluntary activity, so people can put themselves forward. The Department for Constitutional Affairs and the Magistrates' Association have made great efforts to attract magistrates from all sections of society, culminating in a **National Strategy for the Recruitment of Lay Magistrates (2003)**. Initiatives to achieve greater diversity have included advertisements on public transport, local newspapers and radio; and the creation of a **Magistrates' Shadowing Scheme (2004)** for ethnic minorities.

If a person decides to volunteer, the following selection procedure is activated. The candidate will have to complete an **application form**, which must show that the basic qualifications to serve as a magistrate are fulfilled.

- The candidate must be between **18 and 65** on appointment.
- Although there is no national residence requirement, candidates must *not* be in the process of **seeking asylum** and must be prepared to swear an **Oath of Allegiance** to the Crown.
- Following the **Courts Act 2003**, formal rules requiring candidates for the magistracy to live locally to a magistrates' court have been removed owing to changes to the administration of the courts, though in practice they will be appointed to a **local court** (in one of the newly constituted 'local justice areas', replacing the old 'commission areas').
- The candidate must *not* be an **undischarged bankrupt.**
- The candidate must *not* have **serious criminal convictions.** It will be taken into account whether the person has been subject to any criminal or civil orders from a court and all previous convictions, and police cautions, have to be disclosed in the application. Since lay magistrates will deal with many motoring offences, serious or persistent motoring offences will disqualify a candidate for the bench.
- The candidate must *not* have an **infirmity** that might *prevent* him or her carrying out the duties of a magistrate. However, the principal emphasis is placed on ability to carry out the duties: thus, Lord Chancellors have appointed sight-impaired magistrates in recent years and applications

have been welcomed from disabled candidates, taking account of the requirements of the Disability Discrimination Act 1995.

- The candidate must *not* be **disqualified on occupational grounds**, by serving, for example, as a member of:
  - The Police Service
  - The Prison Service
  - The Probation Service
  - The Armed Forces
  - The Traffic Warden Service
  - The Courts Service or Crown Prosecution Service.
- The candidate must *not* have **close relatives** in the **criminal justice system** which might mean that conflicts of interest could arise, or have **close relatives** with **criminal convictions** that might undermine public confidence in the individual.
- Candidates must also be able to demonstrate **'six key qualities'** prescribed by the Department for Constitutional Affairs on appointments to the magistracy:
  - **Good character**
  - **Understanding and communication**
  - **Social awareness**
  - **Maturity and sound temperament**
  - **Sound judgment**
  - **Commitment and reliability.**

  It is seen as important that such personal qualities are 'generally recognised' within the local community where the candidate lives and works.

The selection process is undertaken by **Advisory Committees**, of which there are 109 around the country, which then offer their recommendations about candidates to the **Lord Chancellor**. The Advisory Committees are staffed by existing magistrates and (at least one-third) by non-magistrates. The Advisory Committee, usually consisting of between ten and 12 members, should reflect the broad political opinions of the community (that is, a degree of balance between Labour, Conservative and Liberal Democrat supporters). The benefit of Advisory Committees is that they can bring their local knowledge to bear in making recommendations: they are better placed, at first instance, to recognise suitable candidates within the local community than the Lord Chancellor's officials in the Department for Constitutional Affairs. Aside from examining the applications made, Advisory Committees consider candidates using a **two-stage interview process**. The first stage assesses **personal characteristics** against the criteria of the six key qualities; if successful in this, the candidate will be invited to a second interview where his or her opinions on the criminal justice system will be sought and **judicial aptitude**, in particular, looked for.

An **appointments group** within the **Department for Constitutional Affairs** will deal with, and consider, the recommendations for appointment. Magistrates are ultimately appointed by the Lord Chancellor, on behalf of the Crown.

**Exercise 9.2: The selection of lay magistrates**

*Advise the following individuals whether they meet the necessary requirements to be a lay magistrate.*

(1) An 18-year-old university student.
(2) A retired person of 67 years of age.
(3) A local traffic warden.
(4) A middle-aged person who, earlier in their life, had been declared bankrupt – a status now discharged.
(5) A person, 45, with a number of minor motoring convictions.
(6) A retired academic, with a passion for fox-hunting.
(7) A person, 40, a close relative of the Chief Constable for the local area.
(8) A person, 28, with a physical disability necessitating the use of a wheelchair.
(9) A 23-year-old unemployed, single parent.
(10) A teacher, 35, who has only lived in the area for one year.

For Answers, please turn to pp 339–40.

## The appointment of district judges (magistrates' courts)

**District judges (magistrates' courts)** are *not* lay persons, since they are legally qualified, full-time and salaried. Whilst they can sit with lay magistrates to hear cases, they also hear cases alone, being allocated the most serious and complex work in the magistrates' courts.

The Judicial Appointments Commission announces 'competitions' for the appointment of district judges (magistrates' courts), requiring applicants to have been practising solicitors or barristers for at least seven years. Three main competencies are looked for: judgement; professionalism; and people skills. Suitable candidates recommended by the Judicial Appointments Commission to the Lord Chancellor are referred for formal appointment by the Queen.

## The background of lay magistrates

Despite the fact that anyone meeting the general criteria can volunteer to be a magistrate, the selection process still gives rise to concerns. As **Berlins and Dyer** (2000), in their excellent book *The Law Machine*, have pointed out:

> *. . . there is still criticism that advisory committees, being largely middle and upper-class and 'establishment', tend to choose as magistrates others of their kind, and that the advisory committee system therefore produces a largely self-perpetuating oligarchy from which, in general, the ethnic minorities and working-class people are excluded.*

This public perception has been admitted by the **Magistrates' Association**, but also contested. As the then Chairman, Harry Mawdsley, told the *Times Law Supplement* in 2000: *'The image of the magistracy is a big challenge . . . we're seen not only as middle-class, but upmarket middle-class. The reality is different. On my bench in South Cheshire we have train drivers and postal and hospital workers – not just doctors and nurses'.*

Academic work and statistics on magistrates, compiled by **Darbyshire**, and **Morgan and Russell** (2000), suggest the following:

- That magistrates are overwhelmingly *middle-class*, in that those who volunteer to be magistrates and are in work are from professional and managerial occupational backgrounds.
- That just less than half of all the magistrates are actually *retired* from employment.
- That *almost half* of all lay magistrates are women.
- That *few* applications are made by disabled persons.

The percentage of magistrates from ethnic minority backgrounds (8.5 per cent in 2004) is similar to the percentage of the total population from such backgrounds, but this does not overcome problems where a predominantly white bench sits in an area heavily populated by diverse multi-faith and multi-cultural communities.

There is no doubt that the Department for Constitutional Affairs and the Magistrates' Association are anxious to increase the diversity of the magistracy. However, the **Royal Commission on Justices of the Peace** expressed this view as long ago as **1948**: 'care must be taken to see that there are persons in the commission (area) representative of various sections of the community'. It is remarkable that such an aim remains at the top of the agenda today. For readers with an interest in research on the back-ground of lay magistrates, see 'The lay magistracy: a local court for local people?' by Giles Bayliss (2006) in the *A-level Law Review*, Volume 1, Issue 2, at p 12.

## The role of lay magistrates

Lay magistrates have to sit for between **26 and 35 half-days per year**: they are **unpaid**, but may claim expenses. Part of the problem with attracting magistrates from all sections of society is that some employers resent employees taking off so much time – despite the fact that s 50 of the **Employment Rights Act 1996** permits employees to take time-off for such duties, albeit without an obligation on employers to pay them for it – and the expenses far from make up for lost earnings.

Lay magistrates have to sit on benches of at least two members: in fact, benches usually consist of three magistrates. These are assisted by **magistrates' clerks** (also referred to as **legal advisers**), who assist the bench on legal matters, but do not take part in the decision-making process undertaken by it. However, there are two types of magistrates' clerk: chief clerks (referred to as **justices' clerks**), who have to be legally qualified as solicitors or barristers for a period of at least five years; and assistant clerks (referred to as **court clerks**), who need to have reached the equivalent standard of a law graduate. Specific magistrates' court qualifications are available for those wishing to be clerks. It is the **court clerks** who shoulder the burden of much of the work, raising concerns about the standard of the advice given in the magistrates' court.

The role of lay magistrates divides into two main areas of work, as illustrated by Table 9.2 (see p 188).

Table 9.2 The role of lay magistrates

| *Criminal* | *Civil* |
|---|---|
| • Conducting **first instance criminal trials**, usually in benches of three, for summary criminal offences and either way offences where the defendant has not opted for the Crown Court mode of trial. In such trials, magistrates manage the case, hear the evidence, determine the verdict and pass sentence. Maximum sentencing powers for magistrates generally: up to six months' imprisonment for a single offence and fines subject to statute (£5,000 being the maximum on the standard scale).<br>• Conduct **preliminary hearings of criminal cases**, which may involve **applications for bail** and the **transfer of cases to the Crown Court**.<br>• Sit in the **youth court**, subject to training, for criminal trials of young offenders.<br>• Sit to accompany judges hearing **appeals** from the magistrates' court to the Crown Court. | • Extensive **family law** jurisdiction: to hear adoption cases, cases relating to domestic violence and cases relating to child custody.<br>• **Enforcement of debts**: for example, the magistrates' courts have the jurisdiction to hear cases relating to the non-payment of the television licence and taxes, such as the Council Tax.<br>• **Licensing functions**: providing licences for premises such as betting shops. |

## Training of lay magistrates

As with the judges (see Chapter 8), the body behind the practical training of lay magistrates is the **Judicial Studies Board (JSB)**, which has a specialist Magisterial Committee. Whilst the **Courts Act 2003** gives the Lord Chancellor overall responsibility for the training of lay magistrates, it is organised as locally as possible – by **Bench Training and Development Committees** – based on general standards established by the JSB.

There are effectively two stages in the training of magistrates. The first stage is the **induction** of lay magistrates, which may involve court visits (where the trainee is an observer), visits to penal establishments (such as prisons and young offender institutions), and lectures on the duties and roles of the magistrates in aspects of their civil and criminal work. The first stage should be undertaken *within* three months of appointment.

The second stage relates to the **practical aspects of being a lay magistrate**, and is undertaken by the magistrate to accompany work carried out in the courts. This will take the form prescribed by the **Magistrates New Training Initiative (MNTI)**, a programme devised by the JSB in 1998 and, at the time of writing, in its second incarnation. Each new magistrate will be assigned a **mentor** (usually a senior colleague) to support with the development of a **personal development log** and to carry out between eight and 11 court observations over the **two-year** training period. Magistrates must seek to demonstrate **four competences** through the evidence they gather over the two years:

- understanding of the criminal justice framework;
- application of law and procedure;
- judicial skills;
- working effectively in teams.

In addition, *ad hoc* training sessions will be organised to keep magistrates up-to-date with legal developments; and specialist training is required for magistrates to join the **youth court** or the **family court**, and to attain the position of chairman of the bench.

Since the training is organised locally, there are inevitably differences in the quality of training provision across the country. This is a source of concern, though the central standards of the Judicial Studies Board help to offer some uniformity. It might also be considered whether the training provision is sufficient given that magistrates have no prior training in, or experience of, criminal law and procedure.

## The retirement and removal of lay magistrates

The retirement and removal provisions for magistrates can be found in ss 11–49 of the **Courts Act 2003**. Magistrates may serve on the bench up to the age of 70, with their names added to a **Supplemental List** in recognition of service to the courts.

Magistrates may resign their office at any time. The Lord Chancellor has the power, subject to the agreement of the Lord Chief Justice, to remove a magistrate **'for good cause'**. Few magistrates are actually removed from service on this basis, though removal can be justified on the following grounds:

- incapacity;
- misbehaviour;
- persistent failure to meet standards of competence; or
- neglecting, or declining, to undertake the duties of the office.

In turn, the Lord Chief Justice, with the agreement of the Lord Chancellor, can impose a range of 'formal sanctions short of removal' on magistrates, such as formal warnings, reprimands and suspensions from office.

## Evaluating lay magistrates

As with juries (above), the main points relating to the advantages and disadvantages of the lay magistracy have been placed into categories. The bullet points below summarise some of the main comments made in the text above, and you are encouraged to refer back to those for the purposes of elaboration.

## Advantages

### Trust and confidence in the legal system

- Like juries, lay magistrates have played a significant role in **history**, and from the fourteenth to the nineteenth century, the role of magistrates as 'justices of the peace' provided an important link between the Crown and the local people in the maintenance of the area, the collection of taxes, the distribution of 'relief' monies for the poor and the administration of justice. Although their role is now more limited, the historical thread remains: lay magistrates are local people, often well known in their community, who are responsible for administering justice in the local criminal courts.
- Lay magistrates have an advantage over juries in that they do receive some **training** (jurors are, by contrast, limited to brief instructions and a video of the Crown Court) and they can **consult a clerk** on technical matters.
- Lay magistrates are **representatives of the community**. As Harry Mawdsley pointed out, anybody can volunteer to be a lay magistrate, with the result that the position can be held by members of any occupation, whether manual, semi-skilled or skilled, provided that they can attend the required number of hearings.

### Practical efficiency of lay magistrates

We have seen already that the use of lay magistrates is *less expensive* than the jury system. It is also *more efficient*. Magistrates get through cases quickly and the decisions tend to be accepted, with relatively few appeals as a result. One reason for this is that cases include some of the more routine, less serious criminal offences, such as those relating to road traffic law, and elaborate defences are therefore rare, as contrasted with cases in the Crown Court where the outcomes are much more serious and the trial process takes longer because a person's liberty is at issue.

## Disadvantages

### Lay magistrates are not truly representative of society

- We saw above that despite the voluntary nature of the magistracy, it tends to attract members of the public who represent only a narrow strand of society. Research confirms that magistrates are **overwhelmingly middle class**, and many **retired**. There are obvious practical reasons for this. Many jobs require a level of commitment from workers that prevents them from even considering becoming a magistrate. Moreover, since the lay magistrate is paid expenses only, many people cannot afford to take on such a commitment.
- While men and women are represented almost equally in the magistracy, the number of **ethnic minority magistrates** gives some cause for concern. The figure does reflect the general percentage of minority communities in the population, but this still means that 'white' benches administer justice in areas where communities are much more diverse.

- There is a suspicion that magistrates tend to **favour the police** in particular, a view that gained greater credibility when one magistrate actually admitted this (*R v Bingham JJ ex p Jowitt* (1974)).

Efficiency at the expense of justice

- While it is an advantage to say that the magistrates' courts are more efficient than, say, the Crown Court, this should not be at the expense of justice. The work of the magistrates' courts was famously referred to in one critical report as **'sausage machine justice'** (Carlen, 1978).
- Efficiency in certain areas might also lead to **inconsistencies** that suggest a degree of injustice. Research into the sentencing decisions of magistrates, to take one example, indicates that sentences vary from area to area for similar offences, both in terms of type and severity.

Lack of knowledge to carry out the role

- Lay magistrates receive **training**, but whether this is adequate for them truly to understand criminal law and rules of evidence and procedure is highly debatable. There are also concerns about the way in which the training may differ around the country, given that it is delivered at the local level.
- Certain writers, such as **Darbyshire**, have made the point that magistrates may become too dependent on clerks who are not, in fact, legal practitioners. This is perceived as dangerous, because lay magistrates carry out the bulk of criminal adjudication in this country and yet are being advised by clerks who are arguably ill-equipped to carry out this role. However, the deadline of 2010 has been set for all court clerks to be fully qualified as legal practitioners, subject to certain exemptions' to take into account the experience of long-serving clerks.

## Useful website addresses

| | |
|---|---|
| Auld Review of the Criminal Justice System 2001 | www.criminal-courts-review.org.uk |
| Criminal Justice System (including a 'virtual Crown Court') | www.cjsonline.org |
| Department for Constitutional Affairs | www.dca.gov.uk |
| Home Office | www.home-office.gov.uk |
| Magistrates' Association | www.magistrates-association.org.uk |
| *Materials directly for AS studies:* | |
| John Deft (St Brendan's Sixth Form College) | www.stbrn.ac.uk/other/depts/law |
| Asif Tufal | www.a-level-law.com |

## HINTS AND TIPS

Within the lay persons topic, examination questions might focus *separately* on juries and/or lay magistrates, or allow for a *more general exploration* of the contribution of lay persons to the English legal system. In the broader, general questions, be aware that areas of comparison may be introduced: for example, the **compulsory** selection of juries as contrasted with the **voluntary** nature of the magistracy.

The following areas, of relevance both to juries and lay magistrates, are often included as the subject of examination questions requiring description:

- The **role of the lay person** in the system. For example: 'What do jurors do?'; What are the functions of lay magistrates?'
- The **methods of selection** for lay persons to contribute to the system. For example: 'How are jurors selected?'; 'What is the appointments procedure for lay magistrates?'

In the **juries** topic, you will also be expected to know about the practical aspects of jury trial, from selection through to the verdict (see also Chapter 6 above). While the emphasis will generally be placed on **criminal juries**, the position of juries in **civil trials** should *not* be neglected.

With regard to **lay magistrates**, a number of additional areas might be considered, as follows:

- The **'personal qualities'** required by lay magistrates and the **full appointments process.**
- The **training** of lay magistrates.
- The **retirement** and **removal** of lay magistrates.
- Some comparison between **lay magistrates** and **district judges (magistrates' court).**

In evaluating these lay persons, an understanding of the **advantages** and **disadvantages** of each will clearly be of value. However, also bear in mind the issues raised in Table 9.3.

Table 9.3 Thinking about the role of lay persons

| *Juries* | *Lay magistrates* |
|---|---|
| • The nature of **jury selection**: Should it be compulsory? Were the reforms to jury selection in the **Criminal Justice Act 2003** necessary? Are they causing any problems in practice? | • The **selection** and **appointments process** for **lay magistrates**: Does it produce a representative magistracy? How important is a representative magistracy? |
| • The **alternatives to juries**: Are the alternatives better than the existing system? Should trial by peers be sacrificed to greater efficiency and a more legal approach? | • The **training of magistrates** and **reliance on their clerks**: Is the training adequate for service on the bench? Are magistrates overly dependent on their clerks? |

To complement your studies in this area, two further suggestions seem sensible. First, **keep up-to-date** as far as possible with reforms to juries and lay magistrates. The *A-level Law Review*, *New Law Journal* and the *Times Law Supplement* often contain articles relating to proposed reforms and also suggest new approaches. Secondly, *visit* your local **magistrates' court** and **Crown Court** to see magistrates and juries at work. Practical experience confirms what you have read and, more importantly, brings the law to life!

# The legal profession

This topic enables you:

- To identify the main types of legal personnel in the English legal system: solicitors, barristers, and legal executives.
- To consider the routes available for pursuing a career as a solicitor, barrister or legal executive.
- To recognise the traditional differences between solicitors and barristers, and develop a critical appreciation of the changes that have occurred within the legal profession.
- To consider other branches of legal work, such as the Crown Prosecution Service (CPS).
- To understand the liability implications of advisory and advocacy work.
- To gain a practical introduction to the law as it is practised on a day-to-day basis.

The **legal profession** is essential to the operation of the English legal system. This topic links with many other areas. It particularly informs a *broader understanding* of the following areas in this section of the book: the **workings of the courts structure** and the **role of lawyers in the courts**; the judicial role in courts and **appointments to judicial positions**; and the way in which **legal help and representation** is provided and funded.

## BARRISTERS

### Introduction

There are over 14,000 practising barristers. Barristers are traditionally seen as the senior branch of the profession. The profession is governed by the Senate of Inns of Court and the Bar (known as the **'Bar Council'**, or more formally the General Council of the Bar). Senior members are called 'benchers'. To be a barrister you have to be a member of one of the four **Inns of Court** in London (see 'Profile: Visitor's guide to the Inns of Court' on p 194). Each Inn contains a Great Hall, used for the formal dinners that remain a part of the legal education process for barristers; a church; beautiful and well-maintained gardens; and a number of old, often very grand, buildings that house sets of **barristers' chambers** (from which **self-employed** barristers work, with assistance from **clerks**).

Barristers operate on a *self-employed* basis from chambers, and must accept the **'cab-rank' rule**. The reason for the cab-rank rule is to ensure that litigants have a fair chance of representation. Barristers must accept cases as they are *allocated to them* by the clerk in chambers (thus, barristers are rather

The symbol of Middle Temple

## Profile: *Visitor's guide to the Inns of Court*

The Inns of Court: the entrance to Lincoln's Inn pictured from Lincoln's Inn Fields

- **Lincoln's Inn.** Visitors to Lincoln's Inn (located off Chancery Lane) will recognise this Inn by the *symbol of the Lion* (located upper left on the Inn's coat of arms). This symbol is based on the family sign of a thirteenth-century lawyer who was also the Earl of Lincoln. Lincoln's Inn has had many famous members over the years, including no fewer than 11 Prime Ministers (including Tony Blair) and over 20 Lord Chancellors. Lord Denning was a member of Lincoln's Inn.
- **Gray's Inn.** Visitors to Gray's Inn (located in the area of High Holborn) will recognise this Inn by the *symbol of the Griffin* (a mythical creature with an eagle's head and a lion's body). This symbol is based on the coat of arms (that is, family sign) of a sixteenth-century bencher and treasurer of Gray's Inn.
- **Inner Temple.** Visitors to Inner Temple (located off Fleet Street) will recognise this Inn by the *symbol of Pegasus* (the winged horse). The origins of this are not precisely known, though some link it to an entertainment performed at the Inn during the Christmas revels of the sixteenth century entitled the 'Knights of the Order of Pegasus'.
- **Middle Temple.** Visitors to Middle Temple (again located off Fleet Street) will recognise this Inn by the *symbol of the Lamb and Flag* (*Agnus dei* – the lamb of God). The origins of this date back to the thirteenth century and the Knights Templar (an order of warrior monks founded to protect pilgrims on the way to Jerusalem), though it was adopted by the Inn in the seventeenth century.

When visiting the Temple Inns, fans of Dan Brown's *Da Vinci Code* should not miss the beautiful Temple Church, which dates back to the twelfth century and contains a set of effigies of Knights of the Order of the Knights Templar which Brown features in his novel.

like customers at a taxi-rank; they are expected to take the next one in the queue). The allocation of briefs will depend on a barrister's area of expertise and his or her expectation of a 'reasonable fee'.

In the past, a barrister had to eat 18 **dinners** with senior members of the profession at the Inns of Court before he or she could practise. The justification for dining in the Inns has always been that it forms part of the learning process, encouraging conversation and discussion with senior members of the profession in a formal social environment. (It is difficult, though, to remove the suspicion that there is also a degree of social grooming and elitism perpetuated by these dinners.) In more recent times, however, the dining requirement has been relaxed (it is now 12), with **residential weekends** allowed as an alternative for those taking Bar examinations outside London.

Barristers are identified in court by their **wigs and gowns**. Senior barristers may apply to become a **Queen's Counsel** (QC). This is known as **'taking silk'**. The QC status attracts higher fees. QCs are therefore provided at the client's request and for exceptional cases.

## The role of barristers

The traditional position is that a solicitor selects – or **briefs** – a barrister for his or her client, who will appear on behalf of the client in the courts. Barristers also carry out non-advocacy work as they advise solicitors on legal points, although a lot of their time is actually spent in court.

Barristers are therefore sought mainly for their specialist skill – **advocacy**. The art of advocacy is the persuasive presentation of a line of argument based either on factual evidence, or on legal reasoning before a judge or magistrates. Those who practise advocacy are given **rights of audience** in the courts. Some of the most impressive pieces of historical advocacy have been demonstrated in the criminal trial court – the Crown Court – before a judge and jury (see 'Profile' below).

A business with a long history in London, still providing wigs and gowns for barristers in the twenty-first century

## Profiles: *Famous barristers*

**Sir Edward Marshall Hall**

The legal novelist and playwright, John Mortimer, identified the barrister **Edward Marshall Hall**, at the height of his powers in the first quarter of the twentieth century, as 'undoubtedly the **greatest criminal defender**'. He went on to describe the effect that Marshall Hall had in the courtroom:

> *. . . We can almost see him . . . standing in the cramped Edwardian courtrooms making his final speech to a hushed audience. The two arms were stretched to imitate the scales of justice, evenly balanced, and then into one well-manicured hand, protruding from a gleaming white cuff, Marshall Hall would place the invisible presumption of innocence, the small gold nugget of our criminal law, and the scales would tip inevitably in favour of the accused.*

It is certainly well worth reading through some of the accounts of Marshall Hall's trials. They evoke a style of legal defence that in its time was sensational, and yet today it would probably be dismissed as *too* theatrical. The death penalty awaiting a convicted murderer at that time also added a considerable edge to proceedings. Take, for example, Marshall Hall's defence of a solicitor, Harold Greenwood, who was accused of the murder of his wife by arsenic poisoning. Marshall Hall's closing speech to the jury was, by all accounts, a masterpiece of rhetoric: the jury was reminded, time and time again, that a mistake made by them could not be remedied since a man would, as a consequence, lose his life. He ended the speech with a quote from Shakespeare's **Othello** – *'put out the light, and then put out the light . . .'* – and then the following words to the jury: *'Are you going, by your verdict, to put out that light? Gentlemen of the Jury, I demand, at your hands, the life and liberty of Harold Greenwood.'* The legal writer, Gerald Sparrow, later recounted that *'those who were present said that Marshall's final speech for the defence was the finest they had ever heard at the criminal Bar . . .'*.

**Michael Mansfield QC**

While there are other great defence barristers working today, Michael Mansfield QC is distinct because, as Kevin Toolis, writing in the *Guardian* (1997), pointed out, *'you can buy skills, rhetoric and cleverness, but you cannot buy passion and commitment . . .'*, and Mansfield is famous for these latter qualities. They have informed his practice as a **criminal defender** and advocate in **miscarriage**

**of justice** cases. He is also a great believer in justice. Mansfield's approach to 'miscarriages of justice' is that of supporting the *underdog*, searching methodically through all of the evidence to find the one flaw in the prosecution's case. As Mansfield said in an interview with Toolis, '*the remarkable thing that overturns all these cases is what I call the slender thread which protrudes but a millimetre above the surface of a conviction, but if you pull, unravels the whole case*'. Mansfield was involved in the **Stephen Lawrence murder inquiry** and, among many others, the following 'miscarriage of justice' cases:

**The Bridgewater Three**

Michael Hickey, Vincent Hickey and Jimmy Robertson ('The Bridgewater Three') (plus Pat Molloy who died while serving his sentence) were convicted of the brutal murder of Carl Bridgewater, a boy aged 13. They were sentenced to life imprisonment. However, the Court of Appeal was finally persuaded that the conviction was unsafe. The police had misused their powers in gathering evidence. The three were released after **18 years' imprisonment**, following a great deal of work by the defence team.

**The Birmingham Six**

The case of 'The Birmingham Six' concerned two pub bombings by the IRA in Birmingham, which resulted in 21 deaths and the subsequent trial of six Irish men. The process that brought them to court and the trial itself are often cited as indicative of one of the *worst* miscarriages of justice the English legal system has faced. Confession evidence was seen as unsafe, since police tactics in securing this had been highly questionable, and the forensic evidence used to support the prosecution case was deeply flawed. The six received life sentences; it took **17 years of campaigning** to secure their release, on appeal.

## Talking from experience

**Barristers' chambers**

The chambers of **Michael Mansfield QC** (see 'Profiles' above) can be found at **14 Tooks Court**. This set of chambers has an excellent reputation for *human rights* and *miscarriage of justice* cases, and has gained considerable media publicity. The barristers undertake a range of work. One barrister, for example, spends a great deal of her working life in the Immigration Appeal Tribunal, regarding appeals to enter or remain in the UK.

**6 King's Bench Walk**, the chambers of **Roy Amlot QC**, is listed as one of the leading criminal sets of chambers in the country and specialises in all kinds of criminal cases, from murder to minor criminal offences. Therefore much of the work of these barristers takes place in Crown Courts across London. Barristers' work is wide-ranging, requiring a variety of skills. For example, in addition to advocacy and the writing of opinions for solicitors, barristers have to organise the listing of cases and deal with clients in a sensitive and diplomatic manner.

**Matrix Chambers** is a recently established legal practice involved in international *human rights* (in relation to the retention and use of the death penalty in Commonwealth countries); criminal law (in relation to terrorism cases and serious fraud); and immigration and asylum law. When this set of chambers was founded it attracted publicity, largely as a result of its high-profile members, including the noted QC and high profile political wife, **Cherie Booth**, and David Bean, former Chairman of the Bar Council.

Today the Bar continues in the tradition of great advocates, even though performances are rather more restrained than those associated with Marshall Hall.

One question that is often asked about criminal defence barristers is 'How can they defend somebody who must be guilty?'. The problem with such a question, however, is that it assumes guilt on the part of the defendant, and yet if the defendant is maintaining his or her innocence then it is surely right that he or she is entitled to the best defence possible. The barrister's duty is to the client that he or she receives according to the cab-rank rule. As **Marshall Hall** once said: '*Barristers are public servants and may be called on just as a doctor may be called on to operate on a man suffering from a loathsome complaint*'. If barristers start to question the defendant's story they become judges in effect, and that, after all, is not their role in the criminal trial process.

The Law Society, Chancery Lane, London – the home of the governing body for solicitors

## SOLICITORS

### Introduction

There are over 96,000 practising solicitors. This branch of the profession is governed by the **Law Society**.

Since clients can access solicitors *directly*, offices of small **partnership firms** can be found on High Streets all over the country dealing with routine legal matters. There is a world of difference between these small firms and the huge City of London firms (some with 300 or more partners and offices overseas) that handle international commercial claims and average huge earnings for partners. There is even a so-called **'Magic Circle'** of these firms, consisting of Allen & Overy, Clifford Chance, Freshfields, Linklaters, and Slaughter & May (see 'Useful website addresses' at the end of the chapter).

Clifford Chance, one of the 'Magic Circle' law firms in the City of London

### The role of solicitors

Despite the differences between firms, solicitors generally undertake the following sort of tasks:

- They **advise clients** directly, through interview or by correspondence.
- They **prepare paperwork** (such as legal letters, forms, and so on), often as part of the process of **litigation management**, which involves bringing a case to court and ensuring that the necessary formalities are met.
- They **represent clients** in the lower courts (in the magistrates' courts and county courts) and may seek to gain an **advocacy certificate** to represent clients in the **higher courts** (as solicitor-advocates).

That said, solicitors will tend to specialise in particular areas of work. There are two main types of legal work in the solicitors' office. The first is **contentious work**, which involves disputes that are likely to be resolved in **court**, such as immigration work, divorce, personal injury and general litigation. The second is **non-contentious work**, which largely involves paperwork and dealing with clients in the **office**. Examples include conveyancing, the drafting of wills, financial services and probate.

## Talking from experience
## Solicitors' firms

Work experience in a **local firm of solicitors** will provide a valuable insight into the working practices of a legal office. You will probably undertake a range of clerical duties such as filing, dealing with both incoming and outgoing mail, and operating the fax and photocopying machines. You might also talk to clients on the telephone and attend the local courts.

Solicitor-advocates with the appropriate **advocacy experience** and **qualifications** now have opportunities to apply for **QC status** and also for **appointment to judicial posts** (up to the High Court). However, these opportunities are only available to a small minority of solicitors (by 2004, only 2,000 solicitors had higher court advocacy rights).

## Developing the subject:
## The status of Queen's Counsel

The traditional role of the Lord Chancellor included the appointment of QCs, but there were a number of concerns about the appointments process (as with judges – see Chapter 8 – the suspicion of an '*old boy network*' being maintained through 'secret soundings') and also about the role of the State in conferring the QC status. In 2003, there were 1,244 QCs, of whom only 103 were female and 37 with an ethnic origin described as 'non-white' (*New Law Journal*). The **Commission for Judicial Appointments**, in reviewing the appointment of QCs in 2003, found 'considerable obstacles to diversity' in the process, leading to an impression of the 'silk mould' that, even if it did not amount to bias in practice, gave such an impression to female, ethnic minority and solicitor applicants. Moreover, the **Office of Fair Trading (OFT)** attacked the two-tier system – being especially critical of barristers whose fees rocketed upon being bestowed with this status – and argued strongly that this was another example of anti-competitive practices in the legal profession. The OFT report was part of the Government's own consultation process on the future of the QC system, which was concluded in November 2003. The **Bar Council**, on the other hand, campaigned strongly in favour of retaining the silk status as a 'quality standard' of advocacy and professionalism that operated in the public interest.

To take account of the consultation process, and consider responses, the Lord Chancellor, Lord Falconer, announced a suspension on the appointment of QCs for 2004. He asked the **Bar Council** *and* the **Law Society** to work together to develop a **new selection and accreditation scheme for the QC status**, on the basis that the Lord Chancellor's role would be *withdrawn* in all but the formal process of recommending selected persons to the Queen.

Agreement between the two governing bodies was reached in 2004, with the new scheme announced as a **'fair and transparent means of identifying excellence in advocacy in the higher courts'**. The new system operates with an **independent selection panel** (including lay members), a **written reference system** (to replace 'secret soundings') and a clear **complaints procedure**. The first Chairman of the Selection Panel, in launching the first 'competition' or round of applications in July 2005, told the media that selection would be based on 'merit', that applications would be welcomed from under-represented groups and that applications from solicitors and employed lawyers, with sufficient advocacy experience, were encouraged. The **seven competences** that are looked for in candidates for QC status are:

- integrity;
- understanding and using the law;

- analysis of cases and development of arguments;
- persuasive communication;
- ability to respond to new case developments;
- working with clients; and
- working in teams (not just leadership).

**Talking points:**
- What are the justifications for a two-tier status for lawyers?
- What are the arguments for the abolition of QC status?
- To what extent are the new arrangements likely to address concerns about the QC status?

## Postscript - QC appointments in 2006

The first new QCs to be selected under the revised arrangements for appointment were announced in July 2006. The appointments attracted headlines for all the right reasons: significantly **more women** applied for, and attained, silk than ever before; and all the candidates suggested by the new, independent **Queen's Counsel Selection Panel** were accepted by the Lord Chancellor, without challenge, and recommended to the Queen for formal appointment. The figures for the 2006 appointments round, referred to as the **'first competition'**, were as follows:

| | *Number of applicants for QC status* | *Number of those attaining QC status* |
|---|---|---|
| Males | 375 | 142 |
| Females | 68 | 33 |
| Total | 443 | 175 |
| *Those applicants from ethnic minority backgrounds* | *24* | *10* |
| *Those applicants from the solicitors' branch of the profession* | *12* | *4* |

Sir Duncan Nichol, Chairman of the Queen's Counsel Selection Panel, told BBC News (20/7/06) that he welcomed the 'broad and more diverse list' that had been prompted by the changes in the appointments process. However, application rates from ethnic minority candidates and from solicitors did not show the sorts of increases anticipated. Panel member Karamjit Singh commented that it was perhaps too early to draw conclusions about diversity, but nevertheless expressed his hope that the first competition had sent a message 'that appointment is solely on merit'.

## LEGAL EXECUTIVES

Legal executives work in solicitors' firms as clerks. Some refer to legal executives as 'paralegals', a term which describes all those working in an administrative capacity to support the work of a law firm. However, **legal executives** are in fact a *distinct branch of the profession*, and tend to take responsibility for specific areas of work within the firm, specialising in the paperwork and administration relating to this. A legal executive might, for example, become *specialised* in conveyancing, and will therefore relieve the solicitor of routine tasks and paperwork.

Often, legal executives can be seen doing very similar work to solicitors, and yet their lesser status often leads them to be perceived as 'poor relations'. Nevertheless, experienced legal executives do access partnership positions in firms, and the qualifications set by the **Institute of Legal Executives (ILEX)**, which upon successful completion, enable legal executives to be recognised as **'Fellows'**, are highly regarded and respected within the profession. There are around 7,000 Fellows of the Institute of Legal Executives (and 29,000 Members).

Legal executives can also opt to follow the solicitor career route through taking the Legal Practice Course (see p 202 (Table 10.1) below). While some legal executives go on to become solicitors, experienced specialists may not find it necessary to make this transition since they will have established their expertise within the legal community.

Under s 40 of the Access to Justice Act 1999, ILEX has the authority to grant rights to members to carry out litigation work. Moreover, legal executives have **rights of audience** in certain limited circumstances: these include, in civil proceedings, the rights to appear in the county court and the magistrates' court in family matters. In a step that is seen as bringing legal executives closer, as a profession, to solicitors, legal executives can now also *instruct counsel* independently, rather than having to do so through a solicitor.

## THE CROWN PROSECUTION SERVICE (CPS)

The Crown Prosecution Service (CPS) was set up in 1986 as a result of the **Prosecution of Offences Act 1985**. The CPS was proposed by a **law reform body** (refer back to Chapter 1), the **Phillips Royal Commission on Criminal Procedure 1981**, and Parliament responded with the 1985 Act. The CPS relieved the burden that had previously been shouldered by the police in bringing prosecutions in the two criminal trial courts: the **magistrates' courts** and the **Crown Courts**. Since criminal proceedings are taken in the name of the State – and expressly on behalf of Regina (R), the Crown – the CPS represents the **agency of the State** responsible for this task. It is headed by a senior Government legal officer, the **Director of Public Prosecutions (DPP)**. The DPP is, in turn, accountable to the **Attorney-General** who takes overall responsibility as a Government Minister for criminal prosecutions. Given that the DPP has the ultimate say in whether a prosecution should go ahead, his decision may be subject to judicial review.

The DPP is in charge of an agency that is divided into 42 geographical areas, which share the boundaries of **regional police forces** around the country. Chief Crown Prosecutors are appointed for each of these areas to oversee, in collaboration with Area Business Managers, the work of local CPS offices. It is one of the main aims of the CPS to work 'effectively with others to improve the effectiveness and efficiency of the criminal justice system overall'.

### The role of the CPS

The CPS reviews criminal cases to ensure that there is enough evidence to allow them to proceed. It is still dependent on the police for the resourcing of criminal investigations, and therefore has to work with the evidence produced by the investigative process. On the basis of the evidence at its disposal, the CPS follows the **Code for Crown Prosecutors** when determining whether a prosecution should be pursued (see Chapter 6 at pp 118–19).

**CPS personnel** divide into two main categories:

- **case-workers**, who undertake the case-work to ensure that there is sufficient evidence to support the prosecution in bringing the case to court and presenting it; and
- **Crown prosecutors**, who, as solicitors or barristers, undertake advocacy and therefore present the prosecution case in the **magistrates' courts**; following s 42 of the Access to Justice Act 1999, Crown prosecution lawyers can also act as advocates in the **Crown Court**, though independent barristers are also selected for this role.

The education and training requirements for the **Crown prosecutor posts** are as for solicitors and barristers (see pp 202–3 below). The educational requirements to be a **case-worker** are five GCSEs at grades A–E (with English at grade C or above preferred) and two A-levels.

## QUALIFICATIONS REQUIRED TO ENTER THE LEGAL PROFESSION

Table 10.1 (see p 202) summarises the education and training routes available to pursue a career as a solicitor. Table 10.2 (see p 203) sets out the routes that are available to those wishing to pursue careers as barristers.

The Law Society has recently been engaged in consultation relating to a review of the **education and training framework** for becoming a solicitor. There are a number of pressures for increasing *flexibility* in the education and training framework: the proposed *reforms* to the profession (see coverage of the **Clementi Review** below at pp 205–8), emphasizing high standards of service delivery and 'customer' care; the current *student funding arrangements*, with many students now leaving university in debt; and the efforts at European Union and international levels for *recognition of equivalent qualifications*. The Law Society is mindful of the European Court of Justice decision in the case of *Morgenbesser v Italy* (2003) where a French qualified lawyer was able to rely on EC Treaty rights when she was prevented from practising in Italy because of a rule requiring lawyers to hold a legal qualification from an Italian university.

The Law Society is keen to establish clear competences and formal assessment and performance standards to maximise *flexible* access routes to the profession.

## REFORMS TO THE LEGAL PROFESSION

The calls for reform of the legal profession began to gather momentum in the 1970s, bringing into focus the *monopolies* enjoyed by each branch of the profession and raising the question whether the profession should sustain the

Table 10.1 Education and training: solicitors

| *Post-16 time-line* | *Sixth-form college/FE college* | *Working route* |
|---|---|---|
| Usually **2 years** (completion of AS and A2 Level qualification) | Entrance requirements for Law are generally *high* because of the level of competition for places. Note that the **Law National Admissions Test (LNAT)** will have to be sat for admission to certain universities. | Have at least 4 GCSEs, usually including **English** and **Maths.** Work in a **solicitors' office** doing general clerical work. |
| Undergraduate stage – Usually **3 years** | **University**. Read **Law** or combination subject with Law for a *qualifying* **Law degree**. **or** | Take **ILEX Part I** and **Part II** examinations to become a **Member of the Institute of Legal Executives**. After *5 years* working in a solicitors' office and successful completion of exams (at least 5 core subjects) can be admitted as a **Fellow of the Institute of Legal Executives** (that is, become recognised as a fully qualified **legal executive**). If a career as a solicitor is desired, the next stage is the Legal Practice Course (as for solicitors). |
| Non-Law graduates – **1 year conversion course** | **Study any degree subject** and then take the 1 year conversion course: **Common Professional Examination (CPE)** *or* **Graduate Diploma in Law (GDL).** | |
| Legal Practice Course – **1 year vocational course** | **Legal Practice Course (LPC)** Vocational course to train law students to become practitioners. The training includes: drafting of legal documents; client counselling; and legal accounts. | |
| Training in legal firms – **2 years** | Apply for and undertake **training contracts** with firms. **Qualify as a solicitor.** | |

solicitor/barrister distinction or opt for *'fusion'* of the two roles by recognising just one type of legal professional. Such calls have generally been resisted by the Law Society and the Bar Council, which have – perhaps understandably – sought to *defend* monopolies and specialisation.

In 1979, the **Benson Commission (Royal Commission on Legal Services)** looked into these issues, but did not propose any radical changes. However, by the mid-1980s, the solicitors' profession faced the prospect of reforms, some of which were resisted and some welcomed. The **Administration of Justice Act 1985**, for example, opened the door to **independent licensed conveyancers,** encouraging competition in an area of practice that had been held solely by

Table 10.2 Education and training: barristers

| *Post-16 time-line* | *Sixth-form college/FE college* |
|---|---|
| Usually **2 years** | Same route as for solicitors – complete **AS and A2 Level qualifications**. Note **LNAT** requirements for certain universities. |
| Undergraduate stage – **3 years** | **University**. Study **Law** or combination with Law for a *qualifying* **Law degree**. |
| Non-law graduates – **1 year conversion course** | Same route as solicitors (**CPE/GDL conversion course**). |
| Bar Vocational Course – **1 year** | **Bar Vocational Course**. Vocational course: to train law students to become barristers. Students register with one of the **Inns of Court** during their vocational training, since there is still a requirement that students dine at their selected Inn at least 12 times or attend specified weekend residential courses. Skills developed during the Bar Vocational Course include advocacy; drafting of advice; and legal research. |
| Pupillage – **1 year** | Pupil works with experienced barrister for one year: **observation** for *first* six months, but possibility of managing cases thereafter. The case of *Edmonds v Lawson* (2000) addressed the possibility of having a minimum wage for pupils. Although the Court of Appeal stated that pupils did not have to be paid the minimum wage as they had yet to acquire the status of barrister, the Bar Council, in 2001, *recommended* that all pupils should be paid £5,000 minimum for the first part of their pupillage. For the second part of the pupillage the pupil should receive a guaranteed income. |

solicitors' firms for years; more positively, support was growing for solicitors to have the opportunity to **practise advocacy** in the higher courts (rather than be restricted to the magistrates' courts and county courts, as was the case at the time). Whilst this was welcomed by solicitors, it meant, of course, that the barristers' traditional monopoly over advocacy in the higher courts was being threatened. Alert to the prevailing mood of the times, the **Marre Committee**, a joint Bar Council/Law Society Committee that reported in 1988, suggested a modest extension of the 'rights of audience' enjoyed by solicitors. With the issues clearly in the spotlight, the stage was set for a landmark piece of legislation that would bring changes to the two branches of the profession.

## The landmark reforms: Courts and Legal Services Act 1990

This legislation was steered through Parliament by a free market-orientated Conservative Government intent on *removing* barriers to competition. It sought to ensure that the legal system delivered 'value for money'. Major changes provided for in the **Courts and Legal Services Act 1990** included:

- Building on the 1985 Act mentioned above, powers given to bodies other than solicitors' firms, such as banks and building societies, to practise **conveyancing.** (The Law Society has since resisted these powers and strongly defended the solicitors' role in carrying out conveyancing services.)
- Solicitors firms allowed to *merge with other service providers* (such as estate agents, accountants, and so on) in the form of **multi-disciplinary partnerships**; and to *merge with overseas firms* in the form of **multinational partnerships.** Multi-disciplinary partnerships were also resisted, in practice, by the Law Society at this time.
- A **Legal Services Ombudsman** was established to oversee the handling of complaints by the **Law Society** and the **Bar Council.**
- One of the major changes was that solicitors in private practice (that is, those working for themselves or for the benefit of a partnership) were able to apply for a **certificate of advocacy** that would provide *wider* **rights of audience** for them. These certificates enabled solicitors to represent clients in the Crown Court, High Court and in appeal cases. This meant that the barristers' monopoly on advocacy in the higher courts was being eroded.
- Changes to **legal aid** were envisaged, with **conditional fees** being introduced (see Chapter 11).

By extending solicitors' rights and removing competitive restrictions, the **'fusion' debate** – about the relationship between the solicitors' and barristers' branches of the profession and the extent to which these should be merged or 'fused' – was fuelled by the **Courts and Legal Services Act 1990.**

## Access to Justice Act 1999

This Act reinforced the *erosion of the barristers' monopoly* in respect of **advocacy**, whilst affording **solicitors** and other legal professionals greater rights. Under this Act, s 36 entitles all solicitors to be eligible for **full rights of audience** upon completion of the appropriate training (leading to a **Higher Courts Advocacy Certificate**). Furthermore, s 37 extends rights of audience to solicitors employed 'in house' (those solicitors employed by, for example, major companies, local authorities and charities) and in the Crown Prosecution Office.

## RECENT DEVELOPMENTS

The landscape created by the **Court and Legal Services Act 1990** and the **Access to Justice Act 1999** reflected broader trends affecting businesses and the professions, including an increased interest in value for **consumers.** Even though reforms had taken place, it was still evident that the branches of the legal profession continued to enjoy, and defend, **'restrictive practices'** in what had become a marketplace for legal services. The liberalisation of this market following the 1990 Act, in particular, had meant that other businesses and organisations wanted to get involved in the selling of legal services. The **Office of Fair Trading (OFT)** investigated the profession in 2001 and was very critical of the 'restrictive practices' it identified, making it clear that these were not in the best interests of consumers. A further consultation exercise by the then Lord Chancellor's Department (now **Department for Constitutional Affairs**) initiated in 2002 found that the OFT's misgivings were not without substance: in the words of the Lord Chancellor, Lord Falconer, 'consumers told us clearly that their needs were not being met'. Both the Law Society and the Bar Council could see where this debate was going: *further erosion* of professional monopolies; *more common ground* in the training and work of solicitors and barristers; and *wider provision*, and *greater competition*, in the delivery of legal services. Indeed, one of the Bar Council's early responses was to launch previously prohibited **direct access** schemes so that clients could consult barristers directly, without having to be referred by a solicitor. The Law Society also realised that some of the reforms it had earlier resisted, such as **multi-disciplinary partnerships**, were back on the agenda.

The OFT envisaged a new marketplace for the provision of legal services in which consumers (rather than 'clients') can shop around for the highest quality, or cheapest, legal services from a range of suppliers. This new *competitive marketplace* is often referred to as **Tesco Law**, reflecting the fact that even large supermarkets are keen to offer legal services as part of their expanding product range. The Government's response to the OFT was to order a review of competition and regulation in the legal services market headed by **Sir David Clementi**, a former senior official of the Bank of England.

The **Clementi review** (2004) reinforced the OFT's position on 'restrictive practices' in the legal profession by recognising the new legal marketplace, thus furthering the **Tesco Law** vision of the future. Table 10.3 sets out the pros and cons of this situation.

Table 10.3 Some pros and cons relating to the new legal marketplace

| *Advantages* | *Disadvantages* |
|---|---|
| • Consumers benefit from *increased choice* and *accessibility* of legal services. | • The experience of commercial firms entering the legal services market – particularly certain accident-claims companies – *does not inspire confidence* about the future of legal provision. |
| • Consumers are no longer forced into consulting one particular sort of provider – the new legal marketplace heralds the *end of a 'closed shop'* of legal providers. | • Competition amongst commercial firms may drive traditional high street practices *out of business*. |
| • Consumers always benefit from increased competition because this *keeps prices low*. Competition in the conveyancing market, for example, has forced prices down, to the benefit of consumers. | • Publicly-funded legal services *might be threatened* because they offer limited profit opportunities in a commercial market. |
| • New regulation of the profession (see p 212 below) will *increase efficiency* of *complaints-handling* and *maintain quality standards*. | • The two branches of the profession will lose their respective independence, thus *undermining public confidence* in the delivery of legal services. |

The findings of the **Clementi review** reflect the spirit of the **Courts and Legal Services Act 1990** in encouraging new structures of delivering legal services. The review marks the point, as one Chairman of the Bar Council ruefully commented, at which a traditional legal profession becomes merely part of the 'legal services industry'. **Clementi** welcomes **multi-disciplinary partnerships**, about which the Law Society has long been resistant, with a vision of solicitors and barristers working with other professionals, such as accountants and estate agents, to offer a range of services to the public.

A suggestion that has also proved controversial is that of the **legal disciplinary partnership**, a form of business structure that would allow corporate interests to own law firms. This follows the **Tesco Law** logic of allowing big, successful businesses to have a stake in the new legal services marketplace, the assumption being that such businesses will bring a competitive edge to the market, thus having an interest both in driving up standards of quality and charging affordable rates. There are concerns, expressed by the **Bar Council**, in particular, that corporate interests, and the profit motive in particular, might be incompatible with the independence and integrity that practitioners, and consumers, take for granted under the current arrangements.

Whilst the **Clementi** findings have yet to be implemented, they have clearly influenced Government thinking about the future of the profession, as evidenced by the **White Paper**, 'The Future of Legal Services: Putting Consumers First', published in 2005. A **Draft Legal Services Bill**, containing the Government's plans for implementing the Clementi findings, was introduced to Parliament on 24 May 2006 for pre-legislative scrutiny by a Joint Committee appointed by the two Houses of Parliament.

## Reforms and the 'fusion debate'

Against this context of a changing market environment, it should be remembered that the UK has a divided legal profession (that is, solicitors and barristers), unlike other jurisdictions where the legal functions are fused and there is just one type of legal professional. Many argue for the 'fusion' of the UK profession, with one type of recognised lawyer. It might well be the case that if business structures do change in the way envisaged by **Clementi**, and larger 'one stop shop' firms begin to dominate the marketplace, the distinction between lawyers will become less important.

## Is fusion of the profession a worthwhile aim?

To answer this question, the main advantages and disadvantages of 'fusion' between solicitors and barristers have been summarised in Table 10.4 (see p 207).

Although it is true that the two branches of the profession are becoming somewhat *blurred*, with the growth of solicitor-advocates and barristers increasingly experimenting with direct access schemes, some of the old distinctions continue to be guarded by the Law Society and the Bar Council respectively. It is difficult to find a consensus among commentators. As **David Bean QC** (the then Chairman of the Bar Council) told *The Times* (2001) upon

Table 10.4 Fusion: advantages and disadvantages

| *Advantages* | *Disadvantages* |
|---|---|
| • *Less cost* for legal work, as a fused profession is more efficient and there is less chance of the duplication of tasks. The **Office of Fair Trading** acknowledged this point in its 2001 report. | • There would be *fewer court 'specialists'*, since 'fusion' would encourage lawyers to be 'all-rounders'. Moreover, barristers would seek employment in large solicitors' firms, thus *eroding the independent, self-employed Bar*. |
| • *Removes the 'two-tier' ranking between barristers and solicitors*, and therefore allows solicitors access to higher appointments. Bailey (2002) has observed that solicitors have increasingly been appointed to judicial positions following the reforms to the legal profession (for some measure of this, see Chapter 8). | • The existing system is established and working, so *why* change it? David Mason, a barrister, concluded an article in the *New Law Journal* (2003) with the following comments: 'Some years ago a small African State permitted direct access to the Bar after solicitors were given higher courts access. Both branches suffered. The two professions agreed to go back to a genuinely split profession. That sort of deal seems unlikely in Britain, however desirable'. |
| • More logical regarding legal education as students would have the *same foundation training*, thus gaining the same types of skill. This would mean that neither branch of the legal profession would be closed off to students. They would learn both types of skills and then decide in which area they would like to specialise. | • There is a difference between office skills and advocacy. Specialising in one or the other is difficult enough, but to expect lawyers to be skilled in both might *reduce the overall quality of service* being offered by the profession. Judges are to some extent dependent on quality advocacy, on the one hand, and clients need to know that litigation management and paperwork will be competent, accurate and capable of meeting all the necessary formal requirements, on the other. |
| • Clients can get used to dealing with *one person* throughout the proceedings. As one lawyer would represent the client, rather than having two with differing skills, interests and agendas, there are likely to be advantages in terms of communication and raising the confidence of the client that a clear direction is being set. | • There would be a *loss of the 'cab-rank' rule*. This rule states that barristers must take the next case that comes along, according to their particular area of expertise. The concern here is that while the cab-rank rule currently guarantees representation for the client, there will be no such guarantees with a fused profession. |
| • Fusion would arguably *be better for the client* (as a customer of services), with competition on fees and a wider choice of legal services to consider. Not only are there efficiencies (as identified above) with a fused system, but also the advantages of a relatively free and open market. | • There is a fear that fusion would lead to the creation of *huge law firms* at the expense of the smaller firms. It is unlikely that small firms would be able to retain a barrister, for example, whereas many barristers would be employed in larger concerns rather than making themselves available for self-employed work. |

his appointment: 'I don't see a profession moving towards fusion . . .', whereas **Martyn Day**, of campaigning law firm *Leigh Day & Co* told the *New Law Journal* in 2003 that 'I would be surprised if, in five to ten years, we have not seen the *total abolition of the distinction between solicitors and barristers*'. The changes in business structures associated with the **Clementi** review might necessitate the process predicted by Martyn Day, and there is certainly concern about the future of an independent Bar. However, whether actual fusion ever occurs or not, it is certainly true to say that the reform of the legal profession is an ongoing process. Watch out for further developments on this issue by checking the **updates** section of the **companion website** (**www.routledgecavendish.com/textbooks/9781845680329**) for this book.

## PROFESSIONAL LIABILITY

### Solicitors' liability

As a professional advice-giver, a solicitor must carry **professional indemnity insurance** to cover any claims resulting from inaccurate or inappropriate advice or conduct that has caused loss to a client. Such insurance is important because solicitors will owe legal liability for any errors that they make.

The solicitor is in a **contractual relationship** with the client. Therefore, certain contractual obligations are created on both sides. Hence, a solicitor can sue for fees, and a client can sue the solicitor for breach of contract. A client can also sue a solicitor under the **tort of negligence**. This is because the provision of specialist advice creates a *special relationship* between solicitor and client that places a clear **duty of care** on the solicitor. This special relationship was first identified for professionals in general in *Hedley Byrne & Co Ltd v Heller & Partners Ltd* (1964), in which Lord Morris stated: 'if someone possessed of a special skill undertakes, quite irrespective of contract, to apply that skill for the assistance of another person who relies on such skill, a duty of care will arise'. It was accepted that this situation could apply to solicitors in *Midland Bank Trust Co Ltd v Hett, Stubbs and Kemp* (1979); and an interesting example of a breach of this duty is provided by *Acton v Pearce* (1997), concerning the negligent handling of criminal proceedings by solicitors which had led to their client, another solicitor, being jailed. The client's conviction was subsequently quashed, and he received damages on the basis that reasonable management of the proceedings would not have led to a conviction. The solicitor's duty of care might also extend to others affected by negligence; for example, beneficiaries claiming compensation for lost entitlement under a negligently administered will. This point was established in *Ross v Caunters* (1979) and later followed in *White v Jones* (1995). Other third party situations include the instance in *Al-Kandari v JR Brown* (1988), where solicitors were held to owe a duty to the opposing party when they failed to fulfil an undertaking made to the court to safeguard their client's passport, thus placing the children at the centre of a custody battle in potential risk of abduction by the client.

Solicitors, along with barristers, can be sued for negligent advocacy following the principle in *Hall v Simons* (2000).

## Let's look at cases: *Hamilton Jones v David & Snape (A Firm)* (2003) – an example of solicitors' liability

In *Hamilton Jones v David & Snape (A Firm)* (2003), a firm of solicitors was sued, successfully, in contract and tort when its negligence had led to the client, Hamilton Jones, losing custody of her children. She claimed damages, in contract law, for the mental distress that losing custody had caused her. It was held, in the Chancery Division of the High Court, that she should be entitled to a sum of £20,000 for the distress that she had been caused. This was awarded on the basis that the contract between client and solicitor had been primarily to protect custody of the children and the solicitors' negligence had shattered her 'peace of mind'.

## Complaints against solicitors

The complaints system relating to solicitors is currently administered by the **Law Society**, though the Government's response to the **Clementi review** indicates that a new independent body – the **Office for Legal Complaints** – will take over this role (see pp 211–12 below). This proposal is included in the Government's **Draft Legal Services Bill 2006**.

Initially the complaints system was led by the Solicitors' Complaints Bureau, dealing with up to 26,000 complaints each year (mainly concerning overcharging by solicitors, or relating to the length of time being taken to move proceedings forward). This body was, however, heavily criticised for its own delays and deficiencies. Therefore a new body was created, the **Office for the Supervision of Solicitors (OSS)**, with a mission statement declaring: 'Our aim is to work for excellence and fairness in guarding the standards of the solicitors' profession'. However, in practice it was falling short of these standards. The OSS handled complaints against solicitors relating to delays, costs, lost papers, etc, but was regularly criticised for its own failures, such as poor file management, giving insufficient explanations for its decisions and failing to deliver on promises made to complainants.

In the **Annual Report for the Legal Services Ombudsman for England and Wales 2003/04,** the **Legal Services Ombudsman** expressed satisfaction with just 53.3 per cent of cases handled by the OSS. The Law Society's response, a *re-branding* of the OSS as the **Consumer Complaints Service** in 2004 to deal with 'inadequate professional service', did not impress the Ombudsman, who had not been consulted on the reform. Nevertheless, in the **2004/05 Ombudsman's report**, there was recognition that some progress had been made, with satisfaction expressed with 62 per cent of cases handled, though over 17,000 complaints had been received over this period. The consumer watchdog, *Which?*, pointed out that this meant there was one complaint for every six solicitors in England and Wales and that consumers no longer had confidence in the Law Society's complaints-handling. It welcomed the prospect of an **Office for Legal Complaints**, which would provide quick, fair, accessible, transparent and independent complaints handling, all of which, by implication, the Law Society had been unable to achieve.

In addition to complaints-handling and discipline by the Law Society for matters falling short of professional misconduct, the **Solicitors Disciplinary Tribunal** can *strike off* solicitors found to have committed **serious professional**

**misconduct**. However, whilst this Tribunal can fine offenders, it cannot award compensation to complainants who have lost out because of the solicitor's conduct. The Government's White Paper response to the **Clementi review** and its **Draft Legal Services Bill** suggest that the Law Society will retain some disciplinary powers in name, though subject to standards set and monitored by the **Legal Services Board** (see below at pp 212).

## Barristers' liability

Like solicitors, barristers also take out *professional indemnity insurance* to guard against legal claims. However, they *differ* from solicitors in one respect. Barristers are *not* in a contractual relationship with the client. Therefore, *no* breach of contract claims can ensue, either from the barrister over fees or from the client. For historical purposes, the barrister's fee is actually an *honorarium* (in other words, it is treated more like a 'tip'). If there is a dispute about the barrister's fees, the solicitor can sue the client on the barrister's behalf. Barristers can, however, be sued under the **tort of negligence** both for **advocacy** and for **advice and preparation.**

The established precedent of *Rondel v Worsley* (1969), which gave barristers freedom (or 'immunity') from negligence claims for advocacy work undertaken in the courts, has now been **overruled** by the House of Lords, exercising its discretion under the **1966 Practice Statement** (see Chapter 4), in *Hall v Simons* (2000). The position in *Rondel v Worsley* had been justified on policy grounds. The view that advocates might become overly cautious if subject to the threat of a suit was taken seriously. It was also felt that the advocate's duty to the court would be undermined, clients would seek litigation as an extension of the appeal process, and the floodgates might open, leading to lots of unworthy claims. Academics, such as **Professor Michael Zander**, had long been against such immunity, and there was a suspicion that the profession was effectively looking after itself, even though lawyers have never enjoyed similar immunity with regard to the giving and preparation of legal advice. The House of Lords judges in *Hall v Simons* were *unanimous* in calling for the immunity to be lost in civil cases, but only the majority of their Lordships supported this in relation to criminal cases.

In one of the first major cases to follow the loss of immunity, *Moy v Pettman Smith* (2005) the House of Lords was careful *not* to extend an advocate's liability to advice given 'at the door of the court' where this had been clearly expressed and accepted by the claimant in the course of proceedings. In this case, a barrister had been asked for, and gave, advice on an **offer to settle a personal injury claim.** The claimant followed her advice and did not accept the defendant's offer to settle. However, as the case developed the claimant was forced into settling for much less than he had originally been offered. He sued the barrister, alleging negligence. The House of Lords, in allowing the barrister's appeal against the claim, stated that to hold an advocate liable in these circumstances could send a message to other practitioners that only cautious, defensive advice might be acceptable, which would not, ultimately, be in the best interests of clients.

Barristers may also be sued for **negligent work in preparing for a case.** Therefore, an inaccurate opinion drafted by a barrister may lead to a negligence claim. As Lord Salmon pointed out in *Saif Ali v Sydney Mitchell & Co*

(1980), a case illustrating a successful claim against a barrister for negligent advice, '*if anyone holding himself out as possessing reasonable competence in his avocation undertakes to advise or to settle a document, he owes a duty to advise or settle a document with reasonable competence and care*'.

## Complaints against barristers

A lay **Complaints Commissioner** to hear complaints from the public about barristers was first appointed in 1997. The Complaints Commissioner refers matters to the Bar's **Professional Conduct and Complaints Committee** (PCCC). The Bar Council will award compensation in certain cases where inadequate service has been identified. As with the Law Society, the **Legal Services Ombudsman** also examines the way in which the Bar Council deals with complaints against barristers. In the 2004/05 report, the Ombudsman expressed satisfaction with complaints-handling in 78.7 per cent of cases, a slight historical dip for the Bar Council but nevertheless substantially better than the results achieved by the Law Society in its complaints-handling (see above). The **Complaints Commissioner** dealt with 524 cases during the 2004/05 period. Perhaps understandably, given its reasonable record on complaints-handling, the Bar Council has questioned whether an **Office for Legal Complaints** is necessary, given the likely cost and administration required for the new scheme. However, the Government's post-Clementi White Paper indicates that reform is on the agenda and the Office for Legal Complaints will replace the Bar's own complaints-handling arrangements (see below).

Discipline is largely undertaken by the **Bar Council**. Discipline covers a wide range of factors, such as the duty barristers have to their clients and the way in which *professional ethics* and etiquette are observed in serving the interests of justice.

The Bar Council has the power *to disbar* a barrister in the event of a serious complaint being upheld.

## The Legal Services Ombudsman

One question beloved of those who seek to criticise the law is 'But who regulates the regulators?'. In the case of the legal profession, the office of the **Legal Services Ombudsman** (Zahida Mazoor, at the time of writing) was created to *monitor* the way in which the **Law Society** and the **Bar Council** deal with public complaints against solicitors and barristers respectively. As we have seen, the Legal Services Ombudsman was a product of the **Courts and Legal Services Act 1990**, with the role of the Ombusdman, defined in s 22 of the 1990 Act, being to investigate any allegations, 'properly made', relating to the way in which public complaints to the law governing bodies (including **ILEX**) are handled by these bodies. The Ombudsman can make a series of recommendations based on the investigations undertaken, for which a formal response by the relevant governing body will be required within three months: such recommendations may include requests for the identified governing body to pay compensation in respect of the complaint.

Since February 2004, Zahida Mazoor has taken a further role, in addition to that of Ombudsman, of **Legal Services Complaints Commissioner** (LSCC).

This office had been provided for in the **Access to Justice Act 1999** and monitors the Law Society's planning of complaints-handling, giving the LSCC the power to impose a substantial penalty on the Law Society for failure to submit an adequate plan. In June 2006, *The Times* reported that the Law Society might receive a fine of up to £750,000 for problems with complaints-handling, with the LSCC having already fined the Law Society £250,000 for failures in planning and target-setting with regard to complaints against solicitors.

The creation of a **Legal Services Board** and **Office for Legal Complaints**, as proposed in the Government's post-Clementi White Paper and Draft Legal Services Bill 2006, suggest that the offices of the **Legal Services Ombudsman** and **Legal Services Complaints Commissioner** may be rendered obsolete in the near future.

## The Clementi review (2004) and its implications for the handling of complaints against solicitors and barristers

One of the reasons for setting up the **Clementi review** was to investigate the ways in which the branches of the profession were currently **regulated**, bearing in mind the perceived changes to the market environment in which they were operating. Clementi identified problems with the guarded self-regulation exercised by the Law Society, the Bar Council and ILEX (referred to as **front-line regulators** in the review) and, in considering a range of reform options (including abolition of these bodies), favoured the creation both of an independent **Legal Services Board** (**LSB**) to take over the regulatory role from these bodies and an independent **Office for Legal Complaints** (**OLC**) to investigate complaints against lawyers and enforce awards for financial redress against practitioners up to £20,000, where appropriate. The governing bodies would continue to carry out their representative roles. The Government's 2005 White Paper and **2006 Draft Legal Services Bill** propose that the LSB allow the day-to-day regulation and discipline of legal professionals to remain with the governing bodies provided that they operate within the standards set by the LSB. The OLC, however, may lead to the abolition of the Legal Services Ombudsman and the other current regulatory bodies, and would have sole authority for dealing with complaints about the legal profession.

**Exercise for Chapter 10: Recap quiz on the legal profession**

(1) Of which types of legal personnel are there:

- (a) 29,000 Members, of whom 7,000 are Fellows?
- (b) 14,000 practitioners?
- (c) 96,000 practitioners?
- (d) Case-workers and advocates allocated to 42 geographical areas?

**Options:** solicitors; barristers; Crown Prosecution Service; legal executives.

(2) With which types of legal personnel would you associate the following:

- (a) Inns of Court?
- (b) ILEX?
- (c) Law Society?
- (d) Dinners?

(e) Magic Circle?
(f) Bar Council?
(g) QC status?
(h) Rights of audience?
(i) Rights of audience in the higher courts?
(j) Wigs and gowns?
(k) LPC?
(l) BVC?
(m) Pupillage?
(n) Training contract?
(o) *Hall v Simons* (2000)?

**Options (from which you can choose more than once and in combination with other options where appropriate):** solicitors; barristers; legal executives.

(3) Identify the following proposals associated with the Clementi review:
(a) A new body to investigate allegations of poor service against lawyers?
(b) A new type of business structure which would allow corporate interests to own large law firms?
(c) A business structure that would allow lawyers to work side-by-side and in partnership with other professionals, such as estate agents and accountants?
(d) A new marketplace for legal services on the high street and in the shopping centre?

**Options:** Tesco law; multi-disciplinary partnerships; legal disciplinary partnerships; Office for Legal Complaints.

For Answers, please turn to pp 340–1.

## HINTS AND TIPS

In order to help your revision of this topic, you might wish to devise a **framework chart** in the same style as the one set out at **Figure 10.1** below, and add notes accordingly. This will enable you, at a glance, to note the **main differences** between the legal personnel you have studied and to **understand the contribution of each** to the legal system.

| *Revision criteria* | *Solicitors* | *Barristers* | *Legal Executives* |
|---|---|---|---|
| Governing body | | | |
| Education/training | | | |
| Role/workload | | | |
| Workplaces/examples | | | |
| Liability/complaints | | | |
| Recent changes | | | |

**Figure 10.1** Framework chart for revision

Questions with a greater **analytical/evaluative content** may focus on the last section of this chart, and separate, detailed notes are advised on the **reforms to the legal profession** and the **desirability of 'fusion'**. Since this is an ongoing situation, you should watch out for updates in the media paying particular attention to the Government's **Draft Legal Services Bill 2006**. *The Times* newspaper contained an excellent summary of this: 'Need advice? Visit a supermarket' (Frances Gibb, 25/1/06).

Lastly, one practical point is worth repeating: try to obtain some good, **first-hand experience** of the profession through **work experience** or a **mini-pupillage**. Whilst it is not essential for you to gain such experience at this level of study, it will be of benefit later if you decide to continue with law or are considering this area as a career option. The advantage of carrying out work experience is that it puts theory into practice and allows you to make up your own mind about aspects of the job that are appealing. You should also – if you get the chance – participate in **bar mock trial** or **debating competitions**, as they are not just learning aids but also very interesting and enjoyable.

## Useful website addresses

| | |
|---|---|
| Allen & Overy | www.allenovery.com |
| Bar Council | www.barcouncil.org.uk |
| Clifford Chance | www.cliffordchance.com |
| Commercial Bar | www.combar.com |
| Consumer law firms | www.consumer-solicitors.co.uk |
| Crown Prosecution Service | www.cps.gov.uk |
| Department for Constitutional Affairs | www.dca.gov.uk |
| Family law firms | www.family-solicitors.co.uk |
| Freshfields | www.freshfields.com |
| Institute of Legal Executives | www.ilex.org.uk |
| Law Society | www.lawsociety.org.uk |
| *Law Society Gazette* | www.lawgazette.co.uk |
| Law Society Commerce and Industry Group | www.liggroup.org.uk |
| *The Lawyer* | www.the-lawyer.co.uk |
| Lawyers in Government | www.gls.gov.uk |
| Legal profession (in general) | www.infolaw.co.uk |
| Legal Services Ombudsman | www.olso.org |
| Linklaters | www.linklaters.com |
| Matrix Chambers | www.matrixlaw.co.uk |
| Slaughter & May | www.slaughterandmay.com |
| *Materials directly for AS studies:* | |
| John Deft (St Brendan's Sixth Form College) | www.stbrn.ac.uk/other/depts/law |
| Asif Tufal | www.a-level-law.com |

# Access to justice

This topic enables you:

- To understand the meaning of 'access to justice'.
- To gain an awareness of the sources of legal advice available to members of the public.
- To make the distinction between civil claims that are privately funded and those which require public funding.
- To understand the system that has been put in place for the public funding of civil claims and defending criminal cases.
- To consider the use of conditional fees for personal injury and other civil claims.

This part of the book has focused on dispute-solving within the courts, and also considered the availability of tribunals for some types of legal claim. It has been assumed so far that since there is a clear system for dealing with legal claims then it follows that this system is accessible, or open, to members of the public. However, **does the English legal system provide access to justice, regardless of wealth, background or location?** For example: Can a person with a legitimate legal claim but an uncertain or low-paid job afford to assert his or her legal rights in the civil courts? What sources of legal advice are available to that person? These are some of the questions that this chapter addresses.

## INTRODUCING THE DISCUSSION OF 'ACCESS TO JUSTICE'

In order to explain how the English legal system strives to achieve 'access to justice', this chapter will develop coverage of the legal framework in this area according to the following structure:

- Access to legal information – advice, support and guidance.
- Access to State funding for legal help and representation.
- The role of the legal profession in providing 'access to justice'.

This framework was put in place by the **Access to Justice Act 1999** in order to give coherence to the provision of legal advice and to reform the provision of public funding for legal claims. The old system is evaluated in the 'Developing the subject' box on p 216.

While the new system incorporates aspects of the old, it has shaken up the provision of advice, assistance

> **IT'S A FACT!**
>
> **11.1: The background to the public funding of legal services**
>
> - Provision for legal aid and advice was first made by the pioneering post-war Labour Government led by **Clement Attlee** (1945–51). This Government developed the foundations of the welfare state, including the National Health Service. Whilst some campaigned for a National Legal Service, along the lines of the NHS, the mere fact that people could now claim funding from the State to pursue their legal rights was a great leap forward.
> - The legal aid scheme persisted until the 1990s, when rising costs and Conservative political ideology about the role of the State in legal matters, prompted calls for reform.
> - The Labour Government in 1997 took some of these factors into account when publishing its 'Modernising Justice' White Paper and then creating the current access to justice framework in the **Access to Justice Act 1999**.
> - The Government is obliged to take access to justice seriously as an issue: it is part of the right to a fair trial protected by **Art 6** of the **European Convention on Human Rights**, as incorporated into English law by the **Human Rights Act 1998**.

and representation in the English legal system and a new legal landscape has been formed. The old legal aid system has been replaced by two new schemes:

THE COMMUNITY LEGAL SERVICE ⟶ For civil cases

THE CRIMINAL DEFENCE SERVICE ⟶ For criminal cases

## Developing the subject 11.1: What was wrong with the old legal aid scheme?

As we have also seen with regard to the legal profession (note the main policy aims of the **Courts and Legal Services Act 1990**, for example), the Conservative Governments between 1979 and 1997 had a desire to reduce the role of the State, where it could; reduce direct taxation; and increase efficiency in the delivery of public services. This explains why, in 1992, the Conservative Lord Chancellor, **Lord Mackay**, told the Law Society at its annual conference that the taxpayer should no longer be burdened by the increasing costs of legal aid, running at over £600m at that time, and proposed cuts in legal aid that came to be bitterly opposed.

Costs were undoubtedly an issue. By 1997/98, when the Blair Labour Government came to power, the legal aid bill had risen to £1.5bn, largely as Lord Mackay had predicted. However, this rise in costs occurred despite cuts that removed eligibility for legal aid from millions of citizens. Somehow, a balance needed to be struck between the *demand* for basic legal services and the need to *keep costs under control*. This would include looking at alternatives to legal aid where they provided opportunities for access to justice.

In seeking to shape the future of public funding for legal services, some sense was required of what had gone wrong with the legal aid system. The **Middleton Committee**, set up by the Lord Chancellor to review civil justice and legal aid, provided some suggestions. It was found, in particular, that much of the funding was spent on the expensive fees of lawyers than on meeting the advice and representation needs of the most vulnerable in society. Just as funding had increased, there was evidence that the numbers of people actually receiving help had declined in some areas of work.

The new Labour Government realised, through its emphasis on social justice, that it had a legacy to follow (the post-war Attlee Government's creation of the legal aid scheme) in providing for the most disadvantaged in society, whilst also seeking to make policy that could be justified to taxpayers as 'value for money'. Its resulting policy, following a White Paper called **'Modernising Justice'**, was expressed in the access to justice framework developed by the Act of that name in 1999.

**When you have finished reading this chapter, please attempt the questions that follow Developing the subject 11.2 on pp 225–6.**

## ACCESS TO LEGAL INFORMATION

One of the 'flagship' initiatives at the heart of the 'Access to Justice' framework following the 1999 Act was the establishment of the **'Just Ask!' website**, provided by an important new body called the **Legal Services Commission.** Although this website was subsequently renamed as **Community Legal Service Direct** (www.clsdirect.org.uk), it is clearly a useful source of information for any person seeking advice about his or her legal rights, enabling the public to locate *local networks* of legal providers, known as **Community Legal Service Partnerships.** These are brought together by the **Community Legal Service,** another body created by the 1999 Act. The relationship between the Community Legal Service and the Legal Services Commission is a close one. Table 11.1 illustrates this point.

Table 11.1 Relationship between the Legal Services Commission and Community Legal Service

| *Legal Services Commission* | *Community Legal Service* |
|---|---|
| • The Legal Services Commission is the body that allocates and administers the provision of publicly-funded legal services through the Community Legal Service Fund, thus taking on the role that used to belong to the old Legal Aid Board. | • The Community Legal Service has been set up to provide help, information and advice to the public.<br>• The Community Legal Service Fund has replaced the old system of Legal Aid for civil matters. The Legal Services Commission will manage this fund to ensure that legal services are available to the public. |

NB: The Legal Services Commission stands in a similar relationship to the *Criminal Defence Service*, providing publicly-funded legal services to those involved in criminal investigations or proceedings.

The aim is for the creation of these bodies, and the development of Community Legal Service Partnerships, to result in the relationship of funding bodies with suppliers of legal services in order 'to provide', according to the Legal Services Commission, *'the widest possible access to information and advice'*.

Community Legal Service Partnerships are a combination of three elements:

(**a**) sources of funding;
(**b**) legal service providers; and
(**c**) local interest groups.

See Table 11.2 below.

A *referral network* between providers is encouraged, so that if a member of the public is unable to access the necessary information at one outlet, he or

Table 11.2 The elements of Community Legal Service Partnerships

| *Sources of funding* | *Legal service providers* | *Local interest groups* |
|---|---|---|
| The dominant source of funding is clearly the **Legal Services Commission** that administers the **Community Legal Service Fund.**<br>There are, however, other significant funding sources, such as **local authorities** and **charities**. | The range of providers will differ from area to area, though generally the sorts of providers to be found within such partnerships will include:<br>• **lawyers** (especially **solicitors**)<br>• dedicated **Advice Centres** (such as **Citizens' Advice Bureaux** and **Law Centres**: see pp 218–19 below)<br>• *general* advice centres (such as **libraries** and community centres). | Sometimes **community groups** will also provide input to the work of the Partnership and its contribution to the local public. |

she may be referred elsewhere. The standards of Community Legal Service providers are assured by the **'Community Legal Service Quality Mark'**.

Having established that an umbrella of advice-giving exists via the **Community Legal Service Direct website**, allowing access to information about local Community Legal Service providers, we now focus on each of these providers of legal services.

## Solicitors

The role of solicitors in providing both advice and representation is covered in detail below. However, members of the public who are directed towards certain solicitors or solicitors' firms via the Community Legal Service Partnership scheme (ie, those firms that have been granted the **'Community Legal Service Quality Mark'**) may receive **free services** *or* be **expected to contribute** – to varying degrees – to the provision of the legal services that they require. Some firms, for example, may offer initial interview time with clients free of charge, or ask clients to pay fixed fees rather than fees that change according to the circumstances. The initial interview is usually up to 30 minutes in length.

| Legal Help | Duty Solicitor Scheme |
| --- | --- |
| ↓<br>Pays for legal advice on most civil and criminal matters. | ↓<br>Available to give advice to people detained at a police station or appearing before magistrates' court. |

Solicitors' firms are generally located close to the centres of towns and cities – usually in the vicinity of other offices, such as estate agencies, insurance and accountancy firms – and are therefore accessible by public transport. Some solicitors will take on certain cases on a *pro bono* basis, in other words, they will take these cases for free, either in part or from start to finish.

## Citizens' Advice Bureaux

There are 3,400 **Citizens' Advice Bureaux (CAB) outlets** across Britain, most noticeably in the form of modest advice centres, but also in health centres, schools, prisons, courts, libraries and community centres. The advice centres are located reasonably close to the centres of towns and cities and can therefore be accessed quite easily. CAB offices are funded from a variety of public, private and voluntary sector sources at local level. Each CAB outlet, each a registered charity, is a satellite of **Citizens Advice**, a national charity.

Citizens' Advice Bureaux are staffed primarily by **volunteers** (over 20,000, from a total staff of almost 28,000), though the advisory service they operate is often undertaken in conjunction with participating solicitors and other local agencies, such as consumer groups, probation and youth panel workers. They have certain strengths in advising the public and specialise in areas that affect the most vulnerable members of society, such as welfare benefits, housing matters, employment rights and debt. In 2004/05, CAB dealt with over five million new client problems across England, Wales and Northern Ireland and its website, **www.adviceguide.org.uk**, received over two million visits.

The key point to note about the provision of advice and support from the CAB is that it is *free*. CAB advisers might provide help with composing letters, completing legal and other forms and documents, right through to representing clients in courts and tribunals. Although the volunteer aspect of CAB might not always inspire public confidence, there is no doubt that since their creation in 1939, the Bureaux have helped an enormous number of poor and disadvantaged individuals.

## Law Centres

Law Centres respond to the **'unmet need'**, as suggested by the problems with the public funding of legal claims, by enabling those who are poor, unemployed or otherwise disadvantaged to access information about their rights. These Centres are highly regarded for their advice work in areas such as social welfare and immigration. They aim to offer something akin to a doctor's surgery for legal matters, with a mixture of general and specific information available and advisers on hand to deal with individual cases.

Law Centres, like CAB outlets, currently have a 'shop' presence in 57 locations around Britain, with 22 of these located in London. They are funded from a variety of sources, though the **National Lottery Charities Board** and the **Community Legal Service Fund**, as distributed by the **Legal Services Commission**, are the main contributors. However, between 1991 and 2000, 11 Law Centres had to close, and in each case funding was a key issue. They continue to exist somewhat precariously, though the changes in the **Access to Justice Act 1999** should mean that their value is better appreciated, and therefore that funding is more likely to be released for them.

There are also a number of specialist **Legal Advice Centres** that are operated by charities and campaign groups, such as **Shelter** (for homeless people), **Mind** (with regard to mental health issues) and the **Refugee Legal Centre**.

Law Centres are represented by a national organisation called the **Law Centres Federation**.

## Trade unions

Most trade unions offer free legal advice to *members*, particularly in relation to workplace issues such as statutory employment rights and matters relating to dismissal, redundancy and industrial action. Most unions also issue regular bulletins containing law updates and question-and-answer style advice sections.

## Media

Most national newspapers contain advice columns covering legal issues. For example, the *Times Law Supplement*, which is included in *The Times* every Tuesday, has a legal problems section to which readers write with legal questions, the answers being provided by students at the College of Law. Consumer issues are covered in a great detail in the media, appearing on television (such as **'Watchdog'**), radio (such as Radio 4's 'You and Yours'), and in newspapers and magazines (such as *Which?* magazine, published by the Consumers' Association).

As sources of advice the media have limitations, not least because their coverage is largely in response to particular issues and therefore difficult to predict. However, increasing use of the **internet** has provided greater access to archives of media articles and increased their relevance for members of the public.

## Local authority advice centres

These centres provide advice relating to the provision of local authority services, with housing, welfare and social services being the main areas covered. They are contact points for the local community and provide lots of useful information, not least about the rights of service users and the duties that the local authority owes to them. Such centres are also places in which **Trading Standards** and **Environmental Health Departments** can publicise general consumer rights.

## Specialist organisations

Perhaps the best known examples here are the motoring bodies, such as the **RAC** and the **AA**, which provide members with legal advice and information. Both of these bodies wish to offer a wider range of legal services and it seems likely, following the **Clementi Review** (see Chapter 10), that the RAC will be allowed to expand its legal provision for the benefit of members and consumers in general.

Table 11.3, opposite, summarises the main sources of access to legal information.

# ACCESS TO STATE FUNDING FOR LEGAL HELP AND REPRESENTATION

The new system of funding administered by the Legal Services Commission in allocating the Community Legal Service Fund *replaces* the Legal Aid scheme, which had been in place in one form or another since 1949. Although both the old system and the new system are similar in principle, the new system has been designed to avoid the problems that were evident with Legal Aid. The first point to note is that the terminology has changed, as Table 11.4 on p 222 indicates.

As mentioned earlier, the new system of public funding relates to *both* civil matters and criminal matters. The **Legal Services Commission** administers both schemes.

## Public funding for civil matters – the Community Legal Service

The new provision of funding for legal services in relation to civil matters takes great account of the failings of the old system, such as not providing for the most disadvantaged and needy in society. The new system goes some way to resolving this criticism through two means: first, by *extending* the sorts of claims eligible for public funding; and, second, by creating a new basis of funding for certain sorts of claim, such as personal injury (see p 226 below), through *private arrangements* with certain solicitors' firms.

The **Community Legal Service Fund** will be used to finance **legal help and representation** in civil matters resolved by the courts, by alternative methods of dispute resolution (such as mediation in family cases) and by tribunals in specified areas (eg immigration). Only those solicitors' firms with a **contract** awarded by the **Legal Services Commission** can carry out publicly-funded work, with the contracts process enabling the LSC, in theory if not always in

Table 11.3 Access to legal information: sources

| *Source of legal information* | *Brief description* |
|---|---|
| **'CLS Direct' website** | • Refers members of the public to local providers of help, information, advice and representation. |
| **Solicitors** | • May offer initial interviews.<br>• Provide a range of legal services.<br>• May provide free services, or require the client to pay or contribute to fees. |
| **Citizens' Advice Bureaux (CABx)** | • Many CAB outlets across the UK.<br>• Largely staffed by trained volunteers.<br>• Offer information and services free of charge.<br>• Specialise in areas of particular need, for example, welfare, benefits, debts, etc. |
| **Law Centres** | • Law Centres respond to the needs of the poor, vulnerable and unemployed (the 'unmet need').<br>• There are far fewer Law Centres than, say, CAB outlets, and these are located in largely urban areas.<br>• Law Centres are funded from a mixture of sources. |
| **Trade unions** | • Offer free legal advice to members, particularly on matters of employment law. |
| **Media** | • Newspapers and magazines include columns focusing on employment and consumer rights.<br>• Television and radio programmes also focus on these issues. |
| **Local authority advice centres** | • These provide information relating to local authority services. |
| **Specialist organisations** | • For example, motoring bodies such as the AA and the RAC, which provide their members with advice and information. |

practice, to specify types of work most likely to address 'unmet needs' and match the funding accordingly.

If an individual seeks legal help and representation from a contracted solicitors' firm, a funding assessment will be made of the case to gauge the appropriateness, or **merits**, of the funding. Claims perceived to be in the **public interest** will be given **priority funding**, such as those relating to human rights. There is also a category of social welfare and family cases that attracts priority status because it involves matters of social exclusion, poverty and impacts upon the life and liberty of individuals.

Table 11.4 State funding: terminology

| *Old funding terminology* | *New funding terminology* |
|---|---|
| **Legal Aid** (covering the costs associated with legal representation for the purposes of litigation) | **Legal Representation** |
| **Legal Advice and Assistance** (covering the costs of preparatory work for the client and non-contentious work) | **Legal Help** |

NB: The term **'legal aid'** is still used to refer, in general, to the public funding of legal work.

Full financial support for legal services will be reserved only for those with very **limited means** (in terms of *income* and *capital wealth*); those who exceed certain income thresholds will have to contribute to the services that they require. However, the Community Legal Service Fund will *not* be available for certain types of claim, and in these cases members of the public may have to resort to other means of carrying the case forward. Areas that will *not* be eligible for funding include:

- Personal injury
- Defamation
- Wills and trusts
- Business and corporate law.

Moreover, special rules apply to complex negligence cases – which may be funded in certain circumstances – and other areas such as judicial review where the procedures can be lengthy, time-consuming and expensive.

The Government has been keen to examine the ways in which legal services are delivered by the legal profession and how legal practitioners should be paid out of public funds. Since April 2005, a **fixed fee scheme** has been introduced for large areas of publicly-funded civil work (not including immigration). Under this scheme, solicitors are rewarded for case completion by the Legal Services Commission but at a rate that might not have any bearing on the time spent by practitioners in working on it. The scheme was given a very cautious welcome at the consultation stage by **Citizens Advice**, who issued a press statement (27/7/04): 'We see some merit in proposals for fixed fees (for legal practitioners) for civil work, but unless these are set at a reasonable level, and accompanied by a significant reduction of bureaucracy, more legal aid suppliers will leave, increasing the problem of **advice deserts**'. (**'Advice deserts'** refer to areas in which members of the public are unable to access publicly-funded legal services, thus revealing an **'unmet need'** for basic legal rights.) However, the Legal Services Commission announced in the autumn of 2005 that the scheme will be extended until April 2007, with solicitors reportedly welcoming the news (*Solicitors' Journal* (14 October 2005) and a Minister at the Department for Constitutional Affairs, Bridget Prentice MP, in November 2005 commenting that '(feedback since the scheme's introduction) . . . seem to indicate that it has been a success'. The Lord Chancellor commissioned a review of funding in civil cases, headed by Lord Carter, which has just been completed (see summary below).

## Public funding in criminal cases – the Criminal Defence Service

The **Criminal Defence Service** provides help and representation for those who are the subject of police investigations or actual criminal proceedings. As with the civil scheme for public funding, legal practitioners can only offer these services with a **contract**, and recognition of standards in the form of a **Quality Mark**, from the **Legal Services Commission.** As the following coverage indicates, the funds that are made available can apply to all of the legal work associated with criminal matters, including advice and assistance during detention in custody, through to advocacy on the client's behalf.

The **duty solicitor scheme** is a key aspect of the **Criminal Defence Service's** provision of legal help, with solicitors providing **free advice and assistance** to those detained in police stations or appearing before the magistrates' courts. However, the nature of the advice a person gets will depend on the seriousness of the offence and the circumstances: advice for relatively minor offences is now delivered by telephone, rather than face-to-face.

For **legal representation,** such as advocacy (which may be carried out by solicitor-advocates and barristers), determination of the appropriateness of funding allowed for each case will be based on the perceived **'interests of justice'** of the case (**'merits' test**). This is designed to *filter out* trifling claims for public funding and to recognise those cases where the loss of liberty or some other significant factor merits the allocation of financial aid. Although some safeguards exist to prevent the wealthy from drawing on public funding – including the power of a court to recover defence costs – it is nevertheless still the case that there are some undeserving recipients of public money. The **Criminal Defence Service Act 2006**, s 2, responds to this with provision for **means testing** of those seeking public funding for representation in criminal proceedings, amending the Access to Justice Act 1999 accordingly.

The development of a **Criminal Defence Service** has been accompanied by the piloting of a **'Public Defender' service,** similar in nature to its opposite body, the Crown Prosecution Service. Public Defenders are lawyers, employed by the Criminal Defence Service to carry out legal services for defendants in criminal cases. As for civil legal aid, Lord Carter has also led a review of the way in which public funding should be allocated to legal practitioners carrying out criminal legal aid work.

## Postscript: Lord Carter delivers his report on 'legal aid procurement'

Lord Carter of Coles delivered his final report on the public funding of legal services – specifically the **'procurement' of legal services,** meaning the way in which these are paid for with public money – in July 2006. At present, the total amount spent on legal aid is **£2.1 billion,** costing taxpayers an estimated £100 each per year. Lord Carter's proposals seek to **maintain a limit on total**

**costs.** He has identified **£100 million' worth of cuts and savings** that can be made and argues for the **rebalancing of public spending** so that criminal legal aid, which currently receives the 'lion's share', will be cut-back in favour of **more money for civil legal aid** (including family cases).

Lord Carter's report makes 62 recommendations, which are likely to have the following impacts:

- The provision of all legal aid will be subject to **competitive tendering** by law firms for new contracts to carry out state funded legal services (thus threatening the existence of smaller, less-competitive law firms and favouring larger firms; it is thought that some smaller firms will merge to survive).
- The payment of legal aid to legal practitioners will be on a **fixed fee basis** (or a variant of this) as opposed to the current system of payment based on hourly rates or according to specific work done.
- The rates of pay earned by senior criminal barristers (such as those characterized in the press as 'fat cat QCs') will be cut, whilst junior barristers should see modest increases in the pay rates available.
- The administration of legal aid will become more efficient, with cuts in the running costs of the Legal Services Commission and a better deal being achieved for the taxpayer.

The Lord Chancellor has welcomed the report as a major contribution to **'access to justice'**, but it has been fiercely resisted by criminal law solicitors and barristers. It remains to be seen, at the time of writing, how much of the report the Government will seek to implement.

## OTHER WAYS IN WHICH THE LEGAL PROFESSION PROVIDES ACCESS TO JUSTICE

For those who can afford it, access to justice is not a problem. They will visit a firm of solicitors and **privately finance** any claim that they have. For the poor, on the other hand, 'access to justice' is an issue, but the State will generally fund their claims. Thus, the very poor can bring their claims to court via public funding, and the wealthy can finance their claims themselves. However, a criticism of the old Legal Aid system was that those *in the middle* were often caught out, having *too much* income to be eligible for State funding, but *too little* to finance legal proceedings on their own account. The challenge for policy-makers was to find a *compromise* for those 'stuck in the middle'; and also to ensure that the removal of civil legal aid for personal injury claims did not prevent access to justice for the poor in this specific area. The solution to these problems has taken the form of **Conditional Fee Agreements**.

## Developing the subject 11.2: Evaluating the access to justice framework

*Please refer back to Developing the Subject 11.1 to compare the old legal aid system with the current access to justice framework. This will also enable you to answer the questions in the exercise that follows this piece.*

So has the access to justice framework introduced by the **Access to Justice Act 1999** worked? I have chosen the following criteria to review the current framework: cost; innovation; support of the legal profession; and need for further reforms. I leave the conclusions to you.

*Cost*
The issue of cost has dominated discussion of the new framework. The overall cost now stands at over **£2 billion** per year. There are concerns that spending on criminal legal aid has increased by 37 per cent since 1997 at the expense of the civil justice system, where there remain areas of 'unmet need' that disadvantage the poor and vulnerable. Fees for shorter criminal trials have been effectively frozen for eight years on a fixed fee basis. On the other hand, just 1 per cent of high cost criminal cases can drain 49 per cent of allocated funding. The Lord Chancellor announced in October 2005 that pay rates would be cut in an effort to save up to £140 million per year on criminal legal aid. The Government requested Lord Carter to review the current state of public funding, with particular regard to spending on criminal defence services and report back in 2006. His interim report was published in February 2006 (see summaries: *A-level Law Review*, Vol 2, Issue 1, September 2006, update by Nick Price – www.legalaidprocurementreview.gov.uk/docs/leaflet_pcapp.pdf) and final report in July 2006.

*Innovation*
The access to justice framework contains many innovative features in its provision of advice, including the bringing together of providers in **Community Legal Service Partnerships** and the **Community Legal Service Direct** website. The Public Defender scheme associated with the Criminal Defence Service and the fixed fee approach to civil cases both appear to have met with success.

*Effectiveness*
Although there have been some successes, many of the bodies representing contributors to the **Community Legal Service Partnerships**, such as **Citizens Advice** and the **Law Centres Federation**, continue to identify areas of 'unmet need' and 'advice deserts' in social welfare provision and point the blame at the **Legal Services Commission's** contracting system. This situation contrasts with one of the central themes of the 1999 Act: promoting availability of services, and ensuring that people can secure access to these so as to meet individual needs.

*Support of the legal profession*
Both the **Law Society** and the **Bar Council** have complained about the current state of public funding for legal services and some criminal barristers even went on strike, in the winter of 2005, to express their disgust at the rates of pay being offered. However, the media found it difficult to support the barristers, having identified the first legal aid barrister to be paid more than £1 million per year in fees, James Sturman QC, plus 11 other lawyers – including strike leader, David Spens, QC – earning on average more than £600,000 at the taxpayer's expense (see, eg the *Guardian*, 15/9/05).

*Need for further reforms*
The Government, access to justice agencies and the legal profession are all keen to discuss Lord Carter's vision of the future. The prospect of law firms engaging in **competitive tendering** for public funding contracts from the Legal Services Commission, the impact of the Criminal Defence Act 2006 and the final conclusions of the Carter review dominate the discussion about access to justice, at the time of writing.

**Questions:**

(1) Refer back to Developing the subject 11.1 on p 216. Summarise the problems identified with the old legal aid scheme which prompted the creation of the current access to justice framework.

(2) Compare and contrast this with Developing the subject 11.2, above. Has the access to justice framework solved these problems? List the main successes and failures, in your view, of the access to justice framework, taking into account the article above and Chapter 11 in general.

(3) Imagine that you are the Secretary of State for Constitutional Affairs and Lord Chancellor. You know that the total spending of the Government is £485 billion, of which, for example, £82 billion goes to health, £27 billion to defence and £18 billion for transport (2004 figures: see www.treasury.gov.uk for full breakdown).

(a) Identify as many areas of civil and criminal legal need as you can in the community. Which areas of need should be, in your view, prioritised?

(b) Consider the case for increasing the amount of money allocated to the public funding of legal services. What objections might be encountered?

(c) Develop arguments for and against a National Legal Service, along the lines of the NHS, for the UK.

## Conditional Fee Agreements

Conditional Fee Agreements are also more commonly referred to as **'no win, no fee' agreements.** They represent an agreement between clients and solicitors and were first provided for in the Courts and Legal Services Act 1990, as amended by the Access to Justice Act 1999, ss 27–31, and supplemented by technical provisions contained in statutory instruments. They can be used for *all civil matters*, with the exception of family cases. Given the unpredictable costs associated with civil claims, the conditional fee arrangements enable litigants to lessen their risk of incurring great expense, and are often taken out in conjunction with insurance to achieve further security. **So what is a Conditional Fee Agreement, and how does it operate?**

The first point to make is that the Conditional Fee Agreement does create a **'no win, no fee' situation:** in other words, it is agreed at the outset by the solicitor that if the case is not won, the client does not have to pay anything. This is why it is called a 'conditional fee': the solicitor's fee is payable only *on condition* that the case is won.

So if the case is lost, the situation is simple with regard to the relationship between the solicitor and the client. The client may still have financial obligations if he or she loses – the losing party in a civil case generally has to pay the costs of the winning party – but these are not to the solicitor. Thus, the *obligation* will be owed to the *winning party* and can be covered by **insurance** taken out at the start of the claim.

However, Conditional Fee Agreements also, of course, make provision for the situation in which the **claim is successful.** In making the agreement, the solicitor and client will have come to an agreement on the solicitor's basic fee for the case. The solicitor will, however, calculate a 'success fee', to be added to the basic fee, which the solicitor will claim for winning the case. The 'success fee' may be any amount up to 100 per cent of the value of the base costs incurred by a solicitor in taking the case forward. In *Callery v Gray (No 1)* (2001), the courts suggested that a success fee of 20 per cent would be appropriate for a standard personal injury claim. However, where the claimant solicitors are taking great risks in pursuing claims, a 100 per cent success fee has been upheld (as in *Designers Guild Ltd v Russell Williams* (2003)). It is the **losing party** in the case who will actually **pay this success fee,** since the losing party has to pay all the recoverable costs of the case. The **Access to Justice Act 1999** amended earlier legislation in order to ensure both that the 'success fee' and any insurance premiums paid should be covered by the losing party with responsibility for paying the main costs of the case. The reform achieves the aim that the successful litigant gains the full benefits of any award, rather than paying out a sizeable proportion to a solicitor. This principle was applied in the case of *Callery v Gray (No 1)* (2001).

The costs issue is the main risk associated with financing a civil claim by way of conditional fees. We have seen that if the client's claim is unsuccessful, the client does not have to pay his or her solicitor (the 'no win, no fee' element). However, the client will have to pay the other party's costs in the event that the case is lost. To take this risk into account, the client will take out **insurance** and pay the appropriate premiums in advance. The cost of such premiums can be substantial, and this is recognised by the public funding support provided for the most complex legal claims, such as medical negligence. If a client takes out insurance to cover for the possibility that the case might be lost, and it turns out instead that the case is won, the losing party will cover the cost of the premiums paid.

Conditional Fee Agreements have become a common way of initiating legal claims for civil matters, particularly in the area of personal injury. However, it is open to question whether **Conditional Fee Agreements** are a suitable method for providing access to justice for claimants who are ineligible for public funding under the Community Legal Service.

Table 11.5, on p 229, summarises the general advantages and disadvantages of Conditional Fee Agreements and 'Developing the subject 11.3', again on pp 229–30, considers a recent critical study of this topic.

## *Pro Bono* work

Some lawyers will offer legal services *free of charge* in certain sorts of cases. This is known as *pro bono* work (or 'work for the public good') and will be taken on by both solicitors and barristers. There are *pro bono* groups of solicitors and barristers, and these can be referred to by advice-giving agencies dealing particularly with the most vulnerable members of the community, such as Law Centres. With regard to barristers and *pro bono* work, it should be noted that some QCs have also offered their services – a considerable step given the fees that they can command – though their commitment is limited only to a certain number of days each year. There is also a **Free Representation Unit**, established by barristers (particularly those in training) to provide advocacy services for disadvantaged clients who have been referred to it via the Citizens' Advice Bureaux.

## Let's look at cases 11.1: *Campbell v Mirror Group Newspapers Ltd (No 2)* (2005)

The *Campbell v Mirror Group Newspapers (MGN) Ltd* (2004) case was considered in Chapter 1, relating to the successful action for libel and breach of privacy taken by the supermodel, Naomi Campbell, against the *Daily Mirror* for photographs and a story it had published about her. The significance of this 2005 case is that it focused on the way in which Campbell had brought her law-suit to the House of Lords: via a Conditional Fee Agreement with her solicitors (earlier proceedings had been funded privately).

At the conclusion of the first case, which had been considered by a first instance court and two senior appeal courts, the House of Lords found for Campbell and awarded her £3,500 in damages. In addition, MGN, as the losing party in the case, had to pay Campbell's legal costs. Owing to the length of the proceedings, and the 95 and 100 per cent success fees claimed by Campbell's solicitors and counsel for winning the case under the Conditional Fee Agreement, the costs bill for MGN stood at over £1 million (not including its own costs). MGN therefore challenged the ruling on costs, arguing that it was *disproportionate*, acted as a *gag on freedom of expression* under Art 10 of the European Convention on Human Rights and could not be justified because the supermodel had the 'means' to pay for the legal action herself, without having to rely on a Conditional Fee Agreement.

The House of Lords rejected MGN's arguments, with Lord Hoffmann delivering the leading judgment. The costs award was proportionate because it reflected the reality of Conditional Fee Agreements: the successes under a 'no win, no fee' scheme would make up for the inevitable losses, and thus secured a funding mechanism for legal cases that allowed for access to justice. There was no infringement of freedom of expression: it could not be right for newspapers to have the freedom to print libels at an affordable price. The argument about 'means' did not stand up: there was no requirement in the Access to Justice Act 1999 as to the claimant's means, so it did not matter that Campbell could perhaps have funded the case herself.

**Short answer exercise** *(please refer to pp 226–7 on Conditional Fee Agreements in tackling these questions)*:

(1) What options did Naomi Campbell have for funding a libel case? Why do you think she opted for a Conditional Fee Agreement for her appeal to the House of Lords?
(2) What is a success fee? How does it differ from the basic fee in a Conditional Fee Agreement?
(3) Why was MGN liable for the success fees in Campbell's Conditional Fee Agreement? What is the justification for this position?
(4) Do you have any sympathy with the newspaper's view that costs awards in these circumstances merely serve to stifle freedom of expression?
(5) Had you been one of the Lords of Appeal in Ordinary hearing this case, would you have agreed with this decision, or dissented?

For Answers to Qs 1–3, please turn to pp 341–2. Qs 4 and 5 are included as prompts for thinking and discussion.

Table 11.5 Conditional Fee Agreements: advantages and disadvantages

| *Advantages* | *Disadvantages* |
| --- | --- |
| • Conditional fees represent a new way of providing access to civil justice *without* placing a huge financial burden on the State or its taxpayers. They also provide access for those who are ineligible for State support but are unable to fund their cases privately (such as those of limited means who wish to make a claim for personal injury, which is no longer State funded). | • Because Conditional Fee Agreements represent 'no win, no fee' agreements, in practice solicitors might *refuse to take cases* which they perceive to have a slim chance of succeeding. Matthias Kelly QC, was quoted in the *New Law Journal* in his then role as Bar Council Chairman (2003) as saying 'some lawyers may be reluctant to take on conditional fee litigation unless the prospects of success are at least 75 per cent or better'. He concluded that this did not allow for true access to justice. |
| • Clients *benefit* because they are no longer put off taking legal action by the fees that lawyers charge. Clients will pay to insure against the chances of losing the case and a basic fee if the case is won. | • Since Conditional Fee Agreements are the only available route for taking on personal injury cases, they might still prove *too expensive* for clients with limited means, bearing in mind the need to insure against the possibility that the case might be lost. |
| • Once a solicitor has decided to take a case on a 'no win, no fee' basis, the client can have confidence that the solicitor will be *focused on winning it*: both solicitor and client are therefore committed to achieving a successful outcome. | • Solicitors might pressure clients into *settling the case* at an early stage in order to secure their fees (both basic and 'success fee'), rather than taking the risk of fighting the case and losing it. |
| • Given the need for a solicitor to agree to take the case on a conditional fee basis, *trivial and vexatious claims* can be *weeded out of the system* since no one will take them forward. | • Research into the success of Conditional Fee Agreements suggested that members of the public found them *difficult to understand* and were entering into the Agreements as clients without fully appreciating how they worked. |

## Developing the subject 11.3: Are Conditional Fee Agreements a good alternative to publicly-funded claims? Do they provide access to justice?

Whilst this chapter contains clear evidence of a Conditional Fee Agreement (CFA) that did seem to work in favour of the claimant (*Campbell* (No 2)), a report prepared by James Sandbach of Citizens Advice in 2004, titled **'No Win, No Fee, No Chance'**, provides plenty of horror stories of things that can go wrong with a specific focus on personal injury claims. In the 'consumer experience of "no win, no fee" ' section of the report, Sandbach identifies five major problems that are evidenced by case examples collected by the CAB between 2002 and 2004:

- **High pressure selling** of CFAs by claims management firms and solicitors' firms.
- **Misleading advice** about CFAs.

- **Poor quality of service** provided by solicitors.
- **Disappointing case outcomes for clients,** both with regard to costs that had not been anticipated (including the expense of insurance) and lower than anticipated damages awards.
- **Detrimental impact on the health of clients** (having suffered personal injury plus an unsatisfactory outcome in their claim).

It is clear that some clients lack understanding of the CFAs they are entering into and are being sold on the 'no win, no fee' slogan without realising that they might still incur considerable expense, whether through the insurance agreement they take out, or a misunderstanding of what costs will still have to be paid to the solicitor (and possibly counsel) in the event of a win, or through a disappointing damages award as against the money invested in the claim. Sandbach cites examples of clients who were very much 'out of pocket' at the end of their cases. He also found examples of solicitors 'cherry picking' cases: operating in a manner contrary to access to justice by accepting cases on the basis of their financial potential rather than their basic merit.

Sandbach concluded, on the basis of the consumer experiences, that CFAs for personal injury claims had failed consumers, 'particularly those pursuing low value claims'. Vulnerable people were often pressured into CFAs and linked agreements 'which they do not understand and which are not necessarily the best option for them'.

**Research task**

- Type 'conditional fee agreements explained' (or similar) into an internet search engine for UK sites and compare the quality of explanations you receive from solicitors' firms and claims management firms. Rank the sites in order of the quality of information given. Discuss your results with other members of the class.
- How prepared would you feel about entering into one of these agreements?
- Are you confident that CFAs are delivering access to justice?

**Recap Quiz**

(1) Identify the full titles suggested by the following abbreviations and explain how each of these contributes to the access to justice framework.

(a) LSC.
(b) CLS.
(c) CDS.
(d) CAB.
(e) CFA.

(2) Name at least six sources of legal information. Draw a spider diagram to illustrate these and add this to your notes on the topic.
(3) What is the difference between Legal Help and Legal Representation?
(4) Name the areas of civil law that do not give rise to eligibility for public funding.
(5) In a 'no win, no fee' agreement explain the financial risk borne by the claimant if: (a) the case is won; and (b) the case is lost? (Again, you might wish to create an illustration of how these agreements work for your notes and to aid with revision.)
(6) If a solicitor or barrister has agreed to take on a case on a *pro bono* basis, what does this mean?

For Answers, please turn to pp 342–3.

**HINTS AND TIPS**

A good way to tackle questions on the **sources of legal advice** is to list the sources that you can think of, prioritise these, and then write your answer with some explanatory comments for each. Many of the sources should be suggested to you under the revision title **'Community Legal Service Partnerships'**, which, alongside **solicitors' firms**, include networks of organisations such as:

- Citizens' Advice Bureaux
- Law Centres
- Local authority services (for example, libraries).

It is worth mentioning that links to the local branches of these organisations may be made via the **Community Legal Service Direct website** (formerly 'Just Ask!'). Whether persons seeking legal advice in a civil matter are in a position to pay for that advice or not, solicitors will be consulted either through the Community Legal Service Partnerships, or by direct access by the client who is privately financing a claim.

Broader questions in the topic might require *descriptive* and/or *evaluative* consideration of **legal aid**:

- **Legal advice and assistance** (referred to for public funding purposes as **'Legal Help'**)
- **Representation** (referred to for public funding purposes as **'Legal Representation'**)
- **The legal profession** (that is, the provision of such services by **solicitors** and **barristers**).

In summary, financial support both for Legal Help and Legal Representation is provided by the **Community Legal Service Fund** and the **Criminal Defence Service**, and administered by the **Legal Services Commission**. Solicitors' firms offer Legal Help and Legal Representation in respect of civil cases (under the **Community Legal Service**) and criminal cases (under the **Criminal Defence Service**). Where **solicitors** are accessed via Community Legal Service Partnerships, some will offer free initial interviews and others will offer fixed-fee initial interviews. Some solicitors will also offer some *pro bono* work (that is, they will take on some cases free of charge). It should be noted that some barristers also take preparatory and advocacy work on a *pro bono* basis where clients are particularly vulnerable or disadvantaged. (For further examination-focused reading on the way **criminal legal aid** works in practice, see Nick Price's 'Questions on courts and criminal legal aid' in the *A-level Law Review*, January 2006, at p 30.)

In the absence of public funding for personal injury, save for the more complex types of cases, claimants will have to enter into **Conditional Fee Agreements** with solicitors, often in addition to an insurance policy, to proceed with their claims. This is the **'no win, no fee' situation**, whereby the solicitor takes a basic fee, as agreed with the client, and a *success fee*, paid by the losing party, if the case is won.

The different forms of legal advice and representation available to the general public may be *evaluated* in relation to each other. For example, in terms of ***meeting the needs of the public*** (in providing advice and support on a range of legal issues, including those that affect the disadvantaged; or in the provision of Community Legal Service Partnerships based on a set of 'referral networks' between providers) and in ***facilitating 'access to justice'*** (in terms of location, cost, language and other factors). Recognition of **'advice deserts'** and the **'unmet need'** in your answers will show that you recognise the challenges of public funding for legal services and shortcomings in the access to justice framework. The advantages and disadvantages of the conditional fees system in contrast to straightforward public funding of claims, as provided for by the old Legal Aid system, could also be considered.

## Useful website addresses

| | |
|---|---|
| BBC (re Criminal Defence Service) | www.bbc.co.uk/crime/law/criminaldefenceservice.shtml |
| Citizens Advice | www.adviceguide.org.uk |
| Community Legal Service | www.clsdirect.org.uk |
| Law Centres Federation | www.lawcentres.org.uk |
| The Legal Services Commission | www.legalservices.gov.uk |
| *Materials directly for AS studies:* | |
| John Deft (St Brendan's Sixth Form College) | www.stbrn.ac.uk/other/depts/law |
| Asif Tufal | www.a-level-law.com |

# Introduction to criminal liability

12

This topic enables you:

- To gain an appreciation of the main elements required to establish criminal liability.
- To build on earlier knowledge of the criminal courts (Chapter 6) and juries and lay magistrates (Chapter 9).
- To develop a basic understanding of one area of criminal law: the non-fatal offences against the person.
- To understand the distinction to be drawn between those offences that require *mens rea* and those offences referred to as strict liability.
- To provide foundations in criminal liability for further studies in sentencing (see Chapter 14) and perhaps for criminal law at A2 level.

Criminal law concerns wrongs against the State. These wrongs are seen as sufficiently serious to *cause harm to society in general*, and therefore the **enforcement** of the criminal law is sought by the **State** *on behalf* of its people. The agencies of the State that bring such cases include the **Crown Prosecution Service** (CPS, which prosecutes on behalf of the Police) and other bodies such as the **Trading Standards Departments** of local authorities (which prosecute on matters of consumer protection law).

## TOWARDS A FULLER DEFINITION OF CRIMINAL LAW

Most definitions of criminal law focus on two points: first, that criminal offences are perceived to be **harmful to the State**; and, second, that the only appropriate way of dealing with such offences is through **punishment**. These are harms that are seen as *too serious* to be left to the victim to decide whether or not to claim civil redress in the form of compensation. The search for a single definition of criminal law is, however, complicated by issues such as the law's relationship to morality, which creates a great deal of legal debate.

There is no doubt, on a simple level, that the criminal law enforces morality in its approach to matters such as murder and theft, and thus the relationship between the two certainly exists. However, this relationship is not clear-cut. The moral rule 'thou shalt not kill' is contained in the law only to a certain extent: is it so appropriate, for example, in cases of killings in a time of war, or killings for the purposes of necessity (such as the recent operation to separate conjoined twins, thus killing the weaker twin, in *In Re A* (2000))? As the conjoined twins case shows, sometimes killing is both justified and lawful, and thus the law is departing from 'thou shalt not kill' morality.

Another troubling link, related to the earlier points about morality, is with *justice*. The imagery of justice runs through the criminal law. We also speak of a 'criminal justice system'. But does the criminal law always achieve justice or fairness?

Such difficulties are evident in seeking to frame a definition. However, there are certain themes that provide us with fewer problems. For example, the study of **crime** also necessitates the study of **punishment** (as Chapter 14 clearly demonstrates). In the media, issues of crime and punishment are often referred to as part of the '**law and order**' debate, thus reflecting the association between the criminal law and the upholding of public order. Moreover, the influence of the **European Convention on Human Rights** is significant, highlighting the need for a *proportionate* response in dealing with crime, taking into account private rights and freedoms.

## CLASSIFICATION OF CRIMES

As we have seen in Chapters 6 and 9, the enforcement of criminal law in the courts depends on the **classification** of the crime. Table 12.1 provides a brief reminder of these classifications.

Table 12.1 Classification of crimes

| *Type of offence* | *Mode of trial* |
|---|---|
| Summary (minor offences) | Tried in magistrates' courts |
| Either way offences (intermediate offences) | Magistrates' court or Crown Court (if not allocated to latter, defendant can opt for Crown Court trial by judge and jury) |
| Indictable offences (serious offences) | Crown Court (trial by judge and jury) |

## THE LEGAL CHARACTERISTICS OF CRIMES

Most crimes are said to have two essential ingredients: the *actus reus* and the *mens rea*. There are other sorts of crimes for which the *actus reus* is the only element of the offence that must be proved by the prosecution. These are known as **strict liability** offences. This section will look at these elements in further detail below.

### *Actus reus*

In its simplest form, actus reus means the 'guilty act', but this definition does not adequately cover the range of 'conduct' that can give rise to criminal liability. For example, while the actus reus of most offences involves **doing something** (such as 'appropriating property belonging to another' to constitute the act of theft under s 1(1) of the **Theft Act 1968**), some offences can be committed by way of an omission (as in cases where the neglect of a child by its parents causes grievous bodily harm or even death to the child) and some offences can be committed merely because of the **state of affairs** that exists (as in situations where the status of a person, in a particular place, causes him or her to be acting illegally).

### *Actus reus*: liability for doing something (positive acts)

There are many examples illustrating criminal liability for committing a prohibited act. Take the *actus reus* of **murder**: on one level, murder can be carried out by an **act** of unlawful killing, but as this chapter will go on to illustrate – see coverage of *R v Gibbins and Proctor* (1918) on p 237 – the *actus reus* of murder is actually much broader than this ('the causing of the death of a human being under the Queen's Peace', according to Ormerod, 2006, in the eleventh edition of *Smith & Hogan Criminal Law*). The *actus reus* constitutes the **physical element** of the crime, but it should be noted that the offence of murder would not be established without also showing that the defendant had the required state of mind (*mens rea*) in relation to that offence. For murder, such a state of mind is 'malice aforethought' (in practice, intention to kill or intention to cause grievous bodily harm). As you will see below, the **non-fatal offences** are also crimes with a **physical** *actus reus* element and a **mental** *mens rea* element. For example, the *actus reus* of **battery** is **applying unlawful personal violence on another**, though the prosecution would have to show, in addition, that this was accompanied by the required mental element: either an intention to do so, or recklessness as to the risk of doing so.

Some prohibited acts are also dependent on **particular circumstances** being present. For example, the *actus reus* of **rape** is the penetration, by penis, of specified parts of a person's body, though the circumstance in which this becomes a criminal act is the **absence of consent**. The *mens rea* is intentional penetration, without any 'reasonable belief' that the person was consenting to it.

The following statutory offences provide further examples of criminal liability being imposed for the **commission of prohibited acts**. See if you can identify the *actus reus* elements of these crimes and, by contrast, the *mens rea* elements:

- **Criminal damage** – Criminal Damage Act 1971, s 1(1)
  A person who without lawful excuse destroys or damages any property belonging to another intending to destroy or damage any such property or being reckless as to whether any such property would be destroyed or damaged shall be guilty of an offence.
  Note: consider the circumstance required for this offence – it must be carried out 'without lawful excuse'.
- **Obtaining property by deception** – Theft Act 1968, s 15
  A person who by any deception dishonestly obtains property belonging to another, with the intention of permanently depriving the other of it, shall on conviction on indictment be liable to imprisonment for a term not exceeding ten years.

### *Actus reus*: the voluntary principle

The defendant must have acted **consciously** and in a **voluntary manner** to be responsible for the crime. The law is complex on this question, since the courts have drawn a number of significant fine distinctions between voluntary acts and involuntary acts. Involuntary acts may fall within the category of **'automatism'**. This can be used as a defence by persons accused of crimes to the effect that they were not in control, and not acting voluntarily, owing either to an external factor or to a disease of the mind. The defence has been used in situations where acts have been committed during periods of sleepwalking, epileptic fit, diabetic hypoglycaemic episode and involuntary responses to trauma. In *Hill v Baxter* (1958), for example, a person attacked by bees whilst driving was not held responsible for the breach of road traffic law that followed, his actions were an involuntary response to the trauma of being stung and could no longer be regarded as voluntary 'driving'. Likewise, the defence of insanity might be raised if there is evidence that the defendant's actions were attributable to a disease of the mind.

Occasionally, defendants will be deemed **'unfit to plead'**. The following groups of people may be included in this category: the mentally handicapped, the mentally disordered, and the mentally ill. Those deemed 'unfit to plead' do not have to endure the criminal trial process, though a jury in a separate set of court proceedings will determine the issue as to whether they did or did not commit the specified act.

With regard to a guilty act, the general rule is that, in the absence of a defence of automatism, the defendant must have acted both **voluntarily** and **consciously** in committing the act. However, the 'state of affairs' cases (see p 237) provide an *exception* to this general rule.

### *Actus reus*: liability for omissions

On occasions, **failing to act** may lead to a person being found guilty of a crime. However, this is seen as widening the scope of criminal liability, and English law has been **restrictive** in its approach to omissions. It is clear that criminal liability will not apply to an omission if the offence specifically requires an act. However, some statutes state that an individual may be found guilty if he or she acts or fails to act. This is illustrated by offences where the emphasis is on **'causing'** an outcome, since 'causing' may involve acting or omitting.

The *actus reus* will, however, be satisfied by an omission in circumstances where a particular **duty to act** can be identified. For example, a police officer has a legal duty to act in order to uphold the Queen's Peace. If he or she does not do so then an offence is committed. In *R v Dytham* (1979), a police officer omitted to carry out his duty to uphold the Queen's Peace and stood by as a man was kicked to death by a night club bouncer. He was convicted.

Sometimes the *actus reus* may amount to an omission in circumstances where, though there was no initial duty to act, the defendant's conduct was such that a failure to deal with the consequences of that conduct could attract liability. The classic example of this is where a person, *having created an obvious danger*, proceeds to do absolutely nothing about it. In *R v Miller* (1983), the defendant was a squatter in a house. He fell asleep in the house while holding a cigarette, which was lit. The cigarette, in turn, came into contact with the mattress and set it on fire. The flames from the mattress then woke the defendant, but he did no more than move to the next room to resume his sleep. As a consequence of his inaction, the house caught fire, causing substantial damage. The defendant was convicted of arson.

A further legal duty to act that the courts have recognised on several occasions is that relating to an **assumption of responsibility** for others. A terrible situation to be found in the case law is that of parents, relatives or guardians withholding food from a child, leading to the inevitable consequence of death by starvation. Although omissions can be problematic in relation to establishing causation, it is clear that if the parents omit to offer food to a child, and the child has no other source of food, the resulting death of the child must be attributable to the parents' omission. This is illustrated by the convictions of a father and his mistress for murder in *R v Gibbins and Proctor* (1918), when they both neglected Nelly, the father's seven-year-old child, who died of starvation. Therefore, the point made above, that the *actus reus* of murder is a positive act (unlawful killing), may be viewed as a narrow interpretation, since causing the death of another person may also occur through an omission.

So far the duty to act has been discussed by reference to the **performance of public duties** and **duties owed through an assumption of responsibility**, but the duty will also lie by virtue of certain **contracts of employment** that **raise public expectations in respect of health and safety**. The key authority here is that of *R v Pittwood* (1902), in which the defendant, as a level-crossing guard employed on the railways, omitted to carry out his duty to ensure that the level-crossing gate was closed when a train was passing. As a result of the gate being left open, a hay cart was hit by a passing train, killing the driver of the cart. The level-crossing guard was found guilty of **manslaughter.**

### *Actus reus*: liability for 'state of affairs' cases

In 'state of affairs' cases a person commits the *actus reus* simply by being of a **certain status**, or **being in a certain set of circumstances**. Sometimes these cases appear to *offend justice* because they depend merely on a certain state of affairs existing. They do not, unlike most offences, depend on the person's voluntary conduct (see above) – if the state of affairs exists then it does not matter whether he or she acted voluntarily – neither do these offences depend on that person's state of mind (so *mens rea* will not be required). Therefore, 'state of affairs' cases create **absolute liability**, which can be very harsh for defendants. The Court of Appeal has recently acknowledged, in *R v G* (2006), that absolute offences might well infringe a defendant's right to a fair trial under **Art 6** of the **European Convention on Human Rights**.

However, two cases may be used to illustrate the commission of the *actus reus* by 'state of affairs'. The first is *R v Larsonneur* (1933). Madame Larsonneur had travelled from France to England, and as a consequence of exceeding her permitted stay in the country had been deported to the Republic of Ireland. However, when she got to Dublin, the Irish Police sent her back to England, contrary to her wishes. Upon arrival again in England, she was promptly arrested for being found in the UK as an illegal 'alien' (immigrant), an offence laid down in the Aliens Order 1920. Although she appealed against conviction, the verdict of 'guilty' in this case was upheld.

The decision in Larsonneur has been subject to a great deal of academic criticism, but the courts have actually followed its logic, as *Winzar v Chief Constable of Kent* (1983) illustrates. Here, the defendant, having been discharged from hospital on the grounds that he was drunk, was later found in one of the hospital corridors and the police were called. They removed him from the hospital and set him down on a pavement outside. At this point, the police proceeded to charge the defendant with being found drunk on the highway under the Licensing Act 1872, even though he had 'been found' in such a 'state of affairs' only because they had put him there. The Divisional Court upheld the conviction.

Whilst on the face of it the *Larsonneur* and *Winzar* convictions seem particularly unjust, the defendants in both cases share the common characteristic of being responsible, at the outset, for bringing about the 'state of affairs' they were ultimately to find themselves in, and this should be borne in mind.

Table 12.2 summarises the scope of the *actus reus*.

Table 12.2 Scope of the *actus reus*

| *Actus reus: liability for* ***doing something*** *(positive acts)* | *Actus reus: liability for* ***omissions*** | *Actus reus: liability for* ***'state of affairs'*** *cases* |
|---|---|---|
| For example, the *actus reus* of battery is 'applying unlawful violence on other'. This is a positive act that is against the law.<br>Liability will attach for positive acts that are against the law if they are committed *consciously* and *voluntarily*. | There will be liability for omissions when a 'duty to act' can be identified.<br>The *actus reus* will be formed when such a duty can be identified and there has been a failure to act according to it.<br>Examples include:<br>• Policeman's duty to uphold the peace (*R v Dytham* (1979))<br>• Duty arising from the creation of an obvious danger (*R v Miller* (1983))<br>• Duty arising from the voluntary assumption of responsibility for minors or dependants (*R v Gibbins and Proctor* (1918))<br>• Duty arising from contractual obligations with regard to health and safety (*R v Pittwood* (1902)). | Here a person forms the *actus reus* simply by 'being of a particular status or being in a certain set of circumstances'.<br>Two examples of 'state of affairs' cases are:<br>• *Actus reus* formed by having the status of illegal immigrant (*R v Larsonneur* (1933))<br>• *Actus reus* formed by the circumstances of being drunk on the highway (*Winzar v Chief Constable of Kent* (1983)). |

N.B: For some crimes, conduct alone will evidence the *actus reus*; for others, the *actus reus* will require **causation** to be established ('result crimes').

## *Actus Reus*: causation

It is traditionally said that there are two forms of offences in English criminal law: **conduct crimes** and **result crimes**.

For **conduct crimes**, the prosecution only have to show the **commission of a prohibited act** – that the offender's conduct fell short of the criminal law standard – to establish the offence. Thus a person who intentionally, or recklessly, puts another in fear of immediate, unlawful violence has, by conduct, committed the non-fatal offence of assault.

However, with regard to **result crimes**, the prosecution have to show *more* than just the commission of an act; it is also necessary to show that the **commission of a prohibited act led to a specific harm being caused**. Therefore, for the statutory non-fatal offence of **'assault occasioning actual bodily harm'**, the prosecution not only have to show that the offender's conduct amounted to an assault, but also that the assault occasioned, or resulted in, **actual bodily harm** (physical or psychiatric injury of a minor nature). It is in respect of result crimes, then, that the issue of causation becomes significant.

The subject of **homicide** provides an obvious illustration of **result crimes**. Here, to establish the offences of **murder** or **manslaughter**, the conduct of the defendant must have resulted in the death of a victim. Therefore, issues of **causation** become particularly significant in linking the defendant's conduct to the resulting death of a victim. This link is known as the **'chain of causation'**. As we shall see, the defendant may argue that he or she is relieved of responsibility for a death because of a break in this chain, such as the actions of a third party which intervened in the relationship between the defendant's conduct and the victim's eventual death. However, if the chain remains intact, and the prosecution can show – beyond reasonable doubt – that the defendant's conduct caused the result – death – then liability will be assumed.

For the prosecution to prove that the defendant caused the death of the victim, **causation** must be proved in **fact** and in **law**.

## Factual causation

The matter of factual causation is dealt with by the **'but for' test**. Expressed simply, the test is as follows: *but for* the defendant's conduct, the death would not have occurred in the manner, or at the time, that it did. If the death would have happened regardless of the defendant's conduct then the defendant will not be liable. In *R v White* (1910), the defendant intended to kill his mother by putting a poison, potassium cyanide, into a drink that had been prepared for her. The mother died, but because of a heart attack that arose independently of the poison in the drink. Therefore, the defendant's conduct of poisoning did not cause the death in fact. In practical terms, this would mean that an attempt to prosecute the defendant for murder would fail for lack of causation. The option for the prosecution would, instead, have to be 'attempted murder'.

If the prosecution *can* show that the death would not have occurred in the circumstances without the causative conduct of the defendant, they can show that the defendant was responsible *on the facts*. It is then necessary to turn to the legal aspects of causation.

## Legal causation

Whilst it may be the case that factual causation can be established, a jury would still need to be directed by the judge in a Crown Court trial about the prosecution's need to establish **causation in law**. Legal causation raises three significant issues:

(a) significant contribution;
(b) the thin skull rule; and
(c) the impact of intervening acts.

There is a need to establish that the defendant's conduct made a **significant contribution** to the resulting death or injury, though it is *not* necessary to show that the conduct was the sole cause or the main cause. This is also referred to as the ***de minimis*** principle, meaning that the law does not take into account trivial things.

The defendant must take the victim as he finds him (the **'thin skull rule'**): the defendant cannot escape liability because the victim's injuries are made more severe through personal circumstances. A useful illustration is provided by *R v Holland* (1841), where Holland had beaten his victim with an iron bar, which had led to severe wounds to the victim's hand. As a consequence, the victim suffered blood poisoning and was advised by a surgeon to have a finger amputated in order to treat the poisoning and stem its effects. The victim refused to accept this advice. He subsequently died of a condition known as 'lockjaw', which could have been prevented by the suggested amputation. Nevertheless, Holland was still found guilty of murder. While the defendant might have been unable to foresee how the victim's condition would worsen, he had – as a violent offender – to **take his victim as he found him**.

The same reasoning was applied in *R v Blaue* (1975). Here, the defendant stabbed his victim and she died because, as a **Jehovah's Witness**, she *refused* to accept a **blood transfusion**. Under the **'thin skull rule'**, the defendant had to take the victim as he found her, and could not escape liability by arguing that the victim's religious beliefs were unreasonable.

These cases are indicative of a line of judicial policy to the effect that persons who choose to commit acts of violence on others must **accept the consequences of their actions**, including the fact that some victims are considerably more susceptible to serious harm than others.

There is also a need to establish that the **chain of causation remained intact** as between the defendant and the victim, and that there was **no intervening act by a third party** to *break* the chain of causation (the *novus actus interveniens* principle).

The most obvious examples to illustrate the *novus actus* principle are those in which the **intervention of medical practitioners** occurs between the defendant's conduct and the resulting death of the victim. The courts have distinguished two particular situations. First, if the defendant's act remains the **operative and significant cause of death** then intervening medical treatment, even if it is poor or negligent, will *not* break the chain of causation. For example, in *R v Smith* (1959), the defendant stabbed another man with a bayonet. Thus, at this moment, the chain of causation began (flowing from the defendant's violent conduct). However, the victim was dropped by another soldier while being carried to the medical centre, and when he finally arrived he received inappropriate treatment which did not take account of the fact that he was haemorrhaging (that is, bleeding heavily). The victim died, thus ending the chain between cause and effect. The defendant tried to argue that the inappropriate medical treatment broke the chain of causation. If this could be established then the defendant would be relieved of responsibility for the death. However, the court held that the intervening act of the medical practitioners did *not* break the chain of causation. The defendant's violent conduct – the stabbing with a bayonet – was the 'operative and significant cause of the death' and therefore he was liable for murder.

The logic of this case has been applied in a number of later cases. The following intervening acts have also failed to break the chain of causation between the defendant's conduct and the victim's death:

- where doctors have chosen to turn off life support machines (*R v Malcherek* (1981)); and
- where the medical treatment given to the victim is negligent – for example, where it is based on an inappropriate diagnosis (*R v Cheshire* (1991); *R v Mellor* (1996)).

However, if, to turn to the second situation, the **treatment is so 'palpably wrong'** that it introduces a new and independent element to **break the chain of causation** then this *will* relieve the defendant of liability. In *R v Jordan* (1956), the incident again involved the stabbing of the victim, and again this was the moment at which the defendant's conduct began the chain of causation. However, the medical treatment in this case introduced a new and independent element that may be seen to have broken the chain of causation: the victim was treated with a drug to which he was allergic, and it was this which triggered his death. The **intervening act was of such significance** that the defendant's conduct was *no* longer the operative and significant cause of the victim's death. Therefore, the defendant's conviction for murder was overturned on appeal.

Table 12.3 on p 242 summarises the approaches to causation in establishing criminal liability, with specific examples relating to the 'result crime' of murder.

## *Mens rea*

The *mens rea* is popularly referred to as the **'guilty mind'**, thus equating to **fault**. Motive is, however, irrelevant. It will not provide a defence if the *mens rea* is satisfied. For example, a person may act with the best possible motive – such as relieving the pain of a terminally-ill relative through mercy killing at the relative's request – but this will not relieve him or her of responsibility for murder. There are three main types of *mens rea*:

(a) intention;
(b) recklessness; and
(c) negligence.

### *Mens rea:* intention

This is the most difficult type of *mens rea* to prove. Take a murder trial, for example: it has to be proved by the prosecution, **beyond reasonable doubt**, that the defendant intended to kill the victim. However, where the prosecution have to establish direct intent the matter may in some cases be straightforward. For

Table 12.3 Criminal liability: *actus reus* causation

| *Factual causation* | *Legal causation* |
|---|---|
| To establish **factual causation** (that the defendant's conduct led to the harm suffered by the victim), the ***'but for' test*** is used: the court will ask, *but for* the defendant's conduct, would the harm have occurred?<br><br>If the harm would have occurred anyway, the defendant will *not* be liable: *R v White* (1910) (mother died of heart attack, not because of the defendant's plot to poison her drink). | The **legal principles of causation** also have to be considered:<br>• Did the defendant's conduct make a **significant contribution** to the victim's harm? (Must be a *more than* trivial contribution.)<br>• The defendant will be subject to the **thin skull rule**: a defendant who causes harm must *take the victim as he finds him*. This principle is illustrated by cases in which the victim refuses medical treatment – nevertheless the defendant remains fully liable (*R v Holland* (1841); *R v Blaue* (1975)).<br>• Did a **new intervening act** (*novus actus interveniens*) by a third party **break the chain of causation** between the defendant's conduct and the victim's harm? A typical example of an intervening act would be inappropriate medical treatment, so the courts will look to see whether the defendant's conduct was the operative and significant cause of death (*R v Smith* (1959) contrasted with *R v Jordan* (1956)). |

example, there might be evidence that the defendant had decided to act in such a way as to achieve a criminal outcome. There is intention because the defendant decided upon a desirable outcome that was within his or her power to achieve. The most obvious example of this is where a person decides that a desired outcome is the death of a specified victim – and there is therefore intention – and he or she takes a weapon to that victim to cause the death by shooting, stabbing, and so on.

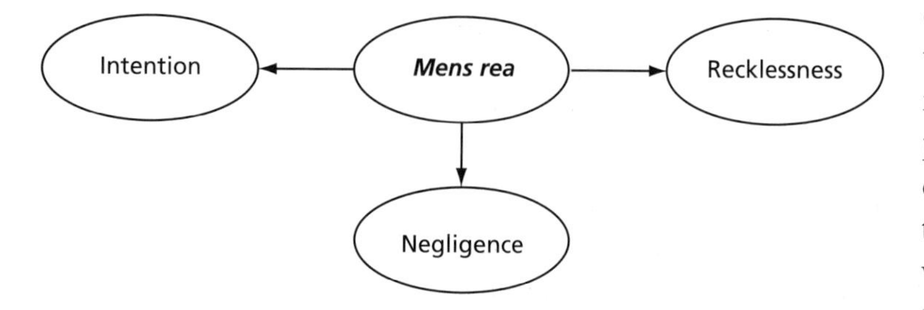


The difficulties with intention arise in cases of **oblique intent.** Put simply, these situations occur when the defendant says, 'I was responsible for the outcome but *I did not intend* that outcome'. The jury is then given the job of deciding whether the defendant had the necessary intention to commit the specified crime. For years there have been legal appeals on the issue of intention, particularly with regard to cases of unlawful killing. This is because a determination of the defendant's intention will mean either a conviction for **murder**, which carries an automatic life sentence, or a conviction for **manslaughter**, where sentencing is left to judicial discretion. In the first instance trials of such cases, the job of explaining the law on intention to the jury is in the hands of the judge. If the judge's directions to the jury are not clear then the jury may send a person to prison for life based on a misunderstanding of the law. This has resulted in a number of defendants having their convictions for murder reduced to manslaughter on appeal. Guidelines on oblique intent have emerged from key appeal cases in this area.

In *R v Nedrick* (1986), the defendant held a grudge against a woman, so he poured paraffin through her letter-box and set fire to it, with the result that the woman's child died in the fire. It was said in this case that the jury should *infer* intention if death or really serious harm was a *virtual certainty* to result from the defendant's act and that this was *foreseeable* by the defendant.

The test has been clarified in *R v Woollin* (1998), which reflects the current legal position on intention. Here a man, in anger, threw a three-month-old baby towards a pram that was positioned next to a wall in the house. The child died after hitting the wall. The defendant was convicted of manslaughter. The *Nedrick* **virtual certainty test** was confirmed, with qualifications. Juries are required, after Woollin, to *find* intention rather than infer it (a more positive requirement) and to be directed that only *results foreseen as virtually certain* will amount to intention.

The *Woollin* test has found recent application in *R v Matthews* (2003). In this case, the defendants were charged with murder following an incident in which they had thrown their victim off a bridge into a river, despite the victim's protests that he could not swim. He died as a result. The defendants argued that while they had been involved in the incident, they had not intended to kill. It was held that the test for intention in such situations was whether the defendant was aware that death was a *virtual certainty* for the victim unless attempts were made to rescue him, and the defendants accordingly had no intention to effect such a rescue.

### *Mens rea:* recklessness

Following a landmark decision by the House of Lords in *R v G and R* (2003) (see Chapter 4 at p 74), recklessness is determined using a **subjective**, rather than objective, test. The **subjective test** was established in the case of *R v Cunningham* (1957). In this case the defendant, in the course of stealing money from a gas meter, fractured a pipe that allowed gas to escape. The gas percolated through a wall to a neighbouring property, endangering the life of the occupant. The defendant's conviction for an offence of 'unlawfully and maliciously administering a noxious thing so as to endanger life', contrary to s 23 of the Offences Against the Person Act 1861, was subsequently quashed because of a misdirection of the law to the jury. To clarify the general ***mens rea*** requirement for this sort of offence, the appeal court therefore articulated a **subjective test**– in Lord Ackner's words (from the joined cases of *Savage* and *Parmenter*) 'the jury should have been left to decide whether even if (Cunningham) . . . did not intend the injury to . . . (the victim), *he* foresaw that the removal of the gas meter might cause injury to someone but nevertheless removed it'.

The test is **subjective** because it will consider whether the defendant had the necessary degree of foresight, based on his or her own personal characteristics. This is the recklessness standard for the non-fatal offences under the **Offences Against the Person Act 1861** (see pp 248–56 below).

### *Mens rea:* negligence

Negligence measures conduct against a certain standard: in this instance, that of the **reasonable man**. Criminal negligence is applied in **road traffic cases** and in situations of **'gross negligence manslaughter'**. A recent example of the latter was provided by the case of *R v Wacker* (2002). Here, a lorry driver, who had conspired to smuggle 58 illegal Chinese immigrants into the UK in the container of his lorry, was grossly negligent in depriving his passengers of air, with the result that all of them died. The driver received a sentence of 14 years' imprisonment for 'gross negligence manslaughter'. The 'reasonable man' is also the standard of negligence used in the civil law of tort (see Chapter 13).

Table 12.4 summarises the types of *mens rea*.

Table 12.4 Types of *mens rea*

| *Mens rea: intention* | *Mens rea: recklessness* | *Mens rea: negligence* |
| --- | --- | --- |
| This is the highest form of *mens rea*, reserved for the most serious crimes.<br>• **Direct intent** can be established when the defendant decides upon a certain outcome and takes action to achieve it.<br>• **Oblique intent** raises the problem where a defendant is responsible for a certain outcome but claims that it was not the intended outcome. An example of the way in which the courts have dealt with oblique intent is provided by the key appeal cases in the area of homicide (see particularly *R v Woollin* (1998) and the **'virtual certainty' test**). | Following the overruling of objective recklessness in the case of *R v G and R* (2003) the recklessness standard is now subjective:<br>• Subjective *Cunningham* recklessness can be established when a defendant **foresees risk** but **goes ahead regardless**. It takes account of the defendant's personal characteristics. | The negligence standard is that of the **reasonable man.**<br>An example of its application is in the area of **'gross negligence manslaughter'** (*R v Wacker* (2002)). |

## Transferred malice and the relationship between *actus reus* and *mens rea*

This may be illustrated by the traditional example of X intending to kill Y with a bow and arrow. X shoots the arrow at Y, but a gust of wind takes it away from Y and it hits Z and kills him. The question therefore must be asked: is X guilty of Z's murder? The concept of **transferred malice** tells us that the answer is 'Yes', since the **malicious intent** (*mens rea*) that X had in respect of Y can be transferred to the ***actus reus*** that took place, namely, the killing of Z.

Transferred malice will not, however, apply if the *actus reus* and *mens rea* do not match for the same crime. This was the case in *R v Pembliton* (1874), where in the course of a fight outside a pub the defendant broke a window using a stone (*actus reus* of the then offence of **malicious damage**) that had been aimed at one of his opponents. Here the malice or intention to hit the person with the stone (*mens rea* for a **non-fatal offence against the person**) could not be transferred to the different outcome of malicious damage.

## The relatiodnship, or 'union', between *actus reus* and *mens rea*: contemporaneity

The point about transferred malice raises the issue of the relationship between *actus reus* and *mens rea* in law. A further rule about this relationship is that the two elements of a crime have to occur **contemporaneously**. This means, in effect, that the *actus reus* and *mens rea* need both to be present at the same time for the prosecution to establish the offence. Some authors also refer to this as the **'coincidence'** of *actus reus* and *mens rea*.

There are a number of *exceptions* to the principle of **contemporaneity**. Judges will recognise that some situations can be interpreted as **one continuing act**. This avoids the possibility of defendants seeking to avoid liability by arguing that the *actus reus* and *mens rea* did *not* coincide. Such exceptions may be illustrated by two cases.

- In *Fagan v Metropolitan Police Commissioner* (1969), the defendant drove, quite by accident, onto a policeman's foot, thus committing the *actus reus* of the offence of battery. However, because this was an accident, there was no *mens rea* for the offence. The *mens rea* developed, however, because the driver, having exchanged words with the policeman, chose to turn off the car's ignition and leave the vehicle on the policeman's foot. It was held that because the *actus reus* of the battery represented a **continuing act**, continuing for as long as the wheel rested on the policeman's foot, then the point at which the *mens rea* was developed represented the necessary **degree of union** between the two elements of the offence. While there was no contemporaneity at the outset, the requirement was substituted, in effect, by the **continuing act**. The defendant was found guilty here.
- The *Thabo Meli v R* (1954) case is different to Fagan on its facts, since here the *mens rea* came before the *actus reus*. Nevertheless it applies the same logic. The facts were as follows. The appellants (to the **Privy Council**) led their victim to a hut where they hit him over the head with the full intent of killing him. He did not die at this point. Therefore, they could be seen to have the *mens rea* of **murder** but not the *actus reus*. In order to dispose of what they thought was a corpse, they decided to throw the victim's body off a cliff. The appellants did not possess the *mens rea* of murder at this point, because they believed that the body they were dispatching from the cliff was already a corpse. On the other hand, the *actus reus* of murder was developed at this stage since the victim actually died from the effects of the fall and exposure suffered on the cliff

face. The Privy Council dismissed the appellants' argument of a lack of contemporaneity and found them guilty. Here, there was clearly a plan by the appellants to kill the victim, and this was pursued through a continuing sequence of acts. This continuing sequence provided the necessary **contemporaneity** to support a conviction for murder.

## STRICT LIABILITY OFFENCES: NEED FOR THE *ACTUS REUS* BUT NOT *MENS REA*

These sorts of offences do *not* require the presence of a guilty mind to accompany the act. The criminal law draws a distinction between (a) those acts which are **criminal in themselves** (that is, because they might be perceived as morally wrong and wicked), for which *mens rea* will be required; and (b) those acts which are made criminal and are prohibited and **carry a penalty simply for the public good** (*Collman v Mills* (1897)). The latter category represents the **strict liability** offences.

The reasoning behind the creation of strict liability is clearly expressed by Mr Justice Channel in *Pearks, Gunston & Tee Ltd v Ward* (1902), who said that these offences were those that Parliament had thought so important to be prevented that they were strictly forbidden; and so if an offender did commit such an act then he would attract a legal penalty, 'whether he had any *mens rea* or not, and whether or not he intended to commit a breach of law'. Moreover, some judges have looked upon these offences as **'regulatory'** or *'quasi-criminal'* in nature. The words of Mr Justice Wright in *Sherras v De Rutzen* (1895) are often quoted in this regard: '[such offences] are not criminal in any real sense, but are acts which **in the public interest** are prohibited under a penalty'. It is often the case, therefore, that these are seen as **'public welfare'** offences.

Businesses, for example, are often subject to strict liability offences to ensure that high standards of care are exercised for the **benefit of consumers** and **society** in general. In *Harrow London Borough Council v Shah* (1999), strict liability was imposed on a shop-owner when one of his employees sold a lottery ticket to a person under the legal age (16) required to buy it. The argument that the sales assistant reasonably believed the customer to be of 16 years of age did not succeed: the act had been committed, and so for reasons of public welfare attracted a criminal penalty.

The courts have also been ready to consider certain **pollution offences**, such as those falling under the Water Resources Act 1991, as strict in order to raise standards of environmental protection by businesses and ensure that prosecutions are not unduly hindered by any need to establish *mens rea*. For example, in *Alphacell v Woodward* (1972), a company was found guilty of 'causing' water pollution when a malfunction in its paper-making process led to an overflow of polluted water to a nearby river. Lord Salmon explained the reasoning behind the strict nature of the offence:

> [If] no conviction could be obtained . . . unless the prosecution could discharge the often impossible onus of proving that the pollution was

**Exercise 12.1: Identifying cases in criminal law and their illustration of key legal concepts**

**Task 1**

*Use the following factual clues to identify the corresponding cases in criminal law.*

(1) A squatter in a house thought it was OK, having set fire to his bed, to move to another room for a night's kip: since the house was badly damaged by the resulting fire, the House of Lords disagreed and upheld his conviction for arson.
(2) A baby died in this terrible case, owing to a father's anger; seen as a landmark case in criminal law.
(3) A fight outside a pub: A throws a heavy stone at B, who ducks, and the stone breaks a window. Was A liable for malicious damage?
(4) When she was deported from England to the Republic of Ireland this unfortunate French Madame was promptly sent back again by Irish police: guilty!
(5) A word of advice: if you do happen to drive onto a policeman's foot, your best next move would not be to turn off the ignition and the leave the vehicle there.
(6) If factories pollute rivers, they will be guilty of an offence, even though the technical reason for the pollution was, for example, faulty equipment.
(7) Another dreadful case: 58 illegal immigrants killed in a lorry container because they were deprived of air.
(8) When this defendant tore a gas meter from a wall to steal money, had he known about the risk of gas affecting others?

Case options: (a) *R v Larsonneur*; (b) *R v Cunningham*; (c) *R v Woollin*; (d) *Alphacell v Woodward*; (e) *R v Pembliton*; (f) *R v Wacker*; (g) *R v Miller*; (h) *Fagan v Metropolitan Police Commissioner*

**Task 2**

*Having identified the cases from the clues, now organise the cases under the relevant headings that follow: Actus reus; Mens rea;* Transferred malice; Contemporaneity; Strict Liability.

For Answers, please turn to p 343.

caused intentionally or negligently, a great deal of pollution would go unpunished and undeterred . . . As a result, many rivers which are now filthy would become filthier still and many rivers which are now clean would lose their cleanliness.

As it was observed in Chapter 3 on statutory interpretation, there is a **presumption** in favour of statutory crimes having *mens rea*. The presumption is necessary to the interpretation process because many offences are silent about whether the prohibited act requires *mens rea* or imposes strict liability. Sometimes judges allow the presumption to prevail, and on other occasions find that the offence is one of **strict liability**. Some recent cases have preferred not to find strict liability, even where relevant earlier cases suggested that this should be applied. However, this should not be taken to suggest that strict liability offences are generally in decline, since they continue to be created, and estimates from legal writers indicate that they make up **half of all criminal offences** and almost a quarter of the serious crimes listed in the criminal lawyer's practice manual, referred to as *Archbold (Pleading, Evidence and Practice in Criminal Cases)*. An attempt, in *Barnfather v Islington London Borough Council* (2003), to argue that strict liability offences imposed such a burden on offenders that they were contrary to the 'right to a fair trial' in the European Convention on Human Rights, Art 6, did *not* succeed. Moreover, the court confirmed the point that Parliament can continue to create new strict liability offences without fear of interference from judges. It remains to be seen, however, if this concludes the matter, with the Court of Appeal in *R v G* (2006) (see earlier comments in this chapter at p 237) recognising the human rights implications of forms of liability that 'might subject a defendant to conviction in circumstances where he had done nothing blameworthy' (Lord Phillips, LCJ).

## OUTLINE OF AN AREA OF CRIMINAL LIABILITY: NON-FATAL OFFENCES AGAINST THE PERSON

So far this chapter has discussed the main elements that inform the operation of criminal law, and it is now appropriate to show how these elements come together by looking at a set of related criminal offences. For the purposes of *applying your knowledge* to real situations, the guidance provided by the **Joint Charging Standard (JCS)**, which was agreed by the Police and the Crown Prosecution Service, indicates the sorts of situation that give rise to some of the offences outlined. Examples from this guidance have therefore been included below. However, examiners will be looking for your ability to **apply the law**, first and foremost, so do not rely solely on the indicative JCS when answering problem questions in this area.

Please note also that the following coverage of assault and battery examines these **separate** offences, though they are both occasionally referred to as **'common assault'**.

**IT'S A FACT!**

**12.1: The non-fatal offences**

According to a quarterly survey of reported crimes (for the period October–December 2004), crimes of serious violence against the person, offences against the person with injury, offences against the person without injury and sexual offences all showed significant increases by contrast with the similar quarterly period in 2003. Moreover, crime patterns in general since 1960 have indicated a significant rise in non-fatal crimes of violence, in particular wounding and acts endangering life, and common assault (loosely referring to assault and battery). (Figures are provided in a report by *The Times*, 22/4/05.)

### Assault

The *actus reus* of assault is an act that places another person **in fear of immediate and unlawful violence**. This can be committed by: **acts alone** (such as raising fists, or brandishing a replica gun); **acts** and **words** (such as raising fists and using threatening language); by **threatening words alone**; or even, in certain circumstances, by **silence**. In *R v Ireland* (1996), the defendant made a series of silent phone calls at night to three women who all subsequently suffered psychiatric illness. This was seen as an assault. Occasionally, however, the precise words used by the defendant might also have the effect of undermining an assault. For example, in *Tuberville v Savage* (1669), the defendant, responding to comments that had been made to him, reached for his sword and said, 'If it were not assize time I would not take such language'. This did not amount to an assault since the effect of the words was to say to his opponent: 'I am angry but I will not take my sword to you in the circumstances' ('assize time' being the time when judges would be available in that area to hear criminal trials). Therefore, the person to whom the defendant had directed his words could not have been placed in fear of violence.

In proving the *actus reus* of assault, the prosecution have to show that the victim had a **fear of violence** at some time. The courts have *moved away* from a strict emphasis on an immediate fear of violence, as the *Ireland* case (above) indicates. Moreover, in both *R v Lewis* (1970) and *Smith v Chief Superintendent, Woking Police Station* (1983), the defendants were found guilty of assault even where their victims, both women, were within the safety of locked rooms and it would have been difficult for any violence to have been carried out against them.

The *mens rea* of assault is an **intention** to place another in fear of immediate and unlawful personal violence, or **subjective recklessness** (see p 243 above) as to the risk of doing this. The courts will look at the *mens rea* in the following ways. First, **intention** may be **direct** (on purpose) or **oblique** (the defendant knows that the consequence of his or her action is virtually certain). Second, the **recklessness** is of the *Cunningham* standard, and so the courts will take into account the personal characteristics of the defendant in determining whether he or she foresaw a risk of placing the victim in fear of violence but nevertheless went ahead and did so.

Assault is a **summary offence**, brought under the **Criminal Justice Act 1988, s 39**. It carries a maximum sentence of six months in prison and/or a fine of £5,000.

## Battery

The *actus reus* of battery is an act of **applying unlawful personal violence on another**. The key point here is that any physical contact can be a battery if it is without consent and therefore unlawful. There have been many authorities to illustrate this point, but everyday contact – for example, in lifts, supermarkets, trains, and so forth – will *not* amount to a battery. So what will? Basically, any **physical contact that is unwanted**, such as an indecent assault (*Faulkner v Talbot* (1981)), or **conduct that is 'hostile'** and cannot legally be excused (such as acts of violence for the purposes of sexual gratification in *R v Brown* (1993)). In *R v Thomas* (1985), the touching, or cutting, of a victim's clothes was held to amount to a battery, even where no actual contact was made with the body. Battery will also be evidenced by hitting, spitting, throwing stones, over-zealously spanking a child, or through the application of indirect force, such as putting acid into the hot air dryer in the school toilets (*DPP v K* (1990)). In *Haystead v Chief Constable of Derbyshire* (2000), the defendant inflicted violence on a mother holding a child. During the course of the attack, the child fell to the ground. The defendant was convicted of a battery on the child. The child's fall was a clear result of the force applied to the mother. Moreover, a battery does *not* have to be accompanied by an assault, so a person who pulls a chair away while someone is about to sit down will have committed a battery.

The **Joint Charging Standard** suggests that the following injuries will amount to this offence:

- Grazes
- Scratches
- Abrasions
- Bruising (minor)
- Swellings
- Reddening of the skin
- Cuts (minor and superficial)
- A 'black eye' (note that an optional charge for this injury could be one of **'assault occasioning actual bodily harm'** under s 47 of the Offences Against the Person Act 1861: see p 250).

**IT'S A FACT!**

**12.2: Non-fatal offences in the news**

Celtic and former Manchester United footballer, Roy Keane was in the news a great deal in 2005, but he made the legal headlines in March of that year when he was charged with assault under s 39 of the Criminal Justice Act 1988. Keane was tried at Trafford magistrates' court after being drawn into an altercation with a student who had earlier shouted abuse at him. The prosecution alleged that Keane had, amongst other things, squared up to the youth, spat in his face and swung a punch. However, the District Judge (magistrates' court) dismissed the case against Keane and he walked free from court.

The *mens rea* for battery is **intention** to apply unlawful personal violence on another, or subjective **recklessness** as to the risk of doing this. As with assault, intention may be **direct** or **oblique**. Since the rules on recklessness are *Cunningham* rules, the prosecution have to show that the defendant acted recklessly (*Venna* (1976)). The case of *Fagan v Metropolitan Police Commissioner* (see the discussion of contemporaneity at p 245 above) shows that an innocent act may become a battery in the course of events, for example, where the motorist, having inadvertently driven onto a policeman's foot, developed the *mens rea* by refusing to drive off.

Under the **Criminal Justice Act 1988, s 39**, battery is a **summary offence** carrying a maximum sentence of six months in prison and/or a fine of £5,000.

## Assault occasioning actual bodily harm

Although the focus of this offence seems to be just on assault, the *actus reus* here is an **assault** *or* **battery** that *causes* **actual bodily harm (abh)**. In *DPP v Smith* (1961), 'actual bodily harm' was held to be a form of harm that was *more than* trivial but *not* really serious. It can refer to **physical harm** (skin, bones, flesh and internal organs) and to **psychiatric harm**.

In *R v Chan-Fook* (1994), the defendant locked a man whom he suspected of stealing his fiancée's jewellery in an upstairs room in order to interrogate him. This frightened the victim to such an extent that he thought his best option was to escape through the window, and he was injured in the process of doing so. The defendant argued that he could not be liable for the injuries, since he did not actually hit his victim. Although the defendant was convicted at first instance, his appeal was allowed, since a defendant will not generally be found guilty of causing 'fear, distress or panic'. However, there will be liability for **psychiatric injury** where this evidences an actual clinical condition. It is for this reason that this area of law has been used to prosecute 'stalkers' and those seeking to distress others through, for example, silent telephone calls (*R v Ireland*; see p 248 above).

Actual bodily harm has also been held to include any **'hurt or injury calculated to interfere with the health and comfort' of the victim** (*R v Miller* (1954)). In this case, the defendant had raped his wife and, in the absence at the time of an offence of 'marital rape', he was convicted of 'actual bodily harm'.

A recent interpretation has been provided by the extraordinary case of *Director of Public Prosecutions v Smith* (2006) (see also Chapter 3 at p 52) in which the Divisional Court of the Queen's Bench Division found that Mr Smith's act of holding down his former girlfriend and cutting off her ponytail with a pair of scissors amounted to harm 'calculated to interfere with the health and comfort of the victim' which was more than trivial. Physical pain is not a prerequisite for establishing the offence.

The **Joint Charging Standard** suggests that the following injuries will amount to this offence (please refer to later coverage in this chapter for the alternative offences):

- Damage to a tooth (loss or breaking of a tooth): an alternative charge here could be one of wounding under ss 18 or 20 of the Offences Against the Person Act 1861.
- Temporary loss of consciousness: an alternative charge here could be one of grievous bodily harm under ss 18 or 20 of the Offences Against the Person Act 1861.
- Bruising (extensive/multiple).
- Broken nose (displaced): alternative charges here could be of grievous bodily harm and possibly also wounding (according to case law rather than the JCS) under ss 18 or 20 of the Offences Against the Person Act 1861.
- Fractures (minor): an alternative charge here could be of grievous bodily harm under ss 18 or 20 of the Offences Against the Person Act 1861.
- Cuts (minor, but requiring stitches): an alternative charge here could be of wounding under ss 18 or 20 of the Offences Against the Person Act 1861.
- Psychiatric injury (more than mere distress or fear): an alternative charge here could be of grievous bodily harm under ss 18 or 20 of the Offences Against the Person Act 1861.

A reasonably typical **'abh' example** is provided by *R v Wilson* (1984), where a driving dispute led the defendant to punch his victim in the face. Whether the injury sustained amounts to actual bodily harm, or grievous bodily harm or wounding (see pp 252–4 below) will depend on its **seriousness.**

The *mens rea* for assault occasioning actual bodily harm is **intention** to commit an **assault** *or* **battery**, or **subjective (*Cunningham*) recklessness** as to the risk, with **actual bodily harm** being caused in fact.

In *R v Savage* (1991), the defendant tried to throw beer over a love rival, but in doing so the beer glass broke, injuring the victim's wrist. The defendant was convicted of assault occasioning actual bodily harm, on the basis that the *mens rea* of recklessness for battery had been satisfied. The prosecution do not have to show intention or recklessness relating to the nature of the actual bodily harm that results from the conduct.

Assault occasioning actual bodily harm is a **'result crime'** and, as with the grievous bodily harm and wounding offences discussed below, raises the issue of **causation.** In *R v Roberts* (1971), the defendant made improper advances to a woman whom he was driving home. These advances included sufficient touching to constitute a battery. The woman, fearing a serious sexual assault, escaped by throwing herself out of the moving car. She was injured in the process. The Court of Appeal made two important points in this case. First, the point later followed in *R v Savage* (1991) (see above) that the *mens rea* required is that for assault or battery, not relating to the actual bodily harm that occurs. Second, the chain of causation between the defendant's conduct and the injury suffered by the victim will be perceived as intact so long as the victim's escape attempt was, in the circumstances, **reasonable.** If, on the other hand, it is 'daft' or 'unexpected' and therefore entirely unforeseeable, such an escape attempt might amount to a *novus actus interveniens*, which will relieve the defendant of liability.

Under the **Offences Against the Person Act 1861, s 47,** this offence is **triable either way,** with a maximum sentence of up to five years in prison and/or an unlimited fine.

## Wounding

The *actus reus* of wounding is an act of **unlawful** and **malicious wounding** on another. There are actually *two* **wounding offences** in the **Offences Against the Person Act 1861**, under ss 18 and 20: both involve unlawful and malicious wounding, and both provide an alternative to the grievous bodily harm offences also found in these sections. However, the **s 18 offence** is reserved for the most serious wounding offences. It therefore has a higher standard of *mens rea* and carries a very heavy penalty, as shown below.

To establish **wounding** there has to be a **breaking of the victim's skin**: this can be anything from a minor cut or graze to a serious wound. Usually wounds are accompanied by bleeding. The case of *JJC (a minor) v Eisenhower* (1984) shows how strict the law is on this point. Here, the defendant fired an air gun and a pellet hit a boy. Although the boy suffered internal injuries there was no wounding, since the skin had not been broken. Some commentators have made the point that this is an odd decision, since it means that a superficial cut, graze or pinprick would amount to wounding, but serious internal injuries would *not*. A broken nose can involve a breaking of the skin if, for example, the inner skin of the nose is broken, leading to bleeding – this follows the logic of a case called *R v Waltham* (1849), in which damage to the lining membrane of the urethra was caused with the result of bleeding. However, if the skin remains intact (as it did in *R v Wood* (1830), where a blow had broken the victim's collarbone but not his skin), the offence options are actual bodily harm or grievous bodily harm.

Wounding may be committed *with or without* the **use of a weapon**. The **Joint Charging Standard** for wounding situations is listed in the grievous bodily harm section at p 254 below, though the need for a **breaking of the skin** clearly needs to be borne in mind.

The *mens rea* for wounding in s 20 of the Offences Against the Person Act 1861 comprises an **intention** to inflict some harm, or **subjective (*Cunningham*) recklessness** as to the risk of inflicting some harm. Intention may again be **direct** or **oblique**. It is not necessary for the prosecution to show that the defendant intended or foresaw that wounding would result: it is enough to show that *some* harm was envisaged. This is illustrated by *R v Mowatt* (1968), which concerned violence that followed an attempt to rob the victim of £5 by the defendant and another. The defendant hit out in response to the victim's attempts to defend himself, and then proceeded to punch the victim repeatedly until the victim was almost unconscious. Here it could clearly be anticipated that harm would result from this behaviour.

However, under **s 18** of the **Offences Against the Person Act 1861**, the seriousness of the offence means that recklessness is not a high enough standard of *mens rea*. Therefore, unlike all the other non-fatal offences where the *mens rea* can be satisfied by intention *or* recklessness (a situation referred to as **basic intent**), s 18 is a crime of **specific intent**. For a s 18 wounding, the defendant must have **intended** grievous bodily harm to result to the victim. Since s 18 is, next to murder, one of the gravest non-fatal offences that can be committed, the **intention** has to be proved to the same standard as murder. Therefore, the *Woollin* test (see p 243 above) is relevant in wounding cases of **oblique intent**: was the really serious harm suffered by the victim a virtual certainty to arise from the defendant's conduct?

Under the **Offences Against the Person Act 1861**, the maximum sentence for the **s 20** triable either way offence is five years' imprisonment and/or an unlimited fine; the maximum sentence for the **s 18** indictable offence is life imprisonment and/or an unlimited fine.

## Grievous bodily harm

The *actus reus* of grievous bodily harm is **inflicting** *or* **causing grievous bodily harm** (**gbh**) *on* another. As with wounding, there are two separate offences under ss 18 and 20 of the **Offences Against the Person Act 1861**, with the **s 18 offence** being the most serious. Grievous bodily harm amounts, in both offences, to **really serious harm.** The offence may be committed *with or without* the **use of a weapon.** An example of serious physical harm can be seen in the case of *R v Brown and Stratten* (1998) where a son, embarrassed by his transsexual father, broke his father's nose and caused bruising, concussion, and knocked some teeth out. In *R v Mandair* (1994), the defendant husband, in the midst of a domestic dispute, threw a container of sulphuric acid at his wife, thus causing her the serious harm of severe acid burns to the face. However, the circumstances do have to be taken into account: *R v Barnes* (2005), see also below, indicates that a late tackle in an amateur football match, giving rise to a serious leg injury sustained by the victim, will only amount to the offence of grievous bodily harm if conduct was 'sufficiently grave to be properly categorised as criminal'. In making this judgment, relevant factors would include: 'the type of sport, the level at which it was played, the **nature of the act** *(actus reus)*, **the degree of force used** *(actus reus)*, the extent of the risk of injury and the defendant's **state of mind** *(mens rea)*'.

As with the offences of assault and battery considered at pp 248–50 above, **serious psychiatric harm** can also amount to grievous bodily harm. In *R v Burstow* (1997), a stalker was responsible for harassing and intimidating a victim, causing her to suffer depression, panic attacks and acute anxiety. Burstow had intimidated and harassed his victim over a period of eight months, and this behaviour had included silent telephone calls, abusive telephone calls and a menacing note; he had also stolen clothes from her washing line and left objects in the garden which were, in the circumstances, unpleasant. The House of Lords held that this behaviour did fall under the offence of 'bodily harm'. The meaning of **'inflict'** in **s 20** after the *Burstow*

**TALKING POINT 12.1: IS A BAD TACKLE A CRIME?**

What distinguishes *R v Barnes* (2005) from a case like *R v Brown and Stratten* (1998)?

The Court of Appeal (Criminal) in *Barnes* (2005) considered factors for limiting the role of criminal law in sport, such as:

- The disciplinary proceedings already in place for organised sports.
- The availability of civil remedies through the torts of negligence or trespass to the person.
- The players' implied consent to risks associated with the playing of contact sports (which makes physical conduct and contact 'lawful').
- The difficulties of applying the subjective recklessness standard to games of football: all defenders, for example, in judging a tackle on an attacker heading for goal can foresee the risk that some bodily harm might result, but the course of play might necessitate that they go ahead regardless.

What do you think? Where should the law stand on serious harm caused in the course of a sports game? Should the defendant have been convicted here for a tackle described by the prosecution, on the one hand, as a 'late, unnecessary, reckless and high crushing tackle' and by the defence, on the other, as a 'fair, if hard (sliding) challenge in the course of play'?

case has broadened to mean both the **direct** *and* **indirect** application of force. Under s **18** this had not been an issue, since the section refers to **'causing' grievous bodily harm** which permits a wider interpretation.

*R v Dica* (2003) provides an interesting recent addition to the case law. Here, the defendant was convicted of 'biological' gbh: even though he carried the *Human Immunodeficiency Virus* (HIV), and knew this, he had gone ahead with unprotected sexual intercourse with two women and infected them with the disease. *The Times* reported, in July 2005, that a woman had also been convicted of this offence when, with knowledge of her condition, she infected a boyfriend through unprotected sex.

The **Joint Charging Standard** suggests that the following injuries should be considered as amounting to grievous bodily harm:

- Severe injury (leading to permanent disability or disfigurement)
- Broken bones/displaced limbs
- Dislocated joints (for example, knee, shoulder, and so on)
- Severe loss of blood from injuries (perhaps requiring transfusions)
- Injuries requiring lengthy treatment, or likely to cause long-term incapacity.

The *mens rea* for grievous bodily harm differs between s 18 and s 20 of the Offences Against the Person Act 1861. Under **s 20**, it is **intention (direct or oblique)** to inflict **some harm**, *or* **subjective (*Cunningham*) recklessness** – a crime of **basic intent.** Under this section, only the suffering of **'some harm'** by the victim needs to be foreseen by the defendant. A number of examples may

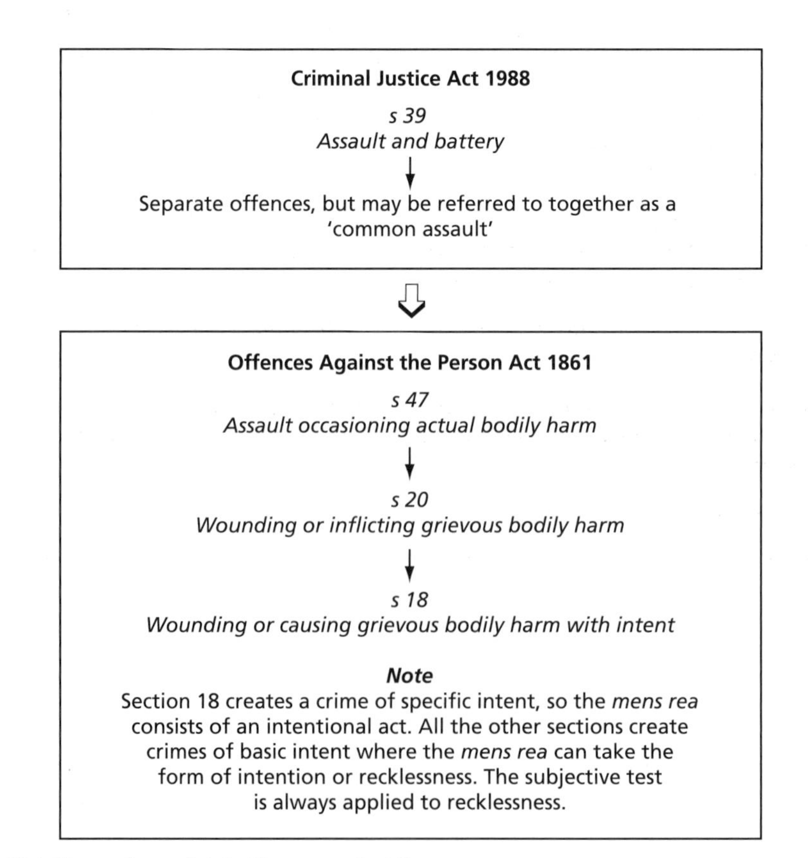


**Figure 12.1** Types of non-fatal offences against the person

be given where the courts have found that the defendant could have foreseen the exit of a theatre and shouting 'fire' (*R v Martin* (1881)); pushing a beer glass into a person's face (*R v Grimshaw* (1984)); inappropriately handling a new-born child (*R v Parmenter* (1991)); and forcing an object into a woman's vagina (*R v Rushworth* (1992)).

However, under **s 18**, only **intention to commit grievous bodily harm** will suffice (a crime of **specific intent**), with intention – as with **s 18 wounding** – at the same standard of proof as for **murder**.

The penalties for grievous bodily harm also differ according to the section under which the prosecution is brought. Under **s 20** of the **Offences Against the Person Act 1861**, the offence is triable either way and there is a maximum sentence of up to five years' imprisonment and/or an unlimited fine. However, the **s 18 offence** is indictable and carries a maximum sentence of life imprisonment and/or an unlimited fine.

**Exercise 12.2: Recap Quiz**

Identify the words, terms or phrases suggested by the clues below to reveal, by the first letters of each, the types of offences that they relate to:

——-/——-/——-: if one of these breaks the chain of causation for a result crime, such as the one in s 47, then the defendant is relieved of liability.

——-/——-/——-/——-/——-: the statute that has resisted reforms since 1861 and still creates much of the framework for this particular area of criminal law.

——-: if this is broken, then s 47 would certainly be relevant, and perhaps – given the circumstances – ss 18 and 20.

——-/——-/——-/——-/——-: you are looking for a case name here (a case that was also considered earlier in the chapter) involving an unfortunate incident involving a motorist and a policeman's foot: the relevant offence is now in s 39 of the Criminal Justice Act 1988.

——-: the *actus reus* of this offence is to place another person in fear of immediate and unlawful violence; it is also used much more loosely, and usually prefaced by the word 'common', in reference to the related offence of battery.

——-: you will probably require lengthy amounts of this, with the threat of long-term incapacity, if you are a victim of a s 18 or s 20 wounding or grievous bodily harm offence (check the Joint Charging Standard if you are unsure).

——-/——-/——-: this requirement, in s 47, shows that the offence is a result crime, not merely one of conduct.

——-/——-/——-: since the victim's skin has to be broken, this is the likely result if you are the unfortunate victim of a wounding offence (again check the Joint Charging Standard if you are unsure).

For Answers, please turn to pp 343–4.

## Useful website addresses

| | |
|---|---|
| Criminal justice system | www.cjsonline.org |
| Crown Prosecution Service (CPS) | www.cps.gov.uk |
| Home Office | www.homeoffice.gov.uk |
| *Materials directly for AS studies:* | |
| John Deft (St Brendan's Sixth Form College) | www.stbrn.ac.uk/other/depts/law |
| Asif Tufal | www.a-level-law.com |

### HINTS AND TIPS

As the structure of this chapter indicates, the topic of criminal liability is a mixture of **concepts to explain** (*actus reus, mens rea*, strict liability) and **apply** (the relationship between *actus reus* and *mens rea*, causation and the specific requirements of particular offences). To make the most of explanations, recognise the various rules relating to each concept – for example, that an *actus reus* may amount to a positive act, or an omission, or a particular state of affairs – and **learn** some **cases** and examples for each.

The **application part** becomes *vital* when you are presented with a **factual situation** – such as X punches Y, giving him a black eye – and asked to identify the criminal offence(s) that X may be charged with and the criminal liability that could attach. It is essential, in these circumstances, to identify the differing **requirements of each offence** and discuss, in an informed way, the charging options that the facts suggest. Examiners will welcome *some* reference to the **CPS/Police Joint Charging Standard** here, since it will substantiate your decision-making if applied appropriately, **provided, of course, that you have *first* discussed, with emphasis, the *actus reus* and *mens rea* of the relevant offence(s) and considered some case law.**

**Table 12.5** below could provide a **useful framework** (perhaps on A3 paper) for you to develop your **revision notes** on the **non-fatal offences** against the person.

Table 12.5 Revision: non-fatal offences against the person

| *Actus reus* | *Assault* | *Battery* | *Assault occasioning actual bodily harm* | *Wounding* | *Grievous bodily harm* |
|---|---|---|---|---|---|
| *Actus reus* examples and cases | | | | | |
| *Mens rea* | | | | | |
| *Mens rea* examples and cases | | | | | |
| Joint Charging Standard examples | | | | | |
| Other comments and features | | | | | |
| Penalties | | | | | |

For further reading, Ian Yule's examination advice in *A-level Law Review*, Vol 1, Issue 1, at p 26 is particularly useful, supporting learning in this topic and providing examples of answers at different levels of attainment.

# Introduction to tort liability

13

This topic enables you:

- To appreciate how the common law develops, with a focus on the tort of negligence.
- To build upon earlier knowledge of judicial precedent (Chapter 4) as the basis of common law development.
- To understand the nature of tort and recognise its contribution to civil law.
- To provide an outline introduction to negligence liability, based on the 'duty, breach, harm' requirements that have been established by the courts.
- To provide a foundation for further studies of the remedies to be awarded in negligence cases (see Chapter 14).

**Tort** is a subject that is not only fascinating but of great practical importance. It affects you, to provide just a few examples, as a **consumer** of manufactured goods; as a **patient** requiring medical services; as a **student** in a school, college or university; as a **passenger** in vehicles; and as an **employee** in the workplace. In these situations the law of tort provides you with **rights**. However, there may also be situations in which you owe **duties** under the law of tort. If you take responsibility for the safety of others, for example, then you will owe such duties.

These rights and duties extend on the basis that accidents are the 'inevitable consequences of activity'. In this sense, tort has an impact on all of our lives.

## THE TORT OF NEGLIGENCE

This is a **civil claim** in the **law of tort**. The test for negligence requires a **claimant** to establish a **breach of a duty of care** owed by the **defendant** that has **led to some harm** being caused. This duty does *not* require a contractual relationship between the parties, though often such claims arise where a contract exists (for example, in accident at work claims the employee will be contracted to the employer).

Therefore, the tort of negligence is the law concerned with a **wrong** that one party has committed and which thereby causes another party or parties

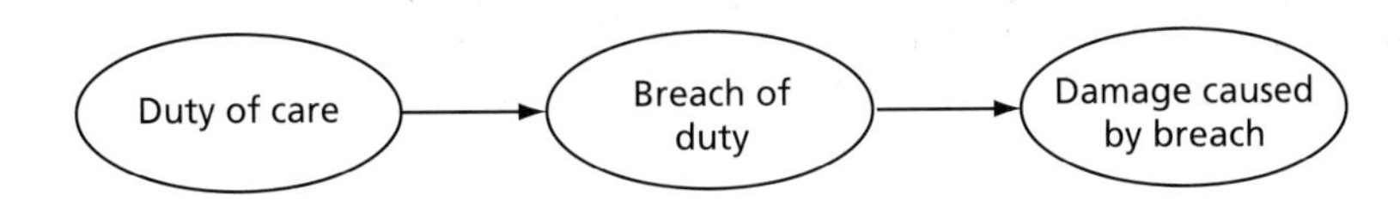

to suffer harm, loss or injury. Negligence law – which is very largely **judge-made** – considers whether it is 'fair' or appropriate for loss to be shifted from the victim to the person who has caused harm. This is expressed by an award of **damages** (in the form of *monetary compensation*) paid by the person who caused the harm (defendant) to the person who has been injured (claimant). Since much of the tort of negligence is underpinned by **insurance**, with compensation claims made against insured parties such as businesses, some have argued that the law of tort fails in its aim of loss-shifting. Instead, the argument goes, it leads to the practical consequence of *loss-spreading*, and this undermines the principle of '**fault**' that lies at the heart of negligence law. Why can this point be made? It is because those who have contributed to an insurance pool are not those who are at fault.

## DISTINGUISHING TORTS FROM OTHER LEGAL WRONGS

### Tort law and criminal law

The comments in Table 13.1 below build on your knowledge of the **criminal law** (see Chapter 12) by providing a basic set of *comparisons* between tort law and criminal law.

The law of tort has been developed by the **common law** and has relied largely on **judicial creativity** for its growth. There are relatively few Acts of Parliament in the law of tort, though a notable example of relevance here is the **Law Reform (Contributory Negligence) Act 1945**. By contrast, while criminal law has also developed through common law, *many more* Acts of Parliament have been passed in that area of law. A number of criminal law statutes are mentioned in Chapter 12, though the most significant for your studies are the **Offences Against the Person Act 1861** and the **Criminal Justice Act 1988**.

Table 13.1 Key features of tort and criminal law

| *Law of tort* | *Criminal law* |
|---|---|
| • Tort is part of **civil law** (injured parties will seek a **remedy** from the person they believe to have committed the wrong against them). | • Criminal law concerns the **punishment of offenders** by the **State**. |
| • Tort ensures that injured claimants can be **compensated** in the form of **damages** (though on very rare occasions damages are used to achieve other purposes: see Chapter 14). | • Criminal law focuses on **punishing the wrong** rather than compensating the harm caused (though sometimes *compensation orders* may be awarded: see Chapter 14). |
| • **Standard of proof** in **tort** is based on the '**balance of probabilities**'. | • **Standard of proof** in **criminal law** is '**beyond reasonable doubt**'. |
| • A **tort lawsuit** is brought by a **claimant** (in a dispute between individuals or companies, for example). | • **State prosecutes the offender** (with very limited scope for private prosecutions). |

Situations may give rise to both **civil** *and* **criminal** consequences. If, to take a very basic example, a driver is not taking care and knocks down a pedestrian, he might be prosecuted for the offence of 'dangerous driving' under the Road Traffic Act 1988 in criminal law; and the injured party could sue him for compensation under the tort of negligence.

## Tort law and contract law

The law of tort may also be contrasted with the law of contract. For example, law (judge-made law, in the main) sets obligations in tort, *whereas* obligations in contract law are set by the parties themselves (based on the principle of 'freedom of contract'). Moreover, compensation in the law of tort differs from that in the law of contract. Contract damages aim to put the party in the position he or she would have been in had the contract been performed. Tort damages, on the other hand, aim to put the claimant in the same position as if the tort had not been committed (for further consideration of tort damages, see Chapter 14).

There are also practical differences between contract and tort. Figure 13.1 below illustrates the chain of contractual liability arising from a defective product sold to a consumer, X. It shows that X is able to sue Y (the retailer) in contract law because the parties have a contractual relationship referred to as **privity**. In turn, Y can sue Z (the manufacturer) on the same basis, taking into account the fact that Z supplied Y with the defective product.

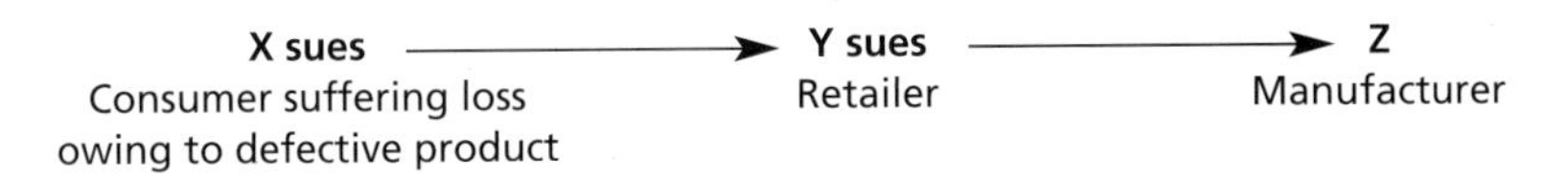


**Figure 13.1** Chain of contractual liability

However, consider now the landmark tort case of *Donoghue v Stevenson* (1932). Here, a friend bought ginger beer for Mrs Donoghue, which was contained an opaque glass bottle. The remains of a decomposed snail were also in the bottle. As a result of Mrs Donoghue drinking the ginger beer she became very ill. **Could she sue under the law of contract?** No – there was no contractual relationship between the retailer and Mrs Donoghue. The contractual relationship was between her friend (the buyer of the drink) and the retailer. **Therefore, what course of legal action could Mrs Donoghue take?** This famous case established that the only action available was under the **tort of negligence**, which enabled her to sue not the retailer but the manufacturer of the ginger beer. However, this sort of action poses difficulties for the claimant. A claimant has the burden of proving the following:

(a) that the defendant owed the claimant a duty of care;
(b) that the defendant was in breach of this duty; and
(c) that such actions by the defendant caused harm or injury to the claimant.

Mrs Donoghue's claim against the manufacturer was successful on this basis. The claim under the **tort of negligence** is illustrated in Figure 13.2 on p 260.

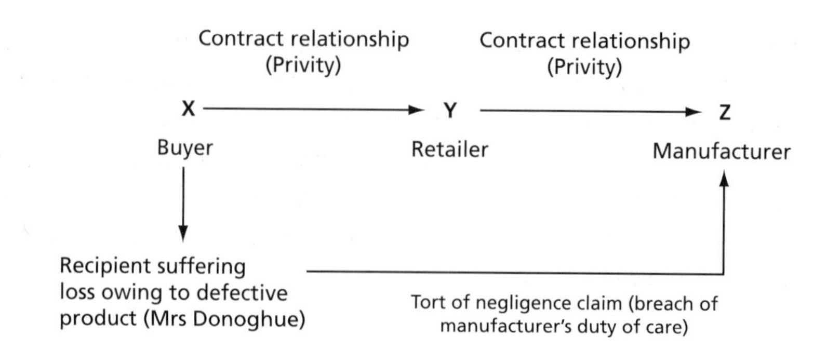


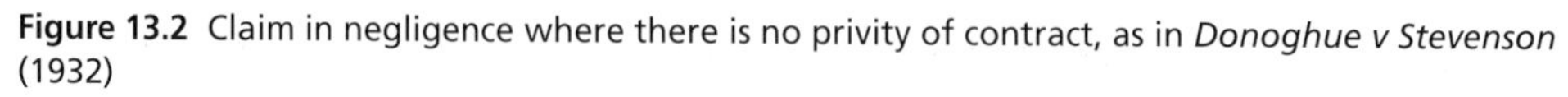
**Figure 13.2** Claim in negligence where there is no privity of contract, as in *Donoghue v Stevenson* (1932)

## THE DUTY OF CARE PRINCIPLE

*Donoghue v Stevenson* (1932) laid the foundations and stimulated the growth of negligence law through the **duty of care principle.** As we have seen, the narrow rule of this case stated that a **manufacturer owed a duty of care to its consumers.** However, **Lord Atkin** developed a *wider rule* in the case, more commonly known as the '**neighbour principle**' or '**neighbour test**':

> You must take reasonable care to avoid acts or omissions which you can *reasonably foresee* would be likely to injure your neighbour. Who then in law is my neighbour? The answer seems to be – *persons so closely and directly affected by my act* that I *ought reasonably to have them in contemplation as being so affected* when directing my mind to the acts or omissions which are called in question. (emphasis added)

This rule provided a principle that could, through precedent, apply to other factual situations. The wide rule has been used to develop the tort of negligence, in that the courts have had to recognise those relationships that satisfy the '**neighbour test**' and those that do not. A professional person is in a *neighbour* relationship with his clients, for example, but a police force is *not* a neighbour of the whole community for the purpose of catching individual criminals. The development of negligence law has been described as an '**incremental**', case-by-case process.

The neighbour test was successfully applied in *Home Office v Dorset Yacht Co Ltd* (1970). This case concerned some troublesome youths who were in a Home Office care institution (known as a Borstal). On a trip outside the institution, the youths were negligently supervised and caused damage to a yacht belonging to the Dorset Yacht Co Ltd. The question for the court here was whether the Home Office was liable in negligence to the Yacht Co Ltd for failing to provide adequate supervision. The court held that the Home Office was liable to the Yacht Co on the basis of Lord Atkin's '**neighbour test**' and that it was reasonably foreseeable that the boys would, if not supervised closely, cause damage to the property of others.

In *Bourhill v Young* (1943), however, the duty of care principle had been *denied*. Here, the claimant, a pregnant housewife, suffered a miscarriage after hearing a fatal motorcycle accident, caused by the defendant, about 50 yards away from her. The duty of care principle in this case did not apply as the consequence, the pregnant housewife suffering a miscarriage, was not foreseeable.

By the mid-1970s, though, the law had developed to the point where the judges had begun to try to assemble the main strands and themes of decisions following *Donoghue v Stevenson*. A leading judgment of Lord Wilberforce, seen as a landmark at the time but no longer viewed as such, in the case of *Anns v Merton London Borough Council* (1978), laid down a **two-stage test for negligence**:

(a) that there be sufficient **proximity** between defendant and claimant that damage to the claimant could be reasonably foreseeable; and
(b) that should such proximity be established, **policy factors** should be considered that might limit or negate the scope of the duty.

This case caused *problems* in the tort of negligence because it led to controversial extensions of the area and prompted some *confusion* among the judges.

## THE CURRENT TEST TO ESTABLISH A DUTY OF CARE: *CAPARO*

The current test that the courts use to establish negligence was laid down in the case of *Caparo Industries plc v Dickman* (1990). This case, on its facts, clarified the scope of the duty of care owed by financial auditors, setting the boundaries between those people who could and those who could not be expected to rely on audited accounts. The test for negligence established in *Caparo* laid down the following **three** stages:

- **Reasonable foreseeability** – that, on account of the defendant's behaviour (ie his or her acts or omissions), injury suffered by the claimant was a reasonably foreseeable consequence of that behaviour.
- **Sufficient degree of proximity between the parties** – that the relationship between the defendant and the claimant was sufficiently close in terms of time, location and context.
- **Whether it is fair, just and reasonable to impose such a duty** – that all the factors of the case need to be considered in view of the scope of the negligence duty and the need for justice to be achieved.

It should be noted, before illustrating each of these stages, that the judges will not generally have to consider the *Caparo* test if the case before them falls within '**established categories**' recognised by the courts (established by **precedent**) as giving rise to a duty of care. These '**established categories**' have been summarised by the legal writers McBride and Bagshaw as follows:

- Situations where the defendant owes a duty of care to others not to act dangerously (for example, motoring situations).
- Situations where the defendant owes a duty of care to others as a result of something done (for example, the giving of advice, the performance of a task, the controlling of another person or animal).

- Situations where the duty of care arises as a result of the defendant's special status or position (for example, as an occupier, employer or teacher).

Although a new factual problem might seem to fit with an 'established category' (and thus might, in practice, be sufficient to identify a duty of care), you are always advised to use the *Caparo* test and apply this to the facts of the case before you. The following authorities provide useful examples to consider when applying *Caparo*.

## Authorities on reasonable foreseeability

The requirement of 'reasonable foreseeability' is central to establishing liability in negligence. The legal writer, Michael Jones, makes the point that 'It is the foundation of the neighbour principle, but is also used as a test of breach of duty and remoteness of damage'.

The case of *Home Office v Dorset Yacht Co Ltd* (1970), as we have seen above, illustrates the 'reasonable foreseeability' principle. Another, more recent example is provided by the case of *Jolley v Sutton London Borough Council* (2000). In this case, the local council owned an area of land close to a block of flats, on which a boat had been left abandoned. The council, as occupiers of the land, had neglected to remove the boat from the land. The area attracted a number of children from the neighbouring flats, and two of these children, the claimant, aged 14, and his friend, decided that the boat could be repaired for the purposes of sailing. In their efforts to effect these repairs, the children used a car jack to raise one side of the boat. However, during this operation the car jack slipped, and the claimant, who had been working underneath the boat, suffered severe injuries when the boat fell down on him. It was held that the local council did owe a duty of care in this situation since it was reasonably foreseeable that the council's omission to remove the boat could lead to harm being suffered by visitors to the land, such as children. The boat was a hazard that would attract children, whether for the purposes of play or repair. The defendant council should therefore have foreseen the potential for harm.

These cases may be contrasted with those in which there is an unforeseeable claimant and the courts have accordingly denied a duty of care. The case of *Bourhill v Young* (1943) (see p 260 above) provides a useful example. Here, there was a claim from a woman who, having heard a fatal motor accident from behind a tram and witnessed its aftermath, suffered 'nervous shock' and a miscarriage. The claim was unsuccessful. As Lord Wright commented in the case:

> *I cannot accept that [the defendant] . . . could reasonably have foreseen, or, more correctly, the reasonable hypothetical observer could reasonably have foreseen, the likelihood that anyone placed as the appellant was, could be affected in the manner in which she was.*

More recently, the Court of Appeal in *French and others v Chief Constable of Sussex Police* (2006) found that a Chief Constable could not reasonably have foreseen that, as a result of a police operation in which a suspect was shot, some officers (the claimants) involved in the operation, but not in the shooting incident, would suffer stress-related psychiatric injury. The claimants had 'no real prospect' of establishing 'reasonable foreseeability'. As the Lord Chief Justice commented:

*'The claimants' case involved postulating a duty of care on the part of employers towards their employees not to cause or permit an untoward event to occur that could foreseeably lead to proceedings in which the employees' conduct would be in issue. It would not be appropriate for a lower court to make such an extension to the law of negligence and (we see) . . . no prospect that the House of Lords would be minded to do so.'*

## Authorities on proximity

'Proximity' means 'nearness in space, time, etc', though its legal definition has been debated by judges for many years. For example, closeness to an incident may be very important in one sort of case, such as the consequences of witnessing an accident, but there can be a 'neighbour' relationship, as we know from *Donoghue v Stevenson*, where the respective parties are not close together at all. The manufacturer and the consumer may be many miles apart; it is the defective product that gives rise to proximity.

Writers on tort differ as to the significance of 'proximity' in establishing a duty of care. Proximity has long been identified as at the core of the 'neighbour principle', and has been recognised as a major element for establishing the duty of care in both the two-stage *Anns v Merton LBC* test and its successor, the current *Caparo* test. However, where the defendant's behaviour directly affects the claimant or the claimant's property it seems that proximity is a less important part of the *Caparo* test, since the duty issue may be based more on the other elements of reasonable foreseeability and 'fair, just and reasonable'. Indeed, some judges have said that clear **foreseeability of damage** can *give rise*, in itself, to a **proximity relationship** (for example, Lord Steyn in a shipping case called *The Nicholas H* (1995); and also Lord Goff in *Muirhead v Industrial Tank Specialities* (1985)). An obvious example of this sort of situation would be the relationship between medical practitioner and patient in respect of an operation. If the operation is negligently performed then harm to the patient is a reasonably foreseeable consequence. It is fair, just and reasonable to hold that the defendant owes a duty to take care in respect of patients. The proximity relationship can therefore, to a large extent, be *presumed* in these circumstances (with medical practitioners and patients clearly falling within Atkin's view of the 'neighbour' principle).

Closer attention will be paid to **proximity**, though, in situations relating to **economic harm caused by negligent advice** and situations of **'nervous shock'** (psychiatric harm). This is because there may be problems with an application of **reasonable foreseeability** in such circumstances. In relation to claims for nervous shock, which arise through the negligence of the defendant, for example, the law insists on a number of proximity factors in respect of secondary victims in order to limit the scope of the duty of care. *Secondary victims* are those suffering shock as a result of witnessing injury to others. These factors include the requirement for claimants to be in a **'close and loving relationship'**

**with the victim** of the defendant's negligence; to be **physically (and geographically) proximate** to the events, thus ruling out shock suffered through transmission of news of an accident via television, radio or mobile phone; and for the claimant to **witness the aftermath** of the incident that has led to the shock.

The case of *McLoughlin v O' Brian* (1983) illustrates the application of these rules. Here, there was a serious road accident caused by the defendant's negligence that badly injured the claimant's husband and two of her children, and killed a third child. The claimant was at home at the time of the accident: she lived two miles away. She received news of the accident one hour later and rushed to the hospital. The scenes that greeted her there were very distressing – the extent of the injuries suffered and the death of the child were revealed at this point – and as a consequence she suffered severe psychiatric injury. The House of Lords allowed her claim to succeed against the defendant because she satisfied the proximity factors. She was, as a mother and wife, in a **close and loving relationship to the victims** of the defendant's negligence; there was **sufficient proximity in time and space** to the incident; and the mother did see the **terrible aftermath of the accident** within a few hours of its occurrence.

To summarise, so far it can be seen that:

- **proximity** does *not* have one precise legal definition;
- the need for proximity *varies* from case to case;
- proximity *overlaps* with the other aspects of the *Caparo* test and is sometimes assumed through the application of **reasonable foreseeability** and **'fair, just and reasonable'** tests; and
- proximity is used to *limit* the scope of the duty of care in some situations. This is seen as an application of **'judicial policy'**, in that the judges are using their tests to justify a particular course of action, for example, avoiding 'opening the floodgates' to too many claims.

In these circumstances, it is difficult to provide a simple example of how proximity works. However, the case of *Hill v Chief Constable of West Yorkshire* (1988) is useful because it illustrates the need for a proximity relationship even where reasonable foreseeability could be established, and also because it considers proximity from its roots in the neighbour test. The case concerned a claim against the police by the representatives ('the estate') of a victim of the multiple murderer known as the 'Yorkshire Ripper'. The claim was that the police owed a duty of care to the public in catching dangerous criminals and thereby preventing the potential for harm to individuals posed by such criminals. While the House of Lords accepted that there was reasonable foreseeability of likely harm to victims if the Ripper were not caught, it could not be said that there was sufficient proximity of relationship between defendant and claimant for the following reasons:

- The Ripper was *not* in custody, so the police had not let him 'escape' (unlike the situation of negligent supervision of disruptive youths by the Home Office in *Home Office v Dorset Yacht* considered at p 260 above).
- The victim was one of a vast number of potential victims and the police could *not* be seen as a 'neighbour' of everybody in the community.

- The victim was not at 'special risk' just by virtue of her age and sex (as Lord Keith pointed out, 'All householders are potential victims of a habitual burglar, and all females those of a habitual rapist': there was *no* special characteristic that would suggest that the defendant owed a duty to that particular victim).
- There were judicial policy reasons to deny the duty of care, including the **'floodgates argument'** (that this would open the floodgates to too many claims) and that the police would have to spend time and resources defending lawsuits and adopting defensive policing strategies.

## Authorities on 'fair, just and reasonable'

The final stage of the *Caparo* test recognises that even though there may be reasonable foreseeability and a proximity relationship, there will be no liability if the application of a duty of care does not seem fair, just and reasonable in all the circumstances. This area inevitably introduces the development of **judicial policy**, with the judges upholding particular principles to take into account the wider circumstances of the cases before them. Professor WVH Rogers in Winfield & Jolowicz on Tort (1998) provides the example of a soldier wishing to claim for injuries sustained due to the negligence of the armed forces during combat with an enemy force. Such a claim will be rejected – as it was in *Mulcahy v Ministry of Defence* (1996), involving a soldier who became deaf allegedly because of the negligence of the armed forces during active engagement in Gulf War combat – because issues of reasonableness are difficult to assess in the field of battle.

We saw above, however, that a number of **established categories of claim** are recognised by the courts as giving rise to a duty of care, though in respect of **'novel' cases** (that is, those new situations that fall outside the accepted categories) the courts will use the 'fair, just and reasonable' element to delimit the boundaries of negligence liability. The extent to which this element of the *Caparo* test is dependent on **judicial policy** is a matter of continuing discussion. This is largely because 'fair, just and reasonable' replaced the two-stage test in *Anns v Merton LBC* which had allowed judges a great deal of discretion to use policy and had, in turn, led both to confusion and the law developing in directions which were not seen as desirable. The judges will still base their decisions on policy grounds under the 'fair, just and reasonable' ground, though this formulation does allow for policy to be reviewed in order to achieve justice in the case. For example, it had been established as 'policy', in *Rondel v Worsley* (1969), that a barrister would be immune from negligence suits for carrying out the advocacy role in court. However, the case of *Arthur JS Hall v Simons* (2000) overruled the earlier precedent of immunity, on the basis that the requirements of policy had changed over time and that barristers could now be sued for negligent advocacy (see Chapter 10, p 210).

The judges will take into account some of the **following factors** when determining whether it would be **'fair, just and reasonable'** to impose a duty of care in the circumstances of the case:

- Whether the case falls within an **'established category'** for which liability will be imposed, or whether it is a 'novel' situation for which liability should be imposed.
- Whether the imposition of liability would **extend the boundaries of liability** beyond reasonable limits.
- Whether the imposition of liability in the one case will **'open the floodgates'** to too many claims from others in similar circumstances.
- Whether the imposition of liability would affect the **practice of professionals** (such as those in the emergency services or public authorities) and interfere with the proper fulfilment of their role. For example, in *Brooks v Commissioner of Police of the Metropolis* (2005), the House of Lords held that the police did not owe a duty of care to a victim or witness during their investigation of a serious crime. Lord Steyn said that an extension of the duty of care in these circumstances 'would have detrimental effects for law enforcement', upholding the general principles established in *Hill v Chief Constable of West Yorkshire* (see earlier coverage at p 264).

## Summary

The main points on establishing a duty of care may thus be summarised as:

(a) the **'neighbour' test** (Lord Atkin in *Donoghue v Stevenson* (1932)); and
(b) the **three-stage test** in *Caparo Industries v Dickman* (1990) (see Table 13.2 on p 267).

For AS examinations in tort, you need only concern yourself with the *Caparo* three-stage test, but it is worth pointing out that tort academics have identified a fourth branch of the duty of care test for those cases where the *general* rule might be that there is no duty: has the defendant voluntarily **assumed responsibility** to the claimant? This is especially relevant where claims are made against public authorities. For example, in *Carty v Croydon LBC* (2006), the Court of Appeal found that local education officers assumed responsibility for children with learning difficulties and therefore – taking account also of the *Caparo* tests – could owe a duty of care to them.

## BREACH OF THE DUTY OF CARE

Once a duty of care has been established, it is then necessary to consider whether the facts of the situation provide evidence of a **breach of this duty**.

## The 'reasonable man' standard of care

What sort of person, or what sort of behaviour, would fall short of the legal standard? The duty of care test is based on the **reasonable man**. Simple constructions of this include 'the man on the Clapham omnibus' and the 'commuter on the London Underground'. *Glasgow Corporation v Muir* (1943) is a landmark case on the meaning of a 'reasonable man'. The facts of the case

Table 13.2 The three-stage test in *Caparo Industries v Dickman*

| *Stage 1: reasonable foreseeability* | *Stage 2: sufficient degree of proximity between the parties* | *Stage 3: whether fair, just and reasonable to impose such a duty* |
|---|---|---|
| Was the claimant's injury a reasonably foreseeable consequence of the defendant's behaviour?<br>Reasonable foreseeability is found in:<br>• *Home Office v Dorset Yacht Co Ltd* (1970) (escaping Borstal boys damage yacht: Home Office liable)<br>• *Jolley v Sutton London Borough Council* (2000) (boy injured when repairing an abandoned yacht: local authority liable)<br>Reasonable foreseeability *not* accepted in:<br>• *Bourhill v Young* (1943) (woman hears accident and suffers shock: no liability) | Was there sufficient closeness in space, time and/or circumstances between the defendant's conduct and the claimant's injury?<br>Proximity can be *presumed* from other *Caparo* factors in some cases, though consider the need for proximity in cases of **nervous shock**:<br>• *McLoughlin v O'Brian* (1983) (mother and wife hears about, and then sees, aftermath of family accident: defendant who caused the accident liable to the mother for her shock)<br>Good illustration of proximity factors denying a claim:<br>• *Hill v Chief Constable of West Yorkshire* (1988) (claim against the Police for failing to catch a murderer – the Yorkshire Ripper: insufficient proximity between the police and victims of the murderer) | Is the application of a duty of care in the circumstances 'just, fair and reasonable'?<br>Indicates the importance of **'policy factors'** to take into account the practical consequences of finding a duty in certain situations, for example:<br>• *Mulcahy v Ministry of Defence* (1996) (soldier injured through negligence of own forces during Gulf War: claim denied – it would not be 'just, fair or reasonable' to impose such a duty in war conditions)<br>The courts will take into account a number of policy factors and keep these under review. |

involved a party at a tea house under the ownership of the Corporation. In preparing the teas for the party, a heavy tea urn was dropped, and as a consequence children were scalded by the hot water. Lord MacMillan defined a 'reasonable man' as one who did not suffer from personal quirks, and exhibited *neither* over-confidence *nor* over-cautiousness. Moreover, in *Blyth v Birmingham Waterworks Co* (1856), Baron Alderson said that negligence was either the *omission* to do something 'which a reasonable man, guided upon those considerations which ordinarily regulate the conduct of human affairs, would do' or an *act* 'which a reasonable and prudent man would not do'.

When establishing whether a breach of duty has occurred, you should ask, has the defendant 'acted as a reasonable man (or woman) in all the circumstances of the case?' In order to answer this question, the courts will take the following issues into account:

(**a**) the magnitude of the risk;
(**b**) the cost and practicality of taking precautions; and
(**c**) the social utility of the act;
(**d**) common practice and the foreseeability of risk; and
(**e**) the degree of skill exercised by different types of person.

Each of these is explained in greater detail below.

## Magnitude of the risk

The magnitude of the risk test for breach comprises two parts: first, the **likelihood of harm** occurring; and, second, the **seriousness of the injury** that could be sustained. The cases that follow illustrate the main rules that have developed.

The case of *Bolton v Stone* (1951) raises issues about the **likelihood of harm.** Here, a cricket ball, which had been struck by a batsman out of a cricket ground, hit the claimant, Miss Stone, who was standing on the highway. Counsel for the cricket club, on appeal, argued it was not negligent because of a number of factors. These included the points that balls had only rarely been hit out of the ground and that precautions had nevertheless been taken, including the erection of a high fence. In view of these facts, the House of Lords agreed. There was *no* negligence here because the club had acted reasonably in the circumstances. The likelihood of harm to members of the public was considered by Lord Reid to be 'extremely small' and did not justify taking out more burdensome precautions. Lord Oaksey said that the 'reasonable man' could be excused some precautions: 'He can, of course, foresee the possibility for many risks, but life would be almost impossible if he were to attempt to take precautions against every risk he can foresee.'

However, *Bolton v Stone* may be contrasted with *Watson v British Boxing Board of Control* (2001), which arose from a championship professional boxing match between Michael Watson and Chris Eubank. In the course of the fight, Watson was knocked down and suffered severe brain injuries. He later sued the British Boxing Board of Control for a breach of the duty of care in failing to provide adequate medical attention at the end of the fight. His claim was successful because here it was highly likely that, in the absence of adequate medical attention, harm would occur. In these circumstances, the British Boxing Board of Control had to accept liability. Unlike in *Bolton v Stone*, the risk here was substantial, and adequate precautions were required accordingly.

The second component of the magnitude of risk test takes into account the **seriousness of the injury** should harm occur. This is illustrated by a series of cases in which the courts have considered that particular care should have been exercised by defendants to ensure that serious harm was not suffered by persons who would appear to be most vulnerable in the event of injury. This test also underlines the point that the duty is owed to **individuals**, whom the defendant must accept as he finds them.

In *Paris v Stepney Borough Council* (1951), Paris was employed by a garage to undertake general manual work on cars. It was not the custom for the employer to supply goggles. However, the claimant was blind in one eye, and the employer was fully aware of this fact. In the course of his work, a metal splinter entered his good eye. This resulted in Paris becoming completely blind. The House of Lords held that the defendant owed the claimant a duty of care: given the claimant's individual problem, and the seriousness of the harm that could result, the employer had a *higher* standard of care to provide him with goggles.

Furthermore, in *Haley v London Electricity Board* (1965), some work was being undertaken on a public highway by electricity board workmen and a hole had been left exposed. The claimant, a blind man, was walking along the pavement when he fell down the hole. The injuries he suffered were such that he became deaf. The defendants were liable to the claimant. Public highways were used by all types of people, and the defendants were under a duty to take precautions suitable for all members of the community, particularly since the seriousness of the injury would be exacerbated in respect of certain vulnerable members of the public, such as the blind. Moreover, the precautions required to avoid such incidents – such as barriers – were practically available and used by other types of workmen.

Lastly, in *Smith v Leech Brain & Co Ltd* (1962), the claimant's husband suffered a burn to his lip during an industrial accident caused by the defendant's negligence. However, the burn triggered the onset of cancer, to which the claimant's husband was especially vulnerable. Owing to the seriousness of the injury sustained – and the fact that the **'egg-shell skull' principle** (that is, the husband's personal vulnerability– see p 277 below) meant that the defendant had to take the victim as he found him – the court found the defendant (an employer) liable for the victim's injury and subsequent death. However, Lord Chief Justice Parker took the view that it was not the consequences of the harm that had to be foreseen by the employer, but rather the *type of injury* that employees in that industry could suffer.

## Cost and practicality of taking precautions

Following on from Lord Oaksey's comments in *Bolton v Stone* (see p 268 above), the reasonable man is under a duty only to act *reasonably*. Indeed, there are occasions when extreme precautions seem unreasonable, given the cost and practicalities of securing them. In *Latimer v AEC Ltd* (1953), for example, torrential rain flooded a factory. The defendant had been powerless to prevent the flooding of the building in these circumstances. The defendant took the decision to keep the factory open, but spread sawdust on slippery surfaces. There was not enough sawdust to cover the whole floor, and Latimer (an employee) slipped and was injured. Could Latimer claim? It was held that there was no negligence here. The employer had done all that was reasonably practicable to avoid risk, short of closing the factory. Lord Denning stated that 'in every case of foreseeable risk, it is a matter of balancing the risk against the measures necessary to eliminate it'. He came down firmly on the side of the employer keeping the factory open.

## Social utility of the act

Sometimes risks are worth taking if, for example, the defendant's purpose has **social utility**. The *circumstances* of the time, and the defendant's *purpose*, are important factors to consider in applying this test. Social utility is particularly relevant in times of *war* and *emergency*. In *Watt v Hertfordshire County*

*Council* (1954), a fire crew was called out to rescue a woman who, in the aftermath of a road accident, was trapped under a lorry. The crew needed a heavy jack for the purposes of lifting the lorry, but because the fire engine used to carry the jack was engaged elsewhere, the firemen loaded the jack onto an alternative vehicle. There was no way of securing the jack on that vehicle, so the firemen steadied it themselves, with the result that the jack slipped in the vehicle and injured the claimant on the way to the rescue. The fireman's claim in negligence failed because the risk incurred was small when balanced against what the firemen were actually trying to achieve. Thus, the social utility of the act *outweighed* the risks.

Nevertheless, the courts have tended to hold against emergency vehicle drivers who have caused accidents. The case of *Ward v LCC* (1938) established the principle that an emergency vehicle that goes through a red light and causes injury to another road user, will generally attract liability. This is because the social utility of attending emergencies has to be balanced against the risk of causing injury to other motorists. The case raised a telling point, which Lord Denning considered in his judgment in *Watt v Hertfordshire County Council*: why bother racing to save lives if other lives are put at serious risk as a result?

## Common practice and foreseeability of risk

Defendants have a duty to take precautions in respect of risks that can be reasonably foreseen. If, however, a risk is unforeseeable, the defendant cannot be held responsible.

The case of *Walker v Northumberland County Council* (1995) is a good example of the former situation. It involved a social worker who had been suffering from stress attributable to the volume of work that he had been given. The employers breached their duty of care when they continued to add to the claimant's workload rather than take steps to reduce it. The risk to the employee was a foreseeable consequence of this conduct, and thus the employers were held liable.

However, there is no such duty to take precautions against 'fantastic possibilities'. In *Fardon v Harcourt-Rivington* (1932), the claimant was injured by flying glass when a dog, locked in a parked car, jumped at and smashed one of the windows. The defendant could not be held liable for this rather bizarre occurrence. *Roe v Minister of Health* (1954) provides further illustration of the unforeseeable risk situation. Here, a patient was paralysed after being given an injection to the spine. The anaesthetic solution used in the injection had become contaminated in storage, though the method of storage was common practice at this time. The Court of Appeal held that there was no liability here. Such contamination had never happened before – the incident occurred in 1947 and research relating to this form of contamination was first published in 1951 – and so this was a risk that could not have been contemplated.

## The level of skill to be exercised by different types of person

This section examines the standard of care applied to people with different levels of skill.

### Persons under 18 (minors)

The rule in tort is that minors *can* be liable for committing torts, though the standard of care expected of minors will not always be as high as that expected of adults. The standard will generally be that of a **'reasonable child'** of the **same age** as the defendant. It is fair to say that the law relating to minors is far less certain than that for adults.

The courts have generally denied negligence claims where minors have engaged in horse-play. In *Mullin v Richards* (1998), for example, two schoolgirls, both aged 15, were fighting each other with plastic rulers. A ruler snapped, hitting one of the girls in the eye. As a result she became blind in that eye. The courts held that since such 'horse-play' was common in classrooms up and down the country, the injury was unforeseeable to persons of that age. The claim for negligence could not succeed. However, there may be a greater readiness to find negligence where children have engaged in 'adult pursuits', such as driving a vehicle. There is persuasive authority to suggest that such conduct will *raise* the standard of care accordingly (*Ryan v Hickson* (1974)).

The courts have been quite severe on child claimants who were seen as contributing to their own injuries, as *Morales v Eccleston* (1991) shows. Here, a boy, aged 11, was playing football and ran blindly into a road to retrieve a ball – at which point he was knocked over by a motorist. It was held that the boy could claim in negligence, but his damages were reduced by 75 per cent (owing to the boy's contributory negligence: see the discussion at p 278 below). If a parent's failure to supervise a child leads to injury to a third party, the parent may be liable for the acts of the child. The parent of the child in the Canadian case of *Ryan v Hickson*, mentioned above, was held liable on this basis. The standard here is that of a **'reasonably prudent parent'**.

Occasionally, third parties have become liable in tort for failing to act prudently in respect of child trespassers. In *Hilder v Associated Portland Cement Manufacturers Ltd* (1961), an occupier of land attracted liability when children, who had been allowed to play on the land, kicked a ball onto an adjacent road and into the path of a motorcyclist, causing a serious road accident.

### Persons in the process of learning a skill

The most obvious example of a person learning a skill is a **'learner driver'**. The case of *Nettleship v Weston* (1971) deals with this situation. Here, the claimant provided a learner driver, his friend, with some driving lessons. During her third lesson the defendant hit a lamp post, injuring the claimant. The court held that the learner driver should be liable to the claimant here. This case clearly illustrates the point that all drivers owe the same duty of care. Although this decision favoured the claimant, the reasoning for it varied as between the judges. One point made was that different standards of care for motorists would result in uncertainty in the law. The courts have therefore tried to provide an **objective test** that is applicable to all motorists. Some commentators have expressed surprise at this outcome, and the High Court of Australia has since refused to follow this decision (*Cook v Cook* (1986)). What do you think?

The same principle was applied in *Wilsher v Essex Area Health Authority* (1988), although this case involved a junior doctor, not a learner driver.

The claimant, born prematurely, suffered damage to his sight which was attributed to the negligence of the defendants. One of the doctor-defendants was junior and had limited experience. The Court of Appeal, whilst acknowledging the difference between consultants and juniors, made the point that the standard of care could not be reduced on this basis since patients had an expectation of, and dependence on, the doctors who treated them.

## Persons with specialist skills

A person who possesses specialist skills in a profession is not judged by the 'reasonable man' test but by **people within the same profession.** This is illustrated by *Bolam v Friern Hospital Management Committee* (1957), from which the **'Bolam test'** derived. In this case a doctor omitted to give a patient a drug to relax the muscles during electro-convulsive therapy. The claimant argued that this resulted in his suffering a fracture. The question for the court was whether the doctor had been negligent. The doctor was held not to have been negligent. Since it could be shown that many other doctors would have acted in the same manner, this doctor could not be held liable. If there is more than one established practice, the doctor will still not be liable if he has exercised the care and skill to be expected of such a practitioner. This decision may be applied to other professions. The standard of care for professional people will be judged to be the standards of ***'a competent body of professional opinion'*** (**'Bolam test'**).

A case in which the **Bolam test** favoured the claimant rather than the doctor was *Clark v Maclennan* (1983). Here, the defendant had performed an operation on the claimant to relieve stress incontinence after the birth of a child, but he did so after one month, contrary to the accepted medical practice of waiting three months. The operation was unsuccessful, and therefore the claimant was able to win damages in the case for the defendant's negligence, since the medical care was contrary to accepted practice and did not demonstrate an exercise of care and skill.

## Summary

In summary, the tests for **breach of a duty of care** are:

(a) establishing the generally applicable **standard of care** (the **'reasonable man'** – see *Glasgow Corporation v Muir* (1943)); and
(b) satisfying the tests for **breach** of the duty of care (see Table 13.3 on p 273).

## DID THE DEFENDANT'S BREACH CAUSE THE HARM?

Once it has been established that the defendant owed the claimant a duty of care and it was breached, you now have to see whether the breach by the defendant caused the harm to the claimant (a **causal link**). This is known as **causation.** It expresses the link between the alleged breach of the duty of care and the consequences that flow from it. Causation is an essential element in determining the person or persons who have legal responsibility for the damage and losses suffered.

Table 13.3 Tests for breach of the duty of care

| *Magnitude of the risk* | *Cost and practicality of taking precautions* | *Social utility of the act* | *Common practice and foreseeability of risk* | *Degree of skill exercised by different types of person* |
|---|---|---|---|---|
| Cases on the likelihood of harm occurring as a result of the defendant's conduct:<br>• *Bolton v Stone* (1951) (cricket ball – claim denied)<br>• *Watson v BBBC* (2001) (boxing injury – claim allowed)<br>Cases on the seriousness of the harm likely to result from the defendant's conduct:<br>• *Paris v Stepney BC* (1951) (one-eyed mechanic made blind – claim succeeds)<br>• *Haley v London Electricity Board* (1965) (blind man made deaf – claim succeeds) | Case illustrating that the defendant has to do only what is reasonable in the circumstances:<br>• *Latimer v AEC* (1953) (worker slips in flooded factory, but employer had done enough to avoid injuries – no claim here) | Cases to illustrate the balancing of risks according to the social utility of the conduct:<br>• *Watt v Hertfordshire CC* (1954) (heavy equipment injures fireman, but small risk compared to goal of saving others – no negligence)<br>• *Ward v LCC* (1938) (fire engines going through red lights will be liable to other road-users if there is an accident) | Case to illustrate liability where a defendant can see a risk but does nothing to prevent it:<br>• *Walker v Northumberland CC* (1995) (stressed worker given even more to do – employer negligent)<br>Case to illustrate an unforeseeable risk, as supported by common practice:<br>• *Roe v Minister of Health* (1954) (paralysed patient owing to contaminated anaesthetic – no negligence, since following common practice) | Cases relating to persons under 18 (minors):<br>• *Mullin v Richards* (1998) (ruler fight between girls – no liability since common horse-play)<br>• *Morales v Eccleston* (1991) (contributory negligence for child retrieving runaway ball)<br>Case relating to 'learners':<br>• *Nettleship v Weston* (1971) (learner driver owes common duty)<br>Case relating to persons with specialist skills:<br>• *Bolam v Friern HMC* (1957) (Bolam test – professionals judged by standards of other professionals) |

## Factual causation and the 'but for' test

In order to establish factual causation the 'but for' test is relevant: it asks, 'But for the defendant's negligence would the harm still have occurred?' If the answer is 'Yes', this relieves the defendant of liability. This is illustrated by *Barnett v Chelsea & Kensington Hospital Management Committee* (1969). Mrs Barnett's husband was poisoned after drinking contaminated tea on New Year's Eve. He was rushed into hospital as he was suffering from stomach pains and was vomiting. He died. Mrs Barnett sued on behalf of her husband, claiming that the hospital had been negligent as the doctor had failed to treat her husband. It was held that although the hospital was negligent in its procedures, it was not held to be liable for the death as the doctor could not have done anything to save the patient – the poison was going to kill him anyway. Thus the question addressed by the court was as follows: '*But for* the hospital's negligence, would the event have happened?' In this case it would. The lack of medical treatment was not the cause of Mr Barnett's death, and therefore the hospital could *not* be held liable.

## Relationship between factual causation and legal causation

Once *factual causation* has been considered, it is also necessary to see whether the conclusion reached is affected by the *legal principles of causation*. Such a process will ultimately result in an investigation as to whether the damage was **too remote a consequence of the breach** (see below). There are several legal principles of causation that will be discussed in the remainder of this section:

- *Novus actus interveniens*
- Material contribution to the harm caused
- *Res ipsa loquitur*
- The 'thin skull' rule
- Remoteness of damage
- Contributory negligence.

### *Novus actus interveniens*

To illustrate this principle, take the *Barnett* case, above. This situation could be complicated by a *novus actus interveniens*. This is when a **new act** may **break the chain of causation**, thereby relieving the defendant of responsibility. A simple illustration should suffice: X is poisoned by Y; however, X's death is not actually caused by Y's poison but by the negligent treatment of Dr Z at the hospital to which X is rushed. The hospital's negligence therefore relieves Y of liability, since it has intervened in the chain of causation. However, the Court of Appeal recently held, in *Corr v IBC Vehicles Ltd* (2006), that an employee who had developed severe clinical depression as a result of the employer's negligence did not break the chain of causation when he committed suicide. Lord Justice Sedley explained that '*It was for a claimant (in this case, the widow of the employee) to establish that it was depression which drove the deceased to suicide, not for a defendant to disprove it. To cut the chain of causation and to treat the employee as responsible for his own death would be to make an unjustified exception to contemporary principles of causation.*'

## Problems in establishing who caused the harm: establishing a 'material contribution'

Problems occur when the actual cause of the harm is not established. This prevents the claimant from succeeding in a case because the tort of negligence is essentially fault-based. It is for the person bringing the claim to prove the fault. This clearly places a very heavy burden on claimants. Nevertheless, some successful claims have been made.

A good example is provided by *Bonnington Castings Ltd v Wardlaw* (1956). This concerned a claimant whose working environment had exposed him to silica dust in the air. As a consequence, the claimant contracted a disease called pneumoconiosis. The silica dust originated from two sources: pneumatic hammers, which the employers had maintained to a reasonable standard; and swing grinders, for which the employers were in breach owing to their use of ineffective dust extraction equipment. It was not known how much dust was created by each of these sources, but the House of Lords held that the swing grinders and the employer's breach in respect of these **materially contributed** to the harm suffered by the claimant. Therefore, the employers were liable for the employee's loss.

In *McGhee v National Coal Board* (1973) the claimant was employed to clean out brick kilns. However, the employers had been negligent in that they had not provided the employee with the necessary facilities for washing. Furthermore, the employee cycled from work to home often in dirty and grime-covered work clothes. He contracted a skin disease, dermatitis, which had been caused by the working conditions in the brick kilns. Evidence also showed, however, that his cycling from work to home in work clothes had significantly contributed to the risk of developing such a disease. Nevertheless, the House of Lords held that the employers were liable in negligence to the employee. As Lord Salmon said (emphasis added): '. . . when it is proved, on a *balance of probabilities*, that an employer has been negligent and that his negligence has *materially increased the risk of his employee contracting an industrial disease* then he is liable in damages to the employee if he contracts the disease . . .'

The House of Lords has recently given approval to the 'material contribution' approach in *McGhee* in the case of *Fairchild v Glenhaven Funeral Services Ltd* (2002). Here the courts were presented with a causation dilemma: could a claimant suffering from an asbestos-related illness make a successful claim when he or she had worked in *more than one place* of employment where exposure to asbestos dust had taken place? The difficulty, acknowledged by the Court of Appeal, was that the claimant would not be able to show which place of employment had caused the harm suffered. Nevertheless, the House of Lords allowed the claim to succeed on the basis that where it could be shown that employer negligence had *materially increased* the risk of developing an industrial disease, that amounted to a 'material contribution' to the harm. Thus, where there were three employers, and each exposed its workers to dangerous dust, a claimant could seek to establish 'material contribution' in *any or all* of these places of employment. The House of Lords has subsequently held, in *Barker v Corus UK* (2006), that the liability of employers, in such circumstances, will be proportionate, with the contribution of individual firms assessed.

## *Res ipsa loquitur*

Breach of duty and causation can, on occasions, be established through the maxim ***res ipsa loquitur***, which means that '*the thing speaks for itself*' (that is, the actionable harm clearly resulted from the event that occurred). In such cases the burden of proof lies with the defendant. In other words, the defendant has to prove that there has been no negligence. Classic examples of the principle in application include *Scott v London and St Katherine Docks Co* (1865), where a claimant successfully recovered damages from the defendant resulting from an incident in which six bags of sugar had fallen from the defendant's warehouse; and *Chaproniere v Mason* (1905), where a consumer successfully sued a manufacturer when she suffered injury because of a stone found in the centre of a bun. However, *res ipsa loquitur* was not allowed in the case of *Roe v Minister of Health* (see p 270 above) because the defendant could discharge the burden of showing that there was no negligence.

## Developing the subject: What are the causal requirements in a 'loss of chance' situation?

The recent tort case law on causation has struggled to find a coherent line of reasoning relating to 'loss of a chance' situations, where claimants seek to assert the view that the defendant's actions caused them to lose out on an opportunity that they would otherwise have had. The cases have been significant because they have forced senior judges to consider the appropriate causal requirements in such situations: for example, should claimants have to establish causation 'on the balance of probabilities' or is it enough for them to show that the defendant's conduct was a 'material contribution' to the harm?

In *Gregg v Scott* (2005), a doctor was sued by a patient who had developed a cancerous lump under his arm and been left without treatment for nine months owing to the doctor's mistaken diagnosis. During the nine month period the cancer grew worse and the patient's chances of recovery had reduced from 45 per cent (if the lump had been treated at the time of the first diagnosis) to just 25 per cent. The House of Lords considered the causal requirement as 'on the balance of probabilities' in such cases – holding that *Fairchild v Glenhaven* (2002) could be distinguished as relating to such situations where the main cause was known, but the actual offending parties were difficult to identify – and accordingly dismissed the claim. The claimant could not say that the doctor's mistaken diagnosis had more likely than not caused a reduction in his prospects of recovery because those prospects of recovery had always been less than 50 per cent.

However, the House of Lords demonstrated its willingness to modify the principles of causation in the earlier case of *Chester v Afshar* (2004). Whilst the House of Lords did not view this case explicitly in 'loss of a chance' terms (and in *Gregg v Scott*, it was considered as limited to its own particular facts); the decision indicates that the courts will extend existing principles in the interests of justice. The facts relate to an operation performed on the claimant's back which, whilst carried out appropriately, led to spinal paralysis. The key point is that the surgeon, who knew that there was a very slim chance that paralysis could occur (0.9–2 per cent), had failed to warn the patient of this risk prior to the operation. The claimant accepted that even if warned she may still have gone ahead with the operation, but she would, first, have sought further advice before committing herself to the date on which the operation had been performed. Although it is difficult to identify causation in this case – the claimant could not establish this on the basis of the general tests – the House of Lords held, by a majority, that her claim should be allowed. As Lord Hope explained, having considered whether justice required the normal approach to be modified and found that it could: 'On policy grounds therefore, the test of causation was satisfied and justice required that the claimant be afforded the remedy she sought, as the injury she suffered at the defendant's hands was within the scope of the very risk which he should have warned her about when obtaining her consent to the operation that resulted in that injury.'

Moreover, in *Fryer v Pearson and Another* (2000) the *res ipsa loquitur* principle was denied to the claimant. Judicial approval was given for the proposition that lawyers should stop using Latin maxims that they do not, in reality, understand. The facts of this case involved a gas fitter who, in the process of doing his job at a client's home, knelt down and found that a needle, hidden in a carpet, had become embedded in his knee. This resulted in a significant disability and he was therefore unable to work. One judge in the case described the incident as 'an unfortunate but freak accident' rather than an incident giving rise to an actionable claim.

## The thin skull rule (also known as the 'egg-shell skull rule')

This principle expresses the view that the **defendant should take the victim as he finds him**, or in simpler terms, that the person causing the injury should be aware that victims may differ as to thresholds of pain, personal circumstances, and so on. The most stark example of this, as referred to at p 269 above, is *Smith v Leech Brain & Co Ltd* (1962). Here it was held that where an employee burnt his lip in an industrial accident at work, which was the fault of the employer, the employer should take responsibility for the injury in full, even though the victim was vulnerable to cancer and later died because of the injury.

## Remoteness of damage

The law on negligence is concerned only with *foreseeable damage*. Unforeseeable damage as a result of a negligent act is seen as **too remote**. It is for the judges to decide whether the damage was foreseeable, based on what a reasonable ordinary person would have thought. The landmark case on remoteness of damage is the Privy Council's decision in *The Wagon Mound (No 1)* (1961). The case concerned a fire that broke out on a wharf, caused by welding activities on a ship. An independent inspection gave the go-ahead for the welding to begin, but because of a mixture of oil and other materials on the water's surface a fire broke out. The resulting tort claim was brought against the welders, but it was unsuccessful on the basis of the 'remoteness of damage' principle. The welders could not be liable since the damage was not 'reasonably foreseeable', a point underlined by the fact of inspection prior to the work being carried out.

Since the Wagon Mound case, *Hughes v Lord Advocate* (1963) has established the point that the rules on reasonable foreseeability will apply even though the injury did *not* occur in the *precise manner* anticipated. In this case, an open manhole and some lamps had been left unattended in a public area. While there was a cover over the manhole, and a set of warning lights surrounding it, a young child was nevertheless attracted to the cover and started playing with one of the lamps that had been left there. The child dropped the lamp into the manhole, causing an explosion, and was badly burnt as a result. Here the House of Lords held that because it was reasonably foreseeable that an unattended manhole and lamps might attract attention, particularly from children, and that these things represented a hazard, it did not matter that the precise nature of the harm – an explosion – differed from that anticipated. However, if the cause of the injury is *entirely unforeseeable* – for example, if an explosion occurs that cannot in any way be envisaged – then the *Wagon Mound* test will apply to deny a claim to the claimant. This was established by *Doughty v Turner* (1964), in which an explosion occurred as a consequence of asbestos materials inadvertently coming into contact with molten metal. This could not have been foreseen by a reasonable person, since the explosive nature of this sort of contact was not known at that time.

The case of *Jolley v Sutton London Borough Council* (2000) (boy injured in attempt to repair an abandoned boat on council land), which we considered at p 262 above, confirms the point made in *Hughes v Lord Advocate*.

**Exercise 13.1: Identifying cases in tort and relationship to duty, breach and harm**

**Task 1**

*Use the following factual clues to identify the corresponding cases in the law of tort.*

(1) When the claimant was hit by a cricket ball, the cricket club was not liable: a high fence had, after all, been erected.
(2) This pregnant claimant suffered a miscarriage when she heard a road traffic accident occur, but her claim did not succeed.
(3) To whom are financial auditors liable when they prepare their accounts? This case tells you, and much more besides.
(4) In this very unfortunate case, did death arise through a contaminated drink or treatment at the hospital?
(5) This case considers the form of action to take if a factory floods: maintain production, albeit with concessions to the circumstances, or keep the factory shut?
(6) The defendant employer in this case really should have ensured that the very unlucky claimant wore some goggles.
(7) An independent inspection had given the go ahead for welding on a ship: a surprise, then, when fire broke out on the wharf?
(8) If you ever get stuck in the cubicle of a public toilet, this case tells you to watch out for the toilet-roll holder if you try to escape.
(9) When you next go to the café, beware of rotting gastropods in dark bottles!
(10) Spilt scalding tea led to the explanation of a very important legal test: on the basis that the test standard applies to both genders, you might wish to ask yourself 'Am I this person'?

**Case options:** (a) *Donoghue v Stevenson*; (b) *Barnett v Chelsea and Kensington Hospital*; (c) *Bolton v Stone*; (d) *Wagon Mound*; (e) *Caparo v Dickman*; (f) *Glasgow Corporation v Muir*; (g) *Sayers v Harlow UDC*; (h) *Bourhill v Young*; (i) *Paris v Stepney BC*; (j) *Latimer v AEC*

**Task 2**

Now sort the cases that you have identified into the appropriate topic categories for an introduction to tort: which relate to DUTY; which to BREACH; and which to HARM? If you are unsure about any of your answers, please have a look through Chapter 13 again.

For Answers, please turn to p 344.

## Contributory negligence

This becomes an issue when the claimant is **also responsible**, with the defendant, for causing injury to himself or herself. The consequence of this is not to deny a claim altogether, but to ensure that the claimant's damages are **reduced.** In some cases, as we saw in *Morales v Eccleston* (see p 271 above), they can be reduced by 75 per cent, and sometimes by even more than that! The **Law Reform (Contributory Negligence) Act 1945** sets out a statutory framework for dealing with such cases.

An amusing example that illustrates how contributory negligence works is *Sayers v Harlow UDC* (1956). Sayers entered a toilet cubicle in a public lavatory, closed and locked the door, and subsequently found that it would not open again. She stood on the toilet-roll holder in a desperate attempt to escape. As a result she fell and injured herself. Although her claim was successful against Harlow Council (as they should have provided an inside door handle), damages were reduced by 25 per cent as Sayers had contributed to her own injury by attempting a rather hazardous form of escape.

In *Froom v Butcher* (1975), the defendant crashed into the claimant's car. However, the injuries sustained by the claimant would have been prevented if he had worn a seat-belt, and he was therefore contributorily negligent. It was stated in this case that if a claimant *fails* to wear a **seat-belt**, in the event of an accident damages would generally be reduced by up to 25 per cent.

In both *Sayers v Harlow* (1956) and *Froom v Butcher* (1975) the claimants' damages were reduced as they had been **contributorily negligent.** However, in *Jones v Boyce* (1816) the court found that the claimant was not, in the circumstances, negligent. Here, the claimant was riding as a passenger on a horse-drawn coach. When one of the reins snapped during the journey, the claimant threw himself out of the coach as he feared a crash. This resulted in the claimant breaking a leg. It was held that the claimant was *not* contributorily negligent here as the defendant's coach had clearly malfunctioned. The court reasoned that a defendant coach driver would be liable where a fault caused the passenger to have reasonable cause for alarm and he took evasive action, as in this instance. He would not, however, be fully liable for a passenger who acted rashly, without thinking, since this would not be a reasonable and prudent act and would amount to contributory negligence.

## Summary

Table 13.4 (see p 280) summarises the tests used by the court to establish that the defendant's breach caused the harm or injury suffered by the claimant.

**HINTS AND TIPS**

The structure of this chapter follows the three elements that a claimant has to prove to establish a claim in negligence. For each of these three elements the courts have developed tests to see whether the claim can be justified:

- Did the defendant owe the claimant a **duty of care**? The courts will consider the *Caparo* test (reasonable foreseeability; proximity; fair, just and reasonable), with an appreciation of the roots of negligence liability in Lord Atkin's 'neighbour test' from *Donoghue v Stevenson* (1932).
- Was the defendant in **breach of this duty**? The courts will consider whether the defendant's conduct satisfied the **'reasonable man'** standard of care taking into account a number of important tests, for example, the magnitude of risk, cost and practicality of precautions, social utility of the act, common practice and foreseeability of risk, and the nature of the defendant's skill and experience.
- Did the actions of the defendant **cause harm or injury** to the claimant? The courts will consider factual causation (the **'but for' test)** and legal principles to establish whether the breach caused the harm, with the rules on **remoteness of damage** being particularly significant. Table 13.4 (see p 280) summarises the legal principles that may be encountered.

Examiners tend to follow the three stages above (also referred to as 'duty, breach and harm') that a claimant must prove to establish negligence, and these stages should provide a structure for your revision. See Ian Yule's 'Tort Law decoded' article in *A-level Law Review*, Vol 1, Issue 2, at p 8.

## Useful website addresses

*Materials directly for AS studies:*

| | |
|---|---|
| John Deft (St Brendan's Sixth Form College) | www.stbrn.ac.uk/other/depts/law |
| Asif Tufal | www.a-level-law.com |

Table 13.4 Tests for causation

| *Factual causation* | *Legal principles of causation* |
|---|---|
| The **'but for' test** asks: '*But for* the defendant's negligence, would the harm have occurred?'<br>If the answer is 'Yes' then the defendant has not caused the harm: it would have happened anyway.<br>See *Barnett v Chelsea & Kensington Hospital Management Committee* (1969) (poisoned man, hospital could not have saved him, so hospital not the cause of death for negligent procedures – 'but for' test applied). | Now turn your attention to the legal principles of causation:<br>• Was there a **new intervening act (*novus actus interveniens*)** which broke the chain of causation? For example, did negligent medical treatment cause the greater harm, thus relieving the defendant of responsibility?<br>• Did the defendant's conduct '**materially contribute**' to the harm suffered by the claimant? Where the actual cause of harm is difficult to establish – for example, where a person has worked in a number of factories and been exposed to the same harm in all these places – the courts will look to see whether the defendant before them has materially increased the risk of harm to the claimant (*McGhee v National Coal Board* (1973) and *Fairchild v Glenhaven Funeral Services* (2002)).<br>• Was this a case of ***res ipsa loquitur* (the facts speak for themselves)**? See *Scott v London & St Katherine's Docks* (1865), where the courts held that the facts spoke for themselves when six bags of sugar fell from the defendant's warehouse onto the passing claimant. However, note the judicial comments in *Fryer v Pearson* (2000).<br>• Does the '**thin skull rule**' apply? The defendant must take the victim as he finds him, as in *Smith v Leech Brain & Co Ltd* (1962) (employee's burnt lip leads to cancer – defendant fully liable).<br>• Is the damage to the claimant **too remote** a consequence of the defendant's breach? Damage that is unforeseeable will be declared too remote (after the *Wagon Mound (No 1)* (1961)), though if damage is foreseeable but the precise type of injury differs from that anticipated, the courts will allow a claim (*Hughes v Lord Advocate* (1963) and *Jolley v Sutton LBC* (2000)).<br>• Has the claimant been **contributorily negligent**? Is the claimant also to some extent responsible, along with the defendant, for the injury suffered? If so, the defendant will still be liable but to a lesser extent, and any award of damages will be reduced accordingly (see illustrative cases such as *Sayers v Harlow UDC* (1956) and *Froom v Butcher* (1975), and the important statutory framework laid down under the **Law Reform (Contributory Negligence) Act 1945**). |

# Sanctions and remedies

14

This topic enables you:

- To distinguish between sanctions in criminal law and remedies in civil law.
- To complement earlier studies of criminal courts, procedures and criminal law.
- To provide elaboration of the roles of magistrates and judges.
- To introduce an area of law – sentencing – where theory is clearly related to legal practice.
- To appreciate the types of sentence that fall within the sentencing framework, leading to an understanding of how these might be applied.
- To recognise the purposes of the damages award in the tort of negligence.
- To broaden understanding of the role of judges in civil cases.
- To identify the differences between general and special damages, and pecuniary and non-pecuniary losses.

This chapter looks at **sentencing** in **criminal law** first, and then moves on to **remedies** in the **tort of negligence**.

**Sentencing** is an outcome of the **criminal justice process**. As a subject of broader study, it includes elements of theory, politics, judicial reasoning and practical application of law. In the law and order debate there is no greater 'political football' than sentencing, and the policy in this area is under constant review and subject to the moods and obsessions of the day. Newspapers, in particular, are keen to pick up on sentences that appear either too harsh or too soft. The area of sentencing is therefore a fascinating area of study, and one that is rarely off the front page.

The remedy of **damages**, taking the form of monetary compensation for the claimant, is the outcome of a successful claim in the **tort of negligence**. As was pointed out in Chapter 13, this process of 'loss-shifting' from the victim (claimant) to the wrongdoer (defendant) reflects a principle that underpins the law of tort, though as we have also seen, it does not always work in practice (see the comments on the problem of 'loss-spreading' by way of insurance at p 258 above). When you read this chapter you should also be thinking about the tort rules that you have studied which have a bearing on the remedies awarded. The issue of **contributory negligence** is especially relevant, since it can *reduce* the damages award to take account of the victim's own contribution to the harm sustained. You should also recall the rules on **remoteness of damage**, in that a victim can claim damages only for injuries that were a reasonably foreseeable consequence of the tort committed. However, the present chapter is about the award of damages as a remedy rather than about the 'remoteness of damage' rule. Damages follow a successful application of the 'duty, breach, harm' rules of negligence, but are not part of these. The award of damages as a remedy is therefore a separate matter, and issues of remoteness are an earlier consideration in determining whether damages should be awarded to the claimant.

**IT'S A FACT!**

**Sentencing as a political issue**

Sentencing became a highly contentious political issue in June 2006 when John Reid, in the position of Home Secretary, criticised the sentence given to Craig Sweeney, who had pleaded guilty to the kidnapping and sexual assault of a child. Craig Sweeney was given a life sentence, but because he pleaded guilty the judge followed sentencing guidelines and cut a third off the initial tariff set (18 years), leaving a total of 12 years; in addition, prisoners become eligible for parole after half the sentence has been served, taking into account any time spent on remand waiting for the trial to be heard. Newspapers seized on the fact that, with these calculations in mind, Sweeney could be recommended for release by a parole board having served just over five years of the sentence, despite the fact that the sentencing judge had told Sweeney that early release was 'unlikely'. Both *The Sun* and *The Daily Mirror* ran campaigns that were heavily critical of the judiciary. The judges, in response, pointed to the legal rules within which they were operating and the guidelines provided by the Sentencing Guidelines Council.

The Government's position was not helped by the fact that the Home Office had been engulfed in controversy following the failure to deport a large number of foreign prisoners at the end of their sentences; and by figures indicating that the prison population was rising year on year, probably to a figure of 85,000 by the year 2010, and yet prison places had not kept up with this increase.

Nevertheless, the Government was able to point to some positive sentencing news during this period. The Attorney General successfully appealed against an 'unduly lenient' sentence of another man convicted of serious sexual assault against a very young child; and the Government's success in legislating for heavy sentences for those who committed murder, and other crimes of violence, on the grounds of race, religion, sexual orientation or disability, led to a judge setting a tariff of 28 years in respect of two men convicted of the murder of a homosexual barman, Jody Dobrowski.

At the time of writing, the Government, Sentencing Advisory Panel and the Sentencing Guidelines Council were engaged in a review of the sentencing discounts that had led to such an outcry in the Sweeney case.

## PUNISHMENT THEORY: THE AIMS OF SENTENCING

When judges or magistrates come to a decision on the sentence to give in a particular case, they will have justified this by the aim of the sentence in relation to the **particular offence** and the **particular offender**. This has traditionally been a field in which the judges have had some discretion – subject to maximum and, occasionally, minimum penalties laid down in statute law – and have developed sentencing principles accordingly. Therefore, when Lord Justice Lawton, in the Court of Appeal case of *R v Sargeant* (1974), named the four 'classical principles of sentencing' as being retribution, deterrence, prevention, and rehabilitation, he gave voice to the often implied justifications for sentencing that the courts adopted. Since then, there has been greater political interest in sentencing and punishment theory has begun to inform Government policy.

Indeed, s 142(1) of the **Criminal Justice Act 2003** sets out, for the first time in legislative form, the **purposes of sentencing:**

- **Punishment** of offenders;
- **Reduction** of crime (including its reduction by way of **deterrence**);
- **Reform** and **rehabilitation** of offenders;
- **Protection** of the public;
- **Reparation** by offenders to the victims of crime.

### Punishment

Punishment reflects the principle of **retribution**. It forces the offender to pay for what he or she has done on the basis of the **'just deserts'** theory. In simple terms, this is the view that serious crimes should lead to serious punishments and the offender gets what he or she deserves. The sentencing framework includes many types of punishments – such as fines, community work and imprisonment – but the use of these will *vary* according to the **severity of the offence** and the **offender's circumstances**.

Basic morality and justice concepts underpin punishment theory. Retribution satisfies a sense of **revenge**, for example. Punishment also contains an element of **denunciation**, to reflect the disapproval, or disgust, of the wider society at the offender's conduct. Certain crimes provoke feelings of revenge and denunciation: those accused of murdering children, in particular, often have to be heavily protected when they appear in court to avoid the attentions of an angry mob outside. While there is a need for those passing sentences to understand the public feeling generated by certain crimes, it is also necessary to consider the other aims of sentencing and ensure that the given response is proportionate.

## Reduction of crime and the reform and rehabilitation of offenders

There are two aspects to the reduction of crime: **deterrence** and **rehabilitation**. These aims might not always seem to be compatible.

**Deterrence** is about persuading individuals, and the public in general, not to offend. There is a distinction between **individual deterrence** (aimed at preventing an offender from re-offending) and **general deterrence** (using examples to society to prevent people in general from offending or re-offending). Deterrence has been used, at times, as a 'knee-jerk response' to particular crimes (through harsh punishments designed to 'make an example' of the offender, a further form of **denunciation**) but is generally a longer-term goal of the sentencing process.

**Rehabilitation** is completely focused on the longer term, with its emphasis on change and reform. Whereas the 'just deserts' approach focuses very much on the severity of the offence, rehabilitation looks more closely at the offender and his or her **potential for reform**. Rehabilitation is associated more with non-custodial, **community sentences** than with imprisonment. If the view is taken that prisons are no more than 'universities of crime', it makes sense to seek to reform an offender, particularly one who is young, rather than encourage association with lots of other offenders who will resent the custodial sentences that they have received.

However, rehabilitation is a costly, and not always successful, option. It also might be seen as an overly **lenient** response to crime, with the public preferring retribution and deterrence. The media image of rehabilitation is, at times, that offenders are 'getting away with it' and avoiding the punishment they deserve, and this is why stronger deterrent sentences are called for to show that offences will be punished strongly. This desire for retribution and deterrence has to be *balanced*, however, against the potential for achieving **long-term reform** of the offender.

## Protection of the public

To achieve this aim, sentences are used which will clearly **prevent** a person from repeating a crime in the future or going on to commit other crimes. There are some offenders, such as murderers, rapists and robbers, from whom the public clearly requires protection, and therefore **long-term imprisonment** is an obvious solution. However, this is not the only way in which sentences can be used to protect the public, and it should be borne in mind that prisons can only hold so many people for so long. There are a number of specific statutory powers to deprive certain offenders of the means to commit crimes, such as **disqualifications** and **exclusions**; **withdrawing licences**; and ordering **curfews, supervision** and **treatments**.

## Reparation

This is the most recent addition to the sentencing theories and involves the offender making up for his offence to the persons affected by it, usually in the form of '**payment in kind**' such as a period of community work related to the type of offence committed. A typical example might be to require a person who has committed criminal damage to help in the repair and reconstruction of the victim's property.

## Sentencing in practice

The purposes of sentencing provide the context for an appreciation of practical sentencing. Sentencing is carried out in two criminal trial courts: the **magistrates' court** and the **Crown Court**.

In a **magistrates' court**, for summary offences and either way offences (where the defendant has not opted for jury trial), sentencing powers lie either with a district judge (magistrates' court) sitting alone, or with a bench of two or more lay magistrates (with benches of three preferred). The magistrates' court is also a **youth court**, and those magistrates who form part of a youth court panel will hear these cases and deliver sentence. Efforts are made in the youth court to provide a bench comprising both male and female magistrates.

In a **Crown Court**, for either way offences (where the defendant has opted for jury trial) and indictable offences, sentencing powers lie with Crown Court judges; or if the matter has been committed from the magistrates' court for sentence, with a judge and two or more lay magistrates. Crown Court judges include High Court judges (who generally hear the most serious criminal cases); circuit judges; recorders; deputy circuit judges; and assistant recorders. The distribution of cases to these judges is based on a classification of offences, the most serious being in Classes 1 and 2 (in the former, offences such as murder, treason and genocide; in the latter, manslaughter, rape and other serious offences).

## The scope of sentencing powers

Unless a penalty is fixed by law (for example, life imprisonment for murder), a maximum penalty is imposed by **statute**. For example, as you will recall from Chapter 12, under the Offences Against the Person Act 1861 the maximum sentence for the offence of assault occasioning actual bodily harm is five years' imprisonment on indictment. The magistrate or judge (hereafter referred to as 'the sentencer') will have regard to the current **tariff**, or 'going rate', for the offence (found from references to past cases and directions from the **Sentencing Guidelines Council**, as established by the Criminal Justice Act

2003). More discretion is allowed for most **common law** offences (murder being a clear exception), though all such offences are capable in law of giving rise to a term of imprisonment.

**Magistrates** can pass custodial sentences of up to **six months' imprisonment** for a single offence (and the **Criminal Justice Act 2003**, at **s 154**, provides for such powers to be increased to **twelve months** in due course, though the Government announced in August 2006 that it was suspending its plans to implement the measure in 2006 owing to 'other priorities') and they can also impose **fines** according to the maximum levels laid down in statute law (the standard maximum being £5,000). Magistrates can also remit a case to the **Crown Court** for sentencing if it is appropriate to impose a higher sentence on a convicted person than their powers will allow. Judges in the **Crown Court** must also observe the statutory criteria and sentencing guidelines for offences, but since they deal with the most serious criminal offences it is clear that their powers can extend to life imprisonment and unlimited fines.

Generally, only those **over 21** may be given a term of imprisonment, whereas those under 21 will instead be detained in a young offenders' institution, or subject to orders relating to detention, training or supervision (depending on their age).

## MAKING THE SENTENCING DECISION (SENTENCING PROCEDURE)

The sentencing decision will generally take into account the following matters.

### The facts

If the defendant pleaded '**not guilty**' but has been found guilty, the sentencer will have all of the facts of the matter at his or her disposal to make the sentencing decision, since the facts will have come out in court as evidence.

If, on the other hand, the defendant pleaded '**guilty**', the prosecution offer a summary of the facts to the court. When sentencing follows a '**guilty plea**' the court must take into account when the plea occurred and must state if this has led to a more lenient sentence.

### The antecedents

Antecedents include evidence of the defendant's age, education, background and financial status, and also **previous convictions** (or 'findings of guilt' from the youth court). The court is entitled to see records of all previous convictions – including those formally 'spent' (that is, where the passage of time has rendered convictions for relatively minor offences effectively void, on the basis of detailed rules in the **Rehabilitation of Offenders Act 1974**) – and recent formal cautions, held in police records, may also be submitted by the prosecution (though these do not have the status of 'previous convictions'). The defendant may also ask for other offences to be 'taken into consideration'. While judges are entitled to take previous convictions into account when determining the seriousness of an offence, there is much judicial and academic debate as to the emphasis that should be placed on such previous records.

## Pre-sentence reports

These are usually prepared by a probation officer or social worker to assist the court in determining how the offender should be dealt with. Such reports contain information on the **aggravating** and **mitigating factors** (see below) that will affect the decision as to the suitability of a custodial sentence or a community sentence.

## Medical reports

Medical reports will be prepared in circumstances where the offender has committed a **very serious offence** of a violent or sexual nature; or where the offender appears to be mentally disordered. Such reports are generally requested by defence counsel, since the medical report may provide evidence of **mitigating factors** and circumstances in relation to the offence or offences committed.

## Mitigation

Pleas in mitigation are those put forward by the defence to the effect that the sentence should *not* be too severe owing to a number of factors, such as previous good behaviour and the likely impact of a harsh sentence. (See further below.)

### Balancing aggravating and mitigating factors

When determining the sentence, the sentencer will attempt to weigh up the **aggravating factors**, being those factors that make the offence worse; and **mitigating factors**, being those factors that reduce the severity of the offence. These factors may be further divided into those that relate to the **seriousness of the offence**, and those **personal characteristics of the offender** that might have a bearing on the seriousness, or circumstances, of the case. In determining the seriousness of an offence, s 143 of the **Criminal Justice Act 2003** requires the court to consider the 'offender's culpability in committing the offence and any harm that the offence caused, intended to cause or might foreseeably have caused'. The lists of aggravating and mitigating factors set out in Table 14.1 on pp 287–8 are not exhaustive, but they contain the most common factors that may be derived from the outcomes of sentencing procedure.

The sentencer will also take into account the **personal** aggravating and mitigating factors of the **offender**. This might include consideration of the offender's **age, background, home-life** (whether, for example, the person has a caring role for dependants in the home), **maturity, intelligence** (and level of formal education), and state of **physical** and **mental health**. As we have seen, account will also be taken of previous convictions, recent formal cautions and responses to previous sentences. The **offender's attitude** about the commission of the offence (whether the offender is remorseful or, on the other hand, unrepentant) and towards the police, the courts and of course the victim will also be influential in weighing up the competing factors when determining the appropriate sentence.

Table 14.1 Sentencing: aggravating and mitigating factors

| *Aggravating factors (relating to the offence)* | *Mitigating factors (relating to the offence)* |
|---|---|
| (1) The type of offence (such as the **use of violence** or the **use of a weapon**). | (1) The **type of offence** (such as a **minor** offence with few, if any, aggravating factors). |
| (2) That the offence is committed against a **public servant** carrying out his or her **duty** (for example, attacks on public transport staff; or on enforcement officers such as police officers or traffic wardens). | (2) That the **offender was provoked** (for example, in the course of a dispute an assault committed in 'hot blood'). |
| (3) That the offence is committed **against a vulnerable person** (for example, children or the elderly). | (3) That the offence was **committed under duress** (for example, the offender was subject to threats to carry out the offence). |
| (4) That the offence was **pre-meditated** (for example, committed in 'cold blood', having been carefully planned rather than having spontaneously occurred in 'hot blood'). | (4) That the offence was **one of need** and *not* motivated by greed. |
| (5) The **part taken by the offender** in committing the act (as a 'prime mover' in instigating the offence, rather than as a person with limited involvement). | (5) That at the time of the offence, **clear remorse was shown by the offender** (for example, in the aftermath of an assault, seeking assistance for an injured victim or calling the emergency services). |
| (6) That the offence represented an **'abuse of trust'** (for example, where a person holds a position of trust over a minor and goes on to abuse that trust). | (6) That the offender was **induced by the police to commit the offence** (for example, where the police investigation involved an element of entrapment). |
| (7) That the offence was committed **whilst on bail** (regarded as very serious, given the fact that bail is the period during which the defendant is awaiting trial for another offence).* | (7) That the offender was only a **minor participant** in the commission of the offence. |
| (8) That the offence was carried out by **a gang**. | (8) That the offender was **intoxicated** when the offence was committed (though this will depend on the circumstances: intoxication will in some instances be a clear aggravating factor). |
| (9) That the offence was one of **greed**. | (9) That the offence was **committed owing to a mistake in law** (for example, when an offender commits a breach of criminal regulations because he or she mistakenly relies on a Government circular). |
| (10) That the **injuries to the victim** that resulted from the offence **were very serious**. | (10) That the offence **did not involve serious injury**, or **did not have a long-term impact**, on the victim. |
| (11) That the **value of property** damaged or stolen as a result of the offence was **considerable**. | (11) That the offence caused only **minor damage** or loss in relation to **property**. |
| (12) That the offence is **prevalent in the area** and offenders need to be **deterred**. | |
| (13) That the offence was carried out in **such a way**, and in **such a time** and **place**, as to **compromise order** and **raise fear in the community**. | |

*(continued)*

Table 14.1 Sentencing: aggravating and mitigating factors *(continued)*

| *Aggravating factors (relating to the offence)* | *Mitigating factors (relating to the offence)* |
|---|---|
| (14) That the offence was **racially motivated** or **aggravated by racism**.* | |
| (15) That the offence was **aggravated** by factors relating to a person's **sexual orientation** or **disability**.* | |

* These are **mandatory aggravating factors** in the **Criminal Justice Act 2003, ss 143–146**.

## THE SENTENCING OPTIONS

The sentencing options are contained within the Sentencing Framework. The Framework originated in the Criminal Justice Act 1991, was consolidated by the Powers of Criminal Courts (Sentencing) Act (PCC(S)A) 2000 and has most recently been reviewed and made much more flexible by the **Criminal Justice Act 2003**. Unless a penalty is fixed by law, the sentencer should look to the statutory maximum penalty and consider the current tariff for that offence. The Sentencing Framework has four general levels of sentence:

- **Discharges** (where punishment would be 'inexpedient').
- **Fines** (where punishment is appropriate, though taking into account the seriousness of the offence and the offender's ability to pay).
- **Community sentences** (where the offence is deemed 'serious enough' and the necessary degree of restriction of liberty is proportionate to the seriousness of the offence, taking into account the suitability of the particular type of **community order** for the offender: s 148(1) of the **Criminal Justice Act 2003**).
- **Custodial sentences** (where the offence is deemed 'so serious' that only a custodial sentence can, in the circumstances, be justified: s 152(2) of the **Criminal Justice Act 2003**).

The length of the sentence will be **proportionate** in respect of the factors outlined.

Greater flexibility has been built into the system through the new approach to community sentences, so that **community orders** can be customised to suit the offender, and through the development of **custody-plus orders** (which adds community licence conditions to a specified period following a short term of imprisonment) and other conditional orders to secure either community works or intermittent custody of an offender.

Using the Sentencing Framework as our guide, the general options for sentencers are therefore as follows:

## Discharges

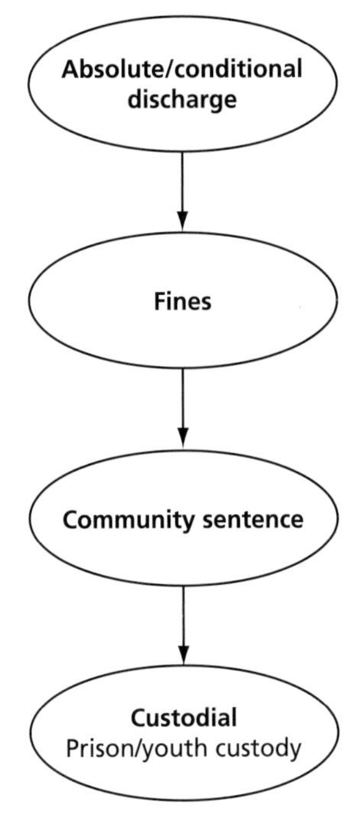


There are two main types of discharges, given where the nature of the offence and the characteristics of the offender are such that punishment is *not* an appropriate outcome.

### Absolute discharge

Here, while the offender has been convicted of the offence (and this will be recorded, unlike an acquittal), the granting of an **absolute discharge** means that the offender will *not* be punished for the offence. The absolute discharge is commonly used to deal with trivial matters, but also where an offender has committed several offences and a distinction is drawn between those offences for which punishment sentences are required and the minor supplementary offences which can be dealt with by discharge.

### Conditional discharge

This discharges the offender but with one condition: that no further offence be committed within the period of the **conditional discharge**. If the offender is convicted of a new offence during the specified period, the court has the power to re-sentence the offender for the original offence when also setting the sentence for the new offence. In order to comply with Art 6 of the European Convention on Human Rights (the right to a fair trial), as incorporated by the Human Rights Act 1998, the offender has the right to expect that the sentencer will give reasons for the conditional discharge.

## Fines

This commonly used sentence means that the offender has to pay a **financial penalty** for committing the offence: the money paid goes to the Treasury. In *R v Baldwin* (2002), the then Lord Chief Justice, Lord Woolf, commented that:

> bearing in mind the stress in our prisons today from overcrowding, if there are good prospects that an offender is not going to prey upon the public again, there are *advantages in using the penalty of a fine* rather than sentencing someone to a further period of imprisonment. (emphasis added)

The amount of the fine will generally be unlimited in the Crown Court, and where businesses have been the offenders, million pound fines have been recorded. As we have seen (p 285 above), the magistrates' court, by contrast, is restricted to fines of up to £5,000, though the magistrates' court can refer cases to the Crown Court for sentencing. Often a statute will set a statutory maximum with reference to the levels of fine outlined below:

| | |
|---|---|
| Level 1 | £200 fine |
| Level 2 | £500 fine |
| Level 3 | £1,000 fine* |
| Level 4 | £2,500 fine |
| Level 5 | £5,000 fine |

* If a statute is silent as to a maximum fine, this will be the presumed maximum.

Fines are used to punish (and so go one step further than the discharge). As we have seen, the sentencer in determining the fine must take account of the **seriousness of the offence** and the **offender's ability to pay**. The offender may be required to provide a **statement of financial circumstances** for this purpose. Young offenders are subject to lower limits than adults, and the parent or guardian can be ordered to pay a fine for a person aged under 16 where the courts deem it appropriate.

Generally, fines may be **combined** with community and custodial sentences as appropriate, though a fine will not be given with a discharge because that would introduce a punishment element where none was perceived to be necessary. The Government announced in March 2005 that it was launching a National Enforcement Service to ensure that fines imposed by the criminal courts would be paid. However, the scale of unpaid fines was revealed in May 2006 by the National Audit Office: a shortfall of £130 million. (See report in *The Independent*, 25/5/06.)

**IT'S A FACT!**

**14.1: Record fine imposed in 2005**

The Hatfield rail disaster, that left 102 injured and four dead, provided the context for a record fine of £10 million imposed on Balfour Beatty, a rail maintenance company, in October 2005. Another company implicated in the disaster, Network Rail, was also fined £3.5 million. Cracks in the rail, which had been detected but not remedied months before the Hatfield incident, were found to have been its main cause. The fines resulted from prosecutions for serious breaches of the Health and Safety at Work Act 1974, though no charges of corporate manslaughter were brought against individual directors.

## Community orders

One of the most radical changes heralded by the **Criminal Justice Act 2003** relates to the overhaul of the community sentences regime, building on existing orders with a flexible and responsive approach to sentencing. The existing orders include:

### Community rehabilitation order

This sentence replaced the probation order and applies to offenders aged over 16. It requires the offender to be placed under the **supervision of a probation officer** or **youth offending team worker** (for offenders under 18). The period of such an order is not less than six months, but not more than three years. The offender is required to maintain contact with the supervisor and to agree a plan that seeks to address the offending behaviour and meet the sentencing aims of prevention and rehabilitation (reflecting the aims of protection of the public and the reduction of crime). Orders may contain special requirements relating to treatment for mental conditions and for drug and alcohol dependency, and may also impose curfew, exclusion and drug abstinence restrictions.

### Community punishment order

This sentence replaced the community service order and applies to offenders aged over 16. It requires the offender to carry out, unpaid, a **specified amount of work for the benefit of the community**. The Probation Service undertakes the organisation of such work. This is a clear alternative to custody for adult offenders, since an order will only be given for offences that have imprisonment as a sentencing option. Generally such work should be completed **within 12 months** and consist of a commitment of **between 40 and 240 hours**. An unemployed person will be able actively to seek work whilst undertaking such an order, and therefore will be entitled to social security benefits as usual.

Community work under this order includes: craft or education projects; garden and conservation projects; manual work (construction, assembly, packaging, and so on) for projects and charities; and working with elderly and disabled people.

### Community rehabilitation and punishment order

This sentence replaced the combination order and applies to offenders aged over 16. This is a mixture of the earlier two orders and involves **supervision** (for a period between one and three years) plus **community work** (for 40–100 hours). These orders are generally reserved for the more serious offences for which community sentences can be given.

However, the **Criminal Justice Act 2003** brings into being a **new flexible regime** that puts into practice the following intention, included by the Government in its 'Justice for All' White Paper (2002): 'All existing community sentences would be available together in a new sentence, allowing sentencers to fit the restrictions and rehabilitation to the offender'. Therefore, where a person **aged 16 or over** is convicted of an offence, the court may now make an **order**, under s 177 of the 2003 Act, that imposes **one** or **more** of the following 'requirements':

- **Unpaid work requirement** (specified work for the benefit of the community to be completed within 12 months, based on a commitment from the offender of between 40 and 300 hours; similar to **community punishment orders**, as created by the Powers of Criminal Courts (Sentencing) Act 2000).
- **Activity requirement** (contact required with a supervisor for up to 60 days, with a plan made to address the offender's behaviour; similar to **community rehabilitation orders**, as created by the PCC(S)A 2000).
- **Programme requirement** (the offender must work to an accredited programme of activity for a period of time to be specified in the community order).
- **Prohibited activity requirement** (the offender must refrain from specified activities on certain days or a period to be prescribed).
- **Curfew requirement** (the offender is placed under curfew relating to specific places and specific times of the day).
- **Exclusion requirement** (the offender will be prohibited from entering a specified place for a period of up to two years).
- **Residence requirement** (the offender will be required to reside at a specified place during a period determined in the community order).
- **Mental health treatment requirement** (the offender must submit, for specified periods, to treatment by a registered medical practitioner or a chartered psychologist).
- **Drug rehabilitation requirement** (the offender must undergo a period of treatment and testing to combat drug dependency, for a period of at least six months).
- **Alcohol treatment requirement** (the offender must submit, for specified periods, to treatment by a person with the necessary experience and qualifications to combat alcohol dependency).
- **Supervision requirement** (the offender is placed under the supervision of a probation officer for a specified period).

- **Attendance centre requirement for offenders under 25** (the offender will attend an attendance centre to receive classes, physical education and learn skills).

Curfew requirements and exclusion requirements *must* generally be complemented by **electronic monitoring ('tagging')**. This sort of monitoring *may* also be sought in conjunction with the other requirements listed above.

For younger offenders, that is those *under* 16, the Criminal Justice Act 2003 amends the PCC(S)A 2000 by creating a set of **Youth Community Orders**. These can consist of: a curfew order; an exclusion order; an attendance centre order; a supervision order; and an action plan order.

## The custodial sentences

Of the custodial sentences, a **term of imprisonment** is the most severe level of punishment that may be delivered by a judge or magistrate. We have seen already that the rules differ according to the age of the offender, so prison is generally reserved for those aged 21 and over. Table 14.2 summarises the custodial sentences available, dependent on the age of the offender.

Table 14.2 Custodial sentences

| *Custodial sentences for those over 21 years of age* | *Custodial sentences for those under 21 years of age* | *Custodial sentences for those aged 12–17 (alternative to YOI)* |
|---|---|---|
| Prison | Young offender institution | Secure training centre or secure accommodation |

Some terms of imprisonment are **mandatory** (for example, life imprisonment for murder, or for a second conviction of a sufficiently serious offence) and some terms will become the **minimum requirement** in respect of offences *persistently* committed (for example, drug trafficking of Class A drugs; domestic burglary). Most commonly, however, maximum sentences are suggested by statute, and the sentencer will have the discretion to determine the appropriate length of the sentence, bearing in mind the **aims of custodial sentences**, identified by Lord Justice Taylor in *R v Cunningham* (1993) as **punishment** and **deterrence**, and the **degree of seriousness of the offence.** In s 152 of the **Criminal Justice Act 2003**, the decision to impose a custodial sentence must reflect the fact that the offence is **'so serious'** that neither a fine nor a community sentence could be justified in the circumstances.

Where custodial sentences are given in respect of two or more offences committed by the same offender, it has to be determined whether these sentences should run **consecutively** (that is, one after another) or **concurrently** (that is, at the same time). The practical implications of each may be explained by the **aggregate totals** achieved. Where series of offences are to run *consecutively*, for example, the court will simply **add up** the total (for example,

5 years + 3 years = 8 years). Where, on the other hand, they run *concurrently* (for example, a 5-year sentence and a 3-year sentence), the sentence served will reflect the **longest of the separate terms**, in this case five years. Table 14.3 summarises the effect of consecutive and concurrent custodial sentences.

Table 14.3 Consecutive and concurrent custodial sentences

| *Consecutive custodial sentences* | *Concurrent custodial sentences* |
|---|---|
| Sentences for a number of offences that take effect one after another. | Sentences for a number of offences that take effect at the same time. |
| The total length of the imprisonment will be the individual sentences added together. | The total length of the imprisonment will be the longest sentence given. |

The Criminal Justice Act 2003, at s 181, provides – with implementation deferred, at the time of writing – for the **custody plus** scheme, whereby short sentence prisoners are provided, via the use of community conditions imposed on the licence period following their release, with community supervision and support. The Act also allows for **intermittent custody orders** (s 183), which find a *balance* between the seriousness of the offence for which some custody is required and the particular circumstances of the offender, for whom a full period of imprisonment might prove particularly damaging. These orders will specify a number of days that *must* be spent in custody by the offender, followed by licence conditions.

On occasions, according to the exceptional circumstances of the case, and where an immediate term of imprisonment *could* have been passed, the court will determine that a **suspended sentence** is the most appropriate penalty. Here, the offender will not be imprisoned as long as no further imprisonable offence is committed during a period prescribed by the court. A suspended sentence may be justified, for example, where the offender committed the offence in the belief that he or she was helping another person, or where the offender's domestic circumstances, such as a caring role for a dependant, are so pressing that prison is not an appropriate option. In the **Criminal Justice Act 2003**, provision is made for the '**custody minus**' scheme at s 189 – a programme in which a prison sentence is suspended and community supervision provided, subject to an automatic return to custody for a failure to comply with its conditions.

## FURTHER POWERS OF THE CRIMINAL COURTS (SHORT OF CUSTODIAL SENTENCES)

### Binding over 'to keep the peace'

This means that at the request of the court an offender makes a **financial commitment** *not* to make a **breach of the peace** for a specified period, often 6–12 months. If a breach occurs, the offender forfeits the committed sum of money, which will represent a 'reasonable sum' at the court's discretion. It is the parent or guardian who will be bound over where the offender is under 16.

**Exercise 14.1: Recap Quiz**

Identify the terms, words and phrases suggested by the following clues to reveal, via the first letters of your answers, the nature of this topic.

_______/_______: from discharges right through to life in jail, this describes the sentencing options available, with the Criminal Justice Act 2003 adding to its flexibility.

_______/_______: a sentence that marks a conviction, but does not punish the offender.

_______/_______: term given to offences of violence such as assault occasioning actual bodily harm, wounding and grievous bodily harm.

_______/_______: the Criminal Justice Act 2003 has introduced this form of sentence, which might be customised to suit offenders of crimes that are 'serious enough'.

_______/_______/_______: also known as intermediate offences, which might be heard, and sentenced, by magistrates' courts or Crown Courts.

_______: the custodial sentence, reserved for offences 'so serious' that a period of detention is required.

_______: on whom the emphasis is placed in rehabilitative sentencing, rather than the emphasis on the offence under the 'just deserts' approach.

_______/_______: this plea might be considered critically at the sentencing stage, since the alternative would have put the defendant in a more favourable light.

_______/_______: a penalty for an offence that would ordinarily justify immediate jail, but owing to the circumstances of the case, is dealt with without detention on the basis that no further offences take place within a specified period.

For Answers, please turn to p 345.

## Compensation orders

In addition to fines, the criminal law also allows for compensation to be paid by the offender to victims in appropriate circumstances. Compensation is a civil law concept rather than a criminal law one (the latter being more concerned with punishment), but if a victim has suffered '**personal injury, loss or damage**' it makes sense, in the process of punishing the offender, to require him or her also to compensate the victim. This is perceived as better than leaving such action to the choice of the victim in civil law once the criminal proceedings have been completed. Where the sentencing option is a fine, and regard has to be had to the offender's ability to pay, the court will give priority to the payment of any compensation over the fine. Generally, where the offender does have the means to pay, both a fine and a compensation order will be imposed. These points make up for the fact that a victim would not benefit from a fine, since this is paid directly to the Treasury.

An alternative source of compensation for victims of physical violence is the **Criminal Injuries Compensation Scheme**. To be eligible to apply for such compensation the victim must meet certain criteria relating to the amount of the claim and their conduct during the incident. Applications, made within two years of the incident of violence, must be sent to the Criminal Injuries Compensation Authority. If the offender has stolen property belonging to the victim, the courts have a further power to make a restitution order to ensure that such goods are returned.

## Reparation

Again, the concept of reparation seems more akin to civil law than criminal law, though it recognises, sensibly, that criminal acts have consequences for the victim. A reparation order is not, however, about monetary compensation but rather some form of **payment in kind** by any offender under 18 to the specific victim or to the community at large. Therefore, reparation can be attached to community sentences, for example in the form of beneficial work for a period of up to 24 hours.

**Exercise 14.2: Sentencing case study**

Imagine that you have the job of sentencing the offender, Jack, in the following situation. Read the case study carefully.

Following a drunken brawl in a pub between rival sets of football supporters, Jack, 25, and two of his friends accompany Bill, who suffered an injury to his wrist and deep cuts to his face during the fracas, to Kingsfield Hospital's Accident and Emergency department. They arrive at 11.45pm, but the department is very busy. Increasingly angry about Bill having to wait for treatment, they become agitated at 12.45am when they see another man, whom they recognise as one of the rival supporters in the pub that night, being offered treatment. They start hurling insults at the man and rush to attack him. Dr Ali, who is treating the man, tries to calm the situation, but he is then subject to abuse relating both to his race and religion, and Jack violently pushes him out of the way. In falling to the ground, Dr Ali suffers bruising and mild concussion. He is also badly shaken up by the incident. Fortunately, nurses and other patients prevent an escalation of the incident. Jack, his two friends and Bill, still untreated, flee from the hospital.

The police later arrested Jack and he was charged with battery. He pleaded not guilty, but was convicted. By statute (Criminal Justice Act 1998), the offence carries a maximum prison sentence of six months and/or a £5,000 fine.

This is Jack's first offence. He is married, with two young children, and works for a garage as a car mechanic. He has expressed his general apologies to the hospital, but not to Dr Ali specifically.

**Discussion points:**

What factors have to be taken into account here?

What are the aggravating factors? What are the mitigating factors?

What are the aims of the sentence to be imposed?

What sort of sentences should be considered for this sort of crime?

Discuss these questions with other members of the group and your teacher. Have you reached similar conclusions? How have you found the process of sentencing: is it an easy task?

# CIVIL LAW: AN OUTLINE OF DAMAGES IN THE TORT OF NEGLIGENCE

## Introduction

The purpose of damages in the law of tort is to put the injured party in the position he or she would have been in had the incident not occurred at all. Thus, tort damages are necessarily *speculative*. The court has to assess how the claimant's life would have progressed in the absence of the harm suffered. Damages are rarely able to provide full compensation for loss, and are used instead to offer *alternative means of satisfaction* for the claimant in living a life the quality of which may have been reduced as a consequence of the tort.

While the victim of a tort might be entitled to financial support from the State in the form of social security benefits and statutory compensation schemes, a successful legal claim in the law of tort will often lead to a much more generous financial settlement. Where a successful claimant has received benefits, the value of these will either be deducted from the damages award, or recovered by the State from the defendant.

All claimants are subject to rules on the timing of the claim under the **Limitation Act 1980**. Claims must generally be brought within six years of the tortious act being committed, or the consequences of the act being suffered. However, in personal injury cases the claim must be brought *within three years* of the damage actually occurring. A longer limitation period will apply if, for example, an occupational disease (such as pneumoconiosis) is contracted through exposure to workplace dust over a long period of time and the claimant's knowledge of this came only at a later stage.

If, as a result of the defendant's negligence, the claimant dies, a claim for damages may be brought either by the claimant's estate (that is, the representatives of the deceased's interests) under the **Law Reform (Miscellaneous Provisions) Act 1934**, or, in certain specified circumstances, by the claimant's dependants under the **Fatal Accidents Act 1976**.

This chapter does not deal with the full range of remedies in the general law of tort, and you will need to look beyond this book for detailed coverage. However, in short, these include forms of damages that are *not* compensatory in nature, such as **nominal damages**, where a small amount is awarded to acknowledge that a tort has been committed by the defendant, but where little or no actual loss has been suffered by the claimant, and **exemplary** or **aggravated damages**, where damages are used – somewhat unusually in civil law – to *punish* the defendant for bad conduct in committing the tort. You will also find in certain torts, such as nuisance, that **equitable remedies** are awarded where damages do not provide an adequate remedy: the **injunction** is a common example, since it can be used to prohibit the carrying out of any activity causing a nuisance. However, it is on the tort of negligence that we place our emphasis here.

## Types of damages awarded

### Damages awarded for personal injury

Tort damages are generally divided into two main categories: **general damages**, reflecting claims for the future; and **special damages**, reflecting those claims up to the date of the trial. The two may overlap in one claim.

**Special damages** represent all *calculable losses* incurred up to the time of the trial. **General damages** are divided into **pecuniary** and **non-pecuniary losses**. Pecuniary losses are losses of a financial nature, such as medical expenses or loss of future earnings. More commonly, non-pecuniary losses are claimed and include such heads of damage as pain and suffering and loss of amenities. General damages are often difficult to quantify (see below).

It is commonly claimed prior to the determination of a damages award that there is a duty on the claimant to **mitigate**, or lessen, the loss suffered. However, the case of *Geest plc v Lansiquot* (2002), concerning the victim of an accident who refused to have surgery, makes it clear that in practice there is no such duty on the claimant in personal injury cases. Instead, it is for the defendant to complain – on the basis of the evidence – that the claimant has acted unreasonably.

### Damages awarded for loss or damage to property

Loss or damage to property awards are relatively easy to calculate and generally form part of a claim for **special damages**. These awards, unlike those for personal injury, are much more likely to reflect full compensation since the *restitutio in integrum* principle (that is, restoring what has been lost) can be applied through repairs or replacements. Such an award will therefore take into account the **value of the property** at the time the tort was committed and the **extent of the loss** sustained. It will also include any additional costs associated with the loss or damage, such as purchase of new parts, costs of repair, transportation costs and consequential losses, that is, other losses flowing from the loss or damage (provided that these are reasonably foreseeable and not too remote).

## Focus on general and special damages

### General damages

Such damages are awarded for losses that are **difficult to calculate** or quantify. This is because the losses do *not* allow for precise value setting. In relation to accidents, for example, how much is the loss of an arm worth in monetary terms? The loss of limbs falls under one of the non-pecuniary 'heads of damage' in that it seeks to put a value on physical loss. While such types of harm cannot be compensated in full – a lost arm will not be restored by a monetary award – there are several **justifications** for giving damages in these circumstances. One of these is that although the damages do not 'cure' the injury, they at least provide some **relief for the victim**. It should also be borne in mind that the harm suffered might have deprived the victim of certain advantages: an award of money will not replace these, but it might provide **access to alternatives.**

There are two main *non-pecuniary* heads of damage:

- **pain and suffering** for physical and/or psychiatric injury; and
- **loss of amenity.**

Damages will be awarded for any pain and suffering that the injury has caused, or for pain and suffering arising from any resulting medical treatment. Psychiatric injury must amount to a recognised form of disorder, and not merely upset or grief. Judges will be conscious of achieving consistency with previous awards through recognition of **precedents** and consideration of the recommended 'going rates' (or tariffs), applied in the courts. However, authorities indicate that damages will not be awarded if the claimant is unconscious and therefore unaware of any pain and suffering, as in *Wise v Kaye* (1962).

Loss of amenity considers the extent to which the loss of a limb, for example, affects the way in which a person has to live his or her life. Again tariffs are used as guidelines, though account will be taken of the particular circumstances of the case – an athlete who loses a leg will clearly be in a worse position than a person in retirement – and regard will be had to examples of previous awards in legal digests such as *Current Law* and *Kemp & Kemp's The Quantum of Damages*. There is no requirement for the claimant to be conscious of the extent of the loss of amenity, and so the rule in *Wise v Kaye* (1962) does not apply to loss of amenity. This is illustrated in *H West & Son v Shephard* (1964), in which a married woman in her early forties suffered, as a result of the defendant's negligence, severe head injuries, paralysis of the limbs, the inability to speak and a reduced life expectancy. The House of Lords held that she could receive substantial damages for loss of amenity, even though her appreciation of her position was limited.

General damages also include **claims relating to the future**, such as **loss of future earnings**, which are by virtue of their nature unpredictable and speculative. Damages for loss of future earnings are known as *pecuniary damages* since they reflect financial, rather than physical, loss. In terms of a personal injury case – for example, an accident that has meant that the victim is unlikely to work again – the judge will use a formula to determine the amount of damages to be awarded. This takes one figure, known as the **multiplicand**, representing the net annual loss of earnings resulting from the claimant's injury, and multiplies it by a figure referred to as the **multiplier**, being the number of years that this loss of earnings capacity represents. The annual interest to be earned on a lump sum payment will also be taken into account (averaged at 3 per cent in *Wells v Wells* (1999)). The same principles of multiplicand and multiplier are used in calculating other forms of future pecuniary loss, such as the costs of ongoing nursing care required as a result of the victim's injury.

### Special damages

Claims for special damages reflect **specific, measurable losses** – such as medical costs, damage to property and lost earnings – which may be calculated accurately. These losses will have been incurred up to the date of the civil trial – thus representing accrued pecuniary damages – and should not be confused with general damages of a pecuniary nature that relate to losses in the future (see above).

Loss of earnings awards reflect the net loss that is, the earnings minus tax deductions (income tax and national insurance) and pension contributions. Medical costs can be claimed so far as these are reasonable. Claimants can expect to be recompensed for any medical expenses incurred through treatment at a private hospital, and so choosing this form of health-care would be seen as reasonable. However, claimants cannot expect to claim an amount equivalent to private treatment if they have actually been treated in an NHS hospital. The term 'medical costs' also extends to special treatments, equipment, appliances and facilities that have been necessitated by the harm suffered.

### In what forms are general and special damages awarded?

The traditional position is that damages in tort are awarded once only and in the form of a **lump sum**. Therefore, damages are awarded in one go, with account having been taken of longer-term factors such as inflation and other changing circumstances. This creates some problems since no judge can tell, with any accuracy, what the longer-term factors might be. As Lord Scarman commented in the case of *Lim Poh Choo v Camden and Islington Health Authority* (1980): 'There is really only one certainty: the future will prove the award to be either too high or too low'. There is also the issue of what might have happened had the harm not been suffered: for example, would certain opportunities have been available to the claimant had he or she remained fit and healthy?

The problems associated with the lump sum approach have long been recognised, both by law reform bodies (Royal Commission on Civil Liability and Compensation for Personal Injury, 1978: the **Pearson Commission**) and by judges (for example, Lord Steyn in *Wells v Wells* (1999)). These calls upon Parliament to introduce awards in the form of periodic payments to relieve the difficulties associated with lump sum payments were heeded, with inclusion of **periodic payments** in s 100(1) of the **Courts Act 2003**. This movement away from the lump sum approach prior to the Courts Act 2003 had been pre-dated by:

(**a**) provisional damages; and
(**b**) structured settlements, providing for periodic payments subject to conditions.

### Alternatives to the 'lump sum' approach

If there is a chance that a claimant's **medical condition will seriously deteriorate** or lead to a **serious disease** as a result of the specific tort, an award of **provisional damages** may be made under the Supreme Courts Act 1981. An example might be a burns victim who faces a 60 per cent risk that the injuries might lead to cancer. Provisional damages are assessed on the basis that the possible deterioration will *not* occur. Thus the award is less than a traditional lump sum since it does not attempt to take into account changing circumstances, but it does allow the claimant to return to court for a further application for damages to reflect the true extent of the loss suffered. Provisional damages are used rarely. They do not apply to cases of *general* deterioration of an injury.

Structured settlements are used in large personal injury awards and consist 'wholly or partly of **periodical payments**', to be determined according to the circumstances (such as for the whole of a person's life, or for a specified period). Prior to the Courts Act 2003, the consent of the parties was required for all types of periodical payments, but now consent is no longer a necessary requirement for future pecuniary losses, such as the costs of care. Orders for periodical payments will only be made where the court can determine that continuity of payment is reasonably secure.

The trend away from from lump sums towards structured settlement awards of damages has been welcomed. As Harlow (1995) has commented, 'the iron law of averages is beginning to overtake the art of fortune-telling'. Furthermore, this change received the support of the Master of the Rolls' Working Party (2002), with Lord Phillips (now Lord Chief Justice) commenting in the *New Law Journal* that 'structured settlements are increasingly seen as a beneficial way of ensuring effective future provision for those who have suffered serious personal injury'. However, 'structured settlements' in their present form are still based on an initial calculation of a lump sum, thus the 'fortune-telling' element has not been entirely removed, and it seems that their applicability will be limited to personal injury cases involving large claims for future pecuniary losses.

**Exercise 14.3: Tort damages – odd one out**

From the three options given for each question, identify the **odd one out**:

(1) General damages – compensation orders – special damages.
(2) Special damages – pain and suffering – loss of amenity.
(3) Special damages – general damages – remoteness of damage.
(4) Loss of amenity – damage to property – *restitutio in integrum*.
(5) Lump sum – structured settlements – injunction.
(6) Pecuniary damages – pain and suffering – loss of earnings.

For Answers, please turn to pp 345–6.

## Useful website addresses

| | |
|---|---|
| Criminal Injuries Compensation Authority | www.cica.gov.uk |
| Home Office | www.homeoffice.gov.uk |
| Prison reform | www.howardleague.org<br>www.prisonreformtrust.org.uk |
| *Materials directly for AS studies:* | |
| John Deft (St Brendan's Sixth Form College) | www.stbrn.ac.uk/other/depts/law |
| Asif Tufal | www.a-level-law.com |

**HINTS AND TIPS**

*Sanctions (sentencing)*

One of the most common types of sentencing question that may be encountered on an examination paper is: 'How do judges arrive at decisions as to what sentences should be imposed on persons convicted of offences?'

The answer requires a balance between:

- **Information factors**: for example, sentencing procedure (that is, facts, antecedents, pre-sentence reports, medical reports, mitigation and reference to the tariff); and, as a consequence, weighing up the aggravating and mitigating factors.
- **The theory**: that is, the aims and objectives of sentencing (the theories of punishment: retribution, deterrence, prevention and rehabilitation).
- **The law**: the range of sentencing options within the four-level Sentencing Framework (discharges, fines, community sentences, custodial sentences) should then be considered and a distinction made between adult and juvenile procedures. Account should be taken of the greater flexibility introduced with regard to community sentences by the **Criminal Justice Act 2003**.

*Remedies (damages)*

Do *not* confuse damages (this topic) with remoteness of damage: they are related within the law of tort, though remoteness of damage is used to determine the extent to which the defendant will be liable whereas damages represent the way in which the liability is calculated and awarded to the claimant. Revision of the remedies section is made easier if you can see the structure of the damages system. One approach to learning this structure involves drawing a table to represent the **various 'heads' of damage** to be encountered in a typical claim arising from negligence. See Table 14.4.

Table 14.4 Revision: the structure of the damages system

| *General damages* | *Special damages (pecuniary)* |
|---|---|
| Difficult to calculate.<br>**Non-pecuniary 'heads' of damage:**<br>• physical and psychiatric pain and suffering<br>• loss of amenity<br>**Pecuniary 'heads' of damage:**<br>• loss of future earnings<br>• cost of future care | **Calculable, accrued up to the date of trial:**<br>• medical expenses<br>• loss of earnings<br>**Damage to property:**<br>• property value at the 'market price'<br>• repairs and transportation costs for replacements<br>• consequential losses<br>• inconvenience caused by loss of use |

You can then go on to revise the way in which the courts award such damages. This allows you to draw upon the content suggested by your table, thus providing some elaboration for each of the heads of damage that might be relevant here. In awarding general non-pecuniary damages under the heads of pain and suffering and loss of amenity, for example, judges try to achieve **consistency** based on a set of 'tariffs' used in the courts and laid down in digests of recent decisions such as *Current Law*. It is also important for you to point out that the award will, in most cases, be made once only and take the form of a **lump sum**.

# Experiencing the law

I am pleased to say that studying the law is not *just* about learning facts and passing examinations. It is also about developing an understanding of the law's role in society, and thinking about *issues* such as justice and morality and the way in which these concepts fit within the existing legal framework. This book is informed strongly by the belief that an enjoyment of law will be shaped by a range of experiences.

The following ways of experiencing the law will be considered below, and I hope you will find, through pursuing some of the suggestions here and your own research, that the law is a relevant, vital discipline:

- The law in **books (fiction and non-fiction)**
- The law on **film** and **television**
- The law and the **internet.**

This chapter concludes with some thoughts about the future, and focuses on the **UCAS process** that follows the completion of the AS year.

## THE LAW IN BOOKS

### Non-fiction

The range of non-fiction law books is huge and includes judicial biographies, court histories, textbooks, books of cases and materials, books about famous trials, critical legal studies, true crime, and so forth. However, the recommendations begin with a practical suggestion. Every law student – as with every law teacher – needs access to a **good law dictionary**. The *Oxford Reference Concise Dictionary of Law* is ideal: neither too weighty, nor too superficial, and with definitions that are easy to locate. A more recent addition to the market, helpfully illustrated and clearly targeted towards to the AS/A2 specifications, is Martin and Gibbins's *The Complete A–Z Law Handbook*.

With practicalities out of the way, I will start with books about law which complement studies directly. Holland and Webb's *Learning Legal Rules* and Fox and Bell's *Learning Legal Skills* are both excellent books to dip into. The former expresses the view that 'studying the law should not be a boring experience' and takes subjects common to the English legal system, such as statutory interpretation and judicial precedent, and then develops them using practical exercises and examples. The latter expresses a similar view: '. . . studying the law should be exciting, challenging and rigorous'. It is a rich feast indeed, and includes extracts, examples and ideas to start us all 'thinking like lawyers'. The book changes with each new edition and has included everything from a modern-day interpretation of the trial of Christ, through to discussion of law films and fiction, differing interpretations of law (for example, feminist, black,

Marxist) and the way in which law is perceived on a day-to-day basis. There is an amusing extract in the second edition, for example, about the way in which American Law Professors routinely break the copyright laws when they provide multiple copies of materials for students. These two books will be good companions throughout your legal studies and come strongly recommended. In the same spirit is Manchester, Salter and Moodie, *Exploring the Law: The Dynamics of Precedent and Statutory Interpretation*, which is recommended for its detailed case studies of the operation of precedent and interpretation in shaping and developing areas of the law.

There are also large numbers of less directly useful, but nevertheless fascinating, collections of legal – or at least law-related – extracts on the market. First, Brian Harris's *The Literature of the Law*, a selection of wise extracts from judgments in cases relating to life and death matters – such as abortion and the decision to withdraw life support from a man in a persistent vegetative state – and a variety of other legal situations. It allows you to see how judges assess competing factors and apply logical reasoning to resolve complex dilemmas. A good book, because it makes you think! Second, John Mortimer's *The Oxford Book of Villains*, which details the exploits of crooks, con-men, traitors and murderers (to name but a few of the categories), using both fact-based and fictional sources. The abridged extract that follows, selected by Mortimer from a biography of the barrister Sir Edward Marshall Hall, about the Old Bailey trial of Frederick Henry Seddon, accused of murdering his lodger with poison (and subsequently convicted and hanged for this offence), provides a flavour of the book:

> *Seddon had a very quick and agile mind: at first his clever parries and retorts were very effective. He had an explanation and a reason for everything. But gradually his very cleverness and his inhuman coolness began to disgust the jury . . . Only towards the end did he break out and lose his composure. When he was asked as to the counting of the gold on the day of [the victim] Miss Barrow's death, he showed his first sign of anger . . . Little by little, Sir Rufus [ie, Sir Rufus Isaacs, the counsel for the prosecution] gained ground, and for all his cleverness the soul of Seddon was laid bare before the Court, if soul it could be called; for its god was gold, and his mean, calculating character, which obviously cared for nothing but Seddon and his worldly possessions, aroused the contempt and loathing of almost everybody in court. Here was a man who would do anything for gain. 'Never,' said an onlooker, 'have I seen a soul stripped so naked as that.'*

In similar vein, *The Faber Book of Murder*, edited by Simon Rae, includes some excellent material under headings such as 'blood', 'knife', 'justice', 'poison', and so on. There is a very interesting section on old legal definitions, including clarification of the meaning of 'malice aforethought' in the *mens rea* of murder from Kenny's *Outlines of Criminal Law*, and a section on hanging. The latter reveals the problems associated with any legal system that attempts to retain a death penalty:

> *Other cases could be cited of innocent men executed, though the official and correct view is 'out of sight, out of mind' and 'dead men tell no tales'. Hansard, of 1881, gives an account of a boy executed at Winchester. The*

*prison chaplain rushed to London bearing a written confession made by a man for the very crime in question. This man was waiting to be hanged on another account. The chaplain could not find the Home Secretary in time; and so the poor boy was hanged.*

Collections of criminal trials are well worth reading, and there are a number of excellent out-of-print volumes which you might find in second-hand shops or car boot sales (fine places to pick up rare, largely forgotten books). John Mortimer's *Famous Trials* is a good introduction, and conveys a number of telling points about the murder trial which help to explain its fascination: 'Murder, like farce, flourishes in the most respectable societies'; 'Murder, like prostitution and the music hall, was one of the great releases for Victorian and Edwardian society'; and, most famously, 'Murder, as is well known, like divorce and Christmas, mainly takes place in the family circle'. These trials tend to evoke a sort of 'golden age' of murder, identified by George Orwell as a period between 'roughly 1850 and 1925' during which murders gave the 'greatest amount of pleasure to the British public'.

A more recent book, *The Trial: A History from Socrates to OJ Simpson* (2005) by Sadakat Kadri is also well worth tracking down. It was clearly a labour of love for the author, whose research is incredibly broad and is packed full of interesting details, stories and historical knowledge. Whilst it is worth reading conventionally, chapter-by-chapter, to take in the broader sweep of the subject, it is also has that wonderful quality where you can dip in almost anywhere and find something remarkable or thought provoking. By tackling the subject in such a wide and varied manner, Kadri has identified a number of patterns to show that societies really do not take sufficient heed of the lessons of history: his coverage of witch-trials, for example, ends not in medieval times but in 1980s America and Britain.

## Talking from experience: New Scotland Yard

There would be no trials without criminal investigation and the gathering of evidence. An insight into criminal investigation may be gained by considering some of the work undertaken at **New Scotland Yard**.

The **Fingerprint Bureau** employs experts with a working knowledge of the characteristics of fingerprints (for example, loops, whorls, arches, and so forth). Fingerprints taken at the scenes of crimes are compared with previous offenders' fingerprints stored on the computer system to see if a match is found. Fingerprint experts will also check a suspect's fingerprints taken at the police station against those on the computer to update the file and to see if the suspect may have committed previous unsolved crimes.

Arch Loop Whorl

Another branch of operations is the **National Missing Persons Bureau**. The Bureau receives reports of persons who have been missing for at least 14 days, or earlier where it is suspected that some harm may have come to the person. The Bureau liaises with Interpol with regard to UK nationals who go missing abroad. There are two main sorts of cases that the Bureau deals with: missing persons; and bodies that are found and unidentified. The records are continually updated by reference to daily telexes, emails and letters from police stations, and in conjunction with the **Police National Computer**. There is a **Metropolitan Missing Persons Bureau** that carries out a similar role to the National Bureau, but only for the London area.

A distinction should be made between the National Missing Persons Bureau and the **Missing Persons Helpline**. The Bureau links all the police stations together so that information can be stored centrally in the form of a database and can be accessed by stations across the country via contact with the Bureau. The Missing Persons Helpline, on the other hand, is aimed at helping and advising those who have been affected by a missing friend, family member or relative. Employees of the Bureau have to write letters to police stations across the country requesting recent photographs and dental records of missing persons. The Bureau also keeps paper-based records relating to missing persons.

For some reason, criminal law is always presented as more interesting than civil law, though as any tort scholar will tell you, the civil law throws up some great human interest stories and acute legal dilemmas. The area of tort known as defamation (that is, injury to a person's reputation in writing, referred to as **libel**, or through the spoken word, referred to as **slander**) is particularly interesting, and there have been some outstanding accounts of libel trials. A recent example, *The Irving Judgment*, details the High Court judgment of Mr Justice Gray in a libel case brought by a historian, David Irving. Irving had sought – unsuccessfully – to defend his reputation against allegations that he was a Nazi apologist who had manipulated historical facts to place Hitler in a positive light and deny the holocaust. This book should be of interest to students of all the Humanities and Social Science subjects, for whom the accurate gathering and presentation of evidence is vital in the pursuit of objective truths.

One way of keeping up-to-date with the law is to buy a daily broadsheet newspaper, or access such a newspaper from a library or the internet. *The Times* is very good for law coverage and contains a *Law Supplement* every Tuesday, which is particularly useful for keeping up-to-date with topics such as the legal profession, the role of the layperson and access to justice. *The Independent*, *The Daily Telegraph* and the *Guardian* also contain legal issues within their coverage of social matters; the *Guardian*'s Marcel Berlins and Clare Dyer are also responsible for one of the best introductory books on the practical workings of the English legal system, *The Law Machine*.

You are also advised, if you can, to keep up-to-date on legal issues by reading the *A-level Law Review, New Law Journal* and Routledge Cavendish *Student Law Review* (available on subscription: turn to the back of the book for a subscription form); and to pick up political and current affairs magazines such as *Private Eye, New Statesman* and *The Spectator*, for wide-ranging views and opinions on some of the legal themes of the day.

## Fiction

The **classics** of law fiction are often stated as including:

- Charles Dickens's *Bleak House* (containing the interminable Chancery suit of *Jarndyce* v *Jarndyce*, as a criticism of English civil justice in the nineteenth century).
- Harper Lee's *To Kill a Mockingbird* (including the great fictional creation of the American lawyer, Atticus Finch).
- Franz Kafka's *The Trial* (a book which uses a legal context to develop broader themes of existence and meaning, and which begins with one of the best opening lines ever: '*Someone must have been telling lies about Joseph K, for without having done anything wrong he was arrested one fine morning.*').

Richard Harrison has also argued that Bram Stoker's *Dracula* is also a great novel about the law (*New Law Journal*, 2002), following the relationship between a firm of solicitors and their most mysterious Transylvanian client.

Perhaps one of the most useful starting points for any discussion of whether we need laws in society is William Golding's *Lord of the Flies*. Equally, a book to show how dreadful it is when such laws are then abused by their makers is George Orwell's masterly *Animal Farm*. Two books that explore the limits of free will, the meaning and implications of murder, and the mechanics of detection are Fyodor Dostoevsky's *Crime and Punishment*, and the less well known, but quite remarkable, *A Report of a Murder* by Yorgi Yatromanolakis. I cannot claim that these books will aid your revision efforts for AS Law but they will invite you to explore issues, challenge accepted strands of logic and think deeply about society and the role of law within it.

There have also been many great plays with legal themes or legal characters, including a large number by **Shakespeare** (with Portia, in *The Merchant of Venice*, being a particularly notable fictional character, famously addressing the Venetian Court disguised as a 'doctor of laws' and defeating Shylock's claim to the 'pound of flesh' of one of his debtors). Some of the great moments of legal drama, however, appear in Robert Bolt's play, *A Man For All Seasons*, about the trial, in the sixteenth century, of Sir Thomas More, Henry VIII's Chancellor. More's crime – described at the time as treason – was to refuse to show his allegiance to the King on a point of religious principle. In the play, More is betrayed in court by Richard Rich, a character whom More had helped in the past, and he is put under pressure by his daughter and her husband-to-be, Roper, to go after Rich:

> **More**: And go he should if he was the Devil himself until he broke the law!
> **Roper**: So now you'd give the Devil benefit of law!
> **More**: Yes. What would you do? Cut a great road through the law to get after the Devil?
> **Roper**: I'd cut down every law in England to do that!
> **More** (*roused and excited*): Oh? (*Advances on Roper.*) And when the last law was down, and the Devil turned round on you – where would you hide, Roper, the laws all being flat? (*Leaves him.*) This country's planted thick with laws from coast to coast – Man's laws, not God's – and if you cut them down – and you're just the man to do it – d'you really think you could stand upright in the winds that would blow then? (*Quietly.*) Yes, I'd give the Devil the benefit of law, for my own safety's sake.

This is a stirring statement for all believers in the **rule of law** and has particular resonance today. Doesn't it remind you of Lord Hoffmann's comments in *A v Secretary of State for the Home Department* (2004) (see Chapter 1 at pp 32–3)? *If we hope to get to the current Devil (terrorists) by eroding our liberties, aren't we giving them the victory?*

It has to be said that much modern law fiction is American, and the best-seller lists are dominated by three names: John Grisham (of course); Scott Turow; and Richard North Patterson. Grisham's fast, pacey thrillers take in a range of themes including the death penalty (*The Chamber*); racism and revenge (*A Time to Kill*); jury independence (*The Runaway Jury*); and corporate greed (*The Rainmaker*). *The Firm*, a particular favourite, presents the reader with a model law graduate, Mitch McDeere, and finds him sucked into a major law firm with criminal connections, thus raising the big question: should Mitch blow the whistle on the firm? The book steps up a gear when it becomes clear that the question is not so much whether he should blow the whistle, but whether he is able to stay alive long enough to do so!

Turow's novels, *Presumed Innocent* and *The Burden of Proof*, are more densely plotted and of the 'whodunnit' variety than Grisham's (and like North Patterson's novels, more consciously political), though perhaps Turow's best work is actually one of non-fiction: *One L: What They Really Teach You at Harvard Law School* should be **compulsory reading** for anyone wanting to read Law at university. His description of lectures by Nicky Morris at Harvard provides a sense of what studying law really can be like: '*Each time I walked into Morris's classroom all that rapturous discovery of the first six weeks returned. And I knew I would leave after each meeting with that same crazy feeling, half-heat, half thirst – the sensation of being nearly sucked dry by excitement*'.

For those interested in American legal fiction, the short-story collection *Legal Briefs*, edited by William Bernhardt, provides an introduction both to Grisham and North Patterson, along with a number of other writers in the genre. All of the above titles fit into the area of 'law fiction', though in the more general **thriller** category David Guterson's *Snow Falling on Cedars* and Donna Tartt's *The Secret History* are excellent reads, the latter – about murderous students! – being one of the most passed-on and recommended books this writer has ever encountered.

The contrast presented by British legal fiction is a stark one. Whilst it has distinguished authors writing in the detective and thriller genres, Britain has yet to produce a Grisham or Turow in legal fiction. It is most welcome, therefore, when a writer such as **PD James** turns her attention to the legal field, and *A Certain Justice*, her tightly plotted story of the murder of a barrister, is a satisfying novel that crosses the genre divide. British legal fiction has tended to be lighter and more whimsical than the American style, and this may seem a little dated by comparison. Nevertheless, it is hard not to find John Mortimer's *Rumpole of the Bailey* irresistible – he of the 'dependable knowledge of bloodstains, blood groups, fingerprints and forgery by typewriter' – and the depictions of life in barristers' chambers and before the judge are charming and gently humorous. Henry Cecil's series of law novels from the 1950s, such as *Brothers in Law, Much in Evidence* and *Sober as a Judge*, are similarly delightful (if the reader makes concessions for the time at which they were written). Indeed, the character of the young barrister, Roger Thursby, is a great comic creation and should be enjoyed by all those who see themselves practising at the Bar in years to come.

## A personal ten top books to have on your shelf as a law student

Whilst I have tried as hard as I can to make this *the* book to have on your shelves, reading more widely, and having the appropriate reference books, will enable you to develop a greater depth of understanding and encourage broader interests in the subject. Please note: these are not the ten top revision guides to pass AS Law, but I believe they will add enormous *value* to your studies.

(1) *Oxford Reference Concise Dictionary of Law* and/or *The Complete A-Z Law Handbook* by Martin and Gibbins.
(2) A further AS Law or English Legal System textbook or revision guide of your choice. (I always like more than one perspective on a subject.)
(3) A good practical companion: *Learning the Law* by ATH Smith or *How to Study Law* by Bradney, Cownie *et al.*
(4) Some topical arguments about the law: try *The Law Machine* by Berlins and Dyer or *Just Law* by Helena Kennedy.
(5) For thinking about taking law further: *One L: What They Really Teach You at Harvard Law School* by Scott Turow.
(6) For general interest: *The Trial: A History from Socrates to OJ Simpson* by Sadakat Kadri.
(7) For fun: anything by John Mortimer (but preferably the *Rumpole of the Bailey* stories) and/or Henry Cecil.
(8) A page-turner: John Grisham – take your pick.
(9) For stretch: William Golding's *Lord of the Flies* or Fyodor Dostoevsky's *Crime and Punishment* or George Orwell's *Animal Farm* or Harper Lee's *To Kill a Mockingbird*.
(10) To place your studies in their historical, constitutional context: Hilaire Barnett's *Britain Unwrapped: Government and Constitution Explained*.

## THE LAW IN FILM AND TELEVISION

Of the books discussed above, some terrific films have been made – for example, *To Kill a Mockingbird* (1962, Dir: Robert Mulligan), with Gregory Peck on superb form as Atticus Finch; and *A Man For All Seasons* (1966, Dir: Fred Zinnemann) – and a number of the Grisham novels also provide superior examples: *The Firm* (1993, Dir: Sydney Pollack), *The Pelican Brief* (1993, Dir: Alan J Pakula) and *The Rainmaker* (1997, Dir: Francis Ford Coppola). In these sorts of films, we tend to find in the hero/heroine characters a demonstration of what the academic HH Koh calls the 'idea of law': '. . . the simple idealistic notion that talented and passionate women and men trained in the law can make our unjust and imperfect world so much better'.

Of all the great films about law, and there have been many, perhaps the US movie *Twelve Angry Men* (1957, Dir: Sidney Lumet) remains the most outstanding. Taking the simple dramatic setting of the jury room for a murder trial (with the defendant facing the death penalty if convicted), 12 men struggle in the summer heat to come to a decision on which they can all be agreed. The jury members each come to the trial with their own personal baggage and prejudices, and the film explores the extent to which important decisions on another man's life or death may be affected by other priorities. One juror, for example, is prepared to go along with any decision so long as it enables him to get out of jury service and to that day's baseball game. The film also illustrates the point that if the standard of proof in criminal law is not kept to 'beyond reasonable doubt' then serious injustices can occur. Henry Fonda plays the character who makes the initially conviction-happy jurors think again, in a series of dramatic scenes in which he points out that 'just maybe' the defendant did not commit the murder. There are some tremendous performances from the cast, and the film has a power and intensity about it which remain with the viewer.

The prize for most **powerful court scene in a film** must go to another US film, *A Few Good Men* (1992, Dir: Rob Reiner). Tom Cruise plays a military attorney who goes head-to-head with Jack Nicholson's platoon commander in a fantastic battle of wits and dominance that retains its impact on every showing. It is a scene that can reduce a law class to silence every time. However, Dustin Hoffman's explosive courtroom performance, under cross-examination, in the custody battle drama, *Kramer v Kramer* (1979, Dir: Robert Benton), runs it very close.

As for British law films, some of the most interesting examples are those of a more gentle nature, such as *Witness for the Prosecution* (1957, Dir: Billy Wilder), notable for Charles Laughton's memorably amusing performance as a barrister; and *Brothers in Law* (1956, Dir: Roy Boulting), an adaptation of the Henry Cecil novel mentioned earlier, and including some charming comic scenes, with Ian Carmichael's performance as the hapless barrister, Roger Thursby, a particular delight. If you think BBC's *The Office* does a good job of both making you laugh and cringe at the same time, try Thursby's first appearance in court, before a very stern Judge Ryman (played by *Dad's Army* star, John Le Mesurier). All would-be barristers should see this.

On a much more serious note, Basil Deardon's *Victim* (1961) is on one level a thriller about blackmail, but it was also courageous at the time of its release in its attempts to highlight the injustices of laws that criminalised homosexuals. Given the social changes that have occurred since 1961 you could be forgiven for thinking that it has lost its capacity to speak to modern audiences, but I think it retains the power to shock precisely because of these changes. Dirk Bogarde's performance as a homosexual barrister, whose efforts to preserve his career and marriage lead to tragedy, is terrific. Another film that retains its capacity to shock and challenge orthodox ideas is Lindsay Anderson's *O' Lucky Man* (1973), which includes a satirical attack on the justice system. Anderson made a series of films attacking aspects of the British institutions, and the law is but one of the many targets in *O' Lucky Man*, which charts the progress of the ambitious Mick Travis, through a series of jobs, adventures and mishaps that provide illustration of his rise and inevitable fall.

## A personal top ten of law films to watch during your AS Law year

To the best of my knowledge the following films are available on DVD/video. The films are best watched for entertainment and the broader issues they raise rather than for strict legal accuracy.

(1) Highly effective and still relevant to your studies: *Twelve Angry Men* (US, 1957).
(2) Another US classic: *To Kill a Mockingbird* (US, 1962) or *Anatomy of a Murder* (US, 1959, Dir: Otto Preminger) or *Inherit the Wind* (US, 1960, Dir: Stanley Kramer).

(3) For sheer joy: *Witness for the Prosecution* (US, 1957) or *Brothers in Law* (UK, 1956).
(4) For best courtroom battle: *A Few Good Men* (US, 1992).
(5) For watching in the presence of the opposite sex: *Kramer v Kramer* (US, 1979) (post-film discussion guaranteed).
(6) For timeless arguments about justice and the rule of law: *A Man For All Seasons* (UK, 1966).
(7) Shocking and thought-provoking # 1: *Victim* (UK, 1961) or *Philadelphia* (US, 1993, Dir: Jonathan Demme).
(8) Shocking and thought-provoking # 2: *Let Him Have It* (UK, 1991, Dir: Peter Medak) or *The Hurricane* (US, 1999, Dir: Norman Jewison).
(9) Good popcorn fodder: any of the John Grisham adaptations (such as *The Firm*, US, 1993).
(10) For campaigning lawyers in action, try the very inaccurate but interesting *In the Name of the Father* (UK, 1993, Dir: Jim Sheridan) or *A Civil Action* (US, 1998, Dir: Steven Zaillian).

Law on British television has ranged from *Crown Court* and Channel 4's *The Courtroom* to *Trial by Jury*; and from *Kavanagh QC* to *Judge John Deed*. There is no doubt that the British public like legal story lines, since whenever one of the major soap operas runs a trial story the nation tends to take sides quite quickly (with encouragement, for the most part, from the tabloid press). Legal dramas are generally very engaging, have strong characters and courtroom scenes, and if they are well written, tend to keep you guessing until the final scene. If it is ever repeated, I urge you to see some episodes of *Rumpole of the Bailey*, with Leo McKern assuming a legal character that rivals Charles Laughton's creation in *Witness for the Prosecution*: a stereotype, but a very jolly one, of the 'Old Bailey hack'.

Perhaps, however, some of you will have been inspired to study law because of US programmes such as *Ally McBeal, Law and Order* and *LA Law*, where working in a legal office is portrayed as consistently fun, glamorous and exciting. While there might be a world of difference between the legal practice depicted in *Ally McBeal* and, say, the conveyancing department of a small provincial English firm, if these programmes entertain and inspire then they have performed a valuable service. Keep enjoying them!

In addition to dramas, television documentaries on legal themes – such as *Dispatches* and *Rough Justice* – can be very useful and thought-provoking. Both the *Law in Action* and *Unreliable Evidence* programmes on Radio 4 are also good guides for keeping up with the law and for their presentation of legal issues (though they do tend to clash with the academic day: schedulers please note). *Crimewatch* is of natural interest to law students, showing how police investigations work in practice and how evidence is gathered prior to proceedings in the criminal justice system. However, UK documentary makers have yet to match some of the US output in recent years, ranging from Michael Moore's *Bowling for Columbine* to Morgan Spurlock's *Supersize Me* (which did make me think again about those obesity law-suits against fastfood chains, which seem to have become somehow representative of a perceived 'compensation culture' by the UK media); and, in much darker and disturbing territory, from *Capturing the Friedmans* (about the impact on a family of dreadful child abuse allegations made against a father) to *Paradise Lost* (providing trial coverage relating to the 'child murders at Robin Hood Hills' and which has led to an international campaign to free the individuals convicted of the crimes).

## THE LAW AND THE INTERNET

As you will have seen, websites that relate directly to information in the chapters of this book and the **AQA**, **OCR** and **WJEC** specifications have been included *within* the text. This stops you having to search through a whole list of websites and feeling perplexed. Others provide you with further reading – if you enjoy a particular chapter you could go on to explore the websites relating to it.

Websites that will guide your further reading throughout this text and any further studies in law are those that enable you to access primary legal sources. Therefore, for access to most of the Acts of Parliament and delegated legislation mentioned in this text, go to **www.hmso.gov.uk/acts.htm**. Case law may be accessed via **www.lawreports.co.uk** and **www.courtservice.gov.uk**. There is an excellent website on European law – European Union Online at **www.europa.eu.int** – with specific links to the institutions and an impressive 'EU at a glance' section, including history, maps and a glossary, to place your studies in context.

Asif Tufal's **www.a-level-law.com** (formerly **www.lawteacher.net**) is an extremely useful site for AS Law students. It is a 'one stop shop' of useful information. It contains links to the AS Law specifications for the main examining boards, so you can make sure, as you carry out your research or revision, that you have covered everything you will need for your examinations. You can also access a law dictionary to assist your reading and post questions on a message board. The site also contains information on the specification topics such as the English legal system, criminal law and the law of tort. It is highly recommended.

Furthermore, students are strongly advised to access **www.stbrn.ac.uk/other/depts/law/index.htm**. It has materials relating directly to the AS Law specifications of the main examining boards. However, before looking at materials on this website, you must look at the terms and conditions of use for the site. This website is also recommended because it contains examples of student work, and hints and tips from former students. I am pleased to acknowledge the work of John Deft and the team at **St Brendan's Sixth-Form College**, since this book hopefully reflects the same spirit as the website: written with enthusiasm to support the efforts of AS Law students in schools and colleges across the country. (See also John Deft's 'ten top websites' in *A-level Law Review*, Vol 1, Issue 1, at p 7 and Dr Peter Jepson's 'Learning the Law: Books or websites?' in *A-level Law Review*, Vol 2, Issue 1, at p 24.)

## THINKING AHEAD . . .

This book concludes with some consideration of the future. It is perhaps too early to decide on careers, but I suspect your school or college will be in the process of preparing you for higher education applications, careers advice, and so on. There follow some comments on the UCAS process, which will gain momentum after your AS examinations. It is important to say, however, that university life will not suit everybody; and that to become a solicitor, for example, you can work your way to the position through experience and commitment as a legal executive (see Chapter 10).

The UCAS process has to be undertaken by all students who wish to study at university. This is a very difficult and stressful time for students; there is the sense that this will determine the next few years of your life, and perhaps a future career, and there is always the lingering doubt that the direction chosen might not be the right one. Moreover, you will have to discuss with parents and teachers the institutions to which you are applying and the course you wish to pursue. Some of you will have more problems convincing parents and teachers of your choices than others. This is not an easy issue to resolve and there are few ready solutions. Experience suggests, however, that many students do win their parents round, largely through hard work and commitment to their respective courses. The strongest point is surely that *you* will be undertaking the next few years at university, not your parents. They should come to accept this in time: fingers crossed!

Once you have decided on your chosen degree, some of you might wish to look at league tables, as they will give you an idea (yes, just an idea) of how good the university is for your course. You must remember, though, that there are many discrepancies with league tables. Universities have differing strengths: some of the older institutions are particularly *research-orientated*, and some of the newer universities are rated highly for *teaching*; some universities are distinguished in both areas. If you are wishing to choose Law, whether on its own or combined with another subject, and have legal career aspirations in mind, you are advised to select a degree that is recognised as a '**qualifying law degree**'. In other words the degree *must* cover the **specified seven core subjects** (each one highlighted below):

- Law of obligations (comprising **contract law** and the **law of tort**)
- **Criminal law**
- **Public law** (also referred to as constitutional and administrative law)
- **Property law** (also referred to as land law)
- **Equity and trusts**
- **EC/EU law.**

As the training routes for solicitors, barristers and legal executives in Chapter 10 illustrate, you do not have to read for a degree in Law to enter the profession. Many students opt for a degree of their choice and then take the one year post-graduate conversion course.

However, for a Law degree, some universities will now require you to sit the **Law National Admissions Test (LNAT)** alongside the UCAS process. These were listed, for 2006 entry, as: **Birmingham; Bristol; Cambridge; Durham; East Anglia; Glasgow; King's College, London; Manchester Metropolitan; Nottingham; Oxford; University College, London.** Whilst there are many skills to consider in attempting to prepare yourself for this experience – albeit in acceptance of the official line that this is a test that cannot be prepared for – I recommend two activities that should stand you in good stead:

- **Competitive debating.** Get involved in the Oxford, Cambridge and Observer Mace competitions. The skills involved (as applicable to public speaking *and* writing) of thinking on your feet, imposing a structure on your examples, opinions and ideas, and delivering a coherent argument will not only help to prepare you for the essay component of the LNAT, but also for examinations and essay-writing in other subjects. Regular debating also brings you into contact with current affairs issues, and topics, that you might not otherwise encounter and so in the process you can become informed in a range of topics.

- **Read quality newspapers** for **news** and for **comment**. Every day of every week, social and political commentators are contributing short essays on topical issues, approaching these from all sorts of angles and perspectives to persuade us of their point of view, or to provoke letters of outrage. Regular reading of these daily polemics will introduce you to aspects of style and rhetoric that you can adopt in your own essay-writing, whilst the reading process itself encourages you to analyse the arguments, pick up on developmental reasoning (or a lack of it!) and respond critically.

While you should be ambitious when applying to universities – and the LNAT universities represent just one group of universities among many – listen to the advice that teachers give about your predicted grades and consider carefully the admission entry requirements and the number of applicants for each place at each institution. Law, for example, is a very popular subject, and the **high entry requirements** underline this point. You should have one or two choices to represent the 'best case scenario' and at least one choice to represent a 'safety net': you should be clearly on course for achieving the grade requirements of the middle choices. It is also important for you to choose courses based on the range of options and course structures featured in the prospectus: what areas of law appeal to you?

You do not have to visit all of the universities you list on the UCAS form, though prior visits will *inform* your choices. Otherwise, you should visit the universities that have accepted you to see whether the course and university really is for you. If you are adventurous and are thinking of moving out, you must ask yourself whether you would like to live in your chosen university town. Does it provide you with the study environment that you need to succeed? Can you **afford** to live in this area?

Students must remember that not all the institutions applied to will accept them. One of the most celebrated and admired criminal defence barristers of our times, Michael Mansfield QC – see the 'Profile' in Chapter 10 – experienced just such a situation: he was initially rejected by Keele University. (In fact, all the universities he applied to rejected him.) Furthermore, Mansfield had to re-sit his Bar examinations as he initially failed them. The determination and perseverance characterised by Mansfield should be borne in mind by all of us, and serve as a great reminder not to give up in the face of short-term difficulties.

## LAST REMARKS . . .

I hope that this book has given you confidence in the subject and that you have found it both interesting and enjoyable to read. I would be delighted to hear about your own experiences of the subject at AS Level (see the **companion website** at **www.routledgecavendish.com/textbooks/9781845680329**). If this book has rescued you on occasion, cheered you up, or merely reminded you of something you had forgotten, it has achieved some of its aims. Good luck for the future!

# Glossary

I am particularly grateful to Minel Dadhania for the inclusion of this section in 'AS Law'.

*The following list identifies some key legal terms that appear in this book.*

**Access to justice** — A phrase that expresses the aim of the Access to Justice Act 1999 and related Government reforms to provide a legal system, and legal services, that are open to all members of the public, regardless of wealth or background.

**Acquittal** — This is when the defendant in a criminal trial is allowed to walk free from court after being found not guilty of a crime.

**Act of Parliament** — This is a piece of written law that has been made according to a series of stages in the Houses of Parliament. An Act of Parliament is also referred to as an example of statute law, or primary legislation.

***Actus reus*** — A guilty act in criminal law, also referred to as the physical element of a crime. However, the *actus reus* also covers omissions and state of affairs cases.

***Ad hoc* bodies** — These are law reform bodies set up from time to time by the Government to investigate particular issues.

**Alternative dispute resolution (ADR)** — This term covers the alternatives that people can use to resolve a dispute – such as arbitration, mediation, conciliation and negotiation – without the case reaching the courts.

**Advocacy** — The act of representing a client in court; developing persuasive lines of argument to explain and support an individual's case in first instance or appeal proceedings.

**Attorney General** — The Attorney General is the Government's chief legal adviser and is politically accountable for the work of a number of State bodies, including the Crown Prosecution Service and its head, the Director of Public Prosecutions. The Attorney General can refer cases to the Court of Appeal where an acquittal is questionable on a point of law or a sentence has been passed which is considered 'unduly lenient'. The Solicitor General is another Government legal officer who acts as a deputy to the Attorney General.

**Bar Council** — This is the governing body of the barristers' profession, formally referred to as the General Council of the Bar.

**Bar Vocational Course** Work-related course to train law students, following their law degrees or completion of a post-graduate conversion course to law (Common Practice Examination/Graduate Diploma in Law), to become barristers.

**Bill** The name given to a draft piece of primary legislation as it goes through the stages of becoming an Act of Parliament.

**Binding precedent** A precedent established by judges in the higher appeal courts that must be followed by the lower courts and by courts on whom previous decisions are binding. The binding element of the judicial decision is referred to as the *ratio decidendi*.

**Burden of proof** The burden falls on the party in a legal action who has to meet the legal standard of proof. For example, in civil proceedings, it is the claimant who has to prove his or her case 'on the balance of probabilities' (civil standard of proof). In criminal cases, the prosecution must prove its case 'beyond reasonable doubt' (criminal standard of proof).

**Byelaws** Form of delegated legislation made by local authorities and other designated public bodies.

**Cab-rank rule** Barristers must accept cases allocated to them by the clerk in chambers. They must take the next case that comes along, rather like the system of a taxi-rank, hence the name 'cab-rank rule'.

**Case law** The type of law that accumulates to form the **common law**. Case law provides the necessary judgments for the doctrine of **judicial precedent** and the **development of principles of statutory interpretation**.

**Chain of causation** The link between the conduct of the defendant and the harm caused to the victim. An expression used both in tort law and criminal law.

**Civil law** Civil law relates to disputes between individuals or businesses. The aim of civil law is generally to compensate the disadvantaged party, but other remedies are available to protect civil law rights, such as injunctions.

**Claimant** The person who brings a **civil claim** (or **lawsuit**) in the courts against a defendant. The old name for this person was 'plaintiff'. Another term that may be used is 'litigant', since the claimant is engaging in litigation.

**Common law** Common law is the law developed by judges in the decisions on cases that come before them in the courts (see case law, above). Common law development is associated with the **doctrine of judicial precedent**.

**Community Legal Service** Body created by the Access to Justice Act 1999 to provide advice and information to the public via Community Legal Service Partnerships. The Community Legal Service represents the access to justice scheme for civil cases.

**Community Legal Service Direct** A website, formerly known as **Just Ask!**, to provide legal information and advice about access to justice.

**Community Legal Service Fund** Created by the Access to Justice Act 1999 to replace the civil Legal Aid Fund. The Fund is managed by the **Legal Services Commission** (see below).

**Community Legal Service Partnerships** These Partnerships represent a mixture of funding, legal service providers and community input for the delivery of local legal services. Legal providers involved in these partnerships have all been awarded the **Community Legal Service Quality Mark.**

**Community sentence** This sentence is passed when an offence is sufficiently serious to merit it, and may include periods of probation (**community rehabilitation orders**), community service (**community punishment orders**) and other forms of order that can be tailored to individual offenders (**community orders**). The idea, following the Criminal Justice Act 2003, is for a **single sentence** to be imposed, with sentencers able to choose one or more orders within it.

**Conditional fees** The Conditional Fee Arrangement is also known as the 'no win, no fee' system. Here the client pays the solicitor a basic fee only if the case is won, but pays an insurance premium to cover costs if the case is lost.

**Constitution** This sets out, in effect, how a country should be run. A constitution does not have to be written but may have evolved over the years: the British constitution is an example of this.

**Contemporaneity** The **relationship or union** between the *actus reus* and *mens rea* for the purposes of identifying whether an offence has occurred in criminal law. It is also referred to as the **coincidence** of *actus reus* and *mens rea.*

**Contributory negligence** This term describes the principles to determine whether the claimant is also responsible, along with the defendant, for an injury he or she has suffered.

**Conviction** A conviction is the result of a 'guilty' verdict in a criminal trial. The defendant will then be sentenced.

**Council of Ministers** The Council of Ministers is an institution of the EU. The main role of the Council of Ministers is to enact EC legislation (often on the basis of co-decision with the European Parliament). Ministers vote according to the Qualified Majority system.

**Court of Appeal** The Court of Appeal has both civil and criminal divisions and hears appeals in these areas. It is second only to the House of Lords in the hierarchy of English courts.

**Criminal Defence Service (CDS)** The body established in the access to justice framework to provide public legal services with regard to criminal cases, with funding supplied by the Legal Services Commission.

| | |
|---|---|
| **Criminal law** | Criminal law relates to offences that are seen as harmful to the State and dealt with by punishing the offender. |
| **Crown** | Takes two forms: the Queen as the monarch or sovereign of the country; and the executive acting on the Queen's behalf by taking the powers that were historically associated with the Queen (**prerogative powers**). |
| **Crown immunity** | Crown immunity reflects the fact that the Crown is a historical body with powers and rights that differ from those of citizens of the State. The term refers to a degree of immunity from legal action in criminal and civil law, subject to the Crown Proceedings Act 1947. |
| **Crown Prosecution Service (CPS)** | The CPS brings prosecutions to court. The CPS reviews criminal cases to ensure that there is enough evidence to allow prosecutions to proceed. |
| **Custody** | This is when a person is kept in a place of security, such as a prison. |
| **Custodial sentences** | For offenders over 21, a custodial sentence will be a term of imprisonment; for offenders under 21, a custodial sentence will be a term in a young offender institution. Offenders aged 12–17 might face custody in an alternative institution, such as secure accommodation under a detention and training order. |
| **Damages** | These will be awarded to an injured party in the civil law of tort, for example, in the form of monetary compensation. In the law of tort damages are divided into **general damages** (compensation for the future, difficult to calculate) and **special damages** (compensation up to the trial, calculable). Furthermore, general damages may be *pecuniary* (losses of a financial nature) or *non-pecuniary* (losses that are not financial in nature, such as pain and suffering). |
| **Decisions** | In EC law, these are pieces of secondary legislation made by the Commission. They are directed towards and bind certain Member States, companies or individuals within those States. |
| **Declaration of incompatibility** | This is a declaration made by judges, under the Human Rights Act 1998, to the effect that a piece of legislation is not in line with an Article of the **European Convention on Human Rights**. This puts pressure on Government and Parliament to make the necessary amendments. |
| **Defamation** | This is a civil claim in **tort** with two parts: **libel**, which relates to attacks to a person's reputation that are in writing; and **slander**, which refers to comments that may cause damage to reputation which are made orally. A jury is still used in this civil area to determine liability and the amount of damages to be awarded. |
| **Defendant** | The person in civil law defending a claim; or the person being tried for an offence in criminal law. In criminal law, the term 'accused' is sometimes preferred over 'defendant'. |

**Delegated legislation** — Delegated legislation is law made by bodies other than Parliament, such as Government Ministers, the Privy Council and local authorities. It is referred to as *secondary* legislation, and most pieces of delegated legislation take the form of **statutory instruments**.

**Discharges** — Discharges are sentences that follow a defendant's conviction, but where punishment would be inappropriate. They allow the defendant to walk free from court, but the conviction is recorded (contrast with acquittal, where the defendant walks free of all charges).

**Distinguishing** — To avoid the strict application of the doctrine of judicial precedent, a judge avoids following a *ratio* by holding that a different factual situation requires a different legal solution.

**Directives** — In EC law, Directives are pieces of secondary legislation. They must be given legal effect in the Member States of the EU, but these States are allowed to implement them in the way they see best. The Directive gives rise to **vertical direct effect**, but not horizontal direct effect.

**Duty of care** — This is a concept associated with Lord Atkin's **'neighbour test'** in *Donoghue v Stevenson* (1932) that a defendant will owe a duty if it is reasonably foreseeable that his acts or omissions would affect a neighbour. The current test to establish a duty of care is laid down in *Caparo Industries plc v Dickman* (1990).

**EC (European Community) law** — The term EC law (or 'Community law') is preferred over European Union (EU) law in this book because the institutional law-making, sources of law and concepts that you study form part of the original EC framework that is maintained as a 'pillar' in the governance of the European Union. However, as the EU is developing as a political and legal entity, many academics are using the broader title of 'EU law'. A reference to EU law on your examination paper can be read as EC law, and *vice versa*, at A-level.

**Equitable remedies** — These are discretionary remedies used by the civil courts where damages might not resolve the problem in the case. For example, injunctions will be awarded in tort cases in the area of nuisance in order to stop an activity occurring, such as offensive farm practices on a neighbouring property.

**Executive** — A term that represents the government of the day, and particularly the Prime Minister and his Cabinet of senior Ministers; it is the administration that runs the country.

**Enabling Act** — An Act of Parliament which delegates power to other bodies to make law. It sets out the parameters for such law-making by other bodies.

***Ejusdem generis*** — A rule of language that is used in statutory interpretation. In English, it means the 'same kind' or 'same class' rule.

**European Commission** — The European Commission is an institution of the EU based in Brussels. It has a number of roles, such as a responsibility for administering EC law and policy; for proposing new EC law; and for enforcing existing law against the Member States in the European Court of Justice.

**European Court of Justice** The European Court of Justice (ECJ) is an institution of the EU. It hears actions brought by the European Commission against Member States for breaches of EC law and hears **Art 234 References** from Member State courts to clarify questions of EC law.

**European Parliament** The European Parliament is an institution of the EU. It is a *directly* elected body, with a significant role in the EC legislative process, though it is not a legislative body in the same way as the UK Parliament. For example, it does not have sole law-making power, though it does have an increasing role of co-decision with the **Council of Ministers**.

**European Union (EU)** The EU was formally brought into being by the Maastricht Treaty 1991 but reflects the social, political, economic and geographical growth of the European project initiated by the Treaty of Rome 1957 and, today, brings together 25 Member States. The EU is governed by four institutions and is responsible for EC law (the EC title being retained to reflect the origins of this law in the European Community – see separate entry on EC Law).

***Expressio unius est exclusio alterius*** A rule of language that is used in statutory interpretation. In English it means the 'expression of one thing is to the exclusion of another'.

**Extrinsic aids** These are aids to statutory interpretation that are separate from the legislation itself, such as a dictionary, or parliamentary debates in Hansard.

**False imprisonment** A tort claim arising from the claimant's movements being restricted by the defendant, for example, through an unlawful arrest. This is a civil area in which trial by jury may still be used.

**Fine** This is the sentence of a financial penalty. The money paid goes to the Government (contrast with compensation in civil law, where the money paid goes to compensate the injured party).

**Fraud** Fraudulent conduct may lead to a claim in civil law (for example, the tort of deceit) or a prosecution for a theft or deception offence. It is one of the few civil areas in which a jury may still be used, though the Government is keen to limit juries in the criminal area of serious fraud.

**Golden rule** A common law rule of statutory interpretation. It is a modification of the literal rule (see below). It is used to avoid absurdity.

**Horizontal direct effect** — This describes the applicability of rights arising from EC legislation. If an EC legal right has horizontal direct effect, it may be *enforced* in the **national courts** against private persons, bodies and institutions. Treaty Articles and Regulations, for example, give rise to horizontal direct effect.

**House of Commons** — The directly elected chamber in Parliament, made up of Members of Parliament (MPs).

**House of Lords** — Parliamentary chamber, referred to as the Upper House. Consists of peers who are either appointed for life, or have power on the basis of their heredity (though heredity is of declining significance). Also includes senior judges and senior members of the clergy (though judges will no longer sit in the legislature when the **Constitutional Reform Act 2005** comes fully into effect).

**House of Lords (Judicial Committee)** — This is the most senior court in the English legal system. It hears the most important civil and criminal appeals in English law. It will be replaced by a **Supreme Court**, predicted to be in place by 2008.

**Indictable offences** — These are serious criminal offences. They are tried before judge and jury in a Crown Court. Some criminal offences of intermediate seriousness, known as **either way offences**, can be tried either as summary offences (by magistrates) or on indictment (Crown Court): the defendant can opt for trial on indictment.

**Institute of Legal Executives (ILEX)** — This is the governing body for legal executives, a branch of the legal profession.

**Intrinsic aids** — These are aids to **statutory interpretation** that are found *within* a statute, such as the long title, headings, side-notes and Schedules.

**Judges** — In all legal cases, the judge's role is to manage the case and to ensure that the evidence is properly admitted and the legal arguments are heard. The roles of the judges differ according to the type of case being tried or appeal being heard.

**Judicial precedent** — This is a legal decision made by a judge in a case that forms a principle for later cases to follow. The precedent system is based on the maxim, 'stand by what has been decided' (***stare decisis***). A precedent is formed by the element of the judicial decision known as the ***ratio decidendi*** (see below).

**Judicial review** — This occurs when a member of the public, a concerned body or pressure group challenges a decision of a Government Minister in the Administrative Court of the High Court (Divisional Court of the Queen's Bench Division) in the hope of getting that decision cancelled. It shows the separation of powers in action, with judges keeping a check on executive power.

**Judicial Studies Board (JSB)** The body responsible for training judges and lay magistrates.

**Judiciary** This is the collective term for the judges who adjudicate on cases before the courts. It represents one of the powers of the British constitution.

**Jury** A jury is the term for a panel of lay members who sit in court to determine the findings of fact in the case before them. In criminal law, they come to a verdict on whether the defendant is guilty or not guilty. In civil law, they determine liability and the amount of damages to be awarded. Generally, juries sit in panels of 12.

**Jury equity** This concept describes the independence that the jury has to determine the outcome of a case, representing the conscience of the community rather than the strict application of law.

**Lay people** Generally speaking, the ordinary man or woman without any specialist legal training. The legal system seeks to involve lay people in the administration of justice. They are neither legally qualified, nor paid for carrying out legal services. Juries and lay magistrates are examples of lay people in the English legal system.

**Law Commission** The Law Commission is an example of a law reform body. It was set up with the specific requirement of keeping the law under review.

**Law reform** This is the process of legal change and development as stimulated by a range of interested parties, groups and bodies, and effected by Parliament. The courts are also responsible for law reform when precedents are set in landmark cases, either taking the law in a new direction or dealing with a new problem or dilemma.

**Law Society** This is the governing body for the solicitors' branch of the legal profession.

**Lay magistrates** Lay magistrates are involved in criminal and civil work. On the criminal side they conduct first instance criminal trials. On the civil side they have extensive family law jurisdiction. Lay people *volunteer* to become magistrates.

**Legal aid** Although the Access to Justice Act 1999 changed the terminology for the use of public money in funding legal advice and representation, 'legal aid' is still the general term used by the legal press and broader media to describe the public funding of legal services in criminal law and civil law.

**Legal executives** Legal executives work in solicitors' firms as clerks. Their work is usually in an administrative capacity, though **Fellows of the Institute of Legal Executives** carry out similar work to solicitors and have some equivalent rights. This is a branch of the legal profession that can be joined upon leaving school rather than following a degree.

| | |
|---|---|
| **Legal Practice Course** | Post-graduate vocational course to train law students, or those students who have converted to law via the Common Professional Examination/Graduate Diploma in Law, to become solicitors. |
| **Legal Services Commission** | Body created by the Access to Justice Act 1999 to replace the Legal Aid Board and administer the provision of publicly-funded legal services via the Community Legal Service Fund (for civil cases) and the Criminal Defence Service (for criminal cases). |
| **Legal Services Ombudsman** | The holder of this post regulates the way in which the Law Society and Bar Council handle complaints. Perhaps to be replaced, in due course, by the **Office for Legal Complaints**. |
| **Legislation** | This is any form of written law. In the English legal system, it can be divided into *primary* legislation, in the form of Acts of Parliament (statute law), and *secondary* legislation, in the form of delegated legislation (mainly statutory instruments). |
| **Legislature** | This is the primary law-making body in the constitution, and in English law it is the Parliament at Westminster. It makes *primary* legislation. |
| **Literal rule** | Common law rule of statutory interpretation. If the wording in a statute is clear, it may be applied literally. |
| **Litigation** | The bringing of legal action by a claimant (litigant). |
| **Lord Chancellor (LC)** | Following the Constitutional Reform Act 2005, the Lord Chancellor's office will be ministerial rather than judicial and combined with the role of Secretary of State for Constitutional Affairs. The Lord Chancellor will continue to have duties relating to the administration of justice, but not in a judicial capacity. (The Lord Chancellor was formerly head of the judiciary and Speaker of the House of Lords, whilst also a Cabinet Minister: he retains just the latter position.) |
| **Lord Chief Justice (LCJ)** | The most senior judge in the English legal system, following the Constitutional Reform Act 2005: **President of the Courts of England and Wales**, and President of the Criminal Court of Appeal. |
| **Lords/Lady Justices of Appeal (LJJ)** | These are the judges to be found in the Civil and Criminal Divisions of the Court of Appeal. |
| **Lords/Lady of Appeal in Ordinary** | These are the 12 senior appeal court judges in the House of Lords who hear the most important civil and criminal appeals. See 'House of Lords (Judicial Committee)' definition above. Will become **Justices of the Supreme Court** in due course, following full implementation of the Constitutional Reform Act 2005 (scheduled for 2008). |
| **Malicious prosecution** | A tort claim arising from the malicious pursuit of the claimant through unreasonable legal proceedings taken out by the defendant. This is a civil area in which trial by jury may still take place. |

**Master of the Rolls (MR)** — This is one of the senior judges in the English legal system (one of the Heads of Division). The Master of the Rolls is the Head of the Civil Court of Appeal.

***Mens rea*** — The guilty mind, or the mental element of a crime. There are three types of *mens rea*: intention, recklessness and negligence.

**Mischief rule** — Common law rule of statutory interpretation that requires the judge to take into account the 'mischief' or problem the Act was aimed at remedying.

**Negligence** — Negligence is a civil claim in the law of tort, based around the concept of the 'duty of care', which provides compensation when a claimant who has suffered harm, loss or injury seeks to establish in the civil courts that it was caused by the defendant's breach of the duty of care.

**Non-fatal offences against the person** — These offences consist of assault, battery, assault occasioning actual bodily harm, wounding and grievous bodily harm. The last three offences are contained in the **Offences Against the Person Act 1861**.

***Noscitur a sociis*** — A rule of language that is used in statutory interpretation. In English, it means that words in a statute should be read in their context.

***Obiter dicta*** — 'By the way' statements made by judges in the course of making a decision in a case before the courts. They are persuasive authority, and therefore do not form part of the *ratio decidendi* (see below).

**Ombudsman** — The holder of this post will investigate the way in which complaints are handled by regulatory bodies, or consider complaints that are raised in respect of certain public or private bodies.

**Orders in Council** — Orders in Council are a form of **delegated legislation** made by the Privy Council.

**Overruling** — With regard to the **doctrine of precedent**, this is where a judge exercises the power to depart from a previous decision and expressly overturns that previous decision so that it is no longer good law.

**Police and Criminal Evidence Act (PACE) 1984** — It provides the framework for police to exercise powers of stop and search, arrest (subject to reforms by the **Serious Organised Crime and Police Act 2005**) and detention. PACE is supported by Codes of Practice.

**Paralegals** — Very general term for those working in a clerical and support capacity in a legal firm (such as legal secretaries).

**Parent Act** — Another name for an Enabling Act (see above).

**Parliament** — This is where *primary* legislation is made in the English legal system: it is the institution that represents the legislature in the constitution. Parliament consists of two chambers: the House of Commons and the House of Lords.

**Parliamentary sovereignty** This theory expresses the view that Parliament is the supreme law-making body in the constitution.

**Persuasive precedent** This form of precedent does not have to be followed, though it may be followed if judges lend the principle weight, through approval and favourable comments, over many years.

**Practice Statement** In the **doctrine of precedent**, the Practice Statement of 1966 enables the House of Lords to *depart* from its own previous decisions, if such a decision is out of date, or if it is perceived to be wrong or has created uncertainty. A Practice Statement is a set of directions from a senior legal figure, such as the Lord Chief Justice, which the courts will follow.

**Presumptions** Presumptions are used in **statutory interpretation**. This is where the court takes a certain situation to be correct, but will then consider if there is any evidence to the contrary.

**Prime Minister** The Prime Minister is one of the MPs of the political party that forms the Government of the day. He or she is elected as the leader of that party and will lead the Government following a general election win. In this role, the Prime Minister is the political leader of the country and head of the executive.

**Prosecution** This describes a legal action in criminal law. Generally the State initiates a prosecution, in the name of the Crown, against a person who has been accused of a crime.

**Puisne judges** These judges are to be found in the High Court.

**Private Bills** Private Bills affect only a limited area/range of persons and come to Parliament through petitions from outside bodies.

**Public Bills** These Bills affect the law in general and include Government Bills and those brought forward by MPs, for example (Private Members' Bills).

**Purposive approach** Broad, contextual common law rule of statutory interpretation, influenced by Continental approaches, that seeks to give effect to the spirit of the law rather than the literal wording.

**Pupillage** The period when trainee barristers, referred to as pupils, work with an experienced barrister for one year. This is the period of training that takes place prior to qualification as a barrister.

**QC** This is the title awarded to senior barristers in recognition of their experience and skills. The process of becoming a QC is known as 'taking silk'. QCs are requested by certain clients and in exceptional cases, and can expect to receive higher fees as a result.

**Qualified majority voting** — This is a system of voting used in the Council of Ministers (European Union) for most decisions, where votes are weighed roughly according to the population size of Member States.

***Ratio decidendi*** — The key to the **doctrine of judicial precedent**: the legal reasoning for the decision in a case and the element of a judicial decision which forms the **binding precedent** for future cases.

**Reference (Art 234)** — A reference procedure is used when a case in the Member State courts raises an issue of significance in European Community law. The Member State court refers the case to the **European Court of Justice (ECJ)** for a ruling.

**Regulations** — In EC law, regulations are pieces of secondary legislation. They are detailed, technical and have immediate legal effect in the Member States of the European Union. Regulations give rise to vertical and horizontal direct effect. *By contrast, in UK delegated legislation, regulations are made by Government Ministers and published as statutory instruments.*

**Reversing** — A judge changes the result of a lower court decision during the course of the appeal process. Unlike the procedure of overruling (see above), the reversed decision affects the parties in the case. For example, a party may win an appeal in the Court of Appeal but lose in the House of Lords.

**Royal assent** — This is the final stage required for a Bill to become an Act. The Queen gives her approval (by convention).

**Rules of language** — Rules are used to assist judges in the process of **statutory interpretation**, particularly with regard to common phrases and constructions in statute.

**Rule of Law** — The 'Rule of Law' is associated with Dicey, the theorist who laid down the principles that no individual is above the law and that checks should be placed on the exercise of power by government.

**Scrutiny Committee** — Made up of members from the House of Commons and House of Lords. Its role is to determine whether statutory instruments (pieces of delegated legislation) have been properly made.

**Sentencing** — It is the role of magistrates or judges to pass sentence on a person convicted in the criminal courts of an offence. The sentencing framework consists of four main types of sentence: discharges; fines; community sentences; and custodial sentences.

**Separation of powers** — This constitutional theory is attributed to Baron de Montesquieu. It requires that the three principal powers in the constitution – the executive, judiciary and legislature – are kept separate so they can exercise checks and balances on each other. In the UK, unlike the US with its written constitution, there is a degree of 'fusion' rather than clear separation (eg, the executive can be found within the legislature).

**Standard of proof** In criminal cases, the standard of proof is 'beyond reasonable doubt'. In civil cases, the standard of proof is 'on the balance of probabilities'. The standard of proof reflects the level of proof that is required to be met by the party with the burden of establishing the case. In criminal law, therefore, the prosecution must satisfy a jury that the case is proved 'beyond reasonable doubt'.

**Statute law** Statute law is otherwise known as legislation. The most obvious example is *primary* legislation, in the form of Acts of Parliament.

**Statutory interpretation** The process whereby judges apply and interpret statutes in relation to the factual circumstances brought before them. A number of common law rules have developed to assist judges in interpreting statutes and intrinsic and extrinsic aids can also be used.

**Strict liability** This form of liability requires only that the defendant's conduct is in breach of a statutory provision; no fault is required in civil law or *mens rea* in criminal law.

**Summary offences** Minor criminal offences. These are tried before a magistrates' court.

**Transferred malice** This occurs in criminal law when the defendant is found guilty of an act even though the victim, or outcome, is not the one intended. For example, A intends to shoot B and commit murder, but actually shoots and kills C, a passer-by.

**Treaty** An international agreement. In EC law, treaties are examples of *primary legislation* and provide broad statements of law in the form of **Articles**. Treaty provisions give rise to vertical and horizontal direct effect.

**Triable either way offences** These are intermediate offences. The mode of trial will vary according to whether the defendant opts for jury trial (Crown Court) or summary trial.

**Tribunal** A less formal institution than a court for hearing certain types of case. Tribunals are established by statute to allow citizens to assert their social, welfare and employment rights.

**Tort** A tort is a civil form of wrong which can be remedied by damages or equitable remedies, such as an injunction. Negligence, defamation and nuisance are all examples of torts.

**Unanimous verdict** When all of the members of the jury agree on the verdict in a case. This is the required form of verdict in a Crown Court trial, though the judge will accept a majority verdict (of 10:2 at the minimum) after two hours and ten minutes of jury deliberations.

**Vertical direct effect**

This describes the applicability of EC rights arising from EC legislation. If an EC legal right has vertical direct effect, it may be enforced in the national courts as against public, or State, authorities or bodies. **Treaty Articles** and **Regulations** have vertical direct effect *and* horizontal direct effect (see above), but **Directives** *only* have vertical direct effect.

# Bibliography

The following books are recommended to you as further reading. Legal publishing is a fast-moving business and law books are constantly being updated, so always check that the book you are reading is the most recent edition of that title. You are also directed to Chapter 15, 'Experiencing the law', which considers a wider range of legal literature.

## GENERAL BOOKS ON ENGLISH LAW AND THE ENGLISH LEGAL SYSTEM

Bailey, SH *et al.* (2002) *Smith, Bailey & Gunn on the Modern English Legal System*, 4th edn, London: Sweet & Maxwell

Berlins, M and Dyer, C (2000) *The Law Machine*, 5th edn, London: Penguin

Cavendish Publishing (2003) *LawCard on the English Legal System* 2003–2004, London: Cavendish Publishing

Darbyshire, P (2002) *Eddey & Darbyshire on the English Legal System*, 7th edn, London: Sweet & Maxwell

Elliott, C and Quinn, F (2004) *English Legal System*, 5th edn, Harlow: Longman

Manchester, Salter and Moodie (2000) *Exploring the Law: The Dynamics of Precedent and Statutory Interpretation*, 2nd edn, London: Sweet & Maxwell

Martin, J (2006) *The English Legal System*, London: Hodder Arnold

McLeod, I (2005) *Legal Method*, 5th edn, London: Palgrave Macmillan

Slapper, G and Kelly, D (2000) *English Law*, London: Cavendish Publishing

Slapper, G and Kelly, D (2004) *The English Legal System*, 7th edn, London: Cavendish Publishing

Ward, R and Wragg, A (2005) *Walker and Walker's English Legal System*, 9th edn, Oxford: OUP

Yule, I (2006) *AS AQA Law Unit Guides*, 2nd edn Philip Allan

## CONSTITUTIONAL LAW AND EUROPEAN LAW

Allen, M & Thompson, B *Cases and Materials on Constitutional and Administrative Law,* 8th edn, Oxford: OUP

Barnett, H (2002) *Britain Unwrapped: Government and Constitution Explained*, London: Penguin

Cavendish Publishing (2003) *LawCard on Constitutional & Administrative Law* 2003–2004, London: Cavendish Publishing

Loughlin, M (2000) *Sword & Scales: An Examination of the Relationship Between Law and Politics*, Oxford: Hart

Turpin, C (2002) *British Government and the Constitution: Text, Cases and Materials*, Cambridge: Cambridge University Press

Weatherill, S (2005) *Cases and Materials on EU Law*, 7th edn, Oxford: OUP

Vincenzi, C and Fairhurst J (2003) *Law of the European Union*, 4th edn, Harlow: Longman

## CRIMINAL LAW, POLICE POWERS AND SENTENCING

Cavendish Publishing (2003) *LawCard on Criminal Law 2003–2004*, London: Cavendish Publishing

Elliott, C and Quinn, F (2002) *Criminal Law*, 5th edn Harlow: Pearson

Fionda, J and Bryant, M (2004) *Briefcase on Criminal Law*, 3rd edn, London: Cavendish Publishing

Jason-Lloyd, L (2005) *An Introduction to Policing and Police Powers*, 2nd edn, London: Routledge Cavendish

Jefferson, M (2005) *Criminal Law*, 7th edn, London: Longman

Ormerod, D (2005) *Smith & Hogan Criminal Law* London: LexisNexis UK

Ormerod, D (2005) *Smith & Hogan Criminal Law: Cases and Materials* London: LexisNexis UK

Roe, D (2002) *Criminal Law*, 2nd edn, London: Hodder & Stoughton

Strickland, C (1998) *Key Issues in A Level Law: Criminal Law*, London: Longman

Wasik, M (2001) *Emmins on Sentencing*, 4th edn, Oxford: OUP

## TORT LAW AND DAMAGES

Bagshaw, R and McBride, N (2005) *The Law of Tort*, 2nd edn, Harlow: Longman

Cavendish Publishing, (2003) *LawCard on Tort Law 2003–2004*, London: Cavendish Publishing

Elliott and Quinn (2003) *Tort Law*, 4th edn, Harlow: Longman

Hodge, S (2004) *Tort Law*, 3rd edn, Devon: Willan

Jones, MA (2006) *Textbook on Torts*, 9th edn, Oxford: OUP

Rogers, WVH (2002) *Winfield & Jolowicz on Tort*, 16th edn, London: Sweet & Maxwell

Turner, C *Contract and Tort Law*, 2nd edn, London: Hodder Arnold

## MISCELLANEOUS

Bradney, Cownie *et al.* (2005) *How to Study Law*, 5th edn, London: Sweet & Maxwell

Goodman, A (2000) *A Walking Guide to Lawyers' London*, London: Blackstone/OUP

Greenfield, Osborn and Robson (2001) *Film and the Law*, London: Cavendish

Kadri, S (2005) *The Trial: A History from Socrates to OJ Simpson*, London: HarperCollins

Kennedy, H (2004) *Just Law: The Changing Face of Justice and Why it Matters to Us All*, London: Chatto & Windus

Mansell, Meteyard and Thomson (2004) *A Critical Introduction to Law*, 3rd edn, London: Cavendish Publishing

Mortimer, J (1984) *Famous Trials*, London: Penguin

Rivlin, G (2002) *First Steps in the Law*, 2nd edn, OUP/Blackstone

Smith, ATH (2002) *Glanville Williams: Learning the Law*, 12th edn, London: Sweet & Maxwell

# Answers

## ANSWERS FOR CHAPTER 1

### Recap Quiz

(1) (a) Separation of powers.
(b) Rule of law.
(c) Prerogative powers.
(d) Parliamentary sovereignty (or supremacy).
(e) Devolution.
(f) EC law obligations under the European Communities Act 1972.
(g) Human Rights Act 1998.
(h) Unwritten constitution.

(2) (a) Pressure groups.
(b) Law Commission.
(c) Private members' Bill.
(d) *Ad hoc* committees.
(e) Common law.

(3) (a) Second reading.
(b) Royal Assent.
(c) First reading.
(d) Report stage.
(e) Third reading.
(f) Committee stage.

## ANSWERS FOR CHAPTER 2

### Suggested answers to the Case exercise

(1) The primary legislation mentioned in this case-note is the Tobacco Advertising and Promotion Act 2002. The secondary (delegated) legislation mentioned in this case-note is the Tobacco Advertising and Promotion (Point of Sale) Regulations 2004. The general term that could be used to describe the primary legislation could be either 'parent Act' or enabling Act.

(2) Regulations are made by Ministers and so the context suggests that the Secretary of State for Health was the Minister authorised by Parliament in the 2002 Act to make the 2004 Regulations. The judicial review challenge to the 2004 Regulations clearly targets the Secretary of State for Health as the law-maker.

(3) The court that heard this case was the Divisional Court of the Queen's Bench Division. Judicial review claims are made to this court. A clue was provided by the title of the judge in this case, denoting High Court status.

(4) The restrictions were seen as reasonable and legitimate because: a democratically elected Parliament had authorised them; no attempt had been made by MPs or peers to annul them; the restrictions merely furthered the objectives of the Act; and they were proportionate to the objectives that Parliament had set out.

(5) Although the method of laying before Parliament is not specified, the mention of annulment suggests the negative resolution procedure. However, no attempt was made by MPs to prevent the delegated legislation being passed – it therefore survived the parliamentary controls.

## Exercise: Revision Quiz

*S*crutiny
*E*nabling
*C*ontrols
*O*rders
*N*egative
*D*elegation
*A*dvantages
*R*egulations
*Y*es

# ANSWERS TO CHAPTER 3

## Exercise: Matching the cases and the rules

| *Number* | *Case name* | *Rule, approach or presumption* |
|---|---|---|
| (1) | *Coltman v Bibby Tankers* | Purposive |
| (2) | *Adler v George* | Golden |
| (3) | *Muir v Keay* | Rule of language: |
| | *noscitur a sociis* | |
| (4) | *Cutter v Eagle Star Insurance Co Ltd* | Literal |
| (5) | *Corkery v Carpenter* | Mischief |
| (6) | *R v Dovermoss* | Literal; use of extrinsic aid |
| (7) | *Lord Advocate v Dumbarton District Council* | Presumption: the Crown is not bound by a statute |
| (8) | *Pepper v Hart* | Mischief/purposive; use |
| | of extrinsic aids | |
| (9) | *Smith v Hughes* | Mischief |
| (10) | *Re Stockport Ragged, Industrial and Reformatory Schools* | Rule of language: *ejusdem generis* |

## ANSWERS FOR CHAPTER 4

### Exercise 4.1: Identifying cases in the precedent topic and their relationship to the courts hierarchy

**Task 1**

(1) (e)
(2) (g)
(3) (a)
(4) (d)
(5) (b)
(6) (f)
(7) (h)
(8) (c)

**Case options:** (a) *R v Gould*; (b) *Central London Property Trust Ltd v High Trees House Ltd*; (c) *Miliangos v George Frank (Textiles) Ltd*; (d) *R v G and R*; (e) *BRB v Herrington*; (f) *Davis v Johnson*; (g) *Young v Bristol Aeroplane Co*; (h) *Commission of the European Communities v Council of the European Union.*

**Task 2**

House of Lords: *Miliangos; R v G and R; BRB v Herrington.*
Court of Appeal (Civil): *Davis v Johnson; Young v Bristol Aeroplane.*
Court of Appeal (Criminal): *R v Gould.*
High Court: *High Trees.*
European Court of Justice: *Commission v Council.*

## ANSWERS FOR CHAPTER 5

### Exercise 5.1: Recap on the European Institutions

*There are four main institutions of the European Union: the European Commission; the European Parliament; the Council of Ministers; and the European Court of Justice.*

**Task 1: Geography of the institutions**

(a) European Court of Justice.
(b) European Parliament.
(c) European Commission.
(d) Council of Ministers.

**Task 2: Powers of the institutions**

(a) European Parliament (in co-decision with the Council of Ministers).
(b) European Commission.
(c) European Court of Justice.
(d) Council of Ministers.

**Task 3: Composition of the institutions**
(a) European Commission.
(b) European Parliament.
(c) Council of Ministers.
(d) European Court of Justice.

**Task 4: Description of the institutions**
(a) European Parliament.
(b) European Court of Justice.
(c) Council of Ministers.
(d) European Commission.

## Exercise 5.2: EC law cases and principles

**Task 1: Identify the following cases from the facts given:**
(1) (a)
(2) (b)
(3) (d)
(4) (e)
(5) (c)

**Case options:** (a) *Van Gend en Loos*; (b) *Factortame*; (c) *Van Duyn v Home Office*; (d) *Marshall v Southampton Area Health Authority*; (e) *Marleasing*.

**Task 2: Sources of EC law**
(1) (c)
(2) (d)
(3) (b)
(4) (a)

Sources of law options:
(a) EC Treaty; (b) Decisions; (c) Regulations; (d) Directives.

**Task 3: The principles of EC law**
*Insert the missing terms/phrases into the following statements:*
(1) Vertical direct effect.
(2) Horizontal direct effect.
(3) UK parliamentary sovereignty.
(4) Francovich.
(5) Entrenched.

# ANSWERS FOR CHAPTER 6

## Exercise 6.1: Identifying the courts

(1) (d)
(2) (e)
(3) (h)

(4) (b)
(5) (f)
(6) (j)
(7) (c)
(8) (g)
(9) (i)
(10) (a)

**Court options:** (a) European Court of Justice; (b) House of Lords; (c) Court of Appeal (Civil); (d) Divisional Court of the Chancery Division; (e) Divisional Court of the Family Division; (f) Divisional Court of the Queen's Bench Division; (g) Queen's Bench Division of the High Court; (h) Crown Court; (i) county court; (j) magistrates' court.

## ANSWERS FOR CHAPTER 7

### Exercise 7.1: Recap on ADR and tribunals

(1) (a) Arbitration.
(b) Negotiation.
(c) Conciliation.
(d) Mediation.

With which methods of ADR would you associate the following:

(2) (a) Mediation, conciliation.
(b) Arbitration.
(c) Arbitration and conciliation in particular, but have a general advisory role.
(d) Arbitration.

(3) The courts have punished parties who have unreasonably refused to consider requests for ADR in their awards for costs. Cases could include: *Dunnett v Railtrack* (2002); *McMillan Williams v Range* (2004); *Halsey v Milton Keynes NHS Trust* (2004) (which did not allow parties to be forced into ADR, but did acknowledge the approach of courts to unreasonable refusals to enter into ADR); and *Burchell v Bullard* (2005).

(4) (a) For example: Employment Tribunals; Mental Health Review Tribunal; Lands Tribunal.
(b) Any form of recognised discrimination (sex, race, disability, sexual orientation, religion, age); unfair dismissal; claims for redundancy pay.
(c) Lots: examples would include the Employment Tribunals; Social Security Appeal Tribunals. Few, if any: Plant Varieties and Seeds Tribunal.
(d) Advisory Conciliation and Arbitration Service.

With which alternatives to courts would you associate:

(5) (a) Public sector ombudsman.
(b) Employment Tribunal (typical remedies).

(6) List three general advantages of ADR over going to court and three disadvantages.

Advantages *such as*: cheaper; less formal; private. (Provide examples in your notes.)
Disadvantages *such as*: ADR can lack clear methods of enforcement and appeal; formality can provide the structure for properly addressing the issues at dispute; and judges, unlike some ADR providers, are clearly accountable for decisions made.

## ANSWERS FOR CHAPTER 8

### Exercise 8.1: Recap on judges

(1) Identify the following judges or judicial titles:
(a) Lord Chief Justice.
(b) Chancellor of the High Court.
(c) District judges.
(d) Master of the Rolls.
(e) Recorders.
(f) Lords of Appeal in Ordinary (or Lady as appropriate).
(g) Lords Justices of Appeal (or Lady as appropriate).

(2) With which aspects of the judiciary topic would you associate:
(a) Training of the judges.
(b) Appointment of the judges.
(c) Removal of judges: note that senior judges have very strong security of tenure and so are very difficult to remove from office, even if not performing well.
(d) Removal of judges – applies to less senior judges, in particular: note, however, reforms to judicial discipline.

(3) Provide the following facts:
(a) 70. (Judges can continue to hear cases part-time.)
(b) House of Lords: 15 years of advocacy rights in the higher courts. Less senior judges: ten years of advocacy rights in the Crown Court or county court (or seven years for district judges).
(c) Constitutional Reform Act 2005.
(d) The Commission for Judicial Appointments was set up by the Government following the Peach Inquiry to monitor the appointments process. The Judicial Appointments Commission was established by the Constitutional Reform Act 2005 to appoint judges.
(e) Judicial review.

## ANSWERS FOR CHAPTER 9

## Exercise 9.1: Quick quiz on post-Criminal Justice Act 2003 jury selection

*All references to the Juries Act 1974 take into account the amendments made by the Criminal Justice Act 2003.*

(1) Yes. In July 2004, the rural affairs minister, Alun Michael MP, became the first Government minister to be called for jury service following the Criminal Justice Act 2003. If an MP objects to carrying out jury service in his or her constituency then the summoning officer can exercise discretion for the service to be carried out elsewhere.
(2) A police officer. Yes. See the case of *R v Abdroikov* (2005) at p 174.
(3) A person with severe clinical depression. Probably not: a person in these circumstances might well fall within the definition of a 'mentally disordered person' and be disqualified from serving (Juries Act 1974, Schedule 1). The Social Exclusion Unit has complained about this aspect of jury selection (2004).
(4) A 75-year-old pensioner. No: 70 is the upper age limit for jury service, under s 1 of the Juries Act 1974.
(5) A 17-year-old student due to take her AS examinations. No: 18 is the lower age limit for jury service under s 1 of the Juries Act 1974.
(6) An 18-year-old student due to take his A2 examinations. Technically yes, though the summoning officer's guidance is to defer the date on which the jury service is to be taken until *after* the examination period.
(7) A 25-year-old asylum seeker. No, since this person does not meet the residency requirements set out by s 1 of the Juries Act.
(8) A person with a recent conviction for assault occasioning actual bodily harm. No, subject to the sentence received: if it was imprisonment or a specified community sentence, the person will be disqualified (assuming that 'recent' refers to a period within the last ten years) under the Juries Act 1974, Schedule 1.
(9) A member of the clergy. Yes. However, those with religious beliefs that are incompatible with jury service, need to provide evidence to support an application for excusal.
(10) A person currently on bail. No, the person will be disqualified from carrying out jury service under the Juries Act 1974, Schedule 1.

## Exercise 9.2: The selection of lay magistrates

(1) An 18-year-old university student. On the one hand, yes: the age at which candidates can now apply for the lay magistracy is 18 years, and a 20-year-old has recently been appointed in West Sussex (who must have applied at 19). However, it remains to be seen whether this candidate will be able to provide sufficient evidence to demonstrate the six key qualities looked for in candidates.

(2) A retired person of 67 years of age. No: the upper age of appointments for lay magistrates is 65, though serving magistrates can retire at 70.

(3) A local traffic warden. No: this is one of the professions that would disqualify a person from applying to the magistracy.

(4) A middle-aged person who, earlier in their life, had been declared bankrupt – a status now discharged. On the face of it, yes (only undischarged bankrupts will be barred from applying) but the candidate's application will be looked at very carefully against the six key qualities to see whether the public could have confidence in this person.

(5) A person, 45, with a number of minor motoring convictions. Most probably, no: a lay magistrate might spend a great deal of time dealing with motoring offences and it is highly unlikely that a person with these sorts of offences would be appointed, since it could undermine public confidence in the authority of the law.

(6) A retired academic, with a passion for fox-hunting. Probably, no: the fox-hunting is the problem. The Lord Chancellor wrote to magistrates in November 2004 to point out that if any refused to enforce the Hunting Act 2004 then they would not be able to stay in office. *The Times* reported in December 2004 that Derek Pearce, a magistrate on the North Avon branch, resigned over this issue, followed in March 2005, by Susan Foster, a magistrate of 30 years' standing from the Telford bench. Clearly, this particular passion might be incompatible with the magistrates' role. (However, Lord Scott of Foscote, a Lord of Appeal in Ordinary, lists 'fox-hunting' as one his recreations in Who's Who and he has not had to stand down, though he will not be allowed to hear any cases relating to the Hunting Act.)

(7) A person, 40, a close relative of the Chief Constable for the local area. No: the relationship with a senior member of the police service indicates the potential for conflicts of interest.

(8) A person, 28, with a physical disability necessitating the use of a wheelchair. Yes, provided that the physical infirmity does not prevent the individual from doing the job and the candidate meets the six key qualities.

(9) A 23-year-old unemployed, single parent. Again, yes, provided the candidate can demonstrate the six key qualities. If the bench is truly going to reflect society, then young single mothers who are willing to volunteer should be considered.

(10) A teacher, 35, who has only lived in the area for one year. Probably, yes, though a demonstration of the six key qualities and a willingness to contribute to the local community would be looked for. (In theory, magistrates now have 'universal jurisdiction', though in practice they will still be appointed to local courts at first instance.)

## ANSWERS FOR CHAPTER 10

## Recap quiz on the legal profession

(1) (a) Legal executives.
(b) Barristers.

(c) Solicitors.
(d) Crown Prosecution Service.

(2) (a) Barristers.
(b) Legal executives (governing body).
(c) Solicitors (governing body).
(d) Barristers (traditional part of the education and training of barristers).
(e) Solicitors (the major group of City law firms).
(f) Barristers (governing body).
(g) Barristers (traditionally); now open to those solicitors performing advocacy.
(h) Barristers, solicitors and, in very limited circumstances, legal executives (the right to represent a client in court).
(i) Barristers (traditionally); now open to those solicitors with a higher courts advocacy certificate.
(j) Barristers.
(k) Solicitors (Legal Practice Course).
(l) Barristers (Bar Vocational Course).
(m) Barristers.
(n) Solicitors.
(o) Barristers and solicitors: by removing the immunity against lawsuits for negligent advocacy against the former, the principle has application to the latter if performing advocacy.

(3) (a) Office for Legal Complaints.
(b) Legal Disciplinary Partnerships (LDPs).
(c) Multi-disciplinary Partnerships (MDPs).
(d) Tesco law.

## ANSWERS FOR CHAPTER 11

### Answers to Qs 1–3 of Let's look at cases 11.1: *Campbell v Mirror Group Newspapers Ltd (No 2)* (2005)

(1) What options did Naomi Campbell have for funding a libel case? Why do you think she opted for a Conditional Fee Agreement for her appeal to the House of Lords?

Naomi Campbell could *not* have claimed public funding for this case, since libel is part of the tort of defamation and the Community Legal Service Fund will not be available for this sort of claim. Her eligibility for public funding would also be called into question by her 'means' – glamorous supermodels do not give the impression of being poor. She *could*, of course, have privately financed the claim (as indeed she did in the proceedings prior to the appeal to the House of Lords), but even then as the costs award indicates, it would have been an expensive case for any individual to take on.

Therefore, the Conditional Fee Agreement was her best option. She could enter such an Agreement on the basis of 'no win, no fee', with her legal team agreeing to take the risk of pursuing the appeal. The onus would only be on Campbell to take out insurance to deal with the possibility of losing the case (an expense she would recoup should the case be won).

**What is a success fee? How does it differ from the basic fee in a Conditional Fee Agreement?**

A Conditional Fee Agreement sets out the fees to be paid to the client's lawyers if the case is won: a basic fee (which the client agrees to pay for the lawyers' work in winning the case); and the success fee (representing an 'uplift' reward for the lawyers' success which the losing party will pay). For high-risk claims, as the *Campbell* case illustrates, a 100 per cent uplift on the lawyers' costs incurred in taking the case forward can be claimed.

**Why was MGN liable for the success fees in Campbell's Conditional Fee Agreements? What is the justification for this position?**

MGN assumes liability in accordance with the Access to Justice Act 1999, ensuring that the losing party pays *both* the success fee relating to a Conditional Fee Agreement and for any insurance expenses incurred. This provision ensures that a successful litigant gains the benefit of the damages award and pays no more to the solicitor than the basic fee.

## Recap Quiz

(1) (a) LSC – Legal Services Commission: body that replaced the Legal Aid Board in order to administer the public funding of legal services.
(b) CLS – Community Legal Service: scheme for the provision of publicly-funded civil legal services.
(c) CDS – Criminal Defence Service: scheme for the provision of publicly-funded criminal legal services.
(d) CAB – Citizens' Advice Bureau, a local provider of free legal advice, staffed largely by volunteers.
(e) CFA – Conditional Fee Agreement, more commonly known as the 'no win, no fee' agreements used to provide access for those wishing to take legal claims where public funding is not available.

(2) Any six sources of legal information from: CLS website; solicitors' firms; Citizen's Advice/CAB; Law Centres; trade unions; media (eg, Watchdog, Which?); local authority advice centres (eg, Trading Standards); specialist organisations (eg, AA).

(3) Legal Help refers to public funding for legal advice and assistance. Legal Representation refers to public funding for bringing the matter to court and advocacy.

(4) Areas of civil law not eligible for public funding are: personal injury; defamation (though the impact of *Steel and Morris v UK* (2005), heard in the ECtHR, might change this position); wills and trusts; business and corporate law. Special arrangements apply to judicial review and very complex negligence cases.

(5) If a case is won, under a 'no win, no fee' agreement, the client will incur only the basic fee for the case, which was agreed with the solicitor at the outset – all the other costs will be borne by the losing party (including

any insurance payments and the solicitor's 'success fee'). Bear in mind that the successful client will probably have been awarded damages, the likely goal of taking the case in the first place.

However, if the case is lost, then the client, whilst relieved from pay ing a fee to the solicitor, is liable for all of the costs of the winning party. As we have seen, the risk of losing can be covered by taking out insurance payments, but these are often substantial.

(6) Taking a case on a pro bono basis means that the legal professionals involved are prepared to work free of charge, for the public good represented by bringing the matter to court.

## ANSWERS FOR CHAPTER 12

### Exercise 12.1: Identifying cases in criminal law (Part 1) and their illustration of key legal concepts

#### Task 1

(1) (g)
(2) (c)
(3) (e)
(4) (a)
(5) (h)
(6) (d)
(7) (f)
(8) (b)

**Case options:** (a) *R v Larsonneur*; (b) *R v Cunningham*; (c) *R v Woollin*; (d) *Alphacell v Woodward*; (e) *R v Pembliton*; (f) *R v Wacker*; (g) *R v Miller*; (h) *Fagan v Metropolitan Police Commissioner*.

#### Task 2

| | |
|---|---|
| *Actus reus*: | (a), (g) |
| *Mens rea*: | (b), (c), (f) |
| Transferred malice: | (e) |
| Contemporaneity: | (h) |
| Strict liability: | (d) |

### Exercise 12.2: Recap Quiz

Identify the words, terms or phrases suggested by the clues below to reveal, by the first letters of each, the types of offences that they relate to:

N*ovus actus interveniens*: if one of these breaks the chain of causation for a result crime, such as the one in s 47, then the defendant is relieved of liability.

O*ffences against the person act*: the statute that has resisted reforms since 1861 and still creates much of the framework for this particular area of criminal law.

*Nose*: if this is broken, then s 47 would certainly be relevant, and perhaps – given the circumstances – ss 18 and 20 (the Joint Charging Standard will help here).

*Fagan v metropolitan police commissioner*: you are looking for a case name here (a case that was also considered earlier in the chapter) involving an unfortunate incident involving a motorist and a policeman's foot: the relevant offence is now in s 39 of the Criminal Justice Act 1988.

*Assault*: the *actus reus* of this offence is to place another person in fear of immediate and unlawful violence; it is also used much more loosely, and usually prefaced by the word 'common', in reference to the related offence of battery.

*Treatment*: you will probably require lengthy amounts of this, with the threat of long-term incapacity, if you are a victim of a s 18 or s 20 wounding or grievous bodily harm offence (check the Joint Charging Standard if you are unsure).

*Actual bodily harm*: this requirement, in s 47, shows that the offence is a result crime, not merely one of conduct.

*Loss of blood*: since the victim's skin has to be broken, this is the likely result if you are the unfortunate victim of a wounding offence (again check the Joint Charging Standard if you are unsure).

## ANSWERS FOR CHAPTER 13

### Exercise 13.1: Identifying cases in tort and relationship to duty, breach and harm

**Task 1**

(1) (c)
(2) (h)
(3) (e)
(4) (b)
(5) (j)
(6) (i)
(7) (d)
(8) (g)
(9) (a)
(10) (f)

**Case options:** (a) *Donoghue v Stevenson*; (b) *Barnett v Chelsea and Kensington Hospital*; (c) *Bolton v Stone*; (d) *Wagon Mound*; (e) *Caparo v Dickman*; (f) *Glasgow Corporation v Muir*; (g) *Sayers v Harlow UDC*; (h) *Bourhill v Young*; (i) *Paris v Stepney BC*; (j) *Latimer v AEC*.

**Task 2**

| | |
|---|---|
| Duty: | (a), (e), (h) |
| Breach: | (c), (f), (i), (j) |
| Harm: | (b), (d), (g) |

## ANSWERS FOR CHAPTER 14

## Exercise 14.1: Recap Quiz

*Identify the terms, words and phrases suggested by the following clues to reveal, via the first letters of your answers, the nature of this topic.*

Sentencing framework: from discharges and fines right through to life in jail, this describes the sentencing options available, with the Criminal Justice Act 2003 adding to its flexibility.

Absolute discharge: a sentence that marks a conviction, but does not punish the offender.

Non-fatal: term given to offences of violence such as assault occasioning actual bodily harm, wounding and grievous bodily harm.

Community order: the Criminal Justice Act 2003 has introduced this form of sentence, which might be customised to suit offenders of crimes that are 'serious enough'.

Triable either way: also known as intermediate offences, which might be heard, and sentenced, by magistrates' courts or Crown Courts.

Imprisonment: the custodial sentence, reserved for offences 'so serious' that a period of detention is required.

Offender: on whom the emphasis is placed in rehabilitative sentencing, rather than the emphasis on the offence under the 'just deserts' approach.

Not guilty: this plea might be considered critically at the sentencing stage, since the alternative would have put the defendant in a more favourable light.

Suspended sentence: a penalty for an offence that would ordinarily justify immediate jail, but owing to the circumstances of the case, is dealt with without detention on the basis that no further offences take place within a specified period.

## Exercise 14.3: Tort damages – odd one out

(1) General damages – **compensation orders** – special damages. Compensation orders may be made by criminal courts as part of the sentencing process and do not have anything to do with the tort of negligence remedies.

(2) **Special damages** – pain and suffering – loss of amenity. Special damages is the odd one out because it describes specific, measurable losses, whereas pain and suffering and loss of amenity are both examples of general damages, which are more difficult to quantify.

(3) Special damages – general damages – **remoteness of damage**. Remoteness of damage is the odd one out: it determines the extent of a defendant's liability in negligence, but not the nature of the damages awarded.

(4) **Loss of amenity** – damage to property – *restitutio in integrum*. Loss of amenity is the odd one out because it refers to the loss of a claimant's ability to live their life in the way they did prior to the harm caused by negligence. However, the other options relate to property losses.

(5) Lump sum – structured settlements – **injunction**. Injunction is the odd one out since it is an equitable remedy for certain types of torts (for

example, nuisance), whereas lump sum and structured settlements provide two ways in which damages under the tort of negligence will be paid to claimants.

(6) Pecuniary damages – **pain and suffering** – loss of earnings. Pain and suffering is the odd one out because it is a non-pecuniary loss, whereas the other two options relate to pecuniary (financial) losses.

# Index